The Color of Success

Politics and Society in Twentieth-Century America

Series Editors

William Chafe, Gary Gerstle, Linda Gordon, and Julian Zelizer

A list of titles in this series appears at the back of the book

The Color of Success

Asian Americans and the Origins of
the Model Minority

Ellen D. Wu

Princeton University Press
Princeton and Oxford

Published by Princeton University Press,
41 William Street, Princeton, New Jersey 08540

In the United Kingdom: Princeton University Press,
6 Oxford Street, Woodstock, Oxfordshire OX20 1TW

press.princeton.edu

Cover photograph: Team USA, also known as the San Francisco Chinese Basketball
Team, 1956. Courtesy of the San Francisco Chinese Basketball Team.

Paperback ISBN: 978-0-691-16802-9

The Library of Congress has cataloged the cloth edition as follows

Wu, Ellen D.
Politics and society in twentieth century America : Asian Americans
and the origins of the model minority / Ellen D. Wu.
pages cm
Includes index.

Summary: "The Color of Success tells of the astonishing transformation of Asians in the United States from the "yellow peril" to "model minorities"—peoples distinct from the white majority but lauded as well-assimilated, upwardly mobile, and exemplars of traditional family values—in the middle decades of the twentieth century. As Ellen Wu shows, liberals argued for the acceptance of these immigrant communities into the national fold, charging that the failure of America to live in accordance with its democratic ideals endangered the country's aspirations to world leadership. Weaving together myriad perspectives, Wu provides an unprecedented view of racial reform and the contradictions of national belonging in the civil rights era. She highlights the contests for power and authority within Japanese and Chinese America alongside the designs of those external to these populations, including government officials, social scientists, journalists, and others. And she demonstrates that the invention of the model minority took place in multiple arenas, such as battles over zoot suiters leaving wartime internment camps, the juvenile delinquency panic of the 1950s, Hawaii statehood, and the African American freedom movement. Together, these illuminate the impact of foreign relations on the domestic racial order and how the nation accepted Asians as legitimate citizens while continuing to perceive them as indelible outsiders. By charting the emergence of the model minority stereotype, The Color of Success reveals that this far-reaching, politically charged process continues to have profound implications for how Americans understand race, opportunity, and nationhood"—Provided by publisher.

ISBN 978-0-691-15782-5 (hardback)
1. Asian Americans—History—20th century. 2. Asian Americans—Cultural assimilation. 3. Asian Americans—Ethnic identity. 4. Asian Americans—Public opinion. 5. United States—Ethnic relations—History—20th century.
6. United States—Race relations—History—20th century. 7. United States—Politics and government—1945–1989. I. Title.

E184.A75W8 2013

305.895'073—dc23

2013019921

British Library Cataloging-in-Publication Data is available

This book has been composed in Sabon LT Std and Italia Std

Printed on acid-free paper. ∞

Printed in the United States of America

For my mother and father,
Anita Mui Wu
and
Paul Pao-lo Wu

The problem of the twentieth century is the problem of the color-line,—the relation of the darker to the lighter races of men in Asia and Africa, in America and the islands of the sea.

—W.E.B. DuBois,
The Souls of Black Folk (1903)

Contents

Acknowledgments

Cataloguing the overwhelming generosity of all who have facilitated this project from start to finish has been humbling and heartwarming. It is impossible to repay all these kindnesses, but perhaps the following sentences can suffice.

I often marvel at how extraordinarily lucky I was to have studied with the best teachers and colleagues at the University of Chicago. My adviser, Mae Ngai, is the consummate mentor, always leading by example. I am continually inspired by her intellectual rigor, commitment to social justice, and dedication to her students. I hope she recognizes her stamp on any convincing parts of this book. George Chauncey's Postwar American Society seminar sparked my curiosity about this period and gave me the confidence to move forward. Kathleen Conzen, James Grossman, Thomas Holt, and Amy Dru Stanley profoundly influenced my understanding of history. Joanne Berens, Diane Brady, and David Goodwine cheerfully walked me through the bureaucratic maze of graduate school from beginning to end. Terry Schulte Scott's companionship enabled me to survive the first year. The camaraderie of Lisa Andersen, Melissa Borja, Michael Carriere, Kornel Chang, Beth Cooper, Mike Czaplicki, Orlando Garcia, Allyson Hobbs, Moira Hinderer, Amanda Howland, Miranda Johnson, Jennifer Lee, Quincy Mills, Meredith Oda, Arissa Oh, Albert Park, Steve Porter, Eli Salazar, Aaron Shapiro, Michael Stamm, Tracy Steffes, and Kyle Volk illuminated the delights of membership in a scholarly community.

I am also indebted to my professors at Indiana University, the University of California, Berkeley, and the University of California, Los Angeles for introducing me to the richness of history and Asian American studies: Nick Cullather, Eugene Eoyang, Yuko Kurahashi, Michael McGerr, Yuan Shu, Steve Stowe, Gin Yong Pang, Steve Louie, Valerie Matsumoto, Don Nakanishi, Glenn Omatsu, Kyeyoung Park, Sandhya Shukla, and Henry Yu. Regrettably, Yuji Ichioka passed away before I could share this work with him, but I hope it honors his efforts as a pioneer of Asian American history.

An army of specialists guided my navigation through the empirical building blocks of this project. For their assistance, I thank the staff members at Chicago's Japanese American Service Committee's Legacy Center, the Chicago Japanese American Historical Society, the Chicago History Museum, the University of Chicago's Regenstein Library, the Brethren

Church Archives, the California Historical Society's North Baker Research Library, the University of California, Berkeley's Ethnic Studies Library and Bancroft Library, the University of California, Los Angeles' Young Research Library Special Collections, the University of California, Los Angeles' Asian American Studies Reading Room, the Hoover Institution, the National Archives and Records Administration in College Park, Maryland, and Washington, DC, the Library of Congress, the Hawai'i State Archives, the University of Hawai'i at Manoa's Hamilton Library, the Harry S. Truman Presidential Library, the Museum of Chinese in the Americas, the Japanese American National Museum's Hirasaki Resource Center, Columbia University's Rare Book and Manuscript Library, the University of Utah's J. Willard Marriott Library Special Collections, the Academy of Motion Picture Arts and Sciences Margaret Herrick Library Special Collections, Yale University's Beinecke Rare Book and Manuscript Library, the University of Michigan's Bentley Historical Library, the Hagley Library, the New York Public Library's Performing Arts Library at Lincoln Center, the University of Iowa Libraries Special Collections, the University of Texas at Austin's Perry-Castañeda Library, and densho.org. The staff members at the Document Delivery Services and Government Information Services at Indiana University's Wells Library clocked countless hours wading through the stacks for me.

I especially thank those who went out of their way to help me put all the pieces of this puzzle together, including Brandon Barton, Matthew Briones, Deborah Mieko Burns, Percy Chu, Miroslava Chávez-García, Winifred Eng Lee, Jim Gatewood, Jennifer Gee, Robert Gin, Reme Grefalda, Merie-Ellen Gushi, Mary Kao, Sojin Kim, Dong Kingman Jr., Cynthia Lee, Marji Lee, Lou Malcomb, Robert Meyer, Brian Niiya, Molly and Yoji Ozaki, Martha Nakagawa, Lisa Nishi, Wei Chi Poon, Jeff Rankin, Judy Soohoo, Randy Sowell, Jim Sparrow, Eileen Tamura, and Judy Yung. Chris Clements, Jason Luna Gavilan, Kristine Krueger, Meredith Oda, Erin Poirier, Katherine Wilson, and Grace Wong provided crucial research assistance. Setsuko Matsunaga Nishi, Jade Snow Wong, Betty Lee Sung, and William Yukon Chang took the time to tell me about their experiences as part of a remarkable earlier generation of Asian Americans. Anne Boylan, Jim Gatewood, Art Hansen, Mary Lui, Greg Robinson, and Henry Yu cordially sent primary materials my way. Charlotte Brooks became a kindred spirit. All the translations of Gilbert Woo's *Chinese Pacific Weekly* that appear here are hers.

Over the years, my thinking evolved through the insights generated by an amazing cross-section of scholars, including participants in the University of Chicago's Reproduction of Race and Racial Ideologies Workshop and Social History Workshop, the Social Science Research Council's 2003 Summer Institute on International Migration, Rutgers University's

Institute for Research on Women's Diasporas and Migrations Seminar, the University of Texas at Austin's Institute for Historical Studies Workshop, Indiana University's Committee for Historians and Intellectual Culture, and the annual meetings of the Association of Asian American Studies, the Organization of American Historians, the American Studies Association, the American Historical Association, and the Society for Historians of American Foreign Relations. A portion of chapter 4 was originally published as "'America's Chinese': Anti-Communism, Citizenship, and Cultural Diplomacy during the Cold War," *Pacific Historical Review* 77, no. 3 (August 2008): 391–422, and I thank the journal editors and referees for their helpful comments as well as the University of California Press for granting permission to reprint the work here. As I faced the daunting task of transforming the dissertation into a book, several protagonists swooped in to provide clarity and direction: Judith Allen, Eiichiro Azuma, John Bodnar, Erika Bsumek, Jason Chang, Susan Ferber, Neil Foley, Matt Guterl, Julie Hardick, Madeline Hsu, Arissa Oh, Naoko Shibusawa, and anonymous readers for Princeton and Oxford University presses. Gary Gerstle's interventions were especially critical.

This book became a real thing due to the efforts of the team at Princeton University Press. I am grateful to Brigitta van Rheinberg and Chuck Myers for seeing the manuscript's promise, Eric Henney and Karen Carter for coordinating the production process, copyeditor Cindy Milstein, and indexer Blythe Woolston. I thank William Chafe, Gary Gerstle, Linda Gordon, and Julian Zelizer, the editors of the Politics and Society in Twentieth-Century America series, for saving me a spot on their list.

Research and writing are resource-intensive endeavors, and I am extremely thankful to all who supported this project through grants and fellowships. At the University of Chicago, a Century Fellowship, a Center for the Study of Race, Politics, and Culture travel grant, a Department of History Freehling research grant, and an Office of Graduate Affairs Doolittle-Harrison Fellowship laid the foundation. Cathy Cohen, Rosalind Fielder, Rolisa Tutwyler, Patrick Rivers, Tony Peffer, Yvonne Weblon, and Bibiana Suarez welcomed me to the Center for the Study of Race, Politics, and Culture as the inaugural dissertation fellow. I also benefited from the Organization of American Historians' Horace Samuel and Marion Galbraith Merrill Travel Grant in Twentieth-Century American Political History, a research grant from the Harry S. Truman Library Institute, and the Society for Historians of American Foreign Relations's Samuel Flagg Bemis Research Grant and its Diversity-International Outreach Fellowship. The resourcefulness of Ann Fabian and Nancy Hewitt at Rutgers University afforded me the stimulating environment of the Institute for Research on Women and the luxury of time to finish my dissertation. At Indiana University, multiple units contributed backing: the

College of Arts and Sciences, the College Arts and Humanities Institute, the New Frontiers in Arts and Humanities Program funded by the Office of President and administered by the Office of the Vice President for Research, the Office of the Vice Provost for Research, and the History and American Studies departments along with the Asian American Studies Program.

I had the good fortune of spending a landmark year at the University of Texas at Austin through fellowships from the Ford Foundation and the University of Texas's Institute for Historical Studies. Thank you to Chris O'Brien and everyone at the Ford Fellowships Office for facilitating my leave. Buoyed by the administrative prowess of Courtney Meador and José Barragán, the Institute for Historical Studies was a super place to write in the company of fellows Venkat Dhulipala, Michelle Moyd, William Nelson, and Stephen Sawyer. I thank director Julie Hardwick for accommodating the particulars of my situation and arranging a crucial manuscript dissection. I acknowledge Madeline Hsu in particular for serving so diligently as my official mentor.

The labors of teacher-caregivers across three states made mine possible. I thank the staff members at the St. Elizabeth's Child Care Center in Jersey City, New Jersey, the University United Methodist Church–Early Childhood Center in Austin, Texas, Wanda and Ricky Ewing, and the Bloomington Developmental Learning Center.

Rutgers University, New Brunswick was a great place to begin my time on the tenure track. I appreciate the collegiality of Chris Brown, Louise Barnett, Paul Clemens, Ann Fabian, David Eng, Leslie Fishbein, Nicole Fleetwood, Angus Gillespie Helene Grynberg, Hilary Hallet, Nancy Hewitt, Alison Isenberg, Catherine Lee, Michael Rockland, Ben Sifuentes-Jáuregui, Edlie Wong, and Ginny Yans.

Myriad coworkers, neighbors, and friends have made the corner of south-central Indiana where I now work not just a pleasant place but also a true community. I am especially indebted to Judith Allen, Nancy Ashley, Peter Bailey, Jim Basore, Alexia Bock, Becky Bryant, Claude Clegg, Denise Cruz, Lesley Davis, Arlene Diaz, Kon Dierks, Michael Dodson, Ben Eklof, Jo Ellen Fitzgerald, Wendy Gamber, Peter Guardino, Blake Harvey, Deke and Glory Heger, Vivian Halloran, Deana Hutchins, Dazhi Jiao, Sarah Knott, Joey Kremer, Jacob Lee, Shera Lesly, Joan Linton, Jun Liu, Arthur Luhur, Manling Luo, Pedro Machado, Krista Maglen, Michael McGerr, Chris and Kelly Molloy, Marissa Moorman, Khalil Muhammad and Stephanie Lawson-Muhammad, Tuli Mukhopadhyay, Matt Murphy, Ashlyn Nelson, John Nieto-Phillips, Mathias Lehman, Amrita Myers, Scott O'Bryan, Don Rawe, Mark Roseman, Nick Roberts, Bret Rothstein, Eric Sandweiss, Sara Schalenghe, Micol Seigel, Rebecca Spang, Steve Stowe, Kirsten Sword, Greg and Sophia Travis, Naoko Wake, Ed and Manasi Watts, Scot Wright, Lanlan Xu, and Sarah Zanti. Catherine Dyar and Gus Hommey immediately incorporated the McWu household into their Bloomington family. Nick and Melanie Cullather, Matt Guterl, and Sandi Latcha reached out to us right away. Karen Inouye and Jennifer Lee were with me from the start. Michelle Moyd and Christina Snyder extended unfailing encouragement and empathy.

I treasure the opportunity that I had to befriend Sophia Travis, a gentle soul, courageous advocate, and the embodiment of fabulosity. Thank you, Sophia, for demonstrating the boundless possibilities of home.

Cherished friends and family nurtured my body and spirit in invaluable ways throughout this project's life span. Many of them offered food, shelter, and company during my research travels; other nourished me when I returned home and picked up when I needed it. Micah Andersen, Eric Amundson, Diana Bocajero, Jenn Chang, Ming Chang, Wen Chang, Janice Chen, C. K. and Mei-Mei Cheung, Denise Cheung, Fay Cheung, Jason Chi, On Chi, Rosa Chi, Pam Chin, Iris Cho, Paul Cho, Sonya Cho, Angela Chu, Corey Ciszek, Biella Coleman, Dana DeAno, Seth DeAvila, Teresa Ejanda-Sano, Amy Fong, Joseph Fu, Villa Fu, Adam Geary, Santiago Giraldo, Sara Herrman, Christine Hsu, Mamoru Iikubo, Leslie Ito, Barnaby James, Steve Johnstone, Josh Kaminker, Sarah Kaminker, Aida Kan, Christy Kim, George Kim, Nancy Kim, Oliver Kim, Vada Kim, Isabella Kwan, Felicity Lao, Nicole Lee, Sean Mizuno, Rachel Mizuno, Susan Nakaoka, Jessica Nimjee, Brad Ottesen, Jimmy Poon, Jim Ross, Talya Salant, Tom Sano, Ellen Tilden, Candy Truong, Frances Tso, Mike Tso, Ben Wan, Edward Wan, Ping Wan, Elaine Wan, Alice Wong, Bobby Wong, Emily Wong, Grace Wong, Henry Wong, Matthew Wong, Shu-Jen Wong, Stanley Wong, Stella Wong, Steve Wong, Ta-Hsiung Wong, Tina Woo, Josh Wu, Phil Wu, Rebecca Wu, Robert Wu, Khai Yang, Rob Yang, Fanny Yee, Jimmy Yee, King Yee, Peony Yee, Linda Yung, and my Nai Nai.

My dearest family gave me the most important gifts of love and perspective. My in-laws—McGraws, McGraw-McClains, Pattersons, Crosses—embraced me from the outset. I am forever indebted to the extended Kwan, Wu, and Indy Chinese families for rallying to lift my brother and me through our darkest times, and for taking us in as their own children.

My brother Simon proved time and again why siblings are irreplaceable.

Paolo and Augie, my beloved sons, made me laugh every day. They fill me with hope, wonder, and joy.

My husband, Jason, anchored me as only a life partner and best friend can. There would be no book without him.

Finally, I dedicate this to my parents, Paul Pao-lo and Anita Mui Wu, two individuals who modeled unconditional devotion and deep commitment to the Christian ideal of service. Ba and Mom, for your bravery, foresight, and guidance, I tell this story for you, with love and longing.

The Color of Success

Introduction

Imperatives of Asian American Citizenship

This is *the* success story of *a* success story.

In December 1970, the *New York Times* ran a front-page article declaring Japanese and Chinese in the United States "an American success story." Both groups had witnessed "the almost total disappearance of discrimination . . . and their assimilation into the mainstream of American life"—a situation that would have been "unthinkable twenty years ago." The *Times* opened with the biography of immigrant J. Chuan Chu as proof. When Chu arrived from China at the end of World War II, he had run into difficulty finding a place to live because of his "Oriental face." Two and half decades later, his race was no longer a handicap. A graduate of the University of Pennsylvania's school of engineering, Chu had risen through the ranks of Massachusetts-based Honeywell Information Systems, Inc. to a vice presidential position. "If you have the ability and can adapt to the American way of speaking, dressing, and doing things," said Chu, "then it doesn't matter any more if you are Chinese."[1]

Chu's experience was hardly unique. In interviews with dozens of Asian Americans, the *Times* heard little of discrimination in housing, education, and the realm of interpersonal interaction. Southerners even considered Asians to be white. By and large, Japanese and Chinese Americans no longer faced "artificial barriers" to high-status professions. Whereas most of the previous generation had had no choice but to toil in menial service work such as laundering and gardening, stars of Asian America's current cohort had achieved nationally distinguished careers: architects Minoru Yamasaki (of New York's World Trade Center fame) and I. M. Pei; multimillion-dollar investment management firm Manhattan Fund director Gerald Tsai; Nobel–prizewinning physicists Tsung Dao Lee and Chen Ning Yang; San Francisco State College president S. I. Hayakawa; and US senator Daniel Inouye. "The pig-tailed coolie has been replaced in the imagination of many Americans by the earnest, bespectacled young scholar," announced the *Times*. Hunter College junior Elaine Yuehy, the daughter of a laundryman, agreed. "My teachers have always helped me because they had such a good image of Chinese students. 'Good little Chinese kid,' they said, 'so bright and so well-behaved and hard-working,'" she recalled. Once despised by American society, "Orientals"—especially

Japanese and Chinese, the two major Asian-ethnic populations at midcentury—had become its most exceptional and beloved people of color, its "model minority."[2]

Indeed, before the 1940s and 1950s, whites had deemed ethnic Japanese and Chinese unassimilable aliens unfit for membership in the nation. Americans had subjected so-called Orientals to the regime of Asiatic Exclusion, marking them as *definitively not-white,* and systematically shutting them out of civic participation through such measures as bars to naturalization, occupational discrimination, and residential segregation. Beginning in World War II, however, the United States' geopolitical ambitions triggered seismic changes in popular notions of nationhood and belonging, which in turn challenged the stronghold of white supremacy.[3] As a result, federal officials, behavioral scientists, social critics, and ordinary people worked in tandem to dismantle Exclusion. Yet such a decision posed a problem for America's racial order and citizenship boundaries. The social standing of Asian Americans was no longer certain, and the terms of their inclusion into the nation needed to be determined. A host of stakeholders resolved this dilemma by the mid-1960s with the invention of a new stereotype of Asian Americans as the model minority—a racial group distinct from the white majority, but lauded as well assimilated, upwardly mobile, politically nonthreatening, and *definitively not-black.*

This astounding transformation reflected the array of new freedoms accorded to Japanese and Chinese Americans by the state and society in the mid-twentieth century. Their emancipation entailed liberation from the lowly station of "aliens ineligible to citizenship," the legal turn of phrase with which lawmakers had codified Asian immigrants as external to American polity and society. Landmark state and federal litigation and legislation in the 1910s and 1920s both drew on as well as reinvigorated the social consensus that peoples of Asian ancestry were wholly incapable of assimilation, because they were racially and culturally too different from white Americans.[4] Under Exclusion, immigrants from Japan and China were subjected to a shock of discriminatory and dehumanizing limitations, from harsh restrictions on entry into the country to the denial of naturalized citizenship along with its attendant rights, including the franchise and property ownership.[5] Their American-born children, birthright citizens of the United States, fared little better. Often forced to attend segregated schools, their career options were narrowly bound to the same peripheral economic niches into which their parents were funneled: truck farming, gardening, domestic labor, restaurants, and laundries. The few who managed to earn professional degrees could only hope to find clients in their Little Tokyo and Chinatown ghettos. The vast majority, however, found it futile to aspire beyond their lot as "professional carrot washers," as one second-generation Japanese American put it, until the demise of Exclusion.[6] With the regime's abolition in the 1940s and 1950s, Asian Americans enjoyed access to previously forbidden areas of employment, neighborhoods, and associational activities. They also benefited from the federal government's relaxation of immigration restrictions and its revocation of their ineligibility to citizenship.[7]

But Asian Americans discovered, too, that various authorities—both within and outside their ethnic communities—checked their autonomy to choose their own futures by pressuring them to behave as praiseworthy citizens. Some gladly complied, others inadvertently went along, and not a few refused to succumb to these demands. All found their lives conscripted into the manufacture of a certain narrative of national racial progress premised on the distinction between "good" and "bad" minorities. The questions at the crux of this book ask: How did this reasoning take hold? What explains the drastic turnaround of the image of ethnic Japanese and Chinese, long regarded by many in the United States as the unalterably strange and despicable "pig-tailed coolie"? Put another way, how did the Asian American success story *itself* become a success story— literally front-page news—edging out other possibilities for understanding their place in the nation? And what did their crowning as model minorities ("the earnest, bespectacled young scholar") mean not only for themselves but also for all Americans?

Answering these queries begins with comprehending the model minority's debut as the unanticipated outcome of a series of intersecting political, social, and cultural imperatives—ethnic and mainstream, domestic and global—that impelled the radical restructuring of America's racial order in the mid-twentieth century. Excavating the origins and aftereffects of this formidable concept therefore necessitates a consideration of the vicissitudes within Japanese and Chinese communities alongside the broader sweep of national and international historical change. In other words, connections between internal and external developments are indispensable to uncovering the birth of this construct; this book moves between these worlds, bringing them into dialogue in order to tell a new story about race making in wartime and postwar America.

The evolution of the political philosophy known as liberalism was foremost among the dynamisms that set the stage for the coming of the model minority. Historians have pointed to liberalism's centrality as well as its "protean" character in US history. The foundational tenets at the core of liberalism—freedom, rational self-interest, and a belief in human progress—have undergirded the nation's political life since the early days of the republic, but Americans have acted on them in ways that have changed decidedly over time. At the start of the twentieth century, the social and economic inequalities resulting from industrial capitalism motivated Progressive Era reformers to redefine liberalism from its nineteenth-century iteration (laissez-faire economics and limited government intervention) to one that valued an activist state attuned to the welfare of its citizens. The impulse to "tame capitalism" dominated liberal thinking through the Great Depression and early years of the New Deal. By the 1940s, however, liberals embraced new priorities cherishing the protection and promotion of the freedoms of individuals as well as social groups.[8]

Mobilization for World War II fostered the advent of *racial* liberalism: the growing belief in political and intellectual circles that the country's racial diversity could be most ably managed through the assimilation and integration of nonwhites. The ideology emphasized federal government intervention in orchestrating the social engineering necessary to achieve civil rights and equality of citizenship for minority groups.[9] Champions of racial liberalism—including many ethnic Japanese and Chinese themselves—pushed the notion that Asians might be something other than indelibly and menacingly alien, and that they deserved to be included in the national polity as bona fide citizens—a giant conceptual leap from the unanimity of previous decades.[10] Liberals of all races invested racial reform with grave urgency: the failure of the nation to live in accordance with its professed democratic ideals endangered the country's aspirations to world leadership. The United States' battles against fascism and then Communism meant that Asiatic Exclusion, like Jim Crow, was no longer tenable. Seeking global legitimacy, Americans moved to undo the legal framework and social practices that relegated Asians outside the bounds of the nation.[11] Certainly, Japanese and Chinese Americans had not lacked in attempts to attain substantive, full citizenship and respectable social standing in the late nineteenth and early twentieth centuries. But their efforts to claim unfettered inclusion only gained traction with the rise of racial liberalism and outbreak of global wars. Japanese and Chinese American fortunes, in short, were tied directly to the national identity politics of World War II and the Cold War.[12]

International imperatives of the 1940s and 1950s anchored the nation's recasting of Asian Americans into *assimilating Others*—persons acknowledged as capable of acting like white Americans while remaining racially distinct from them. Unlike the progeny of turn-of-the century southern and eastern European immigrants who melted into unambiguous whiteness in the crucibles of mass consumption, industrial unionism, New Deal ethnic pluralism, and military service, Japanese and Chinese did not disappear into whiteness after the end of Exclusion.[13] Instead, state authorities, academicians, cultural producers, and common folk renovated Asian America's perceived differences from liability to asset to benefit US expansionism. In the throes of the worldwide decolonization movement, more precisely, Cold Warriors encountered the dilemma of differentiating their own imperium from the personae non gratae of the European empires. As nonwhites, the entrance of Asian Americans into the national fold provided a powerful means for the United States to proclaim itself a racial democracy and thereby credentialed to assume the leadership of the free world. The rearticulation of Asian Americans from ineradicable aliens to assimilating Others by outside interests bolstered the framing of US hegemony abroad as benevolent—an enterprise that mirrored the move toward racial integration at home.[14]

Above all, Japanese and Chinese Americans harbored a profound interest in characterizing anew their racial image and conditions of citizenship, and they often took the lead in this regard. By yoking US officialdom's world-ordering logic to their own quests for political and social acceptance, they actively participated in the revamping of their racial difference. They made claims to inclusion based on the assumption of not only Americanness but also and particularly diasporic Japanese and Chinese identities. Recognizing that the Asian Pacific region loomed large on the US foreign relations agenda, community representatives strategically typecast themselves, asserting that their own ancestries endowed them with innate cultural expertise that qualified them to serve as the United States' most natural ambassadors to the Far East. Therefore, they suggested, admitting people of Japanese and Chinese heritage to first-class citizenship made good diplomatic sense.

Equally decisively, Asian Americans' self-stereotyping convinced others not only because of its payoff for foreign relations but also because it corroborated the nation's cultural conservatism at midcentury. Ethnic Japanese and Chinese emissaries consistently touted their putatively "Oriental" attributes, such as the predisposition to harmony and accommodation, the reverence for family and education, and unflagging industriousness to enhance their demands for equality. These descriptions endorsed not only liberal assimilationist and integrationist imperatives but also the Cold War cultural emphasis on home life rooted in the strict division of gender roles. Self-representations of Japanese and Chinese American masculinity, femininity, and sexuality, purposefully conforming to the norms of the white middle class, were crucial to the reconstruction of aliens ineligible to citizenship into admirable—albeit colored—Americans.[15]

Undeniably, this embrace of Cold War nationalism and traditional values was a politically charged calculation. Japanese and Chinese America were hardly monolithic entities in this period. Rather, they were rife with internal divisions, rival agendas, and disagreements about their collective futures—all of which helped dictate how they would make their way in American society after World War II. External pressures generated commonalities and a modicum of cohesiveness within the two communities, but they also provided the structures that enabled certain individuals and factions to achieve authority and influence. Demographic shifts also mattered. As US-born, second-generation Japanese and Chinese came of age in the 1930s and 1940s, they began to vie with the immigrant elite for leadership positions and the privileges of representing themselves in the public sphere. The winning contenders were those whose politics hewed closest to the reigning dogmas of the day: liberal assimilationism, prowar patriotism, anti-Communism, and respectable heterosexuality. As ethnic spokespersons, the victors in these contests spun flattering portrayals of their peoples to dislodge deeply embedded "yellow peril" caricatures. At the same time, their tales of exemplary Asian American citizenship validated their own political choices and upheld intracommunity power arrangements in their favor. A task of this book is to show how these success story narrators beat out alternative voices including those of zoot-suiters, sexual deviants, draft resisters, those who renounced citizenship, leftists, Communists, and juvenile delinquents—the various entities who did not subscribe to postwar racial liberalism and political-cultural conservatism as the most suitable guidelines for encountering postwar American life.[16]

In the mid-1960s, the assimilating Other underwent a subtle yet profound metamorphosis into the model minority: the Asiatic who was at once a model citizen and definitively not-black. The zenith of liberal racial reform—the 1964 Civil Rights Act and 1965 Voting Rights Act—also marked the beginnings of its collapse under the weight of both progressive and conservative critique. The abolition of de jure apartheid had done little to alter the vast disparities between black and white incomes, housing, employment, and education. Participants in the African American freedom movement urgently pressed for lasting changes to, if not a complete overhaul of, the nation's—and the world's—existing structures of capitalist democracy. Liberals unnerved by blacks' wide-ranging, radical challenges to effect a meaningful redistribution of wealth and power held up Japanese and Chinese Americans as evidence of minority mobility to defend the validity of assimilation as well as integration. Conservatives who feared that black power would go even further than racial liberalism to destroy white supremacy also looked to Asians to salve what they viewed as the decline of "law and order"—wrought especially by black and brown peoples—in American society. Either way, Japanese and Chinese in the United States were catapulted to a new status as model minorities—living examples of advancement *in spite of* the persistent color line and *because of* their racial (often coded as cultural) differences.[17] In recirculating Asian American success stories, both liberals and conservatives grafted the now-familiar postwar tropes of Japanese and Chinese American conduct (patriotism, family values, accommodation, and so forth) onto the new imperative of taming the reach of the Civil Rights revolution.

At its heart, *The Color of Success* concerns the racial order in twentieth-century America—its evolution, consequences, and significance. Japanese and Chinese Americans, the largest ethnic Asian populations, and the two that figured most prominently in the public eye between the 1940s and 1960s, are central to this investigation.[18] Their trajectories unfold separately in order to illuminate their distinct histories. The argument proceeds in alternating chapters to showcase the divergences in their experiences. Yet Japanese and Chinese Americans also appear in tandem to emphasize the many parallels that account for their concurrent emergence as model minorities. As a mix of cultural, social, and political history, this study highlights how the discursive and the material mattered for Japanese American, Chinese American, and ultimately Asian American identity formation from World War II through the "Cold War civil rights" years.

In chronicling the invention of the model minority, this story challenges the black-white paradigm that prevails in histories of race in the twentieth-century United States.[19] To be sure, the question of black racial equality loomed as the paramount social issue of the day, particularly as civil rights activists disrupted the perpetuation of the racial system that had for centuries hinged on white exploitation and degradation of African American people for profit, comfort, and pleasure.[20] This transformation, though, was more complex than its standard treatment as a black-white conflict. A consideration of Japanese and Chinese Americans within the universe of the "Negro Problem," as it was called, demonstrates that the presence and actions of Asians in US society complicated, yet simultaneously reinforced, this central dichotomy. What it meant to be Japanese, Chinese, and Asian American was profoundly shaped by understandings of blackness and whiteness. Just as important, definitions of blackness and whiteness in this period cannot be understood without taking Japanese and Chinese Americans into account. Rather than remaining silent and aloof, as the conventional wisdom goes, Asian Americans were integral participants—and an integral presence—in skirmishes and debates over race in the 1940s through the 1960s.[21]

In this way, then, this chronicle is not simply about race relations but is more fundamentally concerned with race *making*—the incessant work of creating racial categories, living with and within them, altering them, and even obliterating them when they no longer have social or political utility.[22] Two factors for generating and reproducing race are particularly salient here. The first considers the formation of racial classifications as interactive phenomena, contingent on and constitutive of concurrent racial groupings.[23] In the case of Asian Americans at midcentury, the most obvious interdependencies were with whites and blacks.[24] But at various moments, other comparisons also came to the fore, including internal divisions *within* ethnic groups (discrepancies between "loyal" and "disloyal" Japanese during World War II; the state's discrimination between "good" anti-Communist and "bad" pro-Communist Chinese in the 1950s), assumptions about Mexican American waywardness in the 1940s, and contrasts between Native Hawaiians, *haole* (whites), and Asians in postwar Hawai'i.[25] The model minority is a wonderfully telling example demonstrating that racial categories are never static or omnipresent, that they change over time and vary across space, and that they pivot on the contemporaneous making and remaking of other racial categories. It also vividly illustrates how productions of race are crucially determined by confluences with other axes of identification—in this case, gender, sexuality, class, and nation.

The second outstanding element of race making in the following discussion is that of its historically contingent fabrication. Racial ideas do not appear out of nowhere and float around unmoored to social realities. They are consciously concocted and disseminated—if not always accepted without challenge—and are tied to structural developments.[26] Charting the rise of the model minority clarifies how the machinery of race making operated in the mid-twentieth-century United States, when social science, the burgeoning public relations industry, and liberal antiprejudice initiatives coordinated by the state, private foundations, and religious and civic organizations all functioned as puissant crafters of racial knowledge. An examination of these institutional channels offers precision about how green ideologies achieve political and social purchase.[27]

Tracing the course of Japanese and Chinese American racialization in the mid-twentieth century provides a useful way to revise the standard narrative of democratic citizenship in the United States by linking inclusion to racism. The mythology of American democracy depicts liberal egalitarianism as a succession of triumphs over exclusions, and that the circle of those included in the polity as full members of society has continued to widen over time.[28] The ascendance of racial liberalism and its reforms, including the death of the Asiatic alien ineligible to citizenship, would seem to uphold this folklore. Yet the lifting of Exclusion did not result in a teleological progression toward the unmitigated inclusion of Asian Americans in the nation. Rather, the racial logic that politicians, scholars, and journalists deployed to invent the model minority generated new modes of exclusion. Their reliance on culture to explain postwar Asian American socioeconomic mobility re-marked ethnic Japanese and Chinese as not-white, indelibly foreign others, compromising their improvements in social standing. This same reasoning also undergirded contentions that African Americans' cultural deficiencies was the cause of their poverty—assertions that delegitimized blacks' demands for structural changes in the political economy and stigmatized their utilization of welfare state entitlements. The history of the model minority therefore destabilizes the conceptual boundaries between exclusion and inclusion, allowing for a more complete understanding of how the United States and other liberal democracies devise, uphold, and justify social differences and inequalities, even as they expand their boundaries of inclusion and ostensibly progress toward the achievement of universal citizenship for all members.[29] Approaching the model minority as a simultaneously inclusive *and* exclusive reckoning supplies clues to how racism "reproduce[s] itself even after the historical conditions that initially gave it life have disappeared."[30]

Ultimately, the ideas and experiences of Asian Americans offer a fresh perspective on the history of the United States in an extraordinary moment of domestic and global upheaval. By following the careers of Japanese and Chinese American racialization and citizenship from the Pacific War through the Vietnam era, details of how the United States merged its various regional racial landscapes (the North, South, West, and Hawai'i) into a single, national racial order come into sharper focus.[31] As a multifaceted process that operated on local, national, and international registers, Asian America's metamorphosis illuminates the reach of diplomatic concerns into the realm of the everyday as well as the impact of stateside race relations in the ambit of geopolitics. In the end, the fashioning of Japanese and Chinese Americans first into assimilating Others and then definitively not-black model minorities did not only answer the question of Asian American social standing after Exclusion's end. It also worked to square the tension between the planetary spread of decolonization and the United States' designs to propagate its hegemony across islands and continents. Assimilating Others and model minorities performed an indispensable service for the imperative of narrating American exceptionalism to the nation and the world.

Part I
War and the Assimilating Other

The Second World War irrevocably altered the place of the United States in the global arena. American history, of course, had never been free of foreign entanglements despite the isolationist streak firmly embedded in the nation's political culture. Continental expansion, the dispossession of Native peoples, the claim to the Western Hemisphere as its sphere of influence with the 1823 Monroe Doctrine, the annexation of Hawai'i, and the conquest of the Philippines, Puerto Rico, and Guam as spoils of the Spanish-American War in 1898 were all building blocks of US empire. Yet the United States had remained relegated to the second tier of the international pecking order dominated by the European powers before the 1940s. It was not until its anointment as one of "Big Three" Allies that the United States came to be considered—and accepted its responsibilities—as the preeminent world leader. And it was also at this moment that the Asia Pacific region vaulted into a vital geopolitical preoccupation for US officialdom.[1]

These momentous shifts in the United States' international position and its foreign policy priorities undergirded an overhaul of the nation's racial alignments. In the American West and Hawai'i since the mid-nineteenth century, the various immigrant streams from Asia had been racialized together as the "yellow peril"—an alien menace courted for its labor yet despised for its purportedly unbridgeable cultural distance from white, Anglo-Saxon Protestants. With the nation's entry into World War II, however, the conflation of separate ethnic groups as Orientals lost its political purchase. Most saliently, the battles in the Pacific theater forced the disaggregation of Japanese and Chinese American racialization and social standing; the two could no longer be lumped together into one undifferentiated horde. In the wake of the Pearl Harbor bombing, middlebrow magazines famously published tutorials on "How to Tell Your Friends from the Japs." According to *Time*, Japanese were "hesitant, nervous in conversation, laugh loudly at the wrong time," whereas Chinese were "more relaxed" with an "easy gait." *Life* explicated that "enemy Japs"—like Tojo—"show[ed] humorless intensity of ruthless mystics," compared to "friendly Chinese" who wore the "rational calm of tolerant realists."[2]

The wartime rivalry between the United States and Japan along with the concurrent US-China alliance thus obliged the state's and society's divergent treatment of Japanese and Chinese Americans.

In one direction, World War II saw the culmination of the Asiatic Exclusion regime with the removal and incarceration of 120,000 Pacific coast *Nikkei* (individuals of Japanese ancestry), two-thirds of who were US citizens, and half of who were children under age eighteen. President Franklin D. Roosevelt's ostensibly race-neutral Executive Order 9066, signed on February 19, 1942, authorized the secretary of war to "prescribe military areas . . . from which any or all persons may be excluded." The mandate was selectively applied to Japanese Americans in Washington, Oregon, and California—a decision justified by federal authorities on the unsubstantiated grounds that all Japanese Americans were potential fifth columnists by virtue of blood alone. Beginning on March 31, Issei, Nisei, and Sansei (first-, second-, and third-generation immigrants, respectively) left their homes, farms, businesses, and communities for sixteen temporary "assembly centers." By November 1, all had moved again, this time to ten long-term "relocation centers," or concentration camps, in remote locations from Idaho to Arizona to Arkansas. The US Supreme Court upheld the legality of evacuation and detention for the sake of "military necessity" in *Hirabayashi v. United States* (1943), *Yasui v. United States* (1943), and *Korematsu v. United States* (1944). In authorizing, executing, and defending the constitutionality of mass imprisonment, the state effectively classified each and every ethnic Japanese in the United States as "enemy aliens," thereby meriting the utmost instantiation of political and social ostracization.[3]

Irrefutably, Japanese American internment entailed a spectacular denial of civil liberties. Yet to its liberal administrators in the Department of the Interior's War Relocation Authority (WRA), it also presented unparalleled promise for refashioning ethnic Japanese into model *Americans*. Internee life was designed with this goal in mind. Camp school curricula, for instance, prioritized English language instruction and the inculcation of American values, while camp "community councils" trained inmates in the art of democratic governance.[4] The WRA also laid out two pipelines to reentry into American life and fortifying Japanese Americans' station in the national polity. The first of these was postinternment migration throughout the United States, or "resettlement." The WRA envisioned resettlement as an ethnic dispersal, whereby Nikkei would scatter throughout the country in order to prevent the camps from devolving into "something akin to Indian reservations." A geographic fanning out would also inhibit the reconstitution of prewar Japanese enclaves. Just as important, it would push former internees to identify and associate with the white middle class. In theory, resettlement seemed the perfect test case for racial liberalism's incipient solution to America's race problems: state-engineered cultural and structural assimilation.[5]

The resettlement program commenced in October 1942, granting indefinite leaves to qualified applicants (that is, those deemed sufficiently loyal and assimilable by camp administrators) who had secured job offers in areas where their presence would not likely inflame local ire. To expedite resettlement, the WRA established dozens of field offices in intermountain, midwestern, and eastern states; Chicago's was the first to open in January 1943.[6] The authority conducted vigorous public relations efforts within the camps to persuade prisoners to leave, with the hope that all those eligible would be resettled by June 1944. Concurrent policies such as reducing the number of jobs available within the relocation centers and lowering the subsistence allowances were interpreted by inmates as coercive measures designed to force them out. Ironically, the effect was to cool Nikkei receptivity to the idea of resettlement. Other disincentives included economic difficulties, the lack of attractive employment options, fear of racial hostility, the desire to keep families intact, and the yearning to go back to their former homes.[7]

In all, only thirty-six thousand internees—less than one-third of the total—took part in the resettlement program by the end of 1944, starting anew in Denver, Saint Louis, Minneapolis–Saint Paul, Detroit, Cleveland, New York City, and Seabrook Farms, New Jersey, among other places.[8] Resettlers did not comprise a representative sample of detainees; they tended to be college-educated Nisei who were the most familiar with "American" culture. In January 1945, the federal government lifted the exclusion order, and by 1946, 57,251 Nikkei had returned to the Pacific coast, including 5,541 who had first gone eastward. Put another way, just over 60 percent resisted permanent resettlement.[9] If the resettlement program fell short of its objectives in the quantitative sense, the same was true of its qualitative dimensions. Using Chicago as the example, chapter 1 examines the ways in which resettlers defied the WRA's insistence that they forgo ethnic congregation in favor of assimilation.

The second means to restored citizenship promoted by the WRA was military service: surely a foolproof way for internees to authenticate their unswerving loyalty to the United States. After Japanese Americans' tours of duty, federal authorities believed, the public would no longer question their credentials for national belonging. This time, in contrast to resettlement, the prognosis came true. The rehabilitation did not happen without contention and forfeiture, however. Chapter 3 details the benefits and costs to Japanese Americans that accompanied the investiture of the Nisei soldier as the public face of the community.

As with Nikkei, the Pacific War decisively altered Chinese Americans' societal stature. But while the federal decision to intern Japanese Americans characterized the triumph of yellow peril agitation, the 1943 congressional repeal of the Chinese exclusion laws—in effect since 1882—sounded its death knell. This initial step in reversing the marginalization of Chinese in American life was a diplomatic maneuver designed to sinew the Sino-US entente against Japan. For the first time, persons from China were permitted to naturalize their US citizenship, while the legal entry of Chinese resumed—a symbolic elevation to equality with European immigrants.

Just as crucially, the mobilization for total war opened previously restricted avenues for socioeconomic advancement in industry and the armed forces. Until Pearl Harbor, employment options for Chinese Americans had been severely limited. The 1940 US Census found that 62.55 percent of the nation's 77,504 Chinese (including 59 percent of the English-speaking, American-born individuals over age fourteen) were manual laborers, concentrated mostly in restaurants, laundries, and sewing factories. The 20.58 percent who earned their livelihoods as proprietors, managers, and officials were mainly confined to Chinatown's ethnic economy. Another 11.44 percent occupied the semiprofessional, clerical, and sales ranks, while only 2.82 percent held professional or technical positions. This demographic snapshot, though, changed considerably within a few years' time as the wartime labor shortage and booming defense industry drew large numbers from their traditional, segregated niches. Of the 17,782 ethnic Chinese residing in the San Francisco Bay Area, for instance, 1,600 (almost 9 percent) landed war-related work such as shipbuilding by 1942. The war economy provided a lasting foothold for Chinese Americans in the primary labor market, foretelling occupational advances in the postwar period. By 1950, Chinese American men and women had substantially raised their presence in the white-collar world. Chinese in professional and technical fields more than doubled from 1940 to 7.08 percent in 1950, while the percentage working in clerical and sales positions went up to 15.96 percent. Conversely, the proportion of Chinese manual laborers dropped to 51.61 percent. Historians have celebrated World War II as nothing less than a defining instance for ethnic Chinese in the United States, the point at which they "[fell] instep . . . with fellow Americans," and "received a newfound acceptance and stature."[10] Yet while the war undeniably improved their lot, Chinese Americans did not feel fully secure in a society where they still faced racial discrimination. Chapter 2 considers the social and cultural work devoted to realizing the uptick in their social standing as well as second-generation Chinese Americans' continuing uncertainty about national belonging in the late 1940s and early 1950s.

Despite traversing discrete historical paths after 1941, both Japanese and Chinese Americans found themselves recast from aliens ineligible to citizenship to assimilating Others in the crucible of World War II. But the stuff and implications of their assimilation processes continued to play out in unlike ways with the geopolitical reshuffling at the Cold War's genesis. As Japan became America's junior partner against Communism in Asia, and China split into friend (the "free" government exiled to Taiwan) and foe (the People's Republic on the mainland), the absorption of Japanese and Chinese Americans into the body politic encountered new catalysts as well as new blockades unique to each group, as shown in chapters 3 and 4. The excavation of the historically contingent and often-contradictory ideas and practices of incorporation in part I uncovers dissimilarities alongside commonalities that the two communities encountered as they struggled to redefine both their place in the nation and the nation itself.

Chapter 1

Leave Your Zoot Suits Behind

Some 275 young people converged at Chicago's Ashland Auditorium on Saturday evening, November 20, 1943, to attend the Reminiscent Dance of Relocation Days. The soiree was billed as the area's first large-scale public event exclusively catering to second-generation Japanese Americans. All were recent arrivals to the Midwest, having left the WRA's internment camps as participants in the federal government's resettlement program, and eager to reunite with old friends and forge new acquaintanceships. A palpable tension marred the highly anticipated affair, however, as Nisei zoot-suiters, commonly referred to as "pachuke" and "yogore," appeared in droves. Noticing the "sneers on the faces of the stags," one young man worried, "I kept thinking all the time that I was dancing that I would get beaten up because I refused to let them cut in on my partner. Those fellows got very ugly about this and it was an experience that I never want to go through again." Many of the female partygoers likewise disapproved. "I didn't like the crowd at all because it seemed cheap," said one. "The people I saw were mostly the rowdy type. I didn't see any fellow there that looked like he had any ambition. The dance didn't look nice at all." Another confirmed, "A lot of yogores had been drinking and you could smell it all around the room. . . . The cops were there because everybody was anticipating trouble."[1]

The threat of impending conflict shot through subsequent resettler gatherings. "Some of the Los Angeles guys carry knives and they are always waiting to gang up on somebody," surmised a zoot-suiter who frequented the city's Nisei party circuit. "One of these days somebody is going to get hurt." One woman articulated her discomfort at having a stranger "cut in" during her turn on the floor. "I didn't know him and didn't want to dance with him and when my partner tried to continue dancing, the other boy threatened him," she recounted. "I didn't want to create a scene so I consented to dance with the stranger. I'm never going to another dance like that again." In response, event organizers took steps to keep "rowdy elements" at bay. The sponsors of a fete held at the Loop YWCA in November 1944 recruited the Chicago WRA office staff to chaperone and sold tickets in advance to deter spontaneous party crashers.[2]

To resettlement coordinators and many resettlers themselves, the unsavory habits of these rowdy elements jeopardized much more than the attendance and ambiance on social occasions. Yogore hazarded liberals' plans for repairing the damage to Japanese American citizenship wrought by the internment, especially the redistribution of internees throughout the United States so that they might fade into the white middle class. From the perspective of federal authorities, resettlement presented the chance for Nikkei to abandon their injurious typecasting as enemy Japs if they conformed to the default settings of legitimate American citizenship. By embracing orthodox social conventions, normative masculinity and femininity, and reputable heterosexuality alongside explicit avowals of patriotism, Japanese Americans could convincingly exhibit their fitness for inclusion into the national community.[3] Flaunting the flamboyant fashions and irreverent comportment typically associated with Mexican American and African American youths, yogore imperiled this objective by spurning mainstream society's standards of decorum. With no less than the postwar rehabilitation of Japanese American citizenship hanging in the balance, then, the WRA and its partner agencies embarked on a mission to eradicate all trappings of zoot suit culture among resettlers: visual signs (pompadours and ducktails, "drapes" consisting of broad-shouldered, long fingertip coats tapered at the ankles, pleated pegged pants, wide-brimmed hats, and watch fobs) and behavioral indicators (alcohol consumption, casual sex, "loafing," and other conduct deemed highly problematic, if not anti-American).[4]

As the focus of this policing endeavor, the pachuke ultimately served as a constitutive element of Japanese American identity and community formation at a time when the future of Nikkei remained indeterminate. In Chicago, the most popular destination for resettlers, Japanese Americans had numbered just under four hundred on the war's eve. More resettlers were drawn to that metropolis above others for its size, plentiful employment opportunities, and "comparative lack of anti-oriental feeling." By 1946–47, their population peaked at twenty thousand, with scores of ethnic organizations servicing this influx—a surprising growth considering that the federal government had actively discouraged ethnic networks from taking root in the city. Yogore played an integral, dual role in facilitating this momentum. As individuals, they forced the WRA to reconsider its strict assimilationist vision for resettlement. And as symbolic figures, they provided a powerful rhetorical specter that Japanese American spokespersons skillfully invoked to legitimate the establishment of ethnic community structures in the very place where state authorities had hoped to preclude their development.[5]

An exploration of the ways in which Nisei zoot-suiters became a lightning rod for the prescriptions of resettlement's stakeholders illuminates critical features of wartime culture that operated to reset the terms of Japanese American citizenship after Exclusion.[6] A professed political loyalty to the United States unquestionably overshadowed the reimagining of Nikkei as assimilable Others. But other imperatives mattered too. Gender and sexuality especially figured prominently in determining the contours of postcamp social standing. Scattered evidence indicates that community members tagged Nisei women regarded as morally wayward (unwed mothers and prostitutes) as yogore. For the most part, however, the WRA, resettlement agencies, and Nisei themselves imagined yogore as males in their teens and twenties, reflecting the critical importance of masculinity in the midcentury reconfiguration of the Asiatic. The term itself derived from the Japanese verb *yogoreru* (to get dirty). Sociologist Shotero Frank Miyamoto explained that it referred to individuals who were "shiftless, transient, constantly drinking and gambling, hanging around pool halls, always picking fights, visiting prostitutes or attempting to engage in illicit sex relations."[7] Yogore obviously disregarded society's requirements of young men to serve the wartime nation as loyal soldiers and productive workers: they expressed ambivalence, if not outright disdain, toward enlistment; they pursued unsanctioned sexual relations; and they took on employment only irregularly. All told, yogore expressed an alternative masculinity that deviated manifestly from dominant expectations of male citizens during wartime.[8] Resettlement advocates dreaded that such a distinction would torpedo the entire integrationist program by permanently attaching not-whiteness and the enemy alien stigma to all Japanese Americans.[9]

The yogore panic shines new light on the 1940s as the starting point of the forging of a national liberal racial order stitching together the country's various regional systems—a combination personified by resettlement's literal insertion of Japanese Americans into midwestern and eastern locales dominated by black-white relations. The Chicago encounter exemplifies the ways in which state and society's regulation of the yellow peril necessarily dovetailed with the handling of the "Mexican Problem" as well as the Negro Problem. By rejecting directives to discard cultural attachments and mannerisms that deviated from the white, middle-class, zoot suit style invoked instead an explicit kinship between pachuke and working-class brown and black folk. To resettlement advocates, this was an especially worrisome affinity that gestured to the disturbing possibility of a postinternment racialization aligning Japanese Americans more closely with other minorities than with whites. Criminalized conceptions of brownness and blackness, in short, had great bearings on the reconstruction of Nikkei citizenship. Resettlement's zoot suit uproar foretold the ways in which racial conceptions of Japanese Americans would necessarily be redefined as model minorities against other peoples of color in the coming decades.[10]

"Perhaps the zoot suit conceals profound political meaning," mused writer Ralph Ellison in 1943. Though he had African American hipsters in mind, his meditation is apropos for pondering the contests over Japanese American citizenship that unfolded in the realm of the everyday during the war. Among Nikkei who were judged by federal authorities to be loyal to the United States, yogore came to be seen as the most resistant to the state's insistence on the obliteration of ethnic difference. Yet zoot-suiters did not comprise a discrete "underclass" or marginal subculture set apart from the majority of Nisei. In fact, sentimental and behavioral distinctions between yogore and other resettlers were imprecise and even nonexistent at times. The WRA's assimilationist protocol was ignored by many, if not most, of Chicago's resettlers. Underlining this overlap serves as a reminder that the journey from subversive aliens to assimilable Others to model minorities was complicated, disputed, and anything but inevitable.[11]

The Nisei Zoot Suit Crisis

Nikkei elders had long been perturbed by the implications of disorderliness on their collective social standing. This concern dated back to turn of the century, when the Japanese Exclusion regime had not yet rigidified. In partnership with the Japanese imperial state, self-proclaimed immigrant leaders attempted to reform ordinary migrants' habits of body and mind to project civility and morality. Their goal was to avoid the fate of Chinese in the United States—legal-political illegitimacy, cultural degradation, and social marginality—by reassuring white Americans that the Japanese in their midst were *not* like the Chinese. Instead, the aim was to show that they morally resembled middle-class whites and therefore were fit to be embraced as fellow citizens. Issei visionaries attributed anti-Chinese hostilities to the incivility and contemptibility of the Chinese themselves, and scorned the most troublesome Japanese migrants—prostitutes, gamblers, vagrants, criminals, and the penniless—as "Sinicized." On both sides of the Pacific, educated elites spearheaded Americanization efforts to modernize potential and actual immigrants, inculcating bourgeois values to short-circuit any further Sinicization of the Issei masses. In the end, this agenda failed on two fronts. Migrant behaviors, for one, often proved impervious to social discipline. And second, nativists convincingly racialized Issei as aliens ineligible to citizenship by extending the spirit and substance of Chinese Exclusion to cover Japanese and other Asiatics. By 1924, laws and court rulings barred Issei from owning property, marriage to whites, naturalization, and entry into the United States.[12]

The hardening of Japanese Exclusion propelled community leaders to pin their hopes for acceptance on the second generation, which was just beginning to come of age in the 1920s. Many charged their sons and daughters with a unique task: as birthright citizens of the United States, Nisei could function as bicultural "bridges of understanding" between America and their ancestral homeland, not only to maintain transpacific peace and stability, but also to quell racial hostilities between their co-ethnics and whites. Most important, this cultural brokerage entailed a vigorous demonstration of Americanism as the key means to cultivate esteem among middle-class Anglo-Saxon Protestants. The term Americanism in this context denoted not only patriotism toward the United States but also rested heavily on Westernized notions of civility and decency. Elders sought to inculcate this ideal in their juniors through organizational activities, including scouting, athletic teams, and moral training in Japanese-language schools.[13]

Elites and ordinary folk who insisted on Americanism through respectability interpreted inconsistencies with their behavioral recommendations as threatening to the well-being of all Japanese in the United States. The rise of the second generation in the 1930s renewed this sense of urgency. The popularity of associational life among Nisei, especially the plethora of social clubs for boys and girls, spurred a concurrent spike in gang activity as adolescents moved to defend themselves against rival organizations of various ethnic and racial backgrounds, including other Japanese. Community members from Seattle to Los Angeles adopted a range of pressure tactics to keep one another in line: domestic interventions, gossip, ostracism, employer blackballing, and public shaming by outing perpetrators in the columns of vernacular newspapers. The ethnic press loudly reminded the Issei-Nisei public that their indelicacy would certainly preclude any hopes for social equality with whites and full inclusion in the nation.[14]

Japanese Americans who subscribed to these classed, racial, and moral valuations of worthiness upheld the white supremacist underpinnings of citizenship criteria. And indeed, community members deemed troublesome youths as "rowdies" not only because they operated outside social conventions by rejecting ethnic expectations of productive work, marriage, and group responsibility but also due to their attraction to persons of "lower social status," such as African Americans and Filipinos. Los Angeleno Lester Kimura readily fit this bill. During his junior high and high school years, he constantly ran into trouble, committing truancy, shoplifting, burglary, and vandalism. Like many Nisei who lived in diverse urban areas, Kimura fraternized outside the race. All his friends happened to be of Mexican ancestry, and they influenced his fashion sense: "I learned how to dress from the Mexican kids because they really knew how to be classy. They had 'drapes' way before the Nisei heard of such things." Kimura's appearance—unmistakably Chicano inspired—likely reinforced the assumption held by many Japanese Americans that yogore were problematic in part because of their mingling across racial lines.[15]

Incarceration did not these ease interclass tensions but instead heightened their visibility among prisoners, WRA officials, and observers. One internee recalled that "many of the Nisei began to get unconventional in sex attitudes," as manifested by "several cases" of teenage pregnancies and wardens "[catching] the Nisei in actual sex acts in the firebreaks or the empty barracks." Tule Lake center administrators imposed an 11:00 p.m. curfew on dances in an effort to curtail illicit sexual relations among the second generation. At Jerome camp—where there were at least two syphilis outbreaks—the WRA charged internal security officers with the mission of vice control to stop prostitution in the barracks, while the community council passed an ordinance in January 1944 criminalizing affronts to "public decency and morals." Social scientists also recorded myriad cases of violence, organized gambling, and theft perpetrated by both generations.[16]

Yogore were arguably the most visible reminders of deviance among internees. Zoot suit style followed urban prisoners into the camps, where many uninitiated Nisei from rural areas encountered pachuke for the first time. Kimura ran a brisk business at the Santa Anita center altering pants for those following the trend. Sociologist Charles Kikuchi noted at the Tanforan center that "the jitterbug craze is still strong with the young kids and for them nothing else exists. . . . Last night at the dance they were all dressed up in their draped pants and bright shirts. These boys are really extrovert [sic] and many of them speak the special jitterbug language with the facial expressions which they copy from Negroes." For many youths, the boredom of imprisonment likely made zoot culture an amusing way to pass the time. Some perhaps delighted in the shock value of imitating brown and black people. Others possibly embraced the style as a means to amass social capital—1940s' cool—within camp circles.[17]

Sus Kaminaka's wartime testimony provides a glimpse into the lives of Nisei zoot-suiters. Internment completely upended his ambitions. Originally from the farmlands of the Sacramento Delta region, Kaminaka was a studious agricultural college student until the evacuation. On incarceration, he decided hard work was an exercise in futility, and instead concentrated on having "fun like I saw the other kids doing." As one of an eight-member gang at the Stockton assembly center, he spent his days and nights reminiscing about life before imprisonment, chasing young women, and going to camp dances. It was during this time that he acquired his first zoot suit.[18]

FIGURE 1.1 Junichi "Frisco" Yamasaki dressed in zoot suit in the Poston, Arizona, WRA internment camp, 1942.
Gift of Frisco Yamasaki, Japanese American National Museum 2000.418.10

As Kaminaka became steeped in the ways of the yogore, he retreated from his prewar worldview. He used to regard Nisei girls "something sacred" and "never had any dirty thoughts [about] them," but the constant talk of sex freed his libido. Previously intent on earning his college degree, now a goal he considered hopeless, he dropped out of the camp's adult education school. And once "proud of living in the best country in the world," Kaminaka abandoned the idea of registering for the franchise. "I don't think I was too interested in voting anyway because I didn't know what it was all about and my vote didn't mean a thing."[19]

After transferring from Stockton to the relocation center in Rohwer, Arkansas, Kaminaka joined a gang known as the Esquires. For entertainment, they devoured food stolen from the camp's warehouses, drank, played poker, and held nightly bull sessions. "All we talked about was girls and we got to do more and more of this. . . . We would find out who were the most popular girls in camp and then go after them." Their modus operandi emerged as a source of contention among Rohwer's Nisei factions. "The Stockton fellows all went for the Santa Anita girls because they were from the city and this made the Santa Anita fellows sort of sore," he recalled. "That's why there were so many fights at the dances. . . . We went to dances in a gang and we never let anyone cut in on the girls in our group. . . . We would drink before going to the dances and that made us a little cocky."[20]

The Rohwer situation was not unusual. Conflicts between yogore and other prisoners interrupted the daily routines of several, if not all, the camps. In November 1942, the editors of the *Gila News-Courier* bemoaned the disappearance of every single plug from the center's laundry sinks, purportedly swiped for use as improvised zoot suit watch chains. Six months later, they urged their readership to deal with Gila's zoot suit presence through parental guidance and the threat of community censure, lest the center degenerate into "a place unfit for decent people." The following summer, Japanese American Evacuation and Resettlement Study (JERS) anthropologist Tamie Tsuchiyama reported that long-simmering "zoot-suit warfare" was now in "all its glory . . . with incidents of rowdies crashing parties and breaking them up, 'raping' girls, pushing sissies into the swimming pool, etc."[21] Hugely, tensions between yogore and others revolved around issues of impropriety, masculinity, and sexual expression. Camp authorities, investigators, and inmates branded yogore as disruptive *because* of their ill-gotten accessories, extralegal avenues to justice, and performances of masculine identities expressed through gendered, sexualized violence against women as well as "feminized" men—deviations, in other words, from white, middle-class expectations of comportment.

But beyond stability in the camps, pachuke chanced the crux of resettlement's liberal mission. By 1943, the robust zoot suit counterculture (encompassing fashion, jazz and swing music and dance, distinctive argots, and transgressions of race, gender, class, and sexuality boundaries) along with its young brown and black adherents had come to be associated with juvenile delinquency, moral deficiency, and unpatriotic subversion across the country. The zoot suit itself signaled an open defiance of the nation's war effort. The War Production Board banned the sale of zoot suits as a means to ration fabric, and the public deemed its devotees un-American. The eruption of Los Angeles' Zoot Suit Riots during the first week of June, when thousands of white soldiers and civilians violently attacked Mexican Americans, African Americans, and Filipino Americans, undoubtedly fed the anxieties of those committed to facilitating a smooth integration of Japanese Americans into mainstream society. If Nisei came to be widely associated with zoot suiting—and by extension, other racial minorities—Japanese Americans might cement their post-Exclusion social status on the brown and black sides of the nation's color lines.[22]

Against the backdrop of the Zoot Suit Riots and analogous clashes on the Gulf Coast and in Detroit, internment camp newspapers voiced trepidation at the escalating stakes of Nisei zoot suiting. On June 3, the Tule Lake *Daily Dispatch* castigated Nisei zoot-suiters for undermining the resettlement project: "Perhaps they believe that they are Americanized in their manners and in the way they dress. It is high time that someone educated them to the real meaning of the word Americanism." While zoot suiting can be considered a quintessentially American practice, clearly the publication's editors viewed yogore as engaging in the wrong kind of assimilation—into Mexican and African American urban youth culture rather than into the white middle class. Two weeks later, the newspapers of both the Jerome and Manzanar centers noted the patently unfavorable impression made by "rowdy, cheap, and shiftless" yogore in Denver and Chicago. The *Manzanar Free Press* disparaged Nisei zoot-suiters in Ohio and Illinois, "roaming the city streets creating ill-feeling and resentment among American people who are otherwise tolerant and understanding," thereby impeding the rehabilitation of Japanese American citizenship. In the face of this burgeoning crisis, the editors beseeched: "Leave your zoot suits behind. And above all, be an ambassador of goodwill for the sake of the Japanese in America."[23]

Mounting pressure to represent Japanese America did not convince yogore to reform, frustrating resettlement coordinators. They generally faulted Nisei themselves for failing to grasp the importance of conveying properness to others. Their exasperation derived partly from intergenerational disagreements over taste. "I can't understand how these young kids can come out of the centers dogged out as they are in these long coats, narrow trousers that fit tightly around the ankles, and long chains that almost drag to the ground," groused Chicago WRA office director Elmer Shirrell after meeting six Nisei zoot-suiters. "Well, the first one came in and he had one of those funny looking suits on. He told me that he was trying to get a job, so I told him, 'Young fellow, first of all I want to ask you if you think those clothes are appropriate around here. After all, you're out looking for a job, and sure as anything no employer is going to appreciate that kind of outfit.'" The young man paid little heed. When the second arrived, Shirrell's coworker "practically blew up" at the youth's appearance, which daringly flouted middle-class gender conventions. Like their Mexican American counterparts, Nisei zoot-suiters transgressed normative understandings of masculinity and femininity—a move perceived by the agency's administrators as risking the success of the WRA's assimilation objectives. "This one had one of those long hair cuts, and his hair was piled up on top in beautiful curls as if he had a coiffure of a Geisha girl or something," described Shirrell, "and a black silk shirt, with a bright tie, and a zoot suit just like the other fellow. It was more than [the coworker] could bear to look at it, and he just went right after that fellow." Disheartened, he agonized, "I don't know what I'm going to do with them. They're just utterly irresponsible, and all they're doing is hurting the whole resettlement program and the rest of the evacuees who are coming out here."[24]

At the same time, attitudes about appearances and gender performance transcended generational and ethnoracial divides. Rather, an intersection of interests and opinion among the WRA, Japanese American elites, and ordinary Nikkei faithful to the resettlement ideal suggests that they together drove the policing of the yogore. A number of Chicago's Nisei resettlers concluded that zoot-suiters diminished the social standing and assimilation prospects of all Japanese Americans. As one complained, "These damn zoot-suiters get me. Why do nisei have to dress like that anyway? They look like hell and every Caucasian who sees them will think that the nisei are a bunch of rats. People like that make things tough on the other nisei." Another concurred, "Get them out of town!" Joni Shimoda felt strongly enough to write back to Tule Lake camp, imploring the center's leadership to either force yogore to shed their accoutrements and cut their hair before release or withhold consent for them to leave.[25]

The issue was pressing enough to impel both WRA authorities and Nikkei elders to codify preventive and punitive measures. In September 1944, the WRA instructed its personnel to remind delinquent resettlers that habits such as job-hopping, congregating in gangs, and gambling would reflect poorly on all Japanese Americans. That same month, the Butte Community Council, one of the putatively self-governing bodies of the Gila River relocation center's inmates, instituted a formal juvenile code. Among the punishable offenses listed were liquor consumption, attending camp social functions without official invitation, causing disturbances at said events, assaulting young women, and the sporting of zoot suits or ducktail hairstyles by male minors. And in December 1944, the WRA authorized penalties for zoot-suiters, as in the case of one Heart Mountain internee sentenced to a "GI Haircut" as a way to eliminate "badge[s] of an undesirable element" that were "frowned upon by the general public." The administration's justification gestured toward the emerging logic of racial liberalism: "Certainly, it is every youth's privilege to dress as he pleases and follow the current styles, but there is a limit to such practices." For the Japanese American subjects of this state-engineered assimilation project, these limits were set by the federal government, white, middle-class cultural standards, and the prerogatives of community decision makers.[26]

The Symbol of the Pachuke

Ironically, while individual yogore posed obstacles to realizing the objectives of resettlement, the WRA and its partners found it useful to deploy the symbol of the pachuke as a way to discipline potential resettlers. Both the WRA and attendant agencies agreed that the goal of full assimilation entailed "the complete incorporation or absorption into our every community and social activity where only the difference in physical features are noticeable." But as Nisei began to depart the camps en masse, the ominous possibility of reestablishing "Little Tokios" loomed large. "If we fail to prevent in our resettlement program, social, religious, and recreational segregation, we [are] only sowing the seed of future misunderstanding and public resentment," predicted Ralph E. Smeltzer, director of the Church of the Brethren's resettlers hostel in Chicago. "Unless quick action results, the battle against segregation is lost." In the view of resettlement coordinators, the burden of assimilation did not rest on the state, private sectors, or general public; Nikkei themselves were primarily responsible for ensuring its triumph. Each and every one had the responsibility to serve as an "ambassador" for Japanese America. "The decision to relocate rests with you, and you must accept the initiative in adjusting yourself into the community where you plan to reside," WRA director Dillon S. Myer instructed resettlers.[27]

Implicitly and explicitly, coordinators invoked the yogore as a paradigm of misconduct as they screened and prepared resettlement candidates. In leave clearance interviews, required for permission to exit the camps, WRA officials asked Nisei about their willingness to dissociate from large groups of Japanese, forgo speaking the Japanese language, "avoid the organization of any typically Japanese clubs, associations, etc.," and conform to mainstream standards of behavior and clothing to facilitate ready acceptance into "American social groups." Partner organizations implemented analogous evaluation methods. For instance, the Brethren Hostel chose boarders based on written applications and personal interviews. Benchmarks for selection included "good reputation" and "a distinctly 'good' appearance." These criteria suggest that not only were there applicants whose profiles did not align with WRA expectations, especially zoot-suiters, but also that such individuals were not entitled to the opportunity for resettlement.[28]

For those who passed these assessments, managers devised guidelines that similarly raised the specter of the yogore as a shorthand allusion to the possible consequences of errant behavior. The Church of the Brethren's informational brochure, "Helpful Hints to Hostelers," stressed unobtrusiveness: "Don't argue with or antagonize others in public places. Don't get into fights. Observe respectable conduct wherever you are. Don't make yourself conspicuous in any way. Wear conventional clothes and hair cuts. Avoid loud talking and going about town in groups of more than *two or three*. Use your head in situations. Don't get excited." Another handout, the Gila camp administration's "When You Leave the Relocation Center," counseled:

> There may be times when you will find yourself unable to avoid feeling conspicuous in a crowd, but remember, it's a lot better to be conspicuous for being the only boy on the street car to give the old lady a seat [th]an for being the boy with the zoot suit and the duck tail haircut. There is a difference between being conspicuous for doing something commendable and being conspicuous for doing something censurable.

Here as elsewhere, the zoot suit and ducktail haircut stood as salient examples of reprehensible actions that threatened to wreck the entire resettlement project. The figure of the yogore—increasingly coded as a zoot-suiter or pachuke over the course of the war—served as a yardstick against which the federal government measured successful assimilation.[29]

The deployment of the yogore as a symbol echoed parallel strategies in the Mexican American community. There, various interests brandished *el pachuco* and *la pachuca* as potent rhetorical devices to advance a range of social and political agendas during World War II, from curbing the spread of Mexican American youth culture to racial assimilation. Similarly, the WRA and its affiliates found the "imagined pachuke" to be a graphic foil for the assimilating Nisei subject, the embodiment of resettlement gone awry. In the midst of the Zoot Suit Riots and other urban racial conflicts of 1943, coupled with continued wartime anti-Japanese hysteria, the meaning of this sign certainly would not have been lost on the young Nisei arriving in Chicago and other resettlement destinations.[30]

But if the figure of the pachuke stood in marked contrast to the assimilated Nisei, it was also not its polar opposite. The true antithesis to the "100 percent American" person of Japanese ancestry—embodied in the popular imagination by the Nisei soldiers of the 442nd Regimental Combat Team—was the enemy Jap. To be sure, yogore irritated those with an investment in ethnic dispersal and integration. At the same time, the WRA never saw zoot-suiters as a problem in ways comparable to the allegedly disloyal—those internees who refused to "swear unqualified allegiance" to the United States and induction into the armed forces, and in some cases sought re/expatriation to Japan. The WRA subsequently removed all disloyals to Tule Luke and denied them the chance to resettle. By comparison, yogore were not so fundamentally alien to the nation. After all, the government approved the leave clearance of those who eventually migrated to Chicago, Denver, and other places. Yet they remained thorny reminders of the possible alternatives to manly, patriotic citizenship and unadulterated aspirations to whiteness. Ostensibly loyal, the imagined pachuke exposed the fiction of the state's ability to eliminate racial, gender, sexual, and ultimately political waywardness even as the WRA and its assistants wielded the symbol as a way to achieve this containment.

Resettler Noncompliance

Chicago's resettlers tested the WRA's rigid vision of ethnic dispersal right away. Some complied strictly with the WRA's tuition to avoid any type of segregation, clinging to the much-touted possibility of soon achieving full integration. One young man related an uncomfortable incident on the subway after a "typical Jap with buck teeth and glasses" boarded the train and sat down beside him. "I didn't like that so I just ignored him. I didn't talk to him because I didn't want other people to notice us talking. I didn't want them to think that we knew each other." Consequently, he removed his own spectacles and put them in his pocket, because he decided that "two glasses and two buck teeth sitting together was too much and too conspicuous." His response indicates that at least some resettlers truly believed that their every action would affect the overall success of the WRA's assimilationist vision, and that they tried in earnest to dissociate themselves—at least in public—from other Nisei.[31]

Such tendencies, however, appeared to have been displayed by a minority of resettlers. Contemporary researchers noted that Nisei commonly paid "lip service" to the "theory" of assimilation, but that this was more of a token gesture than a lived reality. Whereas the WRA and its helper agencies ranked integration as the topmost priority of the resettlement program, the day-to-day survival issues of finding housing, employment, and friends fully absorbed the attentions of arrivals to Chicago. Most had come without their parents. Between September 1942 and January 1944, only 12 percent of newcomers were Issei. During this early period, most Nisei had few, if any, fellow Japanese American coworkers and neighbors. Facing the hardships of living solo in an unfamiliar city, lonely Nisei readily sought each other out for companionship. Despite the authorities' demands that they cultivate relationships outside the ethnic group, visiting with one another quickly became their preferred pastime.[32]

This disposition reflected resettlers' hesitancy about interacting with whites. The nervousness stemmed from their tenuous status in a society still at war with Japan and the unanswered question of their place in Chicago's racial order. As sociologist Tamotsu Shibutani mused in early 1944, "No one knows precisely where he stands in the new community." Even so, Nisei suspected that their position was probably on par with African Americans, many of whom were also recent transplants. Perhaps their biggest fear was that they were "helpless and at the mercy" of whites. News of the extensive violence perpetrated by whites against blacks during the 1943 Detroit race riots reinforced these apprehensions. Resettlers must have also noticed the bubbling racial tensions between white and black youths in wartime Chicago, including some who were zoot-suiters.[33]

Racial discrimination intensified this uneasiness. Despite the absence of restrictive covenants aimed at Japanese, locating satisfactory housing was the single most difficult task for many resettlers. For the most part, they were only able to rent apartments and homes in restricted areas on the city's Near North Side and Hyde Park–Kenwood on the city's South Side. The dilemma was so widespread that it was documented frequently by the Japanese American press and on occasion Chicago's mainstream media. In addition to housing, resettlers—like the city's other racial minorities—encountered racism in the workplace and other public spaces, including dance halls, hospitals, and even cemeteries.[34]

Rampant fears and alienation elicited a pervasive mood of anxiety among Chicago's Nisei during this period. The reflections of a music teacher epitomized the restlessness felt by many: "Everything seemed so grim and cheerless. It made my morale go way down and I felt low, strange, and alone," she stated. "It is hard to try out an exact path to follow, not knowing what is going to happen next in things which we have no control over. That is why I just live from day to day." With unknown futures, numerous resettlers felt torn between choosing jobs that allowed them to make as much money as possible in the present, or pursuing positions that might yield opportunities for better security and long-term mobility. After the War Department reinstated the eligibility of Japanese Americans for Selective Service in January 1944, Nisei men worried over the possibility of being drafted, prompting more than a few to postpone their plans for studies, marriage, and establishing careers.[35]

Facing these hurdles, countless resettlers readily dismissed the behavioral guidelines set by resettlement coordinators. Nisei zoot-suiters did so especially openly. Kimura recalled his arrival in Chicago: "At first I was very self-conscious and I felt that all of the people were staring at me because I was a Jap. I was wearing my drapes and some of the boochies [Japanese] told me not to wear them as it looked too conspicuous but I didn't pay any attention to them as I didn't see any wrong in it." Tadashi "Blackie" Nakajima spewed English vulgarities and Japanese slang expressions in public, consorted with the North Clark Street yogore gang, gambled, and frequented brothels—clearly not the type of integration the WRA had in mind for resettlers. Some pachuke also preferred to patronize black establishments over mainstream ones. Nakajima often spent his hours after work in black pool halls and theaters, and took his clothes to a black tailor for alterations. "The Negroes don't look at us as much as the *hakujins* [whites]," he explained. On evenings when he felt particularly restless, he would "wander all around the kurombo [black] section all night just thinking about how I will get even with the *keto* [whites] for pushing me around." Unmistakably, Nakajima felt a closer affinity to African Americans than to whites based on common experiences of racial injustice: "I figure that the kurombo should be best friends for [*sic*] the nisei because they have been crowded too." Kimura also articulated this sense of shared oppression: "I guess I sort of belong here [in the United States] just like all of the Negroes and those people who live in slums. There are certain groups in this country that don't get the democracy which they talk about in the schools." And while there is not abundant evidence that yogore maintained regular, meaningful relationships with individual black and Mexican zoot-suiters in Chicago, these material and psychological linkages undeniably contravened the WRA's assimilationist bidding.[36]

Yogore disregard for the federal government's instructions was also plainly evident in their attitudes toward work. Barry Shimizu resettled in Chicago in May 1943 and began working immediately for the Canfield Beverage Company. His supervisors fired him after he represented his coworkers during a strike. He "loafed around" for several weeks before being forced to look for another job after splurging on several new zoot suits. Shimizu then took a position in an area factory, where he quickly advanced to assistant foreman. But at that point, he recounted, "I began to get restless and pretty disgusted with everything. In spite of my promotions at the plant I wasn't satisfied with life. . . . I had too much time to think and I began to feel pretty disgusted with everything." He decided to quit the plant in order to "have some fun" before being drafted, and lived off winnings from racetrack betting and poker games. "I guess I am just lazy and I just don't feel like working anymore," he concluded. "But if I had a good reason to work, I know that I would do it." Shimizu's perception of racial barriers, such as what he believed to be the likelihood of Nisei losing their jobs after the war, deterred him from pursuing steady employment for the duration. His flatmate Kaminaka (the agricultural student-turned-zoot-suiter from Rohwer) narrated a similar outlook. After going through a series of jobs in Chicago, he too concluded that he would "play around" until being drafted, filling his days and nights with Nisei dances, drinking, and sexual exploits. Like Shimizu, Kaminaka expressed a profound ambivalence toward this existence: "I am getting absolutely no place now. . . . It isn't doing me much good. It bothers me a lot and I think of a lot of things I should be doing but I never get ambitious enough to get around to it."[37]

A comparison here between the yogore and African American hipsters illuminates both the commonalities across racial lines as well as specificities of the Nisei example. Malcolm Little (the future Malcolm X) and his fellow zoot-suiters "refus[ed] to be good proletarians," favoring fast-money alternatives such as hustling to the drudgery and alienation of the low-wage, menial wage work options available to them as black, working-class youths. They dodged the draft, prioritized leisure, and took pleasure in music, dancing, and sex as ways to subvert white and black middle-class expectations of patriotism, subservience, and seemliness. They fashioned generational and racial identities that rejected work as the "primary signifier," and instead "reinforce[d] a sense of dignity."[38] Like their African American counterparts, Nisei zoot-suiters rebuffed the government's insistence that they be industrious, compliant participants in the wartime defense mobilization, and looked instead to leisure and pleasure for more immediate gratification.

Yet internment and resettlement also made an appreciable difference. Compared to African Americans, Japanese American newcomers to Chicago were less sure about their social standing during the war. While "having fun" was the zoot-suiters' declared motivation for avoiding wage work, they found the yogore lifestyle ultimately unfulfilling because it did not solve the problem of uncertainty. This helps to explain why pachuke seem not to have been as resistant to the draft as black zoot-suiters. Certainly some yogore adamantly opposed military service. As Kimura opined, "I don't feel like fighting for this country as we have always been kicked around so much. They tell us that they are going to give us a chance to get killed off and then we will be considered loyal, but what good will that do if we are six feet under the ground." But the yogore interviews also reveal a mixed sense of anger, resignation, and even hope. Nakajima declared, "I don't give a s— about the war. . . . If I get taken I'll get taken and that's all there is to that." Kaminaka confessed, "I am willing to fight for the US as I plan to live here always and it is my country in spite of what some Caucasians say. At least I can say that I have a more definite part in the war effort if I were drafted. That's about all the future

I can look forward to now." Shimizu saw induction as a "privilege after the way we have been mistrusted up to now," and believed that he and his fellow Japanese Americans "have to do our part for the war."[39]

In short, Nisei zoot-suiters held a range of positions on the call to arms. Some can be read as oppositional, but not inflexible, given the context of the continuing war against Japan. Others might be interpreted as apolitical or even cautiously patriotic despite their blatant rejection of the assimilationist mandate. This is not entirely surprising given that they had pledged "yes-yes" to the federal government's mandatory survey asking their willingness to serve combat duty and swear unqualified allegiance to the United States—necessary preconditions for indefinite release from camp. Kimura explained that despite pressure from his parents to answer "no-no," he responded "yes-yes." "There wasn't any other way I could answer because I never felt loyal to Japan. Hell, a guy has to answer it in the right way if he were born here, doesn't he?" Shimizu also decided "yes-yes" not only because he "didn't want trouble with the government" but also "because even if we were kicked around, we belong here."[40] Zoot suits, in other words, did not automatically correlate to unchanging anti-American sensibilities for these former internees, even if individual pachuke ignored the WRA's rules for proving Japanese Americans' worthiness of full citizenship.

Significantly, such defiance was not limited to those identified as yogore but rather was expressed by countless Chicago Nisei. As resettlers departed the camps, the WRA had reminded them that the War Manpower Commission required all workers to obtain official releases from their employers or the US Employment Service before leaving their positions for another; Nisei who had neglected to do so were "reflect[ing] unfavorably" on all Japanese Americans. But resettlers understood that the home front faced a worker shortage, and that this scarcity allowed them leverage in the labor market. They continually sought higher-paying jobs, and many did not hesitate to breach their current contracts in pursuit of better opportunities, earning them the moniker "sixty-day Japs." Others quit because they were dissatisfied with their work conditions, including racial discrimination. Again, the common suspicion that Japanese Americans would lose their positions to returning soldiers at the war's end led some to feel less invested in maintaining good relations with employers. For them, their indeterminate status and prospects offset any incentives they had to find regular work. Some entered the illicit economy, as was the case of one Nisei girl rumored to be passing as Chinese and working as a prostitute at the Fairview Hotel.[41]

Thus yogore and nonyogore alike seemed to be marking time until the draft and the end of the war. Kaminaka noted that "most of the Nisei don't feel like working now as it doesn't give them enough time to have fun" after putting in a full day's work. "There's no percentage in that and they feel that they might as well go out and enjoy themselves before the Army takes them. . . . Some of them just quit their jobs without giving any notice and they loaf around for two months so they can get an automatic release and then go after another job when their money runs out." He conceded that these choices might hurt Japanese Americans' postwar standing, but added, "You can't blame some of them for going wild because this is the first chance they have had to have their fling." A fellow resettler agreed, "A part of the Nisei tendency to be restless and to run around a lot now is the sowing of wild oats." Most of his friends were "more interested in getting larger pay checks and spending the money" on clothes and dancing than in saving their earnings, contributing to the war effort, or creating a favorable impression of Japanese Americans in the ways prescribed by the WRA. As he explained, "They felt that they had been deprived of a lot of things during the time they were in camp and this is a relief to them."[42]

Despite federal directives, then, a distinctive Japanese American social world began to coalesce during Chicago's early resettlement period. Characterized by ethnic congregation, this nascent milieu contravened the federal government's expectation that Japanese Americans embrace reliability, honorableness, and normative gender roles. This budding resettler culture endangered the rehabilitation of Japanese American citizenship along the lines of white, middle-class cultural and ideological standards. These flagrant violations ultimately forced the WRA and its supporting organizations to reassess resettlement's guiding principle of assimilation.

Reenvisioning Assimilation: The Chicago Resettlers Committee

Predictably, Nisei's unseemly habits unsettled resettlement coordinators, who feared such conduct would beget an unfavorable image of Japanese Americans and hinder their full inclusion in the larger society. Nisei absenteeism and job-hopping had become widespread enough that a number of Chicago-area businesses expressed an unwillingness to hire Japanese Americans. Sponsoring agencies also noted complaints filed by local residents with the Federal Bureau of Investigation (FBI) charging that "Japanese are forming 'cultural' and 'social' clubs, and loiter on corners on North Clark Street," and fretted that press accounts of "resettler delinquency" had resulted in an "unsavory reputation." Chicagoans' recourse to FBI surveillance suggests that beyond the concerns of gang activity, steady employment, and social assimilation, resettlers' behaviors called into question their national affiliations and political sympathies. Visible ethnic congregations might reinvigorate fears of the enemy Jap that the WRA, some of the Nikkei elite, and many ordinary Japanese Americans had tried to extinguish through Nisei military service.[43]

To counter these setbacks, resettlement coordinators amplified their efforts to impress the importance to resettlers of "accepting the responsibilities of citizenship in the American pattern." Above all, this meant avoiding the resurgence of prewar social organization and the reconstitution of the ethnic community. The Brethren Hostel embraced this approach, requiring boarders to attend discussions that addressed such questions as "What were the mistakes in our social life before evacuation?" "What evidences are there of unnecessary segregation here in Chicago?" and "What can we do to get into Hakujin [white] groups, churches, clubs, professional groups, etc.?" Other organizations worked to achieve the same ends. Volunteers for the Newcomers' Cooperative Committee opened their homes to resettlers for "inter-racial parties," and area YMCAs, YWCAs, and Chicago Public Parks and Recreation facilities recruited resettlers for their programs. The Chicago Church Federation's United Ministry to Resettlers emphasized the imperative of "avoid[ing] segregation *at all costs*" and advised resettlers to "spread out thinly." While these agencies understood their role in resettlement to be that of facilitators of integration, they placed the onus of assimilation on Nisei themselves. This perspective was evident in their definition of segregation, which they considered to be entirely voluntary on the part of Japanese Americans, rather than a consequence of racial discrimination, the anguish of internment, and uncertainty over Nisei's collective postwar citizenship status.[44]

Despite these undertakings, Nisei continued to seek out each other for companionship. Gradually, resettlement coordinators began to accept this situation, albeit with a hope that the motivating factors could eventually be overcome. In November 1944, the American Friends Service Committee and the American Baptist Home Mission Service allowed that "there may be *certain areas of social needs* where racially uniform activity appears inevitable," given the fact resettlers had only recently undergone the experience of being "victim[s] of mass racial discrimination." Still, the two agencies aimed "to cut into this vicious circle in which discriminatory treatment drives a group into clannish withdrawal within itself, thereby inviting further discrimination." Thus, they would continue to devote their resources to fostering "non-segregated on-going life" rather than encouraging "racially segregated activity."[45]

But unacknowledged in this statement were the steps being taken by certain resettlers toward a *politics* of racial integration that differed markedly in substance from the social integration desired by resettlement managers. In May 1945, the eminent sociologist Horace R. Cayton Jr. lauded resettlers nationwide for reorienting themselves within the nation's racial and political order. Devoting one of his *Pittsburgh Courier* columns to the Nikkei's plight, he explained that internment had forced the community to realize that in order advance its "struggle for survival and equality," it needed to join in the "general progressive movement" alongside Jews, African Americans, Mexican Americans, and labor. Japanese Americans were therefore enacting an alternative model of racial integration—one that acknowledged and affirmed their history as an oppressed minority—to the one prescribed by the WRA.[46]

Cayton wrote from firsthand experience. He was one of the most dedicated supporters of resettlers' needs to nurture connections to one another and their desires for ethnic community organizations. As the director of Bronzeville's Parkway Community House, he gave resettlers meeting space for weekly Buddhist services. In 1944, Cayton recruited Setsuko Matsunaga Nishi—herself a new arrival to Chicago—to facilitate Parkway's series of People's Forum discussions on racism. The position provided her "first really close contact with Negroes, who knew so much better than Nisei the destructiveness of the fear and hatred of racial prejudice—which gave me the courage for facing what minorities must." Crucially, Cayton understood that Chicago's Japanese Americans lacked the knowledge and experience to navigate government bureaucracy in order to harness civic resources to their advantage. So he provided Nishi with critical hands-on training by introducing her to the city's social welfare establishment in his capacity as chair of the Committee on Minority Groups of Chicago's Council of Social Agencies, the umbrella organization of municipal social services.[47]

Together, teacher and protégé forcefully advocated for Nikkei. Explaining that the Committee on Minority Groups' purview was not limited in scope to the "Black Metropolis," Cayton encouraged the city's welfare institutions to devote serious thought to the resettlers' conditions. At his behest in December 1944, the Committee on Minority Groups surveyed the various agencies affiliated with the council's Division on Education and Recreation to assess the effectiveness of their outreach to Japanese Americans. The intent, he explained, was "*to provide guidance for the future*," especially as the WRA anticipated a rush of resettlers with the expected closing of the camps in the coming year. Survey data revealed that only 636 of Chicago's 13,000 resettlers utilized the services of the agencies that responded to the questionnaire; 351 of them participated in activities for Japanese Americans only rather than integrated ones. Nishi presented the Committee on Minority Groups' findings to the council in May 1945. Her report detailed resettlers' anomalous predicament: bereft of the "stabilizing factors of family and community ties," Nisei harbored a "sense of futility about their future, a feeling of not belonging, of being outcast." To accentuate these strains, she added that "the Nisei with 'Zoot Suit' and pachuco duck-tail hair cut is not an uncommon sight." She concluded with an "urgent" plea for a "constructive recreational program" to ensure the resettlers' "integration into the social life of the city."[48]

The Committee on Minority Groups modeled its own advice by gathering Japanese American spokespersons and sympathizers to study resettlers' social welfare and make recommendations to the council's directors. Headed by Cayton, the ad hoc conference convened in June 1945. When WRA and Church Federation representatives voiced concerns that resettlers should be "integrated" into mainstream institutions, Cayton affirmed that integration was "desirable," but questioned to what degree it was "practicable," since any group might wish for both coethnic associations as well as "wider relationships." Nishi seconded his remarks by reminding discussants that "enforced integration" had resulted in "psychological difficulties." A "broad program for happiness" struck her as imperative to treat these ills. After several weeks of fact-finding, the conference moved that the Council of Social Agencies should sponsor the formation of a centralized body including Nikkei themselves to oversee "special services" targeting Japanese Americans. In October, the conference formally submitted its proposal to the council to establish the Coordinating Committee on Welfare Services to Japanese Americans. The recommendation strategically foregrounded the disclaimer that such assistance "should be operated with a view to eventual integration" even as Nikkei had the "same right" as others "to form their own volunteer groups." The initiative succeeded. The committee commenced operation, with Nishi on board, in November.[49]

Nishi's "apprenticeship" in "the business of race relations" under Cayton equipped her with the know-how and connections that proved invaluable in laying the groundwork for building viable Nikkei institutions in Chicago. In September 1945, she helped lead a group of fourteen Japanese Americans and allies in establishing the Chicago Resettlers Committee (CRC) "to attend to the unfinished problems of evacuation and resettlement." The formal organization of the Japanese American community was increasingly necessary, the committee argued, as the WRA and other sponsors began to terminate their support programs at the same moment when the final wave of internees arrived in Chicago. The CRC's initial services included assistance with health care, business, employment, and housing, and a varied selection of activities to accommodate resettlers' "dramatic" recreational exigencies.[50]

In late 1946, the CRC appointed the Social Analysis Committee (SAC) to study this distress. With this documentation, the organization hoped to persuade Chicago's Council of Social Agencies to underwrite the creation of recreational programs catering to Nisei youths—the issue that CRC leaders had come to identify as one of the most, if not the most, dire for resettlers. SAC's final report invoked examples of Nisei deviance from correctitude to underline the seriousness of the situation. Crime and delinquency were on the rise, it stressed, no doubt because young, unmarried Nisei were unmoored from "normal home environment and parental guidance." Evidence of maladjustment abounded: fourteen known babies born out of wedlock, climbing numbers of abortion requests, "prevalence of gambling," and "apparent disregard for social conventions." Among the many "individual instances of immorality" were one young convict serving a life sentence for his role in a "hold-up gang," two Nisei arrested for vice trafficking, and an at-large "alleged sex maniac" accused of raping seven women. This "criminal infection," if ignored, would only heighten resettlers' "general dereliction" if the dearth of decent social outlets was left unfilled.[51]

SAC's investigation yielded the following mission statement:

> ON THE EVE of their fifth year of residence in Chicago, many of the 20,000 Japanese American resettlers here have not yet found a world where they can feel at home.
>
> Not only do they not feel at home here, but they are also beset by unwholesome influences that obstruct them from growing in that direction. Those same unwholesome influences may yet claim many more of them as social casualties in 1947.
>
> The challenge now of the unfinished job of relocation is clear. Either the churches, social agencies, and community leadership act with imagination and foresight to provide competing social-recreational outlets for these people, or else we shall surrender them from the potentialities of constructive citizenship.[52]

In striking contradistinction to the white resettlement managers, the CRC placed the responsibility for the assimilation and rehabilitation of Japanese American citizenship on mainstream institutions rather than on Nikkei themselves.

While explicitly acknowledging that "*the ultimate goal [of resettlement] is for the Japanese Americans to become participating members of the Chicago citizenry*," SAC proposed a radically different tactic than the WRA and its partners. SAC maintained that resettlers' "sense of security and self-confidence" needed to be nurtured carefully after the damage of internment in order to cultivate the "well-integrated personalities" crucial for achieving the end result of full assimilation. But restoring psychological well-being was impossible without "identification with some

FIGURE 1.2 Setsuko Matsunaga Nishi, a vocal advocate for Japanese American transplants to the Midwest and a founder of the Chicago Resettlers Committee social service agency. Nishi went on to earn her doctorate in sociology at the University of Chicago, where she spearheaded the interdisciplinary Japanese American Personality and Acculturation Study and wrote her dissertation on Nikkei life postinternment.
Courtesy of the Nishi family archive.

social group," and the only people with whom Nikkei in Chicago consistently identified and associated were other former internees. "If this present identification were suddenly removed," warned the committee, "it would result in further personal disintegration." Therefore, civic leaders had the responsibility "to *gradually* transfer their sense of security in the Japanese American group to groups in the larger society." In other words, resettlers' participation in ethnically exclusive activities as opposed to predominantly white ones could still be used to achieve Japanese American integration. Not coincidentally, SAC's arguments mirrored those of Cayton and Nishi in their campaign for the Coordinating Committee on Welfare Services to Japanese Americans.[53]

The everyday lives of ordinary Nisei thus compelled resettlement's visionaries to reevaluate their brand of assimilationism. Persuaded by the CRC's rationale, WRA director Myer conceded that "insistence on mixed group affairs may serve to deprive [Japanese Americans of] all well managed activity, and to drive them to the very types of recreation" that coordinators viewed as undesirable. An effective resettlement program, Myer concurred, "may well include all-Nisei groups, which if intelligently guided with the final objective always in mind, could contribute to the desired end." The final reports on resettlement filed by the regional branches of the WRA also did not find the spread of ethnic organizations to be problematic, but remained hopeful that "such groups will disappear from the picture as resettlers become more at home in new communities."[54]

Counseled by Cayton, now one of the organization's official advisers, the CRC coupled Myer's endorsement with an invocation of the specter of Nisei delinquency to shore up its proposal for membership in the Council of Social Agencies and for financial support from Chicago's Community Fund. The CRC maintained that it should serve as a liaison between existing community organizations and resettlers in order to encourage Nikkei participation in mainstream social-recreational providers. In addition, it proposed the formation of a citywide Japanese athletic council and other programs in cooperation with mainstream institutions such as YMCAs, YWCAs, the Boy Scouts, and the Girl Scouts. These structured activities, although not racially integrated, provided what the CRC hoped would be attractive alternatives to Nisei "congregating on street corners, [in] pool halls, and taverns" engaged in "drunkenness and fights." Finally, the CRC reiterated that "unless the above-outlined program . . . is vigorously carried forward without delay, the people will find the solution to their frustrations in unsupervised, psychologically isolating activities cut off from the matrix of the larger society."[55]

By pointing to yogore and also portraying the entire Nisei population on the brink of depravity, the CRC effectively revised resettlement's original assimilationist vision to legitimize the institutionalization of Japanese American community life. Once again, this approach paralleled that of contemporary Mexican American and African American leaders in Los Angeles and New York—and of course, Nishi's own work for the Council of Social Agencies' Committee on Minority Groups—who ably mobilized support for their communities by calling attention to their respective zoot suit problems.[56] The imagined pachuke was thus a highly flexible symbol, with the ability to be appropriated for very different ends: to discipline resettlers, shed racialized markers, hurry the assimilation process, and now justify ethnic community formation.

The request effectively moved the Council of Social Agencies to bestow membership on the CRC in September 1946. The council also agreed to provide half the CRC's operating budget for 1947. Admission and the allotment of the monies marked a significant turning point in liberal thinking on Nikkei citizenship. Resettlement authorities and other social policymakers had come to the consensus that ethnic persistence and organization would not necessarily preclude assimilation but instead could function as the most efficacious way to ensure Japanese Americans' full integration into the mainstream community. American society, in turn, had an obligation to its Nikkei citizens to support these efforts.[57]

The Emergence of Chicago's Japanese
American Community

With the backing of both federal authorities and the city's social welfare establishment, Chicago's Japanese American community rapidly organized in the immediate postwar years. During that period, the city was home to several Japanese Christian and Buddhist congregations, Japanese- and English-language community newspapers and magazines, and a range of Nikkei secular organizations—all members of the city's Japanese American Council.[58] Across the country, resettlers and West Coast returnees engaged in similar community (re)building processes out of both necessity and preference.[59]

The CRC reported significant inroads in solving the dilemmas of resettler adjustment in December 1947. Abe Hagiwara, the organization's recreation director, assembled the Citywide Committee on Recreation to oversee an open house series "to provide inexpensive and enjoyable socials for boys and girls" under "wholesome conditions." In addition, the Citywide Committee advised many of Chicago's Nisei organizations, including the Girls Interclub Council and the Chicago Nisei Athletic Association, whose affiliates included softball, basketball, and bowling leagues. By CRC accounts, the rapid proliferation of organized activity successfully directed Nisei youths' leisure time toward "constructive" channels conducive to good citizenship. The CRC's 1948 annual report documented a record 9,363 Nisei participating in the 69 Japanese American groups affiliated with the committee's recreation and education program. By the end of 1949, Nisei began to interact more frequently with non-Japanese through athletic competitions and neighborhood agencies—further steps toward achieving resettlement coordinators' goal of assimilation.[60]

Despite the spread of Japanese American organizations, some Nisei continued to prefer racially integrated associational life. University of Chicago sociology student Eugene Uyeki found that one-quarter of the 62 men he surveyed in 1952 "consciously" sought friendships with whites and joined mainstream organizations to secure their long-term social standing. The American Legion's all-Nisei Rome-Arno Post No. 1183 had difficulty recruiting and retaining membership for these reasons, noted Uyeki, who observed that most Nisei veterans felt that Japanese Americans should pursue the route of affiliating with mainstream institutions as a better means to securing full citizenship.[61]

Nisei deviance, moreover, was not eliminated overnight. SAC called attention to the persistence of "social misfits" for whom "assimilation" meant "floating down into society's gutter." CRC director Yasutake noted continued public intoxication, verbal sparring, and fisticuffs at social functions. A "gang fight" between members of the Ro-babes, a Japanese

American club, and white men in April 1950 prompted the CRC Community Relations Committee to reiterate the necessity of providing appropriate role models for Nisei teens.[62] None of these was hailed as a zoot-suiter problem per se—perhaps because some pachuke must have returned to the Pacific coast after the war, while others probably tired of the look as its popularity evaporated.

By late 1950, however, the CRC was satisfied enough with the general decline in Nisei waywardness to redirect the focus of its recreation program to a more concerted effort at broader social integration. While still maintaining its advisory role to Nisei organizations, the Citywide Recreational Committee discontinued the planning of ethnically exclusive projects in favor of fostering Nisei participation in "inter-group activities" cosponsored by mainstream institutions. Optimistic about the community's progress, the CRC declared in 1953, "Chicago's Japanese Americans have become, relatively more, 'a part of the whole.'" The following year, Hagiwara remarked that "none of [the] problems experienced eight years ago exist today to the same degree. The Nisei today are free to go anywhere and are accepted in public and commercial places of recreation." Hagiwara pointed to the irony of Chicago's "welcoming" environs: "Because of their freedom to select and chose [sic] as they please, the Nisei have unconsciously re-established a self-segregated social pattern."[63]

This self-segregation, though, was not as unconscious as Hagiwara described. From the beginnings of resettlement, Nisei had deliberately rejected the federal government's vision of dispersal and integration. The sum of their day-to-day actions, particularly those read as delinquent, had compelled resettlement coordinators and the city to legitimize the reconstitution of the Japanese American community.

While the fight to correct straying from white middle-class conventions was not the sole factor prompting the formation of Nikkei institutions, it was nevertheless a pivotal one. At a broader level, the omnipresence of yogore—both in terms of real bodies and as politically charged symbols—evinced the salience of brownness and blackness in shaping the course of Japanese American citizenship during as well as after internment. In the context of the war's irrepressible racial tensions, Nisei zoot-suiters conjured up alternative imaginings of Americanism that obstinately resisted the WRA's command to disappear into the white middle class. Their attitudes and decisions, like those of many other resettlers who were *not* pegged as yogore, expanded the viable range of options for postwar identity and community formation. In the process, they helped move perceptions of Nikkei ethnic gathering away from the subversive machinations of perpetually foreign enemy Japs to salutary activity befitting any bona fide American ethnic group.

In a different way, the intricacies of establishing community organizations also revealed the significance of brownness and blackness to the remaking of Japanese American citizenship in the mid-twentieth century. Even as many resettlers—including zoot-suiters—felt conflicted about their black neighbors and coworkers, Chicago's Nisei leaders found African Americans to be some of their most vocal advocates. Epitomized by Nishi and Cayton, these interracial alliances were crucial to positioning Nikkei as a beleaguered minority collectively entitled to civic uplift. By working with African American activists to maneuver through an existing liberal institutional framework devoted to solving the Negro Problem, Japanese American spokespersons deftly instated their version of participation and belonging into Chicago's social welfare structure. Quite remarkably, the CRC and other Nikkei associations effectively challenged the assimilationist orthodoxy espoused by the racial liberals of the WRA and cooperating agencies.

Yet in conceding that assimilation remained the overriding objective of resettlement—if only at the rhetorical level for the sake of social legitimacy and material resources—Japanese American leaders simultaneously validated racial liberalism's ideological underpinnings. Moreover, by deploying the imagined pachuke and threat of Nisei deviance to justify their agenda, Nikkei spokespersons also reproduced the normative positions on gender and sexuality that undergirded racial liberalism. Perhaps they settled on this strategy because it made the most pragmatic sense. Undoubtedly attuned to the political realities of the time, especially as persons of Japanese ancestry living in a country only beginning to recover from a vicious, racially inflected war with Japan, CRC founders must have realized the limitations on the ways they could fruitfully couch their arguments for a rightful existence. Capitulating to white, middle-class expectations of respectability might have been perceived as a small price to pay for the freedoms of being seen and treated as a people with potential for full societal membership. In so doing, the originators of the CRC showed racial liberalism's potential for stretching to accommodate unanticipated situations while simultaneously reinforcing its conservative dimensions within which all racial minorities would necessarily struggle for civil rights and equality of citizenship in the postwar era.[64]

Chapter 2

How American Are We?

The experience of World War II could not have been more starkly different for Japanese and Chinese Americans. Configured as enemy aliens, Nikkei endured mass removal, internment, the effective nullification of their citizenship, and a coercive dispersal.[1] The Chinese, by contrast, enjoyed sounder social footing as a result of their real and presumed ties to China, the nation's partner in the Pacific War against Japan. Thousands of Chinatown residents left the ethnic economy for the first time to take up arms and fill positions in the defense industry. Like never before, the prospect of attaining full acceptance and equality seemed within reach: "The crisis of December 7 has emancipated the Chinese in the United States," declared sociologist Rose Hum Lee in 1942. "No longer do Americans think of the Chinese as mysterious Orientals from a little known land. Most of these Chinese living among them are fellow citizens. The rest of them, as well as their cousins in the old country, are Allies." Social worker Lim P. Lee agreed. "For the first time among the Chinese there is an inter-racial contact, and for the first time, too, the average American has learned to know and highly regard his Chinese co-workers," he told the *San Francisco Chronicle*.[2]

For all these disparities, however, war mobilization impacted Japanese and Chinese American lives in comparable ways. Most fundamentally for both groups, geopolitical forces opened up novel opportunities for national belonging. In the case of the Chinese, many liberals believed that the Exclusion regime could no longer be sustained. Severe immigration restrictions made for "bad diplomacy" at a time when China stood as "the only possibility of an allied offensive on the Asiatic continent," as one federal official brooded. Too, Chinese immigrants and their children needed to be integrated fully into American society. "The war has brought the Chinese out of Chinatown and we should lock the doors behind them," the progressive activist-writer Carey McWilliams declared dramatically in 1943. Articulating the view of many forward-minded persons, McWilliams argued that the global conflict presented an extraordinary incentive for the federal government to intervene immediately in bread-and-butter realms (housing, job training, and education) to ensure "assimilation at the level of full equality of social, economic, and political participation," while simultaneously allowing the "freedom to maintain cultural traditions." Realizing this goal necessitated the redefinition of Chinese American identity in law and society—an aspiration that drove various stakeholders to reorient public opinion before, during, and after the war. Their collective efforts translated into the watershed repeal of the Chinese Exclusion Acts in 1943 and a new emphasis on Chinese *inclusion* in mass culture.[3]

In tandem with the momentous shift in mainline thinking, liberals' avid promotion of Chinese inclusion buoyed changes in the internal dynamics of Chinese America as well. Their championing of acceptance and incorporation helped Chinese Americans break out of the confines of their lives under Exclusion imposed by larger society and traditional immigrant elites, validating the pursuit of greater freedoms and opportunities stateside. Encouraged by the outpouring of wartime racial liberal sentiment, Chinese Americans, especially the native-born cohorts just coming of age, asked new questions and desired new answers about life in the United States. For Chinese Americans, the 1940s was truly a remarkable moment of liberation and possibility.

At the same time, many perceived the next steps as less straightforward, with an uncertain future provoking anxiety as well as optimism. Chinese Americans knew well that their prospects for betterment and belonging remained directly contingent on the United States–China rapport—a shaky situation given the unrelenting strife between Chiang Kai-shek's Nationalists and Mao Zedong's Communists. The advent of the English-language ethnic press in this period opens a window onto this vexed situation. On one level, the bevy of publications founded at midcentury—in part a product of Chinese America's demographic shift from majority foreign to majority-US born—served as the preeminent locus through which rising members of the community jointly grappled with their collective predicament of second-class citizenship. On another level, the creation of Anglophone newspapers and magazines was itself an instantiation of the efforts to resolve the dilemma of Chinese American social standing after Exclusion. Since the late nineteenth century, Chinatown periodicals had been preoccupied with the Chinese nation-state and its partisan disputes. The decision to publish in the common tongue of the United States therefore marked not only a linguistic but also a political departure from decades of immigrant journalism. Fledgling English-language journals, contrarily, evinced an American-oriented sensibility by voicing the aspirations of younger Chinese for recognition and legitimacy within the national community. In this way, the Chinese press in the United States transcended its initial purposes as an intraethnic medium and instrument for the cultivation of a diasporic identity centered on China to become a vehicle for public relations along with the manufacture of new conceptions of *Chinese American* citizenship.

Repealing Chinese Exclusion

For six decades, Chinese had vigorously objected to the matrix of laws and practices that explicitly barred or otherwise impeded their admission to the United States, attainment of naturalized citizenship, and treatment as social equals. In the face of such restrictions, they mounted a gamut of challenges, from lawsuits to economic boycotts to creative strategies for circumventing immigration restrictions. Their protests resulted in a number of important victories, notably the Supreme Court's ruling in *United States v. Wong Kim Ark* (1898) upholding birthright citizenship for all. Yet because of China's attenuated position vis-à-vis the world powers, these measures fell short of overturning exclusion.

Their fortunes began to change in the 1930s. As the Japanese empire expanded into China, the United States offered the Chinese financial assistance and military personnel as a way to secure its own dominance over the Asia-Pacific region. Pearl S. Buck's Pulitzer-prizewinning novel *The Good Earth* (1931) and Metro-Goldwyn-Mayer's Hollywood adaption (1937) introduced sympathetic portrayals of Chinese peasantry to millions of Americans. Publishing magnate Henry Luce, arguably the most influential mass communicator of the day, did the same through moving depictions in *Life* magazine of Chinese women and children suffering at the hand of their Japanese oppressors. *Time*, his other blockbuster venture, crowned China's president along with first lady generalissimo Madame Chiang Kai-shek "Man and Wife of the Year" in 1937. That same year, after Japan's brutal invasion of Nanjing, the circle of US religious workers and businesspeople with firsthand experience in China (including Buck and Luce, both born and raised there by their missionary parents) rallied with Chinese Americans to cultivate public awareness and support for war relief efforts. Myriad agencies banded together as United China Relief, whose trademark "Bowl of Rice" fund-raising festivals, set in the nation's Chinatowns, featured celebrity appearances, parades, Chinese fashion shows, and exotic performances drawing thousands of spectators. The sum of these efforts assured American sympathy for China.[4]

When the United States declared war on Japan in December 1941, China's de facto ally status became formalized. Soong Meiling (Madame Chiang Kai-shek)'s stateside tour in 1943 symbolized and cemented the transpacific relationship by personifying the promise of a new China, and by extension, a new Asia, realized under US tutelage: Christian, democratic, and modern. In projecting a feminized image of China, she no doubt appealed to the United States' sense of paternalistic self-importance. Her beauty, poise, and eloquence enthralled Americans. Speaking before Congress in February 1943, she emphasized the ideological kinship between the two nations. The United States and China, Soong stressed, were "basically and fundamentally fighting for the same cause . . . the Four Freedoms," and the Chinese people were "willing and eager to cooperate with you in the realization of these ideals . . . for ourselves, for our children, for our children's children, and for all mankind." The standing ovation made it clear that her trip was a smashing success for US-China amity.[5]

The sanctified union allowed Chinese Americans to affix a new layer of meaning to their political activities. Their protests, pickets, and humanitarian gestures on behalf of China could now be characterized as complementary to their patriotism to the United States. San Francisco Chinatown's fund-raising drive in 1942, for instance, yielded eighteen thousand dollars for the Red Cross, thirty thousand dollars for US defense bonds, and fifty thousand dollars for Chinese war relief.[6] Kenneth Bechtel, president of Marinship shipyard in Sausalito, California, had this to say about his Chinese American employees: "They are skilled, reliable—and inspired by a double allegiance. They know that every blow they strike in building these ships is a blow of freedom for the land of their fathers as well as for the land of their homes."[7] US officialdom also picked up on the value of this dual orientation. Of the estimated fifteen thousand women and men of Chinese ancestry serving in all branches of the US armed forces, over 10 percent staffed the two all-Chinese American units: the Army Air Force's 14th Air Service Group and the Army Signal Corps's 987th Signal Company.[8] US military commanders regarded Chinese American recruits as culturally literate liaisons between "American" (i.e., white) and local troops in the China-Burma-India theater.[9] Chinese Americans positioned themselves and were positioned quite literally at the nexus of the two nations.

The wartime acme of the Sino-American alliance thus warranted a serious contemplation of rescinding the Chinese Exclusion laws. The liberal internationalist East-West Association led the charge via its newsletter, *Asia*. In February 1942, *Asia* rolled out Far East authority Charles Nelson Spinks's manifesto "Repeal Chinese Exclusion!" a précis of the geopolitical dictates that would structure the campaign in the coming months. Spinks emphasized that of all immigrant groups in the United States, only the Chinese had been "single[d] out" for a "most shameful and categorical form of discrimination." Among other offenses, this disgrace encompassed the necessity that visitors from China must carry special certificates above and beyond the standard passport—a requirement "fully tantamount" to denying China's national sovereignty. Asiatic Exclusion, he argued, contradicted America's open-door policy in Asia—a "fundamental inconsistency" that was now being exploited by the Japanese. Chinese exclusion was not merely a national problem but also a worry of global proportions: "Today the future of the United States

FIGURE 2.1 Winifred Eng Lee, US Navy seaman first class, together with fellow WAVES (Women Accepted for Volunteer Emergency Service). Chinese Americans welcomed the opportunities presented by World War II—particularly the cultural emphases on patriotism, interracial amity, and Allied cooperation—to claim full membership in the nation.

Courtesy of Winifred Eng Lee.

has become more dependent than ever before upon our relations with the millions of inhabitants in Asia." Relegating this part of the world to a permanently unequal status enfeebled America's international standing and ultimately "our efforts to make this a better world for humanity."[10]

Spink's promulgation spurred prominent individuals to sign on, including Buck (the spouse of *Asia* editor Richard J. Walsh) and Minnesota congressional representative Walter H. Judd. Working groups convened in New York, San Francisco, and Los Angeles. Liberal periodicals called attention to the sundry injustices against the Chinese, such as the denial of shore leave for sailors, the "breaking up" of families due to immigration restrictions, and the fearful interrogations of US citizens of Chinese ancestry at border crossings. Proponents compared Exclusion to Adolf Hitler's abhorrent racial ideologies and the Gestapo's terrorist tactics, reminding their audiences that American-Asian cooperation against Japan hung in the balance. In February 1943, New York representative Martin Kennedy introduced the first repeal bill in Congress in a move timed to coincide with Soong's whirlwind visit. At subsequent hearings conducted by the House Committee on Immigration and Naturalization, a parade of witnesses (Buck, Walsh, Washington representative Warren G. Magnuson, and others) testified that the "wall of injustice" would continue to "rise higher and higher," and that Japan would continue to exploit America's hypocrisy for its own gain until the nation intervened.[11] Meanwhile, believers established the Citizens Committee to Repeal Chinese Exclusion (CCRCE) with Walsh at the helm. The committee's tripartite objectives consisted of repealing the Exclusion Acts, setting an annual quota for Chinese entry, and granting Chinese naturalization rights.[12]

The CCRCE orchestrated a national publicity campaign to educate the American public about the necessity of nullifying Exclusion for the sake of US foreign policy. Its 250 members and hundreds of affiliates bombarded the nation with its message in the forms of press releases, letters, broadsides, radio programs, lobbying, and mass demonstrations. One important example was "Our Chinese Wall," a pamphlet that hit all the high notes of the argument: that Tokyo had taken advantage of this weakness in its China-directed broadcasts; that this propaganda might well convince the Chinese to join forces with Japan in a future war against white supremacy; and that exclusion unfairly "humiliat[ed]" Chinese among all immigrant groups. Repeal and Chinese access to naturalization rights were thus a "measure of war expediency" as well as a step to secure the United States' own economic projections by "cementing the good will of a great nation with whom post-war trade will be highly profitable"—a midcentury allusion to America's perpetual quest for the holy grail of the China market. Anticipating detractors' criticisms, the CCRCE confirmed that repeal would neither open floodgates to yellow hordes (the estimated Chinese quota would be set at a miniscule 107) nor reintroduce "cheap coolie labor," promising rigorous state scrutiny of potential newcomers.[13]

The outreach was stunningly effective. National, regional, and niche publications spoke out in favor. The Republican-run *San Francisco Chronicle*, a leader in the nineteenth-century Chinese exclusion drive, ran no fewer than seven approving editorials. The CCRCE's decision to target the Pacific coast, long the stronghold of anti-Asiatic hostility, paid off. A host of organizations and governing bodies resolved to support repeal, including San Francisco's and Los Angeles County's boards of supervisors, California's Congress of Industrial Organizations Council and the state's arms of the League of Women Voters, Veterans of Foreign Wars, and the American Legion. Various interests traditionally sympathetic to the Chinese presence in the United States—business concerns, churches, and progressive entities—championed the cause: the YMCA, the YWCA, other Protestant, Catholic, and Jewish clergy and organizations, and the American Civil Liberties Union, among many others.[14]

Ironically, the CCRCE had purposely distanced itself from Chinese Americans—its most logical constituency—so as not to fall prey to charges that they were being manipulated by Chinese self-interest. Nonetheless, Chinese in the United States actively touted the drive, although more in the form of localized actions rather than in a formally coordinated fashion. Hawai'i's Chinese raised $1,116 for the CCRCE, amounting to over one-fourth of the committee's operating funds. New York's Chinese Consolidated Benevolent Association (CCBA, or the Chinese Six Companies), the umbrella coalition of immigrants' family and district associations, urged Congress to take this critical step toward the "true and lasting friendship between China and the United States," echoing the CCRCE's diplomacy angle. Some individuals exerted behind-the-scenes pressure. Washington, DC resident Arthur Chin sent a heartfelt letter to the CCRCE underlining the moral reasons for abolishing Exclusion. "We Chinese feel that by this unconstitutional law, we are the interlopers in this great democracy and have no voice in its government but, nevertheless, [are] being governed by it." Chinese were eminently qualified for citizenship, he added. Most were not temporary sojourners, as was the common accusation; instead, they came to the United States with every intention of settling permanently. Moreover, they demonstrated exemplary behavior, showing low rates of crime and unemployment along with little tendency to seek relief, even during the Depression years—all indications that Chinese would become outstanding citizens if given the chance. "We do not ask for any extra rights which other people in this democracy do not have, but only to be treated as an equal, within the spirit of the Constitution as set forth by the founding fathers of this great democracy," assured Chin. "In the face of the present world emergency, America must practice what it preaches."[15]

Other Chinese Americans intervened in the debate more independently of the CCRCE. Chinatown newspapers encouraged readers to petition their congressional delegates on this "most vital legislation." Theodora Chan Wang, president of New York's Chinese Women's Association, made a special plea to first lady Eleanor Roosevelt, underscoring her community's love for the United States: "There is no Chinese in this country who would not go far beyond the contribution now so freely given, in the sacrifice of his fortune, and his very life, to preserve the ideals of America, the traditional friend of China." The Left-leaning Chinese Hand Laundry Alliance helped to convince a coalition convened by the American Committee for the Protection of the Foreign Born and the New York Guild of Lawyers to endorse repeal. The alliance's organ, the *China Daily News*, opined on multiple occasions that Chinese Americans should mobilize one another and the public to rally behind the cause, with its editors increasingly emphasizing the issues of equality and democracy over the foreign policy arguments accented by the CCRCE.[16]

In late 1943, the campaign reached its tipping point. A nationwide poll conducted by the Office of Public Opinion Research found that 65 percent of its 1,200 respondents favored repeal, while only 26 percent were opposed.[17] A dispatch from President Franklin Delano Roosevelt to Congress affirmed its mission with his executive imprimatur. Repeal would not only "correct a historic mistake and silence the distorted Japanese propaganda"; it would also furnish "additional proof that we regard China not only as a partner in waging war but that we shall regard her as a partner in days of peace." The outpouring of endorsements sufficed to persuade the US Senate and House of Representatives, and Congress finally countermanded the Chinese Exclusion laws with the Magnuson Act of December 17, 1943.[18] With it, foreign-born nationals of Chinese ancestry became eligible for naturalization rights as well entry into the United States under a token yearly quota of 105 persons.

Chinese Americans received the decree with guarded optimism. Several months prior, San Francisco journalist Gilbert Woo had sarcastically remarked that "107 Chinese" (the initial proposed figure for the annual quota) were "in number . . . not enough . . . to make up a full set of mahjong tiles." By December, however, he conceded that repeal was a "fortunate occurrence," the timely outcome of the Pacific alliance against Japan and a wartime labor shortage that aligned to "silence" the "antiforeign clique in America." Still, some continued to criticize the government's implementation of what amounted to a *global* race quota that channeled persons of Chinese ancestry into the yearly allotment regardless of their place of residence or nationality as "a new discrimination in itself" and a violation of those countries' national sovereignty. (Jus solis ethnic Chinese citizens of Latin American republics, for instance, could not enjoy the same rights to limitless entry granted to all other inhabitants of the Western Hemisphere.) Others protested that repeal left intact the state's exceptionally harsh naturalization procedures, border-crossing obstacles, and other racial injustices.[19]

Yet there was no doubt among many, if not most, stateside Chinese that repeal was truly an event of "extraordinary" consequence—a landmark decision that protended newfound prospects for national acceptance. On the eve of the repeal's enactment, San Francisco's *Young China* predicted that "a new era is about to arrive." Similarly, the *China Daily News* waxed optimistic. As voting, taxpaying citizens, Chinese now had "many direct opportunities and advantages to solve the problems and to promote the welfare of the Chinese community" along with the United

States as a whole. Demonstrating this potential, Hawai'i's Chinese population kicked off a "gratitude" war bond drive, raising over one million dollars "to give concrete evidence of their thanks to America." With repeal, Chinese in the United States brightly stepped forward into a new phase of their history—one that promised to be framed by emancipation rather than ostracization from the body politic.[20]

Chinese Inclusion

The mission to defeat fascism that spurred Americans to overturn Exclusion catalyzed an unheralded receptivity to Chinese *inclusion* in the country's mass culture. Government authorities looking to differentiate the United States from its totalitarian adversaries welcomed ethnic Chinese into the national fold. Countless other Americans endorsed the state's charge to forge and sustain national unity through the eradication of racial as well as religious discrimination. Together, these imperatives spawned a new, viable conception of Chinese in the United States as assimilating Others—people becoming, or capable of becoming, legitimate citizens in spite of their racial distinctiveness from whites—further buttressing the sense of sureness that Chinese Americans gained from repeal.

The appearance of cultural pluralism as a fundamental aspect of national identity in the late 1930s and early 1940s is key to grasping how a cultural revision of Chinese American citizenship became thinkable. Ideologies of assimilation and cultural pluralism first emerged around the turn of the century as rival paradigms for managing the millions of immigrants streaming into the United States to fill the labor needs of industrial capital. Assimilation quickly became attached to the nativist-tinged, totalizing approach to Americanization that left little room for ethnic retention. Philosopher Horace Kallen, a German-born Jew, balked at this insistence and instead advocated what he dubbed cultural pluralism: the desirability of multiplicity in American life, in which a "democracy of nationalities" worked harmoniously together through "common institutions." Meanwhile, the liberal social scientists who took part in the Carnegie Corporation's "Americanization Studies," including University of Chicago sociologist Robert E. Park (famous for his theory of social interaction that posited competition, conflict, accommodation, and assimilation as the four stages of encounter between two groups), concluded that ethnic newspapers and organizations might serve as worthwhile vehicles to Americanization, and that assimilation was not necessarily unidirectional; rather, it was an organic "mutual giving and taking" between old hands and newer stock. Just as important, in the 1920s and 1930s, Columbia University anthropologists Frank Boas, Margaret

Mead, and Ruth Benedict took the conceptual leap of divorcing culture from race—in other words, rejecting biological determinism. In elevating culture as the best mechanism to explain human behavior, they argued for tolerance of diversity.[21]

Cultural pluralism languished as a minor strand in American social thought for several decades. Its obscurity was hardly accidental. The xenophobic nationalism of World War I and reactionary 1920s preordained immigrant communities from being perceived as anything but menacing. By the late 1930s, though, escalating ethnic conflict and the rise of fascism in Europe jolted civic leaders, opinion makers, and cultural producers into action to prevent a similar fate from befalling the United States. Fearful that Old World tensions might be replicated in the New, liberals tried to preempt tensions and foster national comity by redefining American identity vis-à-vis totalitarianism. Inclusivity was central to their vision of peoples of varied ethnoreligious backgrounds coexisting peacefully through shared core values such as democracy and freedom. Fueled by the wide-reaching efforts of educators, intellectuals, policymakers, and other influential figures, a valorization of cultural pluralism swept through American culture, gathering momentum as the United States officially entered the war. Literature, visual art, music, radio, film, photography, theater, public festivals, and social commentary all showed the blooming enchantment with touting the country as a "nation of nations," in the words of writer Louis Adamic.[22]

On the war's cusp, cultural pluralist productions presciently urged America to accept Chinese as fellow citizens. In 1938–39, the US Department of the Interior's Office of Education broadcast the twenty-six-part radio series *Americans All, Immigrants All*, celebrating immigrant and minority groups as a means to foster national cohesion. Episode sixteen honored the myriad contributions of Chinese to American life: provisioning California gold rush miners, building the transcontinental railroad, advancing agriculture and the arts, and modeling an enviable "Oriental temperament" through disciplined parenting and the extreme rarity of juvenile delinquency in the nation's Chinatowns.[23] The following year, singer Paul Robeson recorded "Ballad for Americans," a Popular Front ode to the nation's working peoples: "Irish, Negro, Jewish, Italian, French and English, Spanish, Russian, Chinese, Polish, Scotch, Hungarian, Litvak, Swedish, Finnish, Canadian, Greek and Turk, and Czech and double Czech American." The release was a huge hit, performed by schoolchildren nationwide, and even sung during the Republican and Communist Party national conventions as well as the New York World's Fair in 1940.[24]

With the outbreak of hostilities, liberals steadily drummed the message of Chinese inclusion for all to hear. Photographer Alexander Alland's

American Counterpoint (1943) spotlighted visual montages of the national mosaic, placing Chinese alongside Yugoslavs, Italians, Danes, and other ethnic groups. "These are the children of America," read an excerpt published in the *New York Times Magazine*. "None of them looks like the others. . . . Yet they are all Americans. Why? Because they live the dream that is America, the dream of all peoples living together in peace."[25] Not surprisingly, racially progressive organizations especially drove home this point. San Francisco's International Institute included Chinese in its KSFO radio series *Americans All*, a commemorative documentary of the region's polyglot pioneers.[26] The Common Council for American Unity, a leading cultural pluralism advocacy group, introduced up-and-coming Chinese American voices such as writer Jade Snow Wong in its journal *Common Ground*, a celebration of the multiracial, multiethnic nation.[27] *Common Ground* also pushed explicitly for Chinese American equality with such articles as "Citizen Kwong" (1943), written by CCRCE leader Carl Glick. "Citizen Kwong" related the plight of a Chinatown patriarch whose dream of US citizenship could only be realized vicariously through his native-born son's experiences of voting and military service. Granting Kwong the right of naturalization would reward him and his fellow immigrants for the "part they have played in our democracy."[28]

Reaching the widest audiences of all, mass-market serials celebrated ethnoracial diversity by suggesting that difference was a means to assimilation versus an end in itself. *Ladies' Home Journal*'s "Americans All" (1943) starred three families—Chinese, Polish, and German—beckoning readers to "see for yourself how successfully they have become Americans." The Halls of Los Altos, California, incarnated the telos of immigrant striving. Grandfather Sam had once worked as a cook, but had envisioned a better future for his offspring. Son James did not disappoint; a graduate of Stanford medical school, he presently served as chief of staff for San Francisco's Chinese Hospital. The younger Hall exemplified national promise with his prosperous white-collar career, suburban address, and active, bicultural civic engagement (Masons and the Chinese American Citizens Alliance). Through his own example, James hoped to instill in his child the "best of two worlds—American flexibility combined with Chinese integration with family and responsibility for its good name."[29] *Reader's Digest* (1944) also rolled out its version of Chinese melting into the pot. Like Sam Hall, immigrant Goon Mah had aspired to an existence beyond menial labor. Quitting his houseboy job, he moved his family from San Francisco to Boston Chinatown, where he opened a restaurant until competition forced them to fold. Undaunted, the Mahs relocated yet again to Hartford, Connecticut. Weathering the loss of their savings during the Depression, they soldiered on, and were now proud owners of a thriving eatery. "It's a good thing that we did fail in Boston," reflected Mah. "You see, if we had stayed in Boston's Chinatown, the children would not have had the chance to expand which they got from living in a non-Chinese settlement." Their children's accomplishments offered proof. The eldest son, an MIT doctoral candidate, was part of the 81st Chemical Battalion; two daughters were nurses, and a third held a "responsible" war industry position; a middle son flew in the US Army Air Forces; another was completing the premedicine track at the University of Chicago; and the youngest daughter had recently been plucked to be the poster child for Hartford's war bond drive. Here was a household of US citizens, "proud of their Chinese background," but "prouder still to be Americans."[30]

Even the most visible embodiment of Chineseness—Chinatown—was more American than Chinese in these wartime renderings. "To get behind the tourist front," *Look* magazine (with likely encouragement from the Office of War Information, the federal government's domestic propaganda agency) commissioned renowned Chinese American photographer/cinematographer James Wong Howe to capture images for its "Chinatown, San Francisco" (1944) pictorial feature. Howe's portraits included shots of the American Legion Cathay Post 384, a grandmother eating lunch during her shift at an area shipyard, nightclub dancers, and teenagers hanging out at a neighborhood soda fountain. The takeaway message: "Chinatown still appears Chinese, but beneath its Oriental façade it is as American as a piping plate of Boston baked beans."[31]

In preaching the ethos of ethnoracial tolerance for the sake of national unity, these stories presented a Chinese America spiritedly acceding to wartime's heightened obligations of citizenship. Chinese Americans, suggested their advocates, were motivated to serve the nation not by the coercion of the state but rather by inmost patriotic feelings. The omnipresent Glick affectionately recast the community as eager Americans in *Shake Hands with the Dragon* (1941), a lighthearted guide to the world of Chinese in the United States. The book and its *Reader's Digest* snippet recounted the enthusiasm of the thousand young men of New York's Chinatown who reported for duty before the crack of dawn on the first day of Selective Service registration in 1940.[32] *Independent Woman* answered this masculinist parable with a celebration of female participation in the war effort, applauding the myriad doings of the "Chinese Daughters of Uncle Sam": mechanics, clerks, Women's Army Corps members, nurses, doctors, nurses' aides, crop corps workers, and bond sellers.[33] Metropolitan newspapers, too, ran occasional features about area Chinese Americans' military and home front impact, doing the same work as national magazines on a local scale.[34] *San Francisco Chronicle* columnist Bill Simons, for instance, praised his city's Chinese denizens for their multifaceted engagement as air raid wardens, Red Cross disaster relief

FIGURE 2.2 This captioned photograph appeared in *Look* magazine's 1944 pictorial feature "Chinatown, San Francisco" to illustrate the commonalities between ethnic Chinese and other Americans: "Sunday afternoon at the Shee Wong Chan's is much like that of any other American family. Grandpa Chan is well established behind the Sunday paper, sharing it with his grandchildren. Like his wife, he invests in War Bonds, has sold many."

Photograh by James Wong Howe. Courtesy of the Bancroft Library, University of California, Berkeley. 1996.014:25-PIC.

coordinators, draft registrars, and enlistees. "That's what Chinatown has been doing for America," he raved. "Next time you're eating or drinking in the district, don't let the fancy neon lights, the Cantonese talk or the Oriental architecture fool you. These people are American through and through."[35] The meaning of this discourse was unequivocal: as cheerful, dedicated servants of the nation, Chinese deserved recognition and inclusion.

The groundswell of cultural pluralist sentiment emboldened Chinese Americans to demand acceptance and equality, albeit within the constraints of liberalism's assimilationist stipulations for legitimate membership in the nation. In a guest column for the *San Francisco Chronicle*, historian William Hoy reported that the daily habits of Chinatown residents looked increasingly like those of their fellow Americans. Coffee was consumed in "staggering" amounts, bridge was just as popular as mah-jongg, and basketball teams abounded. "Chinatown . . . is growing up to confound many who used to cry that the Chinese were unassimilable, and eventually it will take its place in this 'Nation of Nations,'" Hoy predicted. Speaking to the liberal readership of the *Survey Graphic* in 1942, Rose Hum Lee told of the thrilling changes undergone by Chinese Americans since Pearl Harbor. Previously confined to the ethnic service economy, they could now happily be found in shipbuilding, aircraft factories, and the armed forces. For a community that included "fourth-generation Americans"—those who spoke only English, cultivated close relationships with their white neighbors, and enjoyed the same pastimes as any other citizen—partaking in the war effort was "another stepping stone toward complete assimilation." Echoing African Americans' "Double V" campaign for victory over fascism abroad and racism at home, Lee called on the nation to eliminate anti-Chinese discrimination: "With the absorption of the Chinese in industry and the proof that they are good workers, loyal citizens, and faithful to the United Nations' cause, racial barriers and prejudices should break down now and for all time."[36]

Chinese American spokespersons strategically deployed a pair of loaded symbols—the coolie and the soldier—to illustrate their distance from the alien ineligible to citizenship, their capacity for assimilation, and their deservedness of inclusion. Paul Yee and Dr. Min Hi Li, the two community witnesses who testified in the US House of Representatives' repeal hearings, underlined this juxtaposition. Both emphatically distinguished their Chinese American contemporaries—defense workers and dedicated combatants—from "coolie labor," whose admission they unhesitatingly opposed. By disavowing the coolie, the embodiment of ineffaceable foreignness, they affirmed Chinese America's embrace of the assimilationist standards for citizenship set by the architects of the nascent liberal racial order.[37] Journalist Charles L. Leong, writing for the US Army Air Forces Training Command's *Buckley Armorer* newsletter, summarized the argument forcefully by spotlighting Chinese Americans' faith in the promise of democracy, deepened by the heady experience of military service: "The average Chinese GI Joe likes and swears by the army. . . . To GI Joe Wong, in the army a 'Chinaman's Chance' means a fair chance, one not based on race or creed, but on the stuff of the man who wears the uniform of the U.S. Army."[38]

The state's emphasis on national unity in diversity during the war meant that Chinese Americans could make these claims with their feet as well as their words. Some of the most visible of these demonstrations were the I Am an American Day and like celebrations that took place around the country each May. As the Office of War Information explained, the purpose of such events—sponsored by the Immigration and Naturalization Service and cooperating agencies—was to recognize newly naturalized citizens and "re-dedicat[e] all Americans to the ideals of American citizenship." Chinese Americans welcomed these chances to perform inclusion on the public stage. In 1941, Los Angeles' Mei Wah Girls' Drum Corps and Chinatown Boy Scout Troop 817 proudly marched in the city's I Am an American parade, while Chinese San Franciscans performed in the multiracial Cavalcade of Democracy sponsored by the local Council for Civic Unity the same week. The following year, Chinese American high schoolers partnered with students of other races to stage an Americans All–themed talent show at the San Francisco Chinese YWCA. Meanwhile, across the bay, fifteen-year-old Florence Gee won the *Oakland Post-Enquirer*'s I Am an American Essay Contest. In 1943, San Francisco's Chinese joined twenty-one other ethnic groups to fete the holiday with a "pageant of all nations," art displays, and food and gift sales to benefit the US Department of the Treasury's war bond drive. The *Chinese Press* urged its readers to attend, guaranteeing, "It will be a show long to be remembered and it will be history making for San Francisco—and for all America."[39]

The repeal of the Exclusion Acts and liberals' cultural valorization of ethnoracial diversity marked the two most important developments for the course of Chinese American citizenship during World War II. Both projects, however, were meant first and foremost to bolster the United States' moral legitimacy in the fight against fascism, rather than to secure full rights and entitlements for Chinese Americans per se. Thus, they left the question of Chinese America's domestic social standing wide open after the war's end. The undeniable sea change in American popular sentiment on race—inviting the country to take a more inclusive approach to the articulation of national identity—inspired many young Chinese Americans to revisit the enduring problem of belonging. As a robust, freewheeling conversation about the issue unfolded within the community, members of the second generation forged a fresh, upbeat perspective on life in the United States. In the process, they also began to wrest control from the immigrant elites that had long dominated as Chinatown's representatives to America at large. The flowering of Chinese America's English-language print culture at midcentury heralded both this shift in perspective and the changing of the guard—a dual refashioning that prefigured a new kind of relationship between the ethnic community and outside world.

The Rise of the Chinese American Press

Chinese immigrant communities boasted a long tradition of journalistic output dating back to the 1850s. The earliest ventures tended to be spearheaded by missionaries and entrepreneurs to boost their religious and commercial interests. By the turn of the century, Chinese-language newspapers throughout the United States took on a new raison d'être: the modernization of China. With the exception of a few notable independent publications, most were closely affiliated, if not run, by China's major political factions. Regardless of their leanings, the signal characteristics of the Chinese immigrant press in the early to mid-twentieth century were its use of the Chinese language along with its singular focus on China. The matter was not simply one of intellectual debate. Exclusion had forced Chinese in the United States to rely on the Chinese nation-state to secure their life chances in such a hostile environ.[40]

This is not to say that Chinese in the United States were unconcerned with more conventional or expected means of immigrant incorporation. In the half century before World War II, native-born Chinese Americans in particular sought acceptance and legitimacy as members of the American nation even in the face of systemic marginalization. In 1895, for instance, a number in San Francisco organized the Native Sons of the Golden State (later renamed the Chinese American Citizens Alliance) "to fully enjoy and defend our American citizenship" through the franchise, the courts, economic boycotts, and social and cultural activities. The Hawaiian Chinese Civic Association, founded in 1925, harbored analogous aspirations for islanders.[41]

The English-language community media was born out of this desire for equality and mobility within a US framework as the first critical mass of educated, native-born Chinese came of age in the 1920s and 1930s. Hawai'i led the way in 1926 with the introduction of the bilingual *Hawaii Chinese News*. The newspaper noticeably contrasted to Cantonese-language productions by focusing squarely on local affairs, social events, and athletics. After its six-year life span, the territory's *United Chinese News* filled the gap with a short-lived English section until the 1937 appearance of the *Hawaii Chinese Journal*, billed as the "Voice of 27,000 Chinese." As Hawai'i's Chinese were "becoming more and more Americanized"—84 percent of Chinese islanders were native born—the editors insisted that the paper be produced in English and that it place greater weight on the coverage of domestic over international happenings. These decisions were as much about prescribing a Chinese American identity as they were about pragmatically responding to demographic shifts in the community.[42]

San Francisco's *Chinese Digest*, the first mainland English-language periodical, boldly underscored this ambition from the outset of its run (1935–40).[43] Founders Thomas W. Chinn and Chingwah Lee[44] envisioned the newsmagazine as an engine of assimilation for the second generation. The premier issue laid out their multipronged ambitions for the project—nothing less than "a full-sized battle" to be waged on "five fronts" to reset the terms of Chinese American citizenship. The manifesto "Killing a Celestial" stated the founders' intent to dispense with degrading anti-Chinese stereotypes. "The Truth Is Our Battle Cry" assured accurate information about the ongoing Sino-Japanese conflict. The piece "Bridging the Pacific" pledged the cultivation of appreciation for classical Chinese arts and culture as a means of "enrich[ing] American life." *Chinese Digest* also aimed to cultivate "Inter-Trench Communication" among Chinese Americans across the land, given their common experiences as members of a racialized minority group. Finally, "The War on Neglect" vowed to fight for the expansion of career options for "Young China" in the United States by promoting Chinese-friendly employers and businesses—a move reminiscent of the contemporaneous "Don't Buy Where You Can't Work" campaigns among African Americans.[45]

Despite the confident tone and decidedly US tilt of such pronouncements, *Chinese Digest* staff members had no illusions about the tension between their desires for full citizenship and the sociological reality of segregation. As associate editor Hoy put it, "Is there a place for us in America? Or must we return to the land of our fathers to build our future?"[46] With gravely limited options in the United States, many young Chinese Americans seriously considered relocating to China, where they believed they would find more favorable opportunities in tandem with aiding the struggle against Japanese aggression. In 1936, the *Chinese Digest* revealed the acute resolve of such inclinations when it reprinted the winning entries to an essay competition sponsored by New York City's Ging Hawk women's club on the prompt "Does My Future Lie in China or America?"[47] First-place contestant and Harvard University student Robert Dunn advocated staying in the United States for a number of reasons, including the "social estrangement" that would result from the inevitable East-West culture clash. He conceded that securing remunerative employment was difficult, but added that it was not impossible. Dunn did not disavow the obligation to serve China felt by many of his cohort. Rather, he argued that he could contribute to the cause by "building up a good impression of the Chinese among Americans."[48]

Incensed at Dunn's reasoning, the Stanford University Chinese Students' Club fired off an open letter to him in the *Chinese Digest*. The Stanford students criticized Dunn for lacking true understanding of Chinese culture—a misperception of the US color line, and a willingness to shirk conflict, hardship, and ultimately responsibility for China's "salvation."[49] In a surprising twist, Dunn confessed that when he began penning his essay, "I immediately and instinctively chose the side favoring a future in China." But given the stated criteria that compositions would be evaluated on their "originality of thought," he switched to the other side in order to approach the topic from a novel perspective. His original argument was thus more of an intellectual exercise than a reflection of his personal views. In reality, he concurred that China was "really 'the line of least resistance' for young Chinese Americans." True to his word, Dunn moved to Chungking (Chongqing) shortly thereafter to work for the Chinese ministry of affairs.[50]

As the exchange in the *Chinese Digest* made clear, numerous Chinese Americans envisaged China to be the most attractive solution to the "Second-Generation Problem." University of Washington student Kaye Hong articulated this shared desire to "'Go Further West, Young Man.' Yes, across the Pacific and to China" in his essay that won the runner-up prize. Disillusioned by American racism, Hong dubbed China a "land of opportunity" for Yankee "go-getter[s]."[51] According to one estimate, approximately 20 percent of American-born Chinese did migrate to China in search of work opportunities during the 1930s, suggesting that Hong's view had a significant number of sympathizers within the community.[52] Yet for others, neither China nor the United States was an attractive option. New Yorker Grace W. Wang expressed an inveterate pessimism. In her assessment, low standards of living as well as the challenge of language and culture precluded China from being a viable option. There also seemed to be no end in sight to racial discrimination in the United States.[53]

While these different positions on the Second-Generation Problem had their adherents, most young Chinese Americans decided to remain in the United States. As one San Francisco social worker observed, "Practical life tells us that only a small percent has gone and will go back. . . . The majority of American Chinese have their future in America instead of in China."[54] The contents of the *Chinese Digest* corroborated her thesis. Editorials exhorted the readership to improve San Francisco Chinatown's image to boost tourism.[55] Regular columns presented investigative features on pressing issues of the day, including substandard housing, alien land laws, labor unionization, public health, and women's challenges. In 1939, the *Chinese Digest* revamped its editorial policy to stress its commitment "to aid the second generation Chinese to understand their position, social and economic; to point out their potentialities; to publicize their achievements; and to make known to them their inherent responsibilities toward working for the present and future welfare of their race and generation *in America*."[56] Such a pronouncement left little doubt that the organ's editors believed the future of Chinese American citizenship would be grounded in the United States.

This was the vision embraced by the *Chinese Digest*'s immediate successor, the *California Chinese Press*—a continuity due in part to an overlap in editorial personnel.[57] In November 1940, *Chinese Digest* editor Hoy teamed up with San Francisco journalist Leong to launch the

California Chinese Press, soon rechristened the *Chinese Press* to better reflect the paper's national scope.[58] As an organ "Dedicated to the Social and Economic Welfare of the Chinese in California," the inaugural editorial placed assimilation squarely at the forefront of the *Press*'s agenda: "The California Chinese today are predominantly Americans, either through privilege of birth or by derivative citizenship. As Americans of Chinese descent their future is the future of America, and their social and political ideals are those of the American democracy." Their professed outlook was manifest in the publication's substance. Periodic announcements implored readers to vote in upcoming elections, and advertisements by local and state candidates of both parties dotted the pages during political campaign season. As the United States prepared to enter the global fray, the *Chinese Press* also spotlighted Chinese Americans' home front participation.[59]

More than anything, war presented the *Chinese Press* with an unsurpassed opportunity to simultaneously encourage Americanism among its readership as well as tell outsiders—including state authorities—about the usefulness of Chinese Americans for the national mobilization. In July 1942, Bradford Smith of the federal Office of War Information approached Leong about reprinting summaries of China-related news distributed weekly by the agency. Leong gladly obliged, emphasizing the *Press*'s bicultural outreach: "Our circulation ranges from strictly Chinese readers to many Americans who are interested in Chinese affairs, and whatever information the government wants to distribute will have a double-barrel effect." He further offered to run their approved editorial cartoons, include the Office of War Information on the *Press*'s regular mailing list, and promote any "pro-democratic meetings" targeting Asian immigrant communities being planned by the office.[60]

The *Chinese Press* stressed Chinese American patriotism most ardently by regularly reporting on military-related issues. The front page of the debut issue named San Francisco's first four Chinese called for training. The following week, the journal profiled New York City Chinatown's premier draftee.[61] For three years, the *Chinese Press* churned out a steady stream of news about inductees, including the recurring "Roll of Honor," letters from soldiers, the efforts of the Army Air Corps, US Navy, Women's Army Corps, California's Chinese State Guard Unit, and the Merchant Marines to recruit Chinese American volunteers, and the goings-on of the American Legion's all-Chinese veterans' association. When Hoy left for the army in July 1942, he initiated a weekly column chronicling the everyday experiences of Chinese Americans in uniform.[62] In the aggregate, these tidbits of information posited that many Chinese not only accepted the call to duty, but also understood their service as a springboard to acceptance as constituents of the nation entitled to equal treatment.

Yet for all of its explicit avowals of assimilation and enthusiastic support of the war effort, the *Chinese Press* did not advocate the wholesale embrace of American identity at the expense of Chinese kinship. Like the *Chinese Digest*, the *Chinese Press* also recognized the affinities that many in its target audience felt for their ancestral homeland. Cognizant that US-born Chinese desired to participate in the building of "a greater China to come," the editors vowed to provide updates on the Sino-Japanese hostilities and ongoing reconstruction of "Free China."[63] News of China occupied ample space in the *Press*, including occasional political commentary, guest submissions by Chinese dignitaries, matters of historical interest, and even special souvenir editions generated for San Francisco's 1941 Rice Bowl and Soong's visit in 1943.[64]

The *Chinese Press*'s attentiveness to China politics gestured to the lingering ambivalence held by many young Chinese Americans toward the United States. On the eve of World War II, the Second-Generation Problem had shown little sign of dissipating. Contemporary observers, to the contrary, found that the employment situation was only worsening. Various mass-circulation journals deplored the "Chinaman's chance" plaguing Chinese American college graduates in the mainstream labor market—a "crisis" comparable in magnitude to the Negro Problem in the South. A *Chinese Press* forum in May 1941 on the seemingly intractable Second-Generation Problem confirmed these reports. Hoy summed up the predicament: "We belong to this country and not to China; but . . . we are treated nevertheless with intolerance and prejudice and looked upon as foreigners still." Participants variously opined that the route to full citizenship in the United States could be found in interracial collaboration and understanding, and that neither birthright citizenship nor a Western education could "make a person an 'American'" if racial discrimination persisted. For some, China still offered better prospects for individual "progress."[65]

The experiences of World War II did not resolve the Second-Generation Problem, despite the momentous gains for Chinese Americans. In light of repeal and cultural pluralism's ascendance, there was a striking degree of similarity between the prewar, wartime, and postwar iterations of the debate among young Chinese Americans. As voiced in the pages of *East Wind* magazine (1945–48), many second-generation Chinese saw their inclusion as incomplete. The brainchild of Henry S. Louie, Paul Louie, and young Christian liberals, *East Wind* aimed to "organiz[e] . . . our potentialities to a more distinct union and understanding of ourselves and other Americans," thereby filling the void left by the suspension of the *Chinese Press* in October 1943.[66] Based in Cleveland, *East Wind* was the first Chinese American publication to move beyond a Northern California emphasis by drawing on a phalanx of volunteer field correspondents from over twenty metropolitan areas throughout the United States and Canada. As a quarterly, its style also differed from the *Chinese Digest* and *Chinese Press*; the articles tended to be longer and more detailed about topics. But *East Wind*'s contents, despite these distinguishing features, bore a marked resemblance to its precursors. In its three-year run, the familiar puzzle of the Second-Generation Problem along with its attendant issues of identity, assimilation, and race relations endured as the journal's primary preoccupation.[67]

East Wind plainly demonstrated the lack of agreement among Chinese Americans about the condition of their citizenship at the war's close. In its first issue, the magazine recounted the conversation among several youths responding to the query "How American Are We?" Citing examples of Chinese Americans in the armed forces and their entry en masse into the mainstream labor market, one concluded, "Everything about this war proves it. I never realized it so much before, but we're Americans. Solidly." Others disputed his contention—"Look at Johnny, a Ph.D. in economics. What did they make him? Assistant cook"—and predicted that the occupational advances made by Chinese Americans would recede in peacetime. Pointing to the continued segregation of Chinese Americans in various arenas, they concluded, "We can't call ourselves Americans or feel that we're part of this country until all these social and economic barriers are removed."[68] On this last point the majority of *East Wind*'s contributors and readers agreed, although they diverged, as in the past, on how to redress this inequality. China remained both a psychic and real option. As correspondent Shelley Mark observed, the ubiquity of racism meant that "we've never felt a true sense of belonging in our American environment." Chinese Americans needed to push past the stage of "wishful thinking" about China as many had done for so long and commit to the move. "The era of reconstruction is conceivably near at hand," he stated, and the "challenge" to building a "new China" was "now being thrown directly at us."[69]

Mark's summons prompted a deluge of responses. As before, proponents underscored the duty of all those equipped to aid China's reconstruction.[70] A few adopted a more diplomatic stance. Editor Henry Louie emphasized the importance of those working to transform China into a "true world power," thus elevating US public opinion "in our favor by having a strong-voiced mother country." In the meantime, those who remained stateside ought to further the "tremendous inroads" made during the war.[71] Associate editor Paul Louie called on Chinese Americans to serve as China's "cultural ambassadors" while simultaneously "fulfill[ing] our duty to America" as "decent and law-abiding citizens."[72] Others completely rejected the notion of "going back," either skeptical that Chinese Americans could advance without proper connections or because they insisted that their generation should pursue integration into the broader US society.[73] Contributor Richard Quey advised readers to seek social interactions across racial lines, cautioning that an "interest in China and things Chinese shall not obstruct, hinder, or encroach on time and energy which properly should be devoted to America and things American."[74] By its final issue in summer 1948, neither readers nor writers had reached a consensus.

The termination of *East Wind* coincided with the resumption of the *Chinese Press*'s publication, and with it, a continuation of the searching meditations on race, citizenship, and opportunity. Like its predecessors, the revitalized weekly tackled the socioeconomic conundrum of the US-born cohort, regularly tracking developments in fair employment practices, documenting the persistence of anti-Chinese discrimination in the labor market, and counseling job seekers.[75] Conspicuously absent from the postwar *Chinese Press* was the notion of "returning" to China, however. The long-running impasse of China versus America broke after the 1949 Chinese Revolution. With the severing of diplomatic relations between the embryonic People's Republic and the United States, a future in China was no longer an option, real or imagined. San Francisco Chinatown community leader Lim P. Lee unambiguously assessed the upshot of the Communist victory: "When the [Chinese] pioneers found America too rough, they returned to China for security and old age. Such a path is closed to the Chinese-Americans today. . . . Our future is in this country." Rose Hum Lee similarly pronounced, "Today, the doors are closed. Young Chinese must learn to adjust themselves to the society here as never before; even China-borns must." Lee emphasized personal adjustment to the demands of the labor market as a means toward "becom[ing] an integral part of the American society" in this unforeseen context. The responsibility for dismantling discrimination lay not only in the hands of "larger society" but also with Chinese Americans themselves, she argued, so long as they adopted a flexible approach to job hunting, a willingness to take on various types of work, and cooperated with fellow employees of "all races and creeds."[76]

Building on her advice, the *Chinese Press* featured the series "Chinese-Americans on the Job," profiling individuals flourishing in a range of non-traditional occupations: engineer-designer, bus driver, post office superintendent, naval supplier, college cafeteria director, and narcotics agent.[77] Showcasing a world of newfound possibilities in the post-Exclusion era, the sequence layered an additional register of significance on workplace integration. By "doing our best on the job" within interracial settings, Chinese Americans could aid in dispelling Communist propaganda that charged the United States with race discrimination against minority groups. Acts of patriotism would affirm their loyalty to the United States, and by implication, prove that the "the majority of Americans of Chinese ancestry are coming of age as full-fledged American citizens . . . working side-by-side with his white fellow American."[78] Integrated labor, underscored the *Press*, was not merely an issue of individual advancement but also one of proving the group's capacity for full citizenship.

Alongside earning, voting stood as a pillar of the *Chinese Press*'s formula for the attainment of unmitigated inclusion in postwar US society.[79] The 1948 elections held special import for the community, observed the editors, given the thousands of individuals who had recently joined the electorate's ranks. As the "best weapon" against the remaining structures of racial discrimination, the *Press* implored Chinese Americans to descend on the polls en masse. After the ballots were cast, the *Press* noted delightedly that San Francisco Chinatown voters had made their strongest showing yet, and reminded readers that "when each of us cast our vote, we are helping to shape the destiny of our country."[80] Over the remainder of its life span, the newspaper repeatedly beckoned Chinese America to exercise the franchise, prodding readers to back candidates and propositions that would yield immediate benefits to the entire community, such as the building of public housing in San Francisco Chinatown and immigration reforms to permit the nonquota entry of war brides from China.[81]

Beyond urging voter turnout, the *Press* cultivated a US-oriented political sensibility in myriad ways: delivering news of local- and state-level candidates, publicizing speeches, rallies, and appearances, running political advertisements, following campaign developments, and eventually announcing its own endorsements, reminding readers of Chinatown voters' potential to swing municipal competitions.[82] Stories of individual Chinese Americans active in party politics were intended to inspire as well as inform readers.[83] More than once, the staff encouraged Chinese Americans to run for high-profile seats, especially on the San Francisco Board of Supervisors.[84] "The [continued] development of sound political leadership among younger Chinese is of utmost necessity," advised *Press* contributor Stanton Jue. "Chinese Americans cannot afford to be politically inert."[85]

Admittedly, the prospect of a Chinese American on the San Francisco Board of Supervisors likely seemed far-fetched at a time when Chinese often faced resistance when attempting to move into white neighborhoods and even seeking burial in nonintegrated cemeteries.[86] But if read as aspirational pronouncements, such political discussions uncovered the public relations function of the English-language Chinese American media. Indeed, the *Chinese Press* pioneered Chinese Americans' postwar strategy of refashioning their collective image through the circulation of information in the public sphere. As during World War II, editor-publisher Leong positioned the weekly to reach both mainstream readers as well as ethnic subscribers. "There's a genuine need for a newspaper that can serve as an interpretive medium for Chinese, Chinese-Americans, and Americans," stated the press release announcing the resumption of publication in 1948. "The *Chinese Press* will endeavor to provide that service."[87] (Notably, Chinatown's Sinophone newspapers acknowledged the unique niche filled by the *Chinese Press*.)[88] Leong deftly coordinated a promotional blitz to generate fanfare celebrating the *Press*'s return. Prominent public figures sent congratulatory messages, including San Francisco mayor Elmer E. Robinson and US senator William F. Knowland.[89] At least forty news outlets throughout California, Oregon, Washington, and even Chicago heralded its comeback. *Fortnight: The Newsmagazine of California* and Beverly Hills's *Script* ran flattering interviews with Leong to coincide with the revival—an auspicious rebeginning to what was undoubtedly a risky financial venture. Aiming to reach a circulation of over ten thousand, the *Chinese Press* got off to a running start; the initial run of five thousand represented a substantial increase from the peak of twenty-seven hundred before the newspaper went into hiatus in 1943.[90]

Leong characterized a new breed of ambitious young self-starters vying for the privilege of speaking on behalf of Chinese America in the post-Exclusion era. Before World War II, Chinese communities throughout the United States had relied heavily on the merchant-elite-dominated CCBAs to act as intermediaries between Chinatown, the state, and the larger society. The CCBAs worked primarily through the legal system and diplomatic pressures to challenge the myriad injustices levied against their constituencies.[91] The few attempts by Chinese to stop their marginalization and dehumanization in Anglophone mass communications, though significant, were virtually drowned out by the forces of yellow peril xenophobia.[92] It was not until the 1930s and 1940s that the coincidental emergence of racial liberalism, cultural pluralism, and a critical mass of native-born, American-university-educated Chinese who had come of age presented untrodden openings for self-representation in media, literature, and social science.

Leong's curriculum vitae primed him to take full advantage of these gateways. A native of Watsonville, California, he attended San Jose State College, where he edited the school newspaper and moonlighted for a local daily. After completing a master's degree in journalism at Stanford University, Leong applied for a reporter position in his hometown but was turned down for racial reasons. To recover from this "especially bitter and emotional pill to swallow," Leong looked to San Francisco as the "best escape route to forgetfulness." In the city, he landed a job crafting publicity stories for the Democratic Party headquarters, and over time went on to write for the *San Francisco Chronicle* and United Press

FIGURE 2.3 San Francisco journalist and public relations man Charles Leong (middle), who strived to remake the social standing of Chinese Americans through his English-language periodicals the *Chinese Press* and *Chinese News*. Both publications enjoyed a readership well beyond the ethnic community.
Photograph by Chester Gan. Courtesy of the Asian American Studies Collection, Ethnic Studies Library, University of California, Berkeley.

wire service while managing a small publicity concern. From there, he cofounded the *Chinese Press* with Hoy. In 1943, Leong put the *Chinese Press* on hold to join the Fourteenth Army Air Force "Flying Tigers" in the China-Burma-India theater as the unit's sole Chinese American combat correspondent. Other wartime service included contributions to *Yank* magazine, an editorial position at the Shanghai outpost of *Stars and Stripes*, and a direct field commission as public relations officer in the US Army's Chinese Combat Command. At the end of the war he stayed in China to do public relations work for the UN Relief and Rehabilitation Administration and its China correlate, the China National Relief and Rehabilitation Administration. Leong returned home to San Francisco in 1947, where he established Charles L. Leong and Associates, a public relations firm and publisher's representative specializing in connecting American companies and Far Eastern media. Meanwhile, he resurrected the *Chinese Press*.[93]

With Leong having amassed both practical experience and business capital, the *Chinese Press* stood apart from its Chinese American forerunners and contemporaries with its comparatively high levels of professionalization as well as visibility. Years of working in mainstream and government media had afforded Leong the faculty to forge valuable connections to white opinion makers. For instance, the *Chinese Press* counted among its subscribers the influential *San Francisco Chronicle* columnist Herb Caen, who periodically repeated Chinatown anecdotes relayed by Leong. As the first Chinese American member of the San Francisco Press Club, Leong also boasted the distinction of stewarding the only ethnic-Chinese-targeted publication to membership in the California Newspaper Publisher's Association and the National Editorial Association. Entrenched into these professional networks, the *Chinese Press* provided an effective vehicle through which Leong and his staff could regularly telegraph the Americanism of their people to the general public. An early assessment showed that the postwar iteration of the *Press* was well received: "We have forty-nine more issues coming, but we can report that so far, the inscrutable Chinese are getting less so every week," concluded *Script* magazine in July 1948. A 1951 Herrick Award bestowed on the *Chinese Press* by the National Editorial Association Convention's Better Newspaper Contest for the expression of "the ideals of Americanism and the workings of American democracy" offered further evidence. But the money shot may have been a telegram sent by President Truman himself (extracted via Leong's contacts) to commemorate the journal's tenth anniversary: "Please accept my congratulations on this happy event and the fine job that the press has done in promoting sound American ideals," read the dispatch.[94]

In February 1952, the *Chinese Press* shut down abruptly—a casualty, it appears, of Leong's personal troubles.[95] Undeterred, he reinvented himself as the founding editor of the *Chinese News: America's Chinese Newsmagazine*, with his friend Jake W. Lee on board as publisher. The *Chinese News* resembled its antecedent in big ways. Like the *Chinese Press*, the *News* aimed to "speak for and by" Americans of Chinese ancestry, promising to "take up the editorial battle for the legitimate aspiration of the Chinese as American citizens"—which in the Cold War context, meant espousing "vigorous anti-Communism" and "support[ing] the constructive policies" of the US government. The *Chinese News* accordingly put interracial outreach at the front and center of its mission. While the *Press* had undeniably incorporated a public relations agenda, the *Chinese News* made it an even more explicit objective. It hoped, for example, to foster an appreciation for China's traditional arts and culture among "other Americans as an expressive medium of friendship between the Chinese and American people." Self-advertisements promoted subscriptions as "Good News! For Chinese Americans and Their Other American Friends."[96] In his business correspondence, Leong accentuated the role of his magazine in filling the "need for an English language publication edited and published by Chinese-Americans to distribute among our fellow-Americans as a very graphic proof of our adherence to the American way of life."[97]

For Chinese Americans, the notion of public relations made good political sense in the age of McCarthyism. Interventions in the public sphere—especially ones that took advantage of Leong's extensive professional connections—could do much to secure their citizenship in the insecure political climate, especially after the entry of the People's Republic of China into the Korean War. Thus a *Chinese News* story about the participation of Manhattan Chinatown's American Legion Kimlau Post in New York City's 1953 Loyalty Day parade was not merely an objective description of an event but also a deliberate rendering of ethnic Chinese as patriotic members of the nation. The recurring "Roll of Honor" (a holdover from the *Chinese Press*) noted the whereabouts of individual Chinese American soldiers and veterans while reminding readers of the sacrifices made by the community to the cause of democracy.[98] The *Chinese News* also offered six-month subscriptions gratis to all servicemen and women as a show of Cold War Americanism.

The public relations modus operandi of the *Chinese News* was to clarify for "Other Americans" their stake in the acceptance of Chinese Americans as full citizens while persuading them to financially support the magazine. One way was to grant sellers of goods and services access to a potentially lucrative yet untapped buyers' market. In courting prospective advertisers, the *Chinese News* underlined its uniqueness as the sole venue "to offer a blanket coverage of the high standard of living of Chinese Americans throughout the U.S." That is, the *Chinese News* depicted Chinese Americans as middle-class consumers to both attract advertising dollars as well as suggest that the denizens of Chinatown (and increasingly, suburbia) comprised an integral part of the postwar "Consumers' Republic"—the "complex shared commitment on the part of policymakers, business and labor leaders, and civic groups to put mass consumption at the center of their plans for a prosperous postwar America."[99] Leong concurrently promised a Chinese American *voters'* market by proposing that the magazine run "properly slanted stories" favoring California's Democratic slate in 1954. For the price of forty-five hundred dollars for three special election editions, Leong offered party officials a hand in the "shaping of editorial materials to best achieve the objectives of winning over all the Chinese-American votes"—a sound investment, he added, given that the nation's Chinese looked to California for "leadership." A decisive victory there would yield "the added impetus . . . of winning over

Chinese in other parts of the United States to the Democratic vote."[100] Always the entrepreneur, Leong put himself and the *Chinese News* forward as conduits for a new, post-Exclusion Chinese America whose inclusion in the nation augured benefits for all.[101]

Besides market share and electoral pull, Leong pitched the significance of Chinese America and the *Chinese News* at the high-stakes level of international relations. He donated five hundred copies of the *Chinese News*, for instance, to the China Club of Seattle, a staunch advocate of Sino-American amity, undoubtedly in hopes of attracting subscribers, yet also to show "Chinese-American enterprise in the field of reflecting the problems, progress, and opinions of the Chinese-Americans, a small but important group in the overall field of Chinese-American relations."[102] This was the point in the March 1953 editorial favoring the admission of Hawai'i to statehood. The entrance of the majority Asian-populated territory to the Union would likely result in the election of Chinese Americans to the US Senate and House of Representatives, the *Chinese News* conjectured. Diplomatically, the payoff would be huge: "In this uncertain unpeaceful [*sic*] era of the Pacific cycle in American global growth, Congress can skilfull [*sic*] use the opinions and backgrounds of any qualified American of Asian ancestry in U.S. foreign policy."[103] Leong forwarded the piece to Secretary of State John Foster Dulles, alerting him to the "potential value of the Asian-American" for foreign affairs, adding, "We hope that our editorial comments may be of some service to you in your program and as a magazine dedicated to public service we shall be happy to . . . furnish you any other type of data relating to the over-all question."[104] This was his 1950s' rebuttal to the decades-old question "Does My Future Lie in China or America?" in which the rendering of Chinese Americans as valuable transoceanic intermediaries would be a boon for their citizenship aspirations, America's Cold War objectives, magazine sales, and Leong's own professional cachet—a win-win-win-win situation.

Leong's ambitions for *Chinese News* ultimately seem to have outpaced the journal's fiscal realities. Despite notable successes, including a Freedom Foundation Award for editorial writing, the final issue appears to have been released in summer or fall 1954.[105] The truncated duration of *Chinese News*, however, belies the significance of Leong's ventures and Chinatown's Anglophone print culture more generally for the post-Exclusion trajectory of Chinese American racialization and citizenship. English-language ethnic periodicals were useful, much-craved platforms for the younger generation of Chinese Americans to appraise their life possibilities when US-China relations and domestic race relations inescapably structured their aggregate destiny. The Chinese American press became a virtual movement between the mid-1940s and mid-1960s with an explosion of publications directed at those who preferred English to Cantonese. Three of San Francisco's five Chinese-language newspapers unveiled English sections in this period: the *Chinese World* (1949–69), the *Chinese Pacific Weekly*'s *Pictorial* (1952), and *Young China* (1962–66), for which Leong himself would serve as editor.[106] The *Hawaii Chinese Journal*, established in 1937, held steady until 1957 and was briefly replaced by the *Hawaii Chinese Weekly* (1957–58). In addition, Chinese American youths all over initiated small-scale serials, including Detroit's *Chit-Chat*, Houston's *Yip-Yap*, and Augusta, Georgia's *Oriental Wind*.[107]

Leong recognized this internal utility as a way to create a professional opportunity for himself within the field of journalism at a time when minorities' avenues for advancement were limited. More than that, he grasped the potential of the Anglophone press to project Chinese Americans' own visions for the terms of their inclusion into the public domain—an editorial vision that would later be emulated by the *Chinese-American Times* (1955–72), a New York–based monthly newspaper published by William Yukon Chang, himself a former contributor to the *Chinese Press*. In the course of producing the *Chinese Press* and *Chinese News*, Leong honed his public relations proficiency—a skill set that he would tap throughout the postwar period to mold mainstream discourse about Chinese in the United States. The *Chinese Press* and *Chinese News* therefore were important examples of the ways in which Asian American spokespersons shaped their own racialization in the mid-twentieth century. Such efforts had a distinct parallel within the Nikkei community in the form of the Japanese American Citizens League's (JACL) controversial invention and promotion of the Nisei soldier.

Chapter 3

Nisei in Uniform

Tempers flared at JACL's first postwar national gathering in early 1946. At the Denver meeting, delegates thundered about an "embarrassing situation" as Japanese Americans returned to the Pacific coast from the WRA camps. Among those repairing to their former homes were the Tule Lake renunciants, some five thousand internees who had forsworn their US citizenship during the internment. These "troublemakers" stood at odds with the patriotic proclivities of JACL, the organization that had promoted Nikkei cooperation with the federal government during the war. JACL leaders dreaded that local residents would confuse the renunciants with Japanese Americans of "unquestioned loyalty." Given the less than welcoming reception that many returnees faced, whites' failure to distinguish between the disloyal and loyal would likely precipitate "ill will," thereby further damaging the already-precarious state of Nikkei.[1]

Painful, unresolved ideological fissures over loyalty and citizenship, rooted in the crisis of incarceration, lurked beneath this distress. JACL's wartime accommodation to federal policy along with its calls to hyperpatriotism and military service as the means to demonstrate Japanese America's unequivocal allegiance to the United States had incited bitter criticisms from many Nikkei. Consequently, both its intracommunity reputation and membership numbers had plummeted drastically. But as the widely acclaimed heroism of Nisei soldiers in the European combat theater began to improve the image of Japanese Americans, the organization felt it decisions justified. Still, as this goodwill continued to grow, JACL stalwarts agonized that the renunciants would reap the benefits without having "risked anything." They fretted that the league and Nisei veterans would not be rightfully credited for realizing this shift in public sentiment.[2]

Convention delegates wrestled passionately with JACL policy toward the renunciants as well as the Nisei draft resisters known as the Heart Mountain Fair Play Committee. Some pressed the *Pacific Citizen*, the league's organ, to drop its reporting on the two groups, arguing that the coverage denoted tacit support. Accusing the dissenters of "belittling" Nisei soldiers, veterans demanded "no sympathy whatsoever." They called for immediate deportation and recommended that said offenders carry special identification papers in the meantime. Such measures were necessary because renunciants and conscientious objectors would continue to spearhead not only "anti-America" but also "anti-J.A.C.L. movements."[3]

JACL national officers finally determined that the league would abide by the government's ruling regarding the renunciants' quest to reinstate their US citizenship. With the verdict still under deliberation, they confirmed that the *Pacific Citizen* would continue to follow the cases in the interest of journalistic integrity. Delegates conceded, too, that mandating legal distinctions between different sectors of the Nikkei populace might result in similar acts of discrimination extending to all Japanese Americans, subjecting the entire community to unending humiliation.[4]

Yet even with these ostensibly neutral resolutions, JACL adopted a position that was far from impartial. The national board declined to shoulder renunciants' legal battles. More tellingly, it excluded them from JACL membership. By refusing to back the renunciants' appeals, JACL aimed to delegitimize any alternatives to the organization's carefully constructed representation of Japanese Americans as cooperative, loyal, and patriotic.[5] At the same time, by barring these dissidents from joining, the organization precluded them from wielding any power to dictate the league's postwar political agenda. The alarm over the renunciants and draft resisters, in short, exposed JACL's uneasiness regarding its own future as well as that of Japanese America—two destinies that its leadership deemed fundamentally inseparable.

A rattled JACL made repeated, concurrent efforts to lift its faltering position within the Nikkei community and secure Japanese American citizenship more broadly during and after World War II. JACL leaders believed that the organization's survival hung in the balance just as they grasped the shakiness of Japanese Americans' life prospects in the United States. In response, the league embarked on an ambitious program to fulfill the dual purposes of ensuring its own continuity and fostering the unencumbered participation of Japanese Americans in the polity and society. This multifaceted lineup included the recruitment of Nisei for the armed forces, the memorialization of Japanese American veterans, monetary reparations for internment-related losses, property and naturalization rights for Issei, and the brokering of US-Japan relations in the 1950s.

To achieve these objectives, JACL leaders waged an extensive public relations campaign anchored by the figure of the Nisei soldier, an intentionally crafted archetype of Japanese American manhood that foregrounded the notion of martial patriotism—unwavering loyalty to the United States demonstrated through the sacrifice of military service. (In real terms, the 33,000 Japanese Americans who served in the armed forces during World War II amassed an indisputably distinguished record; the army's all-Nisei 442nd Regimental Combat Team accumulated seven Presidential Unit

Citations and earned 18,143 individual citations while suffering 9,486 casualties totaling over 300 percent of its original infantry strength. Japanese Americans also enlisted in the Women's Army Corps and the US Air Force; others labored as medics, mechanics, and clerks in the Quartermaster Corps, instructors and interpreters for the Military Intelligence Service Language School, and Army Map Service staff; and a number worked in the Office of Strategic Services as well as the Office of War Information.)[6] In the context of a widespread valorization of veterans and global realignments, this strategy effectively undergirded the organization's program by providing a persuasive basis for making claims on society and the state. In the eyes of many Japanese Americans, the resulting victories—particularly the end of legal Exclusion—vindicated the league's accommodationist approach to internment and salvaged JACL's damaged repute within the ethnic community.[7]

The iconic Nisei soldier, JACL's brainchild, thus answered a constellation of race and citizenship imperatives in the 1940s and 1950s. For all Japanese Americans, Nisei fighters guaranteed their claims to assimilability and national belonging by responding to the call to arms, recasting them from enemy aliens to loyal citizens in the process. As the pinnacle of wartime masculinity, soldiering allowed Japanese American men in particular to rebut deep-rooted popular beliefs that the gender identities of "Oriental" men were feminized, ambiguous, or deviant—notions that had served to justify Exclusion.[8] The public recognition of Issei "Gold Star Mothers"—those who sacrificed the bodies of their sons to the war—also provided a compelling, if secondary, means for Japanese American women to claim full citizenship as virtuous maternal nurturers of family and nation.[9] For JACL, the ascendance of the warrior persona, recognized and lauded by the public and policymakers, offered reassurance that its orientation was indeed the righteous path to redemption for both itself and the ethnic community. And for the nation, the Nisei soldier modeled liberal prescriptions for managing racial difference. The Nisei soldier's willingness to abide by the rules of assimilation as well as civic obligation bespoke the type of minority behavior deemed the prerequisite for white acceptance and social equality. That the state's postwar implementation of civil rights reforms for Japanese Americans were framed as rewards for Nisei military service only reinforced this paradigm.

In the long run, however, the Nisei soldier could not resolve all the problems of Japanese American social standing. The league's reliance on *racialized* martial patriotism to rehabilitate Nikkei citizenship was a concession that Japanese Americans could not eradicate their difference from whites (and hence remove lingering status disparities) but instead could only hope to endow this difference with positive meanings. The emergence of the heroic Japanese American warrior thus captured both the freeing and constricting potentialities of racial liberalism. Moreover, JACL maintained a serious investment in renewing Japanese Americans' racial dissimilarity. After all, despite its perennial avowals of assimilationism, the league could only flourish so long as Japanese Americans remained a distinct group. Its very power derived from its claims to the mantle of racial "spokesorganization." In an era of volatile fluctuations in US-Japan relations, this reproduction of otherness was a risk that league leaders assumed in their quest to retain their position atop the ethnic community's hierarchy.

JACL's Contested Rise

The league's twinned postwar ambitions originated in the interwar decades of the 1920s and 1930s. As second-generation Japanese Americans came of age, many pondered the effects of the Pacific coast's anti-Japanese agitation on their life chances. In 1923, a number established the California-wide American Loyalty League to "create a better understanding" between whites and Japanese. To realize this aim, the group encouraged Nisei to embrace their citizenship obligations, especially voting. The organization also developed a public relations approach, with local chapters inviting civic officials to their functions, for example. Despite a strong start, the league lasted only five years, lacking popular appeal among the majority of Nisei, who were considerably younger than the group's founders.[10]

The American Loyalty League's legacy, though, proved much more enduring. Its two-pronged methodology for solving Nisei's collective predicament—Americanism and public relations—became the template for JACL. Between 1928 and 1930, former members of the American Loyalty League and Seattle's Progressive Citizens League, a second group formed in the 1920s with comparable objectives, reorganized the fledgling Nisei movement as the Japanese American Citizens League. The desire at the outset to obtain political and economic security for Nisei formed the crux of JACL's mission; Americanism campaigns and public relations were two preferred means to these ends. The leadership's calls to the second generation to relinquish its dual citizenship (Japan and United States) to signal Nisei's American patriotism exemplified this strategy.[11]

As practiced by JACL in the 1930s, Americanism did not preclude internationalism in the form of ties to Japan. The league received financial assistance from the Japanese consulate and its Issei-run affiliate, the Japanese Association of America. Nisei leaders also espoused the view that their generation could serve as "bridges of understanding," or cultural brokers, between the United States and their ancestral homeland to maintain transpacific peace and stability. Rank-and-file members, too, supported their ancestral homeland in the Sino-Japanese conflict by raising money for the Japan Red Cross's military relief fund.[12]

But as US diplomacy and public opinion turned against Japan in favor of China, JACL necessarily narrowed its definition of Americanism. Loyalty became an increasingly important dimension. After the official start of the Sino-Japanese War in 1937, JACL heads generally concurred that Nisei needed to maintain neutrality as evidence of their sympathies with the United States. The league also spearheaded more proactive expressions of allegiance, such as backing universal military conscription and the federal government's fingerprinting of Issei under the Alien Registration Act.[13]

With the prospect of war looming on the horizon, JACL leaders ratcheted up their public relations work. Local chapters held patriotic rallies and coordinated speakers' bureaus to impress on non-Japanese the sincerity and substance of Nisei patriotism. In 1941, the national board hired the organization's first full-time staff member, Mike Masaoka, an energetic young Nisei from Salt Lake City, Utah, to coordinate a far-reaching outreach operation. As a first step, Masaoka drafted avowals of JACL's stance on Americanism, such as the "Japanese American Creed," read before the US Senate in May 1941:

> Because I believe in America, and I trust she believes in me, and because I have received innumerable benefits from her, I pledge myself to do honor to her at all times and in all places; to support her constitution; to obey her laws; to respect her flag; to defend her against all enemies, foreign or domestic; to actively assume my duties and obligations as a citizen, cheerfully and without any reservations whatsoever, in the hope that I may become a better American in a greater America.

JACL clearly aimed these gestures at white opinion makers, legislators, and dignitaries. Masaoka distributed thousands of reprints of the creed and related documents among the White House staff, Congress, state-level officials, civic organizations, media outlets, and others.[14]

While the league's main concern remained the imminent confrontation in the Pacific, the leadership devoted scrupulous attention to organizational development. By the mid-1930s, national officers had designs for the league to become the most prominent Nisei organization nationwide. JACL had made considerable strides on the eve of World War II toward achieving this goal, growing from eight charter chapters in 1930 to fifty-five (and a membership roll of over eight thousand) in November 1941. Despite these gains, JACL never successfully courted the bulk of its presumed constituency. Only 20 percent, according to one estimate, of all Nisei men belonged. Demographic differences between the leaders and most Nisei partly explained this inability to attract greater numbers. JACL founders and leaders' personal backgrounds (older, university-educated, middle-class businesspeople and professionals) contrasted markedly with most Nisei, who came from working-class families. JACL also had no shortage of detractors. Its conciliatory stance toward race relations, political conservatism, and claims to represent the entire community repelled many Nisei, especially intellectuals, liberals, and progressives. The league's Americanism outlook, furthermore, alienated the Kibei, those Nisei who had been born in the United States but raised overseas and therefore were more likely to identify with Japan. Thus JACL was far from attaining the unequivocal leadership of the second generation. Intracommunity public relations efforts, including a speaking tour by Masaoka in fall 1941 and the consistent editorial support of the *Pacific Citizen*, sought to remedy this problem.[15]

JACL finally achieved its objective of becoming Nisei America's preeminent organization in the months leading up to President Roosevelt's signing of Executive Order 9066 in February 1942. In the immediate aftermath of the Pearl Harbor bombing on December 7, 1941, the FBI commenced its roundup and detention of Issei community elders. The heads of the league immediately stepped into this void and claimed to represent all Japanese Americans. Local, state, and federal officialdom validated this assertion by granting the league special powers to act in this regard. In Los Angeles, for one, the US postmaster authorized JACL to censor the city's Nikkei press.[16]

Even as the federal government targeted purported enemy alien Issei for imprisonment in the opening weeks of the war, JACL held out the hope that Nisei, as birthright citizens, would be spared this treatment if they could prove to authorities that they were sufficiently loyal to the United States. On December 7, JACL national headquarters wired President Roosevelt, pledging Japanese America's "fullest cooperation" with the United States and denouncing Japan. National, district, and local leaders continued their practice of distinguishing the second generation from immigrant Japanese by rooting out allegedly disloyal elements among their elder co-ethnics. Some even cooperated with the Naval Intelligence Bureau and FBI to identify potentially subversive Issei. The Los Angeles chapter formed the JACL Anti-Axis Committee to foster Nikkei cooperation with the government, coordinate intracommunity action, and "secure National unity by fair treatment of loyal Americans." The Anti-Axis Committee also continued the familiar public relations strategy in the desperate effort to convince white policymakers of Nisei loyalty.[17]

JACL's chosen course ultimately came at a heavy cost to itself. On the one hand, it succeeded in becoming the most powerful organization within the entire Japanese American community, Issei included. On the other hand, the popular perception that JACL leaders had acted as *inu* (dogs or stool pigeons) in their vigorous push to promote Nisei loyalty destroyed their credibility among their fellow Nikkei. Even within the league itself, some disagreed with what they believed were certain individuals' extreme tactics. On February 19, the day that Roosevelt issued Executive Order 9066, JACL member Togo Tanaka rallied fifteen hundred Los Angeles–area Nisei to form the United Citizens Federation. Tanaka intended the federation to provide a forum for Nisei to express competing viewpoints and catalyze the installation of new spokespersons to mediate between the community and state. The bid failed; JACL leaders refused to relinquish any of their power and moved forward as self-proclaimed community representatives. In this capacity, they maintained that wholesale internment violated the "integrity" of Nisei citizenship. They also resolved to cooperate with the evacuation and relocation for the sake of "military necessity" in order to demonstrate their fealty as well as warrant a humane transition to the camps.[18] In so doing, however, the league further cemented its reputation as a government collaborator—not an entirely fair depiction, as historians have noted, but a notion nonetheless held as truth by many of their coethnics. This notoriety would profoundly shape the JACL's course along with the trajectory of Japanese American citizenship during and beyond internment.

The Birth of the Nisei Soldier

JACL began internment in a paradoxical position, having attained the power to act as Japanese America's liaison to the federal government, but without strong backing from the community as a whole. The WRA's legitimization of the league as the voice of Nikkei, coupled with JACL's continuing reliance on Americanism and public relations to secure Japanese American citizenship—including and especially military service—would only aggravate intraethnic tensions throughout the duration of the war.

From the outset of evacuation, the federal government validated JACL's claim to being the representative head of Japanese America—a recognition that fomented discontent and distrust among the prisoners. Eager to demonstrate their willingness to cooperate with the authorities, JACL leaders volunteered to help set up the camps. In recognition of their efforts, administrators granted them access to the most desirable jobs, particularly white-collar and supervisory positions, in the centers—a move that rankled many internees. The administration privileged JACL above other internees in other ways as well. It permitted to league to operate out of Salt Lake City, allowed for the continued publication of the *Pacific Citizen*, authorized JACL members to control the contents of camp newspapers, and tapped JACL leaders to serve as advisers on center policies. By contrast, the WRA further undermined Issei's authority by initially banning them from staffing the "community councils" (instituted as part of the WRA's policy of democratic "self-government") and mandating that camp governance meetings be conducted in English rather than Japanese.[19]

In acting as spokesorganization, JACL stuck by its established tenets of Americanism and public relations. On April 6, 1942, Masaoka presented the WRA with an eighteen-page letter detailing the league's recommendations for carrying out internment. JACL believed that the "tragedy" of internment could be redirected into an opportunity to "create 'Better Americans in a Greater America'"—a stance that matched the WRA's own approach of liberal assimilation. Masaoka pinpointed several avenues that JACL hoped the administration would follow to reach this destination, including the facilitation of Nikkei interaction with whites as well as an education curriculum that would "inculcate" students "with the spirit of Americanism and democratic processes." He also advocated a triple-pronged public relations campaign reaching the general public, internees, and various arms of the federal government to persuade all three that Japanese Americans were loyal and assimilable, internment could be an effective vehicle for the Americanization of Nikkei, and the WRA deserved support for its efforts in this regard.[20]

Above all, JACL's suggestion to open the armed forces to Nisei comprised the cornerstone of its vision for rehabilitating Japanese American citizenship. In March 1942, the War Department had forbade any further induction of West Coast Nisei into the armed forces, and by July of that year, the Selective Service System had officially designated Nisei as "4C," or enemy aliens, rendering them ineligible for military service. JACL leaders, anxious to reopen the doors of this important venue for proving Japanese American patriotism, pressed federal authorities to end this "unwarranted and unjust discrimination" that placed their "loyalty and allegiance" under suspicion. At a special emergency meeting convened in November 1942 in Salt Lake City, JACL delegates from all ten WRA camps unanimously resolved to ask the War Department to reclassify Nisei "on the same basis as all other Americans."[21]

JACL's view of military service as Japanese Americans' entering wedge into the national polity was not without precedent. The league had just recently led the successful drive to obtain naturalization rights for World War I veterans of Asian ancestry. The passage of the Nye-Lea Act in 1935 had shown that martial patriotism had the power to eclipse racial nativism, if only momentarily. This victory had been possible because the state had placed enormous weight on allegiance to the United States, demonstrated by a willingness to participate in the armed defense of the country, as a necessary precondition for citizenship during and after World War I. Even the American Legion, a vocal proponent of Asiatic Exclusion, supported the cause as part of a broader move to ensure recognition and benefits for veterans at a time when both were insecure. Thus JACL could hold out hope that soldiering might once again counter racial animosity and be used as proof of the Nikkei's fitness for national belonging. Enlistment would afford Japanese Americans the immediate opportunity to fulfill this highest obligation of citizenship and therefore force Americans to recognize Nisei as one of their own.[22]

JACL's arguments resonated with the considerations of several high-level decision makers, including WRA director Dillon Myer, Assistant Secretary of War John J. McCloy, and Office of War Information director Elmer Davis. Both Myer and McCloy championed the idea of Nisei induction. Since the state could not keep Japanese Americans imprisoned indefinitely, they thought, military service could be an effectual means to begin reintegrating the internees back into the larger society and restoring their badly damaged public image. Davis lobbied President Roosevelt to allow Nisei enlistment in order to counter Japanese propaganda that the United States was fighting a "racial war." Finally, on January 1, 1943, the army approved the formation of an all-Nisei volunteer combat team.[23] JACL leaders hesitated at first over the concept of a "Jap Crow" regiment, but were eventually persuaded by the War Department's reasoning that "by forming an all American-Japanese combat team on a voluntary basis, the American people will be presented with the incontrovertible fact that there are loyal American-Japanese who are willing to fight for the United States."[24] As a show of the league's support, Masaoka was the first to enlist in the 442nd Regimental Combat Team.[25]

Reception of the news within Japanese American circles was a different story. Sixty-three Nisei from Poston camp, critical of JACL's position, wrote to President Roosevelt stating that they would be willing to serve only when the federal government reinstated their rights as US citizens. Others turned to violence to express their contempt for the league. When JACL leader Fred Tayama returned to Manzanar from the organization's conference in early December, a number of internees beat him severely enough to warrant his hospitalization. The next day more than two thousand inmates gathered to demand the release of one of the suspected assailants detained by the WRA and express their frustrations with internment more generally, not least what many felt to be the collusion between authorities and the league. They placed the names of Tayama and other JACL leaders on a death list, and those named barely survived by fleeing the center.[26]

Despite these objections, the WRA continued with its plan to assemble an all-Nisei regiment. Such a task, however, required the federal government to devise a system to distinguish "loyal" from "disloyal" inmates. To do so, authorities administered a loyalty questionnaire, officially known as the "Application for Leave Clearance," to all internees over the age of seventeen to determine who among the population would be suitable for military service and resettlement. The most controversial portions of the appraisal were questions 27 and 28, which inquired, respectively, "Are you willing to serve in the armed forces of the United States on combat duty, wherever ordered?" and "Will you swear unqualified allegiance to the United States of America and faithfully defend the United States from any or all attack by foreign or domestic forces, and forswear any form of allegiance or obedience to the Japanese emperor, or any other foreign government, power or organization?" Both questions sparked widespread upheaval and turmoil among internees, fearful of the unknown consequences of answering either "yes" or "no." At Tule Lake, to take one example, mass protests resulted in the arrests of over 100 prisoners at gunpoint for violation of the Espionage Act; 49 percent of Nisei and 42 percent of Issei either repudiated registration or answered "no" to question 28.[27]

Among allegedly loyal internees, reaction to opportunity for military service was less than enthusiastic. Many who answered yes-yes declined to sign up. The recruitment drive within the ten camps yielded only 1,181 volunteers, far short of the 3,000 anticipated by the War Department. In May 1943, enlistees began their ten-month training period at Fort Shelby in Mississippi. On witnessing the commendable showing on the European front by the Hawaiian-Nisei men of the 100th Battalion (who had begun active duty in August 1943), the military deliberated whether or not to conscript additional Nisei. After a protracted debate, the War Department announced the reinstatement of selective service for Japanese Americans in January 1944; draftees would serve as replacements for the 442nd.[28]

Tensions continued to run high in the camps. News of the severe casualties suffered by the 100th further eroded internee confidence in the WRA-JACL plan. The resumption of the draft was itself an admission that the volunteer combat team had failed to inspire support. Of the 315 Nisei who refused compliance, 263 were convicted and jailed, including the 63 resisters known as the Heart Mountain Fair Play Committee.[29]

JACL turned to intracommunity public relations to defuse the prevalent unrest, especially after the 442nd began active duty in June 1944. The *Pacific Citizen* devoted ample space to reporting Nisei combatants' exploits.[30] Another tactic was the utilization of individual soldiers to speak before camp audiences. At the behest of the WRA, JACL sponsored the Japanese-language lecture circuit of Private First Class Thomas Higa, a 100th Battalion veteran, in September 1944. According to JACL, the purpose of the tour was to educate friends and family members about the "facts" of Japanese American soldiers' experiences overseas as well as quash rumors that Nisei soldiers were being used as "cannon fodder." President Saburo Kido reported that Higa's appearances drew "huge audiences," and "helped to build the morale of the Nisei and the parents of Nisei soldiers in the relocation centers."[31] Yet internees' lukewarm and even hostile responses to an analogous tour of the camps by Army Air Corps technical sergeant Ben Kuroki several months prior suggest that Kido's account may have been exaggerated.[32]

Nevertheless, the embrace of martial patriotism by segments of the Nikkei population indicates that not a few Japanese Americans warmed over time to JACL's perspective. New York City's Japanese American Committee for Democracy, an activist group dedicated to "mobiliz[ing] all loyal Americans of Japanese ancestry and Japanese residents of our community loyal to the United States for the defense of American democracy," endorsed Nisei military service in its *NewsLetter*. "The re-opening of selective service [to Nisei] . . . will bind the Japanese in America closer and deeper to this country and this country's stake in the war," opined the Japanese American Committee for Democracy in February 1944.[33] On the ground, community members around the country demonstrated their support through such activities as letter writing to 442nd soldiers and the establishment of United Service Organizations centers to provide entertainment to Japanese American GIs. At Rohwer and Jerome camps in Arkansas, for example, Nisei hostesses coordinated dances, variety shows, and other amusements for troops training at Camp Shelby and other nearby locations.[34]

Meanwhile, JACL simultaneously directed its publicity efforts outward to tell the nation about Japanese Americans' battlefront contributions. In fact, the league, fearful that the war's impending shift to the Pacific front would likely lead to "greater hatred" against Nikkei, named public relations its top priority for 1944. One project that JACL pursued with particular zeal was its use of Kuroki to personalize the Nisei soldier. The league distributed fifteen thousand copies of "Ben Kuroki's Story," a transcript of Kuroki's February 1944 address to San Francisco's Commonwealth Club. The speech detailed his upbringing in Nebraska along with his fifty-eight completed missions as an aerial gunner over North Africa and Europe. In it, Kuroki argued that there were "two battles to fight—against the Axis and against [in]tolerance"— a statement reminiscent of African Americans' Double V campaign. Reminding his audience of Nisei currently in the service, he underscored, "I do believe that loyal

Americans of Japanese descent are entitled to the democratic rights which Jefferson propounded, Washington fought for, and Lincoln died for."[35]

In many ways, the interests of JACL and the state merged in publicizing the contributions of Nisei soldiers. JACL national secretary Masaoka was the most salient embodiment of this intersection. As public relations officer for the 442nd, he generated more than twenty-seven hundred stories about his comrades in action during his tenure. Masaoka recalled that his primary objective as the regiment's media contact was to

> underscore the points that Japanese Americans had volunteered because we were Americans, that we believed in democracy, that we would be willing to fight against Japan as well as any other enemy of the nation, that even though our families were in detention camps as the result of a wartime aberration[,] the 442nd was an example of democracy in action, and that in a period of hate and misunderstanding we sought only a chance to prove our Americanism.[36]

Federal officials, too, had a vested interest in exposing the accomplishments of Nisei troops. In addition to their desire to offset international criticisms that the nation was fighting a race war, political leaders remained wedded to using internment and resettlement as vehicles for Nikkei assimilation. State agencies circulated narratives highlighting Nisei service to prime whites to welcome Japanese Americans as future colleagues, neighbors, and friends. Take, for example, the informational booklet "Nisei in Uniform," issued in October 1944 by the Department of the Interior (the WRA's parent agency) in conjunction with the War Department. Prefaced by President Roosevelt's declaration that "no loyal citizen of the United States should be denied the democratic right to exercise the responsibilities of his citizenship, regardless of his ancestry," "Nisei in Uniform" embraced racial liberalism's tenets, emphasizing that "men whose parents come from Japan are showing that devotion to America and gallantry in action are not determined by the slant of the eyes or color of the skin." It noted that the Nisei fought not only to defeat the Axis but also to "prove" that there was no difference "in attitude or loyalty" between Japanese Americans and other citizens. Scores of photographs displayed "American soldiers with Japanese faces"—including the famous Kuroki—in the field, at rest, and on leave. Besides the 442nd and 100th, the publication also featured Japanese Americans serving in the Marines, Coast Guard, and Women's Army Corps, and snippets of articles from newspapers and magazines around the country praising enlisted Nisei.[37]

The mainstream media proved amenable to this campaign. Just days after the military announced that it would begin to draft Nisei, *Life* featured

Figure 3.1 This WRA publicity photo from 1945, featuring Private First Class Noboru Hokame holding the WRA pamphlet "Nisei in Uniform," underlined the martial patriotism of Japanese American soldiers. The accompanying text highlighted the testimony of Hokame's friend Private First Class Charles P. Carroll (left): "I'd rather fight with just one unit of Japanese-Americans than an entire Army of ordinary soldiers. These boys mean business, and you have a better chance of coming out of a battle intact with them than anybody else I know in the Army."
   Photograph by Hikaru Iwasaki. Courtesy of the Bancroft Library, University of California, Berkeley. 1967.014 v. 52 FI-805-PIC.

"American hero" Yoshinao "Turtle" Omiya, a Hawai'i-born veteran blinded in combat. The same week, both the *Los Angeles Times* and *Time* ran celebratory profiles of Kuroki, stressing his Americanism. The National Association for the Advancement of Colored People (NAACP) magazine, *Crisis*, editorialized that "our fellow citizens of Japanese ancestry . . . deserve every line" of this publicity, lamenting only that African American soldiers were not receiving the same type of favorable reporting. These depictions suggest that the liberal notion of accepting Japanese Americans as members of the national community had started to gain a toehold among white and black Americans during the latter part of the war.[38]

Reactions to these messages, however, were uneven. In January 1944, NBC officials canceled a scheduled radio appearance by Kuroki, citing a concern over the "highly controversial" standing of Japanese Americans in the western United States. Congressperson Clair Engle pushed for a congressional investigation of the WRA's dissemination of such "propaganda," charging the agency with a "ridiculous expenditure" of public monies. Certainly many Americans continued to feel enmity toward Nikkei, as several polling organizations found, leading one *Washington Post* columnist to advocate for even more publicity of Nisei soldiers' war record to assuage hostilities.[39]

Ironically, one of the most visible opportunities for alerting the public to Japanese American sacrifice stemmed from an attempt to deny recognition to Nisei soldiers. In November 1944, the Hood River, Oregon, post of the American Legion removed the names of Nisei enlistees from the town's honor roll. The erasure generated a flurry of local and national criticism, with some three hundred GIs writing to the *Hood River News* in protest. New York City's American Legion Brooks post extended an invitation to the deleted Nisei to join its ranks.[40] In denouncing the Hood River post's decision, mainstream publications reminded readers of the exemplary patriotism of Nisei in the military and their deservedness of full membership in the nation.[41]

The press churned out an additional slew of sympathetic portraits following the outbreak of anti-Japanese hostilities as internees began to return to the West Coast in January 1945. *American Mercury*'s June 1945 article "Japanese-American Soldiers Make Good" (later abridged in *Reader's Digest*) was typical of this surge of exaltation. The story illustrated the myriad ways in which army Nisei fought not only to defeat the Axis powers but also "to prove that Japanese-Americans were basically no different in attitude or loyalty from American citizens whose forebears came from other lands." Nisei resented others' attempts to differentiate them from white soldiers. Vetoing a proposed design of a yellow fist for their group insignia, the Nisei soldiers favored a white one instead. "They prefer to be called Americans, or if they must be distinguished, Japanese-Americans, or JA's," noted the writers.[42]

They were right. In 1940s' America, Nisei soldiers could not avoid being identified on the basis of race. But the second half of the war marked a turning point when many whites did not automatically construe the differences that they perceived between themselves and Japanese Americans as negative or threatening. Journalists, social watchers, and state authorities increasingly identified singularizing characteristics among Nisei as strikingly complimentary. Racial liberalism's arrival had opened up the possibility not for the expunging of racial distinction but rather for a recasting of the alien into the assimilable Other. The *American Mercury* contributors, among many, did precisely that in finding Nisei to be uniquely set apart from other troops by virtue of their "superior soldiership." The 100th Battalion boasted not only the absence of a single desertion but also instances of "AWOL-in-reverse"— wounded men who left their hospital wards to resume fighting before having fully recuperated. Not to be outdone, the 442nd endured the most grueling of conditions, including sleep deprivation and extreme food shortages, yet served as "the spearhead of the spearhead," clearing the way for other units of the Fifth Army.[43] Such descriptions buttressed JACL's claims of Nikkei national belonging that would come to dominate the postwar reconfiguration of Japanese American citizenship.

Memorializing the Nisei Soldier

Poignant eulogies of the loyal Nisei soldier alone, though, could not ensure Nikkei equal treatment as full citizens as they resumed their lives outside the camps. Many struggled to locate housing, find employment, and re-create their households and community networks in the face of racial antagonism. Japanese Americans returning to rural areas on the Pacific coast especially confronted shootings and arson attempts by white vigilantes. In summer 1945, the anti-Japanese movement resurfaced in California in the guise of Proposition 15. Adherents sought to make the Alien Land Law, originally passed in 1913 to prevent Japanese immigrant farmers from purchasing land, a permanent fixture of the state constitution.[44]

Keenly aware of these difficulties, JACL's national officers proposed expanding the league's external public relations efforts at the 1946 Denver convention. Without an intensified crusade, emphasized President Kido, the "ultimate objective for which we are all working"—that is, Japanese Americans' "complete integration into American life"—would be even harder to achieve, since many Americans remained ignorant of the Nikkei's plight. Kido and his cabinet argued that legal reforms, such as the repeal of racially based exclusions in immigration and naturalization law, reparations for losses incurred during the internment, and the nullification of discriminatory legislation directly targeting Nikkei, were necessary to secure Japanese Americans' full citizenship standing. Persuaded, the conferees resolved to strengthen JACL's contacts, cultivate new supporters, and educate the masses on Japanese American issues.[45]

With this mission articulated, JACL launched a fortified publicity campaign underlining the "contributions of Nisei in uniform" to rouse the needed backing to fulfill its legislative objectives. It made sense for JACL to pursue this strategy for myriad reasons. League leaders undoubtedly read the conviction with which many Americans linked liberal contentions for racial tolerance to the sacrifices of Japanese American GIs as good reason to maintain this focus. The awarding of the 1946 Pulitzer Prize to Mississippi journalist Hodding Carter, author of "Go for Broke," an essay foregrounding the valor of Nisei troops in a passionate plea to the nation to accept Japanese Americans as equals, distilled this sincerity.[46] Japanese American warriors continued to capture the public's interest, as evinced by the thousands who turned out to witness the 442nd parade through the streets of Washington, DC, en route to receiving one of the first Presidential Distinguished Unit Citations in July 1946. More broadly, the passage of the Serviceman's Readjustment Act of 1944, popularly known as the GI Bill, signaled the veneration of soldiers in American culture and society by granting sweeping entitlements to World War II veterans.[47]

JACL hastened to build on this trend, worried that "every passing day the record of the Nisei soldier become[s] less and less interesting to the average congressman and the people at large." As a first step, it funded an extended national tour by Kuroki to continue his "59th Mission" against racial intolerance. The league promoted the sale of Kuroki's biography, *Boy from Nebraska* (1946), touting it as "the kind of book every Japanese family ought to have, and every friend of the Japanese people too ought to include in their library." *Boy from Nebraska* received favorable reviews in the mainstream press, attesting to the continuing allure of Nisei in uniform.[48]

The league concurrently initiated a series of Nisei veteran commemorations. Masaoka's efforts led to the placement of a bronze marker near the city of Bruyeres, France, in October 1947, saluting the 442nd's rescue of the "Lost" Texas Battalion at the Vosges Mountains in 1944. JACL also worked with the army to rename its troop ship *USAT Wilson Victory* as the *USAT Pvt. Sadao Munemori* (after the posthumous Nisei recipient of the Congressional Medal of Honor) and stage memorial services at Arlington National Cemetery in June 1948 to coincide with the burial of the first Nisei soldiers to be interred at the prestigious site.[49]

JACL's designation of October 30 as Nisei Soldier Memorial Day suited the gamut of the group's objectives. At one level, the yearly event paid homage to the sacrifices of Japanese Americans in the armed forces with observances around the country.[50] At another level, Nisei Solider Memorial Day functioned as purposeful outreach to encourage public support for the elimination of anti-Japanese discrimination. In advance of the observances in 1950 and 1951, National Director Masao Satow urged chapters to involve churches, veterans organizations, and area newspapers, "playing up" the "supreme sacrifice" and "the necessity of giving immediate citizenship rights to their parents as a matter of justice." Newspaper reportage nationwide suggests that this was a fruitful strategy.[51]

At still another level, the league fashioned the occasion to serve as "an important medium of public relations" for itself within Japanese American circles. As Satow observed, the hope was that as many Nikkei as possible would participate, "even if people are anti-JACL."[52] If individuals did not actively take part, coverage of the event in the ethnic press nevertheless could serve as a reminder that the "magnificent" Nisei combat record—made possible, of course, by JACL's wartime maneuvering—was "the most compelling reason" for Japanese America's improved social standing.[53] In advance of the observances in 1950 and 1951, Satow encouraged league representatives to call on families of the deceased to offer reassurance that JACL had "pledged all our resources to insure that the sacrifices of their sons will not have been in vain."[54] But the Nikkei public did not sign on unquestioningly, indicating that JACL's take on assimilation continued to be divisive. Somewhat counterintuitively, Seattle's Nisei Veterans Committee passed a resolution in November 1949 urging JACL to eliminate the event: "The American ex-soldiers of this group desire no special 'Memorial Day,' no segregated observance; but desire only to participate whole-heartedly in the events of the day set aside for *all* soldiers of this nation."[55] This type of push back must have impressed on the league's directors the imperative to carry on JACL's internal *and* external public relations drive.

Go for Broke!

JACL rose to the occasion with *Go for Broke!*, Metro-Goldwyn-Mayer's 1951 feature film and the most prominent undertaking of the league's postwar publicity offensive. Written and directed by Robert Pirosh, *Go for Broke!* chronicled the wartime experiences of the 442nd, told through the eyes of Lieutenant Michael Grayson (played by Van Johnson), a white Texan unhappily assigned to command the all-Nisei platoon. Over the course of the movie, Grayson's attitude decidedly transformed as he developed relationships with his soldiers and witnessed firsthand their valor during their rescue of the "Lost" Texas battalion, the outfit to which Grayson had previously belonged.[56] The moral of the tale unmistakably echoed JACL's take on martial patriotism: that Nisei had proved beyond a doubt their Americanism through their "baptism of blood."[57]

JACL leaders forecast that *Go for Broke!* would "do more good for persons of Japanese ancestry from a public relations aspect than any other single program or project we can think of." Masaoka actively assisted during the filming as a "special consultant." Postproduction, the national JACL coordinated a promotional blitz to milk the "opportunities" that "should result in goodwill locally for every person of Japanese ancestry." Officers advised chapters not only to encourage their theaters to book the film but also to issue press releases with the names of area 442nd veterans, and arrange for the attendance of Nisei soldiers' parents, widows, and other guests of honor at the first showing. The issue was not simply to foster a positive image of Japanese America as an end in and of itself; it was to build an outpouring of mass support for immigration and naturalization reform. "Perhaps local newspapers might even be willing to run an editorial," they added, "pointing to the fact that the parents of these 'Go for Broke' boys cannot be American citizens because of race."[58]

The fanfare surrounding the various premieres of *Go for Broke!* (Tokyo, Honolulu, Los Angeles, and Washington, DC) evidenced the hand of JACL. The league's capital office hosted a special screening—complete with a hundred-piece Army Ground Forces band—for members of Congress, Supreme Court justices, and sundry federal officials.[59] The Hollywood premiere boasted a festive lineup including the 442nd Color Guard, 442nd Purple Heart recipients, Brigadier General Henry K. Kellogg, and a tribute to Mrs. Nawa Munemori, the mother of Congressional Medal of Honor recipient Private First Class Sadao Munemori. Programs and press books featured profiles of the individual Nisei actors and a triumphant history of the 442nd.[60]

Released Memorial Day weekend, *Go for Broke!* garnered enthusiastic reviews everywhere. The *Chicago Tribune* dubbed the movie "warm and arresting" while the *Oakland Tribune* lauded the "capital performances" of the film's Nisei actors, all of whom were 442nd veterans. Critics were receptive to *Go for Broke's* lessons of racial liberalism. "As a thinking American citizen, the moviegoer . . . will obviously want to cheer the picture for what it says. And that is, in the words of Franklin Delano Roosevelt, that 'Americanism is a matter of mind and heart. Americanism is not, and never was, a matter of race or ancestry,'" applauded the *Los Angeles Daily News*, parroting the quote that graced the film's opening sequence.[61]

JACL correctly predicted that the movie would refresh the memory of Nisei wartime heroism. Reviewers recapitulated the 442nd's achievements. Some, like the *Youngstown Indicator*, rehearsed the battalion's record: "two invasions, seven major campaigns, casualties 9,486 (314% of original strength); seven Presidential Distinguished Unit citations;

individual decorations 18,143, including 6,300 Purple Hearts." Others, including the *New York Journal-American*, extolled the accomplishments of individual Nisei, such as local Kei Yamato (Silver Star and Purple Heart with two clusters), who was "ready" to "bear arms again" in Korea if called.[62]

Go for Broke!'s reception in Cincinnati illustrated the reach of JACL's campaign. Both the *Cincinnati Post* and *Cincinnati Times-Star* endorsed the picture. The *Times-Star* also followed the city's 442nd veterans, not only to bring attention to their battlefront accomplishments, but also to inform readers of the discrimination still faced by many Japanese Americans. The paper noted that Issei remained barred from naturalized citizenship, landownership in some of the western states, and access to old-age pensions. But many Nikkei hoped the film would "help right these wrongs," in the words of Cincinnati JACL branch president Masaji Toki. The chapter's outreach efforts prompted Mayor Albert D. Cash to proclaim an official Go for Broke Week and encourage his constituents to see the movie, "to form a just appraisal of the valor and loyalty of our Japanese-American citizens."[63]

JACL leaders were delighted with the overall response to the film. "This . . . epic was the greatest public relations boost we persons of Japanese ancestry have ever received," testified Masaoka at the league's 1952 national convention.[64] *Pacific Citizen* editor Larry Tajiri concluded with satisfaction that *Go for Broke!*'s "popular success"—measured by sellout crowds and impressive box office returns—clearly served as a "barometer of the public attitude" toward Nikkei.[65]

As for refurbishing JACL's image *within* Japanese America, however, *Go for Broke!*'s effect was below all-out glittering. In Denver, the league's plan to preview the movie to encourage attendance at its April 1951 regional conference grossly backfired. When news of the special showing broke in the Japanese American press with a mention that seats would be limited to conference registrants, conflict erupted. According to an internal report, "anti-JACLers . . . raised a terrific hue and cry" about the arrangements. Denver's American Legion Cathay Post, a veterans' organization dominated by Chinese and Japanese Americans, furiously condemned JACL for acting as gatekeeper and insisted that members of the 442nd should have first priority. Issei parents of fighters, "led to believe that they were being barred," bombarded the local JACL office with complaints. Ultimately, JACL and the Cathay Post worked out a compromise that allowed all area veterans fair dibs. But the controversy marred what should have been a glorious moment.[66]

Few voices disrupted the glowing consensus about the film's narrative, but one in particular merits consideration because it also glimpsed intraethnic dissension and competing visions of Japanese American citizenship. George Yamada, a World War II conscientious objector, scathingly denounced the movie in the January 1953 issue of the *Crisis*. In his view, *Go for Broke!* was a "dismal failure" rife with "contradictions" by trafficking in racial "clichés." He held up the love affair between the lead, Grayson, and the film's Italian ingénue as a case in point: its presence in the film contrasted sharply with the absence of romance between any Nisei and the local women. From personal experience, he knew that plenty of signorinas had fancied the men of the 442nd, yet Hollywood's discomfort with interracial courtship instead reduced this portrayal of Japanese Americans to "stoical Oriental[s] unpreoccupied with such peccadilloes." The upshot was that "*Go for Broke* is Uncle Tom," and with its "expedient acceptance of popular stereotypes," it in effect perpetuated white supremacy.[67]

Yamada's indictment of *Go for Broke!* was really a rebuke of JACL and its martial patriotism approach. Though he never identified the league by name in the review (referring to it only obliquely as "rabid flagwavers" and "rabid apologists"), he made clear his distaste for the organization's politics interwoven throughout the film. While acknowledging that the "valor" of the 442nd had favorably impacted the public's view of Japanese America, he questioned whether military service had truly vindicated JACL, considering the heavy casualties suffered by the regiment. He also reminded his readers that the 442nd was not truly a "volunteer" battalion, as was the common claim. Under the league's direction, he bemoaned, Nisei had become a "200 percent American . . . obsequious conformist . . . timorous sycophant of the political and cultural *status in quo*." *Go for Broke!* was but another instantiation of that impoverished orientation that did nothing to solve the "critical plight" of all peoples of color in the United States.[68]

Yamada's analysis of *Go for Broke!* thus presented an important counterpoint to the dominant conversation about Japanese American citizenship after World War II. His critique gestured at the diversity of Nikkei views regarding the terms of their belonging in the nation. Yet his assessment should be read as a minority report of sorts; written for an African American journal, and published one and half years after the film's debut, the review likely did not carry the necessary weight needed to force a serious debate within the ethnic community. By the early 1950s, JACL's strategy for the rehabilitation of Japanese American citizenship via the Nisei soldier had become a powerful, hegemonic idea, just as JACL had assured its position as the preeminent Nikkei spokesorganization. Detractors would find both nearly impossible to dislodge.

JACL's Push for Legislative Reform

JACL's multifaceted hallowing of the Nisei soldier laid the cultural groundwork for the organization's concurrent push for legislative reform. In the league's view, revamping the law books served a dual purpose: it would move Japanese America closer to full citizenship, and it would bolster the organization's position within the Nikkei community. Resonating with the rise of racial liberalism's emphasis on the state as guarantor of racial equality, JACL's approach successfully met these two goals while reinforcing its power to dictate the trajectory of Japanese American citizenship. More precisely, in utilizing lobbying, congressional testimonies, court cases, and anti-Communism as the vehicles through which to make its claims of national belonging, the organization redefined the meaning of Japanese American identity to include political moderation—a shift that would have lasting consequences for the nation's racial landscape.

Given the debacle of the wartime loyalty questionnaire and its aftermath, JACL's reputation within the Nikkei community remained tarnished at the outset of the postwar period. In Chicago, Nisei indifference and antagonism toward the organization led one contemporary sociologist to doubt that the league could establish itself in the city, despite the fact that it was home to one of the largest Nikkei populations at the war's end.[69] One Los Angeles recruiter enrolled only four of the three hundred people who he approached to join the league, while the Cincinnati chapter attracted merely a quarter of the area's hundred Nisei by mid-1946.[70]

JACL leaders suffered no delusions about the status of their organization and agreed that their greatest challenge ahead was boosting their membership rolls. At the 1946 Denver convention, national officers contended that there needed to be "concrete evidence" of the league's work and its payoff for Japanese America. To coordinate the lobbying necessary to influence congressional legislators, JACL unveiled its Washington, DC–based Anti-Discrimination Committee (ADC) in July 1946, with Masaoka at the helm as national legislative director.[71]

In founding the ADC, JACL leaders adopted what one described as an "exploratory and conciliatory" approach to antiracist work—in essence, a continuation of their wartime methodology. This political orientation not only reaffirmed the league's assimilationist stance but also aimed to ensure that "the door of receptivity" remained open to Japanese Americans.[72] Furthermore, a legislative campaign meant that JACL leaders could build on their established relationships with federal authorities in order to shore up JACL's claim to be the sole spokesorganization of the Nikkei community.

Fortuitously for JACL, its political aims aligned closely with those of President Harry S. Truman's civil rights agenda. In December 1946, Truman convened his Committee on Civil Rights. Although the bulk of the committee's attention focused on the situation of African Americans, its members entertained issues facing other minority groups. At the request of Masaoka himself, the committee invited him to participate as an expert on Japanese American issues, providing JACL an incomparable opportunity to push for its legislative goals.[73]

Predictably, Masaoka turned to the figure of the Nisei soldier to buttress his appeals to the state. In defense of the Evacuation Claims bill, intended to provide restitution for economic damages incurred during the internment, he cited Truman's declaration that it would be a "tragic anomaly if the United States were, on the one hand, to acclaim and decorate with honors the brave Nisei troops who fought so valiantly and at such sacrifice overseas, while, on the other hand, it ignored and left unaddressed the very real and grievous losses."[74] Masaoka argued that the legal designation of Issei as aliens ineligible to citizenship continued to deprive the immigrant generation of means of livelihood. He cited the case of the parents of one soldier killed in action who were barred from "inheriting" the land that they had purchased in their son's name to circumvent California's Alien Land Laws. Ineligibility to citizenship also disqualified Issei, including the mother of a Congressional Medal of Honor recipient, from receiving old-age pensions and relief payments. Such discriminations "threaten[ed] those fundamental concepts of decent living that so many fought for overseas."[75]

Masaoka's suggestion that Nisei had earned the full entitlements of citizenship through their wartime bloodshed proved a shrewd rhetorical move. The landmark final report of the President's Committee on Civil Rights, *To Secure These Rights* (1947), reveals the indelible imprint of his influence. The committee recommended the repeal of state laws targeting aliens ineligible to citizenship, establishment of a procedural body to process the internment-related property loss claims of former internees, and restructuring of naturalization laws to remove restrictions based on race and national origins.[76] Its findings even quoted a firsthand account from Masaoka himself—identified only as a "Japanese American veteran"—to draw attention to the "moral impact" of such discrimination:

Most of us fought as we did because we felt that, in spite of the way we had been kicked around, America was still the land of opportunity for all of us. I know my mother sent five of her sons. Every one volunteered for combat. One was killed. The rest of us were wounded. We have over thirty individual decorations and

medals among us. Well, my mother wants to become a citizen. It is
for people like my mother and for a lot of Americans of good will
throughout the United States who have a lot of confidence in us and
our loyalty that we did the job we did.

The inclusion of this passage and similar others indicates that JACL's espousal of martial patriotism was a sound way to make claims on society
and the state after World War II.[77] In so doing, the league tapped into
the tried-and-true strategy of generations of veterans seeking reciprocity
from the federal government.[78]

Indeed, public opinion seemed amenable to reenvisioning Nikkei as US
citizens entitled to equal treatment before the law. In November 1946,
Californians defeated Proposition 15 by 350,000 votes—the first time in
the state's history that residents blocked an anti-Asian referendum from
passage. The ADC's steady dissemination of information to media outlets
had most certainly facilitated the appearance of over fifty newspaper editorials, national magazine features, and major radio programs supporting Japanese American civil rights. Numerous local-level organizations
voiced approval as well—in Chicago, the City Club, the Chicago Civil
Liberties Committee, and the Church Federation of Greater Chicago,
among other groups, adopted resolutions in favor of JACL's drive.[79]

This shift in thinking impelled a string of legislative and judicial victories for JACL and Japanese Americans. The league led the push for Public
Law 213 (1947), allowing Japanese war brides to enter the United States,
and Public Law 863 (1948), conceding to Japanese nationals the right to
petition the attorney general to suspend deportation orders. When California continued to escheat Japanese American properties even after the
defeat of Proposition 15, JACL successfully questioned the Alien Land
Law's constitutionality in *Oyama v. California* (1948). The league brought
a second case before the Supreme Court, *Takahashi v. California Fish and
Game Commission* (1948), in which the bench ruled that aliens ineligible to citizenship—that is, Japanese immigrants—could not be barred
from obtaining commercial fishing licenses in California. Both *Oyama*
and *Takahashi* upheld the application of the Fourteenth Amendment for
Issei noncitizens as well as citizens. Along with the landmark *Shelley v.
Kraemer* (1948), the ruling that outlawed racially restrictive housing covenants (for which JACL filed a supporting amicus curiae brief), *Oyama*
and *Takahashi* signaled the majority court's resolve to strike down laws
that discriminated against Japanese Americans—crucial steps toward the
final dismantling of the Asiatic Exclusion regime.[80]

The triumphant mood at JACL's national convention in September
1948 contrasted markedly to the somber tone of the previous gathering.
Masaoka proudly announced that Congress had approved the Evacuation

Claims Act, which not only provided compensation for internment-related property losses but also indicated the government's "confidence" in the Japanese American community.[81] To be sure, JACL had much cause to be encouraged. For one, the organization had garnered a host of accolades for its achievements. Masaoka, in particular, gained more than a modicum of fame. *Common Ground* saluted Masaoka as a "lobbyist extraordinary" and enthusiastically remarked that Japanese Americans had "moved ahead with greater strides" in 1948 than ever before. In 1949, *Reader's Digest* hailed Masaoka as "Washington's Most Successful Lobbyist," boasting a legislative record in the eightieth Congress unmatched by any of his peers on the Hill.[82]

This winning streak enabled the league to speed the rescue of its intra-community reputation. In Chicago, resettlers were increasingly willing to admit that JACL served their collective interests. Chicago's chapter had even amassed a cadre of supporters by the late 1940s to form a local branch of the ADC. Membership swung upward nationwide: the league claimed 5,782 in 1947, and by the 1948 national convention, the roster counted 6,700.[83]

Yet the league's recovery was far from finished. For some, the wartime rifts had never healed. Journalist Jimmie Omura, among the most vocal of the league's skeptics, put it most bluntly: "We need something besides the JACL." A longtime discontent, Omura had been one of the few Japanese Americans to object openly to the imminent incarceration in the days after President Roosevelt issued Executive Order 9066—a decision that led Masaoka to dub him the league's "Public Enemy Number One." Omura spent the war as a newspaper reporter in Colorado, criticizing JACL and the induction of Nisei into the armed forces, and throwing his support behind the draft resisters of the Heart Mountain Fair Play Committee. He followed up with a succession of anti-JACL screeds in his brief postwar tenure as English editor of Denver's *Rocky Shimpo* in 1947. In his view, the league's failure to defend the rights of Nisei who did not conform to its Americanist vision, refusal to acknowledge the multiplicity of Nisei political orientations, and "leech-like grip on national leadership" had rightfully earned its leaders the "censure of the Nisei at large." Although conceding that the JACL-ADC "has already performed magnificently in Washington," he nevertheless charged that the league first and foremost served its own interests rather than those of the entire community. Omura thus urged Nisei to resist the league's designs to "complete domination" over all of Japanese America.[84]

Total authority, however, remained out of the league's grasp. In June 1949, *Crossroads*, a Los Angeles–based Japanese American weekly, canvased a cross-section of Nisei on the question "Do you believe the Japanese American Citizens League is doing an effective job?" Respondents conveyed a mix of impressions. College student Fred Oyama, the most exuberant, was also perhaps the least impartial, given that the league had recently defended him in the successful *Oyama v. California* lawsuit: "I witnessed JACL demand and win rights for the Nisei as Americans—the very thing the Nisei once felt the JACL failed to do during evacuation." Others were more circumspect, but also held the "Nisei public" responsible for the league's direction. Some wished that the organization would do more to address bread-and-butter issues such as juvenile delinquency and employment opportunities.[85]

While JACL leaders might have dismissed such remarks as isolated occurrences, organized forces vying for influence posed more much of a threat. The most prominent challenge came from a few hundred leftists in New York, Chicago, San Francisco, and Los Angeles who rallied as Nisei for Wallace to support former vice president Henry Wallace's run for the presidency on the Progressive Party ticket in 1948. Dissatisfied with the reactionary, militaristic, and "oligarch[ic]" direction of Truman Democrats, Nisei for Wallace campaigned for the aspirant it saw as most committed to "America's role in the preservation of world peace and economic well-being." Wallace enthusiasts felt particularly drawn to him for his uncompromising stand in favor of unabridged rights for all minority groups. At the Progressive Party's national convention in July, Nisei delegates successfully swayed their colleagues to incorporate Japanese American–specific planks into the platform: immediate statehood for Hawai'i, blanket compensation for internees' losses moving beyond the limitations of the JACL-backed Evacuation Claims Law, and the right to naturalization for Issei.[86]

Undeterred by its candidate's defeat in the November polls, Nisei for Wallace reinvented itself as the Nisei Progressives to "carry on a program of political action and education that would protect and advance the general welfare and the economic, social, and political interests of the Japanese American community." Beyond its general vision of "peace, abundance, and freedom for all," the group also targeted five "special" issues to which it was devoted: naturalization and immigration rights, employment, housing, "equitable" evacuation claims, and the growing "Youth Problem" in the Nikkei community.[87] Over the next few years, the Nisei Progressives took up a diverse array of causes, joining forces with African Americans to oppose the city of Los Angeles' eviction of Nikkei and black tenants from Little Tokyo, condemning a congressional antisubversive bill for "embodying the concept of guilt by association," pleading with Indian prime minister Jawarhalal Nehru to mediate the Korean War, supporting the admission of the People's Republic of China to the United Nations, and boycotting Florida products after NAACP leader Harry T. Moore was slain there in 1951.[88] While the Nisei Progressives' communications (the Los Angeles chapter's *Independent* newsletter and the New York chapter's *Bandwagon* magazine) betrayed few overt spats with JACL, their sustained activism proved beyond a doubt that the league did not speak for all of Japanese America.[89]

The Cold War End of Japanese Exclusion

If the rehabilitation of JACL's intracommunity reputation remained incomplete, so, too, did its political agenda; Issei remained legally classified as aliens ineligible to citizenship. An important reorganization of congressional priorities after 1948, however, translated into improved prospects for this linchpin of JACL's postwar legislative campaign. Under the direction of Senator Pat McCarran, the Senate Judiciary Committee undertook an exhaustive investigation of the nation's immigration apparatus in the name of safeguarding the United States' "internal security" from the menace of Communism. This was precisely the opening that JACL needed to make what might be seen as a special interest issue, relevant only to Japanese Americans, appeal to the broadest possible audience.

In usual form, Masaoka deftly sculpted JACL's call for reform to fit the national obsession with containing Communism. Speaking on behalf of the ADC, Masaoka repeatedly emphasized the foreign policy implications of eliminating racial barriers to immigration and naturalization, particularly with regard to the Far East. Testifying before US senators in 1951, he reminded his audience of Japan, Korea, and Southeast Asia's critical roles in America's battle against Communism. Overturning racial restrictions in immigration law, he argued, would provide a "dramatic and concrete demonstration of our regard for our fellow freemen who are enlisted with us in the great war for survival against the Communist threat" in the Asia-Pacific region. Such a move could well be the "tiny spark needed to ignite the torch of freedom in the Orient." Conversely, congressional inaction would leave the nation vulnerable to Communist propaganda criticizing the United States for its racist policies.[90]

Masaoka connected the plight of Issei to the United States' desire to reconstruct Japan as "our bulwark of democracy in the Orient." He not only posited that immigration and naturalization policy carried tremendous weight in terms of the US-Japan relationship but also noted that the reform impulse was particularly timely with the impending signing of the peace treaty between the two nations. On the one hand, should the United States continue to stall, Japan could "fall prey to the Communists, especially in that transitional period following the signing of the peace treaty." Changes to the law, on the other hand, would welcome Japan "into the family of democratic nations"—a smart move toward cultivating a "mutual confidence."[91]

Other supporters advanced the same argument. *Reader's Digest* editor Blake Clark, a dedicated champion of Japanese American equality, joined the Cold War rationale to the notion of Issei women as republican mothers. Clark pointed to the example of Mrs. Munemori, "denied citizenship by the country for which her son sacrificed his life." Like Masaoka, he maintained that perpetuating such discrimination would severely "damage" US relations with Asia.[92] Inserting the text of Clark's article into the *Congressional Record*, Representative Judd added, "How much longer will we jeopardize the lives of Americans by failing to remove the insult which denies us the full trust and good will of a billion people?"[93]

Not much longer, as it turned out. On June 27, 1952, Congress narrowly overrode President Truman's veto of the Immigration and Nationality Act, ending at last the career of the alien ineligible to citizenship. Also known as the McCarran-Walter Act, the new law allotted Japan a token yearly immigration quota and permitted persons of Japanese ancestry the rights to naturalized citizenship.[94] Delegates to JACL's national convention in San Francisco ecstatically greeted Masaoka's arrival the next day, waving banners that read "Well Done, Mike!"[95] For weeks afterword, the *Pacific Citizen* sang the praises of its parent organization and especially the lobbyist's "legislative genius" in realizing this "highwater mark." JACL gladly credited Masaoka for the "realization" of the "Issei Dream."[96]

Hitching its political fortunes to the McCarran-Walter wagon, though, presented JACL with hazards as well as returns. A fierce conservative, McCarran had sought to tighten the provisions of his namesake 1950 Internal Security Act that had empowered the federal government to exclude, deport, and denaturalize Communists along with other alleged subversives. The 1952 law as it was passed reflected this reactionary agenda. Many liberals judged its racial implications to be equally disturbing. They read the levying of token quotas on colonies—especially those in the British Caribbean—as a draconian move to keep blacks from emigrating to the United States. The bill also introduced the "Asia-Pacific Triangle" to keep the inflow of Asian peoples to a minimum. All individuals of Asiatic ancestry, regardless of birthplace or residence, would be "charged" to the Asia-Pacific Triangle's relatively stingy annual ceiling of two thousand admittees. Finally, the legislation did nothing to overturn the national origins quota system, first imposed by Congress in 1924 as a means to block southern and eastern European immigration. Together, these features offended a large swath of liberal-leftist America, including

Figure 3.2 Tsukasa Kiyono, a retired Issei flower grower, presents a check for two thousand dollars to JACL's Mike Masaoka (right) in September 1956. Kiyono's donation expressed his appreciation for league's leadership in postwar civil rights reform benefiting the Nikkei community. By the early 1950s, JACL had repaired much of the reputational damage that the organization had suffered as a result of its contentious wartime decisions.

Photograph by Toyo Miyatake Studio. Gift of the Alan Miyatake Family, Japanese American National Museum. 96.267.364

some Japanese Americans. The Nisei Progressives, for one, lobbied President Truman to veto the act. Virtually alone among immigrant, ethnic, and civil rights associations in backing the legislation, JACL risked alienating itself from its political bedfellows.[97]

The league's greatest gamble was the potential loss of constituents within Japanese America. A decline in Nikkei support for its programs could lead to a drop in the organization's power to represent the ethnic community. JACL's push for Issei citizenship rights undoubtedly had the enthusiastic backing of many Japanese Americans—Hawai'i Nikkei alone raised more than a quarter million dollars for the effort. But the league's decision to throw its weight behind the McCarran-Walter bill disappointed others. University of Chicago linguist S. I. Hayakawa aired perhaps the most visible critique in a series of open letters to JACL published in the *Chicago Shimpo*, one of his city's Japanese American organs. After the ratification of the McCarran-Walter Act, Hayakawa informed the league that he no longer wished to contribute to the JACL-ADC fund. The league had been celebrating the decision as a "milestone of liberal progress," but Hayakawa begged to differ. In his view, the league had committed a "profound disservice" by securing Issei naturalization rights "at the cost of all the questionable and illiberal features of the Walter-McCarran bill." Such a compromise, he bristled, was "an act of unpardonable short-sightedness of cynical opportunism." *Chicago Shimpo* editor Ryoichi Fujii introduced Hayakawa's missive during public hearings conducted by President Truman's Commission on Immigration and Naturalization in fall 1952, noting that "several Japanese Americans have expressed a similar opinion." Even in JACL's greatest moment of triumph, dissenters continued to dog the league.[98]

JACL's Vexed Relationship to Japan

The assertions advanced by Masaoka for JACL in favor of the McCarran-Walter Act pointed to the paradoxical nature of Nikkei citizenship at midcentury: Japanese Americans could not break free from an automatic association with Japan. Just as the Pacific rivalry between Japan and the United States had dictated the terms of belonging for Nikkei during World War II, geopolitics continued to undergird those conditions in the postwar period. In the case of immigration reform, this configuration had worked to their advantage. But as the US occupation of Japan drew to a close in the early 1950s, many Japanese Americans continued to worry that the nature of their citizenship remained tenuously positioned, subject as ever to the mercurial forces of international relations. The ratification of the US-Japan peace treaty and withdrawl of Allied forces in 1951–52 consequently catapulted JACL's role in US-Japan affairs to the forefront of the league's policy agenda.[99]

Though JACL had long trumpeted Americanism as its political orientation, the organization had never fully divorced itself from Japan-related issues. The ADC pushed both the Senate Foreign Relations Committee and President Truman to expedite the signing of the peace treaty with Japan. Masaoka participated as an unofficial observer at the 1951 San Francisco Peace Conference, where the accord was finalized, during which he discussed the "Japanese American point of view" with representatives of both lands. At JACL's 1952 national convention, the organization's National Public Relations Committee recommended sending Masaoka to Japan as the league's envoy. The committee foresaw US-Japan relations as continuing to scaffold the terms of Japanese American citizenship, and contended that Masaoka might forge valuable contacts in the government and private sector.[100]

The proposition ignited a heated disagreement among conference participants. One attendee pointed out that the recommendation seemed to contradict the fact that JACL was "primarily established for the welfare and security of persons of Japanese ancestry *in America*." Former president Kido warned that JACL jeopardized its future by risking being "used as a tool" for Japan. Some put forward the possibility of allowing Masaoka to go, but not under the auspices of JACL. Others favored the pitch, maintaining that a familiarity with Japanese affairs would enable Masaoka to better "protect" JACL. The delegates ultimately tabled the proposal, leaving unresolved the larger issue of JACL's involvement in international relations.[101]

But league officials knew that the question could not go unanswered indefinitely. JACL felt internal and external pressures to formulate a clear position on the subject as well as the imperative to be prepared should Japan fall "in the red orbit." Thus, at the September 1954 national convention, the National Public Relations Committee introduced a tentative statement articulating JACL's official stance on foreign affairs.[102] The document outlined members' various standpoints: the league should function as an "international bridge" between the United States and Japan; JACL should work on maximizing Japan's economic development and popularizing Japanese culture in the United States; and JACL definitely should not involve itself in all "things Japanese."[103] After weighing these different options, the National Public Relations Committee concluded that JACL "cannot afford to risk the chance of becoming identified with Japan." It reasoned that if Japan once again assumed enemy status by becoming Communist or strengthening ties with Red China, Japanese Americans, by association, would again suffer. The committee reminded delegates that the federal government had permitted JACL to operate during the war only because it had "carefully avoided contact and association with Japanese officials and organizations" in the years before Pearl Harbor—a claim, of course, not entirely veracious. Convention delegates approved the charge to refrain from "participating or intervening in any matters relating to the international relations of this Government, including those with Japan," unless the "welfare" of Japanese Americans was directly imperiled.[104]

But even if JACL opted to distance itself from international relations, it could not divest itself or Japanese America entirely from the association with Japan. Some of these linkages were voluntary. The league maintained a liaison with the embassy of Japan, for instance, to discuss matters of import to Japanese Americans. Others were not. Such was the case with the story of Iva "Tokyo Rose" Toguri d'Aquino. Toguri d'Aquino, a Nisei visiting Japan in 1941, had been unable to return to the United States after the Pearl Harbor bombing. To support herself during the war, she accepted a position at Radio Tokyo, where she was one of several Anglophone female disc jockeys collectively known as Tokyo Rose. The women broadcast popular American music and comedy routines to US military personnel stationed in the Pacific, often playfully subverting the Axis propaganda that they were assigned to deliver. After the war, the Department of Justice wrongfully singled out Toguri d'Aquino as *the* Tokyo Rose and charged her with treason. In a sensationalized trial, the federal government convicted her and revoked her US citizenship. Lincoln Yamamoto of Pasadena, California, wrote to *Newsweek* in February 1956 to comment on Toguri d'Aquino's release from federal prison. In his view, Nisei "consider[ed] ourselves citizens of Japan, regardless of where we're born," and d'Aquino Toguri was simply "doing her duty" to her country as Tokyo Rose. "We niseis [*sic*] are proud of Iva D'Aquino and we're going to give her a heroine's welcome."[105]

Yamamoto's assertion laid bare the divergent possibilities of Japanese American identity that JACL had labored carefully to suppress. One was embodied in the figment of Tokyo Rose, portrayed in the US media as a seditious siren, irresistible to the American GI and capable of derailing the Allied mission in the Pacific. In every way, she embodied the opposite of the Nisei patriot in arms—female, sexual, and turncoat. Moreover, the type of womanhood that she represented vivified tenacious associations in popular culture between Asian females, hypersexuality, and prostitution. This, of course, ran counter to JACL's promotion of Issei women as the Cold War mothers of the republic.[106] Yamamoto symbolized yet another alternative to JACL's version of palatable Nikkei identity: a Japanese American man with no history of service in the US armed forces and whose wartime political allegiances aligned unequivocally with Japan. Both threatened to unseat the loyal Nisei soldier as the public face of the community. To JACL, a columnist for the *Palo Alto Times* made plain this risk in an opinion published three days later. The editorialist warned that the "brass-band homecoming" planned for Toguri was "ill-advised" since it would "reinforc[e] the prejudices of those who feel that the Nisei are pro-Japanese under all circumstances."[107]

Fearful that such a displacement could be ruinous to their organization and the Nikkei community at large, JACL leaders swiftly refuted Yamamoto's declaration. Peter Nakahara, president of JACL's Northern California Sequoia chapter, complained to the *Palo Alto Times* that Yamamoto spoke "only for himself in his irresponsible and misguided fanaticism." The offending writer agreed to clarify the misunderstanding.[108] The *Pacific Citizen* condemned Yamamoto's letter as a "great disservice to Nisei everywhere" and called for his deportation. The league goaded the FBI and US Post Office to assist in locating Yamamoto, charging that the issue was libelous and a "violation of our civil rights." Unable to confirm his existence, the fruitless search led JACL leaders to suspect—or perhaps just conveniently claim—that he was actually a "fictitious character." Masaoka implored *Newsweek* to make amends for its "irresponsible journalism" by "affirm[ing] your confidence in the loyalty and allegiance of Americans of Japanese ancestry in this country." Individual league members wrote to the magazine, lambasting Yamamoto's "fanatical outburst" and reiterating the undivided loyalty of Nisei to the United States. The JACL respondents turned once again to martial patriotism to substantiate the latter point. As one put it, "Instead of giving Iva D'Aquino a heroine's welcome it is our conviction that men like Hiroshi Miyamura of Gallup, N.M. and Sadao Mumemori [*sic*] of California, both winners of the Congressional Medal of Honor, are the heroes of the Japanese Americans in the United States." And in case *Newsweek* missed the point, JACL legal counsel Frank Chuman informed its board of directors that they should expect a lawsuit if they failed to retract the claim or publish a correction.[109]

The league's pressure tactics yielded rapid results. *Newsweek* ran eleven of the JACL letters accompanied by an apology reiterating that "Americans of Japanese descent have proved themselves, both at home and on the battlefield, as citizens who yield to no one in their loyalty to their country." Support for the protest revealed the scope of JACL's influence. Stockton, California's American Legion Karl Ross Post passed a resolution reproaching *Newsweek* and expressing "confidence" in Nisei veterans' patriotism. On the floor of the US Congress, Senator Thomas H. Kuchel and representatives James Roosevelt and Charles Gubser denounced Yamamoto's remarks while affirming the "splendid record" of Japanese American soldiers.[110]

JACL leaders reviewed the hullabaloo with mixed feelings. As Masaoka pointed out, *Newsweek*'s concession was an "unusual" move for any publication, and as such, "I suppose that we should be thankful for that much." Yet it could not reverse the fact that "the damage has been done." Members of Congress continued to hear from constituents skeptical of Nisei loyalty, and Masaoka conjectured that "it will be a long time before this is forgotten." The problem also concerned more than the image of Japanese America. The other issue at stake was JACL's claim to act on behalf of all Nikkei. Masaoka reported that Wimp Hiroto, a contributor to the Nikkei weekly *Crossroads*, had "laughed at the JACL's concern and Nisei indignation" in a recent essay. What if other "supposed Nisei spokesmen" carried on the same way? Should *Newsweek* or Congress learn of such remarks, "they would wonder what kind of people we are to write such smears against *ourselves* and *our* national reputation." The victorious outcome of the Yamamoto incident seemed more pyrrhic than decisive, and Masaoka urged "something drastic" to discipline future contrarians.[111]

Within a few months another "alarming development" arose to put JACL on the defensive yet again. At the league's 1956 national convention, Masaoka noted apprehensively the spread of boycotts against Japan-made textiles and other manufactures. He worried that this hostility would soon be redirected toward Japanese Americans. "Much of the goodwill which American GIs brought back from Japan has been lost and even the goodwill from the Nisei war record is being slowly dissipated," cautioned Masaoka. Anticipating even greater animosity in the coming months, he predicted that the "Nisei position" would soon become "even more difficult."[112]

Anxieties inflamed, convention delegates resumed the consideration of the league's stance on international affairs. Knowing well that "international incidents mold public opinion at home," the league's Interim Public Relations Committee urged JACL to intervene in questions of "general welfare." Two of the conference's keynote speakers made similar appeals. Maxwell Rabb, cabinet secretary to President Dwight D. Eisenhower, encouraged Nisei involvement in US-Japan relations to stave off Communism's encroachment in the Far East. Edward Ennis, general counsel to the American Civil Liberties Union and JACL, suggested that JACL "formulate a new perspective" on Japanese America's role in diplomacy, and urged Nisei to foster trade between the United States and Japan as a means to cultivate the latter as a key Cold War ally.[113]

Masaoka took these words to heart. Less than three weeks after the convention, he testified before the House Ways and Means Committee to voice objections to tighter import limits on Japanese goods. He argued that the United States should foster business with Japan for geopolitical as well as monetary reasons. "The real importance . . . is that we weaken the communist lure by strengthening the vitality of the Japanese people and their confidence in us as sincere allies," he exhorted. "This certainly is not the time to drive our friends and allies into the enemy's camp by imposing trade restrictions which will jeopardize their ability to remain free." Masaoka's commentary drew coast-to-cast media attention, from the *Wall Street Journal* to the *Fresno Bee*.[114]

Immediately, Fresno JACL member Fred Hirasuna circulated a withering attack on Masaoka and the league. Outraged that newspaper coverage had identified Masaoka as a "spokesman for Japanese Americans" and "the Japanese American Citizens League," Hirasuna fumed, "What individual, or individuals, in the JACL are to be authorized to decide and make known the collective stand of all Japanese Americans, or even of just the JACL members, on such controversial matters?" Hirasuna demanded more transparency and integrity on Masaoka's part. "If he is expressing the collective opinion of Japanese Americans, or of the JACL, it behooves him to be sure that he is truly expressing that opinion. It is a tremendous responsibility. It is a public trust that should be put beyond any suspicion of the motive of private gain," he asserted.[115] Hirasuna alluded to the fact that Masaoka had resigned as full-time director of JACL's ADC in 1952 to open his own public relations firm, Mike M. Masaoka Consultants. Masaoka kept JACL as his main client, but added a host of others to his roster, including numerous Japanese concerns aspiring to access the US market.[116]

Reading Hirasuna's rant, the national directors panicked that it might cause "unpleasant repercussions" for the association if leaked to the ethnic public.[117] Indignant, Masaoka refused to "dignify the letter with any kind of acknowledgment." He nonetheless denied that he was "not a paid lobbyist for any Japanese interest, textile or otherwise," although he confirmed that he represented "Americans who import Japanese exports." Masaoka insisted he only accepted lobbying accounts that did not conflict with JACL objectives and that any related to Japan had to be "in the national interest of the United States," especially those of Nisei. Furthermore, he maintained that he had "earned the right" to league members' confidence to speak for them as he saw fit in accordance with the organization's declared policies.[118]

While Masaoka's explanation made sense to other JACL officers, it could not negate the uncomfortable truth that the league's credibility within the community continued to be undermined by skepticism and mistrust—sometimes by its own card-carrying members. Hirasuna was not alone in his criticism. Writing in *Crossroads*, Kango Kunitsugu, legislative committee chair for JACL's Pacific Southwest council, called on the league to recuse itself from "matters international," except in cases with direct bearing on Nikkei in the United States. Those with an abiding interest, he added, ought to operate independently of JACL. *Crossroads* writer Hiroto bluntly opined that JACL had no right to speak for all Japanese Americans, particularly as pertaining to US-Japan dynamics.[119] These ruminations helped move what had started as a discussion internal to JACL outside the league's circle. The pressures pushed Masaoka and other league directors to solidify their plans to establish an autonomous organization to handle global concerns.[120]

In December, the debate spilled onto the national scene when the *Saturday Evening Post* revisited the proceedings of JACL's national convention. The *Saturday Evening Post* charged that Ennis had gone too far in endorsing the "complete liberty in peacetime" of minority groups to shape US policy regarding their ancestral homelands. "The danger is not that they will hang back, but that some will carry their activities too far," the editors warned. As with the *Newsweek* controversy, JACL directors rushed to admonish the magazine, arguing that it had taken Ennis's remarks out of context, and asserting yet again that the "primary and fundamental loyalty" of Japanese Americans was to the United States. Unlike *Newsweek*, however, the *Saturday Evening Post* refused to retract its opinions.[121]

In the wake of this incident, JACL rank and file demanded an unambiguous resolution. Individual members, local chapters, and regional districts aired competing views for more than a year in the *Pacific Citizen*.[122] Some complained that Masaoka rather than the national board dictated JACL's decisions. They also requested a list of Masaoka's private accounts so that they could determine for themselves whether or not he had conflicts of interest.[123] Ever the naysayer, Kunitsugu blasted JACL in the pages of *Crossroads* and the *Pacific Citizen*, critiquing what he perceived as a double standard in the organization's drift: the advocacy of internationalist interventions while shying away from assisting African American civil rights organizations on issues with more "direct bearing" on Japanese Americans. He also insisted that Nisei deserved to know whether the league would become "propaganda machinery" for either US foreign policy or Japanese business, and whether its leaders stood to profit from such dealings.[124] In May 1958, the Hollywood, California, branch voted that JACL should refrain entirely from engaging in US-Japan relations.[125] By then, the dispute had escalated to the point that national JACL president Roy Nishikawa dubbed it "one of the most controversial problems ever confronting the organization."[126]

The matter finally exploded at that year's national convention when the league's top officials decided that the impasse risked JACL's standing as the country's paramount Nikkei organization. Harold Gordon, chair of the league's Legislative-Legal Committee, argued that the present policy was "too restrictive" for JACL to maintain its current station. He cited an editorial published in San Francisco's *Hokubei Mainichi* enjoining JACL to take a firm position on Japan as opposed to "the cowardly stand of 'no comment.' "[127] To short-circuit the exodus of intracommunity supporters, Gordon proposed the formation of a standing national committee on international relations. Masaoka spelled out the stakes even more explicitly. "If the JACL does not go into this field of United States-Japan affairs and if you refuse to take a position . . . you are inviting to have some other group take over by default," he warned. "If the group does not have the same interests as ours, we are giving to another group the right if they want to speak for us. This I think is too dangerous and too high a price to pay."[128] This line of reasoning sufficed to convince the majority of the delegates, who then authorized the establishment of JACL's National Committee on International Relations.[129]

With perhaps unintended irony, Masaoka also announced the founding of the American Committee on Japan (ACJ), a body independent of JACL. For years Masaoka had steadfastly clung to the belief that Japanese Americans should be involved in US-Japan dealings and that there was "no question" that JACL should take the helm. But he had also worried that "competitive, self-seeking" Nisei organizations devoted to this cause would threaten the league's authority, particularly if his beloved organization remained paralyzed about the issue. As early as 1954, Masaoka proposed a possible solution: select JACL members should form a separate entity "to safeguard JACL's position" even if the league continued to adhere to its policy of nonparticipation in international affairs. His inkling now came to life with the ACJ's arrival. Its objective echoed that of the league's expansion into international affairs: "to prevent any group from taking over" the lead as Nikkei spokesorganization in regard to US-Japan relations. While ostensibly a separate entity whose raison d'être placed it in direct competition with JACL, the interests of the two organizations, along with those of Masaoka as an individual, were by no means detached. Masaoka himself served as executive secretary of the ACJ, and former JACL president Kido presided as chair. Their formation of the ACJ betrayed their continuing investment in wielding power as mediators between Japanese America and the peoples and governments of the United States *and* Japan. Acting under the auspices of the ACJ rather than (or in addition to) JACL offered several advantages to Masaoka and Kido. For one, the simultaneous emergence of the league's National Committee on International Relations presented the duo an opportunity to speak out twice on issues.[130] Just as crucially, the ACJ allowed them the freedom to engage in foreign relations while sidestepping additional controversy surrounding the appropriate purview of the league and Masaoka's leadership role. The ACJ also afforded another avenue through which Masaoka in particular could cultivate his identity as a transpacific intermediary. Masaoka had a personal financial stake in US-Japan trade, and did not hesitate to exercise his influence via the ACJ and JACL to foster economic development along these lines.[131]

The Japan debate forced JACL to confront the persistent tension head-on between assimilation and ethnic identity that endangered its lock on community leadership. During World War II, the league never wavered from espousing assimilationism as the preferred strategy for repairing the damages to Japanese Americans' collective citizenship standing. Racial liberalism's assimilationist imperatives validated this approach. After 1945, the United States' reconstruction of Japan reconfigured the terrain of possibilities for rehabilitating Japanese American citizenship. While JACL leaders did not abandon their mission of conveying to the public the Nikkei's loyalty and Americanism, they now embraced the opportunity to portray themselves as the best-qualified ethnic experts to broker US-Japan relations in the name of democratic cooperation. JACL, in short, had an investment in depicting Japanese America as *both* the same and different from whites—assimilating Others—in order to simultaneously vindicate its political decisions, make claims on the state, and shore up its hegemony as *the* voice of the ethnic community. Yet this remained a precarious equilibrium that could be disturbed at any time by geopolitical recalibrations.

Reintroducing the Nisei Soldier

The eruption of anti-American sentiment in Japan as the 1960 deadline for the renewal of the US-Japan security treaty approached brought this delicate balance between assimilation and ethnic retention into stark relief. In the late 1950s, many unapologetically expressed their antipathy toward the unequal terms of US-Japan relations, widely regarded as furthering American Cold War interests at the expense of Japanese sovereignty. Millions took to the streets to stop the ratification, and the ensuing riots resulted in the cancellation of President Eisenhower's visit to Tokyo in June 1960.[132] Worries about the potential repercussions of these clashes permeated the proceedings of the league's national convention that summer. As Masaoka grimly assessed, "The carefully built up image of the new Japan as an orderly, responsible, civilized nation [of] . . . courteous, law-abiding, grateful people" was now "badly tarnished," if not "completely destroyed," among the general public.[133]

For Japanese Americans, this turn of events seemed to undo the progress that they had made in rebuilding their collective social standing since the war's end. The backlash, according to Masaoka's count, had proliferated at a distressing pace. Politicians increasingly demanded boycotts of imports while American businesses had begun to terminate dealings with Japanese companies. Ordinary Americans were contacting JACL to ask "why 'we' didn't do something to control 'your people.'" Masaoka determined that "the painfully and painstakingly developed 'image' of the Japanese American as a brave and loyal American that was created during and immediately after World War II" was now being dangerously conflated with "Japanese in Japan," decried again by many as a treacherous race. In the view of JACL leaders, this "grave crisis, the greatest since December 7, 1941," was no less than an emergency with potentially devastating repercussions for all Nikkei. Just as had been the case during World War II, Japanese Americans' "welfare" and foreign entanglements were "inextricably intertwined."[134]

The league attempted to defuse the situation by fortifying its budding international relations agenda and underscoring its capacity to serve as a liaison between the two countries. For example, JACL began working with the US Information Agency to design displays for overseas exhibition of American life spotlighting the Nikkei's "unique contributions" to "United States culture." The organization also advised the State Department on how to assess the potential harm of anti-Japanese Hollywood movies on US-Japan relations.[135]

JACL leaders, of course, were also painfully aware of the pitfalls of an internationalist strategy during moments of US-Japan tension. Thus, in the face of an unknown and fearful future, they simultaneously recommitted themselves to reinvigorating their domestic public relations efforts to "assert and re-establish the 'true' image or picture of Nisei as *Americans of Japanese ancestry*." In order to carry out this charge, the league's National Public Relations Committee proposed a comprehensive program to trumpet "elements of Nisei Americanism, loyalty, the war record, high level of good citizenship and responsibility, their socio-economic status in the community, [and] the traditions and cultural heritage of their race as adapted to the American society." Convention delegates approved these objectives and designated public relations as JACL's top priority in the decade ahead.[136]

In keeping with this mandate, the National Public Relations Committee unveiled plans for a special ceremony at Arlington National Cemetery in 1963 to commemorate the twentieth anniversary of Japanese American military service during World War II.[137] JACL assembled a special subcommittee to coordinate the event, inviting Hawai'i senator Inouye, a veteran of the 442nd, and Hawai'i congressperson Spark Matsunaga, a veteran of the 100th, to serve as honorary cochairs. The subcommittee executed an extensive information campaign to promote the event. Publicity materials accentuated the dramatic change in Japanese American standing over the past two decades from "suspect" to "fully accepted and respected citizens of the United States." JACL attributed this "dramatic reversal" first and foremost to the "unparalleled record of loyalty and gallantry of Americans of Japanese ancestry in World War II."[138]

The occasion attracted national attention, as hoped by the organizers. The ceremonies, held on June 2, 1963, at Arlington National Cemetery, featured distinguished speakers, including General Jacob J. Devers, former commanding general of the US Army Field Forces, Inouye, and Matsunaga. Following the tributes, national JACL president K. Patrick Okura, accompanied by Mrs. Munemori, mother of Congressional Medal of Honor recipient Sadao Munemori, laid wreaths at the tombs of the Unknown Soldiers. The services then continued with a tribute to the Japanese American veterans of the Spanish-American War and visits to the gravesides of Nisei soldiers. The commemoration resumed the day after with a visit by Munemori, Masaoka, Inouye, Matsunaga, and additional JACL representatives to the White House to meet President John F. Kennedy and Vice President Lyndon B. Johnson.[139] The following week, twenty-three members of Congress paid tribute to the contributions of the Nisei soldiers of World War II—with some using the very language supplied by JACL, such as Oregon representative Al Ullman: "Their record of outstanding citizenship during wartime is matched only by their records during peacetime. The Japanese Americans in my own district are noted for their industriousness and model citizenship." Perhaps just as important, various representatives also applauded JACL and Masaoka for "promot[ing] and foster[ing] a responsible and interested citizenry" along with "visionary and statesmanlike leadership."[140]

At the league's 1964 national convention, President Okura described the commemoration as "probably the most important public relations project in the past decade" in terms of JACL's "external image." Such an assessment tellingly underscored yet again the ways in which the standing of JACL and the condition of Japanese American citizenship were mutually contingent after World War II. Indeed, the 1963 memorial testified to both the resurgence of JACL from its nadir of unpopularity and the refashioning of Nikkei into exemplary citizens. The Nisei soldier had become the face of Japanese America, recognized by the nation's most powerful political leaders. In occupying this position, he obscured competing conceptions of Nikkei masculinity and political identity—renunciants, draft resisters, zoot-suiters, and others who deviated from the league's script—and buttressed JACL's hegemony within the ethnic community.

Yet martial patriotism was also a defensive posture, deployed by JACL whenever challenges to the legitimacy of Japanese American claims to national belonging arose. In the end, the Nisei soldier and all that he personified—loyalty, patriotism, and unequivocal Americanism—remained unstable and vulnerable to changes in the sociopolitical milieu. As the social movements of the 1960s unfolded, and the Right and Left forcefully interrogated racial liberalism's usefulness for solving the "American Dilemma," JACL would find its ideological hallmarks and the limits of its power to shape Japanese American identity and citizenship tested as never before.

Chapter 4

America's Chinese

Ethnic Chinese throughout the United States greeted the news of the People's Republic of China's entry into the Korean War in October 1950 with immense trepidation. "Like others of Oriental ancestry, they remember only too well the plight of 125,000 persons of Japanese ancestry after an infamous December 7," observed the *Washington Evening Star* of the District of Columbia's Chinatown residents. "[They] cannot help but wonder if the larger community may some day turn upon them, especially if a more violent war should engulf China and the United States." Reverends Albert Lau and Wun Bew Wong of Los Angeles' Chinese First Presbyterian Church and Chinese Methodist Church, respectively, told of similar fears among their city's coethnics, as did San Francisco journalist Gilbert Woo. In light of McCarthyism's rapid rise, their apprehensions were not unfounded. The month before, Congress had passed the McCarran Internal Security Act, authorizing state detention of persons suspected of espionage or sabotage in the event of an invasion, war, or insurrection. Almost overnight the prevailing images of Chinese in the American public eye had metamorphosed from friendly (if weak) Pacific allies to formidable, threatening foes. Businesses reported losses as nervous clientele began canceling orders. Individuals became targets of verbal harassment and physical assaults, as was the case of one unfortunate Texan who was shot when mistaken for a "Communist."[1]

Community members did their best to diffuse these hostilities in various ways. Some rushed to enlist as a show of support for the United States' intervention in Korea. At a Los Angeles restaurant, a bartender who overheard patrons muttering "Let's get out of here, this place is run by Chinks," informed them he had brothers serving in the armed forces. San Francisco's *Chinese Pacific Weekly* urged the cultivation of relations with liberal, sympathetic whites as well as the importance of being law-abiding citizens. Gerald H. Moye, the "unofficial mayor" of Chicago's Chinatown, flatly affirmed the loyalty of the city's Chinese: "We don't like those Reds." The Chinese Consolidated Benevolent Association of Washington, DC, issued a statement emphasizing that it stood "wholeheartedly behind the United States Government and with all the free peoples of the world as they engage the menace of communism." New York's

Chinese Nationalist Daily published a list of talking points to stress in discussing the Korean War with "American friends":

1. We, the Chinese-American citizens, pledge our loyalty to the United States.
2. We support the Nationalist Government of Free China and her great leader, President Chiang Kai-shek.
3. We support the United Nations Charter and the efforts made by the United Nations troops who are fighting for a united, free, and independent Korea.
4. The Chinese Communists are the stooges of Soviet Russia. Those who are invading Korea are the Chinese COMMU-NISTS, not the peace-loving people of Free China.

Area merchants followed the editors' suggestion to display the list in their store windows "for all to see."[2]

Chinatown's Korean War Red Scare dramatized the ways in which the Cold War structured the reconfiguration of Chinese American citizenship in the post-Exclusion era. The ascendance of anti-Communism as the defining paradigm of US foreign policy after World War II introduced new imperatives to clarify Chinese America's social and political standing. For the community, fears of blanket criminalization and mass persecution impelled the need to make plain Chinese Americans' loyalty and patriotism to the United States. For the state, geopolitical exigencies presented incentives to legitimate Chinese Americans' belonging in the nation. As the United States assumed the leadership of the "free world," federal officialdom believed that the country's treatment of its minority groups, including ethnic Chinese, had significant bearing on perceptions of US democracy around the world.

To address these problems, both parties looked to the identification of Chinese in the United States as "Overseas Chinese"—that is, members of a global Chinese diaspora with ties to each other and China.[3] In the early 1950s, the Chinatown elite launched a nationwide campaign to publicize Chinese America's anti-Communism. It emphasized loyalty to both the United States *and* Nationalist or "Free" China, the regime ruled by Chiang's Kuomingtang Party, exiled to Taiwan after its defeat by Communist forces in 1949. This strategy, of course, had worked well for Chinese Americans during World War II, when they had enjoyed heightened levels of national belonging by virtue of association with their ancestral homeland. The hope was that the community could continue to benefit from this affiliation.[4]

For Chinatown leaders, Overseas Chinese was not only a rhetorical construction but also a real political attachment with material consequences.

Pledging allegiance to Nationalist China paid transnational dividends. The Kuomingtang Party, eager for support within the United States in order to maximize its leverage in the global arena, reciprocated by placing CCBA executives in positions within the party and Nationalist government. This formalization of ties between Chinatown powers and Chiang's administration underscored the overlap between Chinese American and Overseas Chinese identity during the early years of the Cold War.

It was in this capacity that Chinese in the United States experienced unprecedented validation as members of the American nation. While Chinatown's anti-Communist push offered reassurance that Chinese enclaves in the United States were subversion free, the federal government worried that other immigrant Chinese populations, particularly those residing in the Asia-Pacific region, were especially susceptible to political seduction by the People's Republic of China.[5] In this context, the Overseas Chinese became a significant target of US cultural diplomacy that stressed integration—in terms of both local assimilation and the manufacture of affective bonds between the United States and peoples of the decolonizing third world—as a positive counterpoint to containment.[6] The US State Department therefore found it politically expedient to peddle narratives of successfully assimilated Chinese Americans—the United States' own Overseas Chinese—as evidence of the superiority of liberal democracy to communism. This calculus, moreover, spurred federal authorities to employ Chinese American individuals as channels through which to deliver this message abroad to audiences. By utilizing Chinese Americans as official representatives of the nation, then, the state acknowledged their long-standing claims to full citizenship in powerful, highly public ways. In other words, Cold War geopolitics offered Chinese in the United States fresh opportunities for inclusion.

At the same time, this legitimization compromised Chinese Americans' midcentury gains in social standing. The thinking underpinning the state's integrationist imperative simultaneously justified new modes of exclusion. Significantly, the terms on which Chinese Americans served as ambassadors for nation and the state during the Cold War—as racial minorities and Overseas Chinese—also served to propagate their otherness. Their displays of anti-Communism along with their involvement in cultural diplomacy initiatives re-marked them as not-white and indelibly foreign, even after the ending of Asiatic Exclusion.[7] By assuming that Chinese American identity always included a transnational dimension as Overseas Chinese, the State Department fed a logic that resulted in severe consequences for the entire community. In the mid-1950s, federal officials charged that the United States was in danger of being infiltrated by a vast network of Communist Chinese spies entering the country on counterfeit papers. This accusation supplied a potent justification for the state to intensify its surveillance of the Chinatown Left as well as initiate a concerted, terrifying campaign to police Chinese American immigration from which few, if any, community members were immune.

Chinatown's Anti-Communist Crusade

Since the beginnings of Chinese immigration to the United States in the mid-nineteenth century, Chinese in America had been continually associated with China in the public imagination. To be sure, these migrants willingly forged and sustained transoceanic connections with their families and communities of origin. Furthermore, they understood that as subjects of a relatively weak nation-state, they had little diplomatic recourse through which to counter the myriad exclusions they faced in the United States. Believing that building a strong, modern China free from imperial interventions would lead to their better treatment by the US government and American people, Chinese in the United States actively engaged in political events unfolding across the Pacific. China's political parties encouraged their involvement by claiming migrants in the United States, Canada, the Caribbean, Latin America, and Southeast Asia as Overseas Chinese; Sun Yat-sen, the first provisional president of the Republic of China, hailed Overseas Chinese as "the mother of the [Chinese] Revolution." As Overseas Chinese, many Chinese in the United States supported various factions in China, including Chiang's Kuomintang Party (KMT) and Mao's Chinese Communist Party (CCP), by making financial contributions, staging demonstrations, and publishing party organs.[8]

On another register, the linkages that the American public presumed to exist between China and Chinese in the United States worked to racialize Chinese Americans as perpetual aliens. This understanding justified the exclusion of Chinese Americans from the national community through the 1920s. Recall that in the 1930s, prevailing notions of Chinese immigrants began to shift as Americans' views of China itself underwent transformation—an evolution driven by the United States' strategic interests in China. The experience of fighting Japan, a common foe, during World War II added to this momentum. Yet even with this radical change in US attitudes, most whites never dissociated Chinese Americans from notions of foreignness. Thus, despite increasing recognition of their membership in the national community, Chinese Americans remained tethered to China in the public imagination. While they could not break free of this link, the simultaneous existence of a "bad" China (the People's Republic) and "good" one (the Nationalists on Taiwan) after 1949 meant that Chinese Americans could position themselves as anti-Communist Overseas Chinese committed to both the KMT and United States.[9]

Chinatown leaders seized this opening as they launched their nation-wide crusade against Communism. The movement signaled three distinct, if related, messages intended for both the greater public and state, which together accentuated both the community's Americanness and its location within the Chinese diaspora. The first was Chinese Americans' loyalty to the United States. As Mo Chong Way, president of Portland, Oregon's CCBA, put it, "We are American Chinese and we want to be American even though we are Chinese by descent. We don't desire to help or support anyone who fights against America." Houston's On Leong and Hip Sang Associations, together with the Dragoneers, a Chinese American youth organization, published a letter in area newspapers avowing their faith in the principles of the US Constitution, pride in US citizenship, and pledge to serve the nation in the event of war.[10]

The second revelation was the denunciation of the People's Republic of China. In December 1950, the Los Angeles branch of the Chinese consulate, the city's CCBA, and thirty-one other area Chinese American organizations together telegrammed President Truman to declare their "absolute opposition" to Mao's authority, and emphasize that the Chinese in the United States remained law-abiding, peace-loving, and faithful to democracy. Honolulu's Chinese Chamber of Commerce and United Chinese Society followed suit, condemning Red China's "aggression" against UN forces in Korea.[11]

The third point was Chinese America's strident support for the KMT-Nationalist regime. Sacramento's CCBA, for example, contacted the UN Security Council to protest the People's Republic of China's seating in the UN General Assembly, arguing, "The only legitimate representation of China is that of the Chinese Nationalist government." Many Chinese Americans continued to commemorate Double Ten Day, the anniversary marking the birth of the Republic of China, rather than October 1, the founding date of the People's Republic of China. According to the *Chinese World*, San Francisco's 1951 Double Ten celebration, sponsored by the Six Companies, drew thousands of spectators to witness the processional of floats symbolizing "the struggle against communism." One of the most impressive was the forty-by-eighty-foot flag of Nationalist China carried by Chinese American women into which onlookers tossed money to support war relief efforts, reminiscent of Chinatown's activities during the Sino-Japanese War.[12]

New York City Chinatown's Free China Day in November 1951, staged as part of the national Clothes-for-Korea Drive, epitomized the interlacing of the campaign's various objectives along with its simultaneous production of Chinese American and Overseas Chinese identities. Free China Day showcased Chinese American patriotism to the United States and Nationalist China. The *New York Times* reported that more than two hundred Chinese children, "led by a noticeably under-age dragon" sporting denim and gym shoes beneath its "resplendent oriental silks," marched down Mott Street with bundles of donations. The ceremonies featured Korean consul general David Y. Namkoong, along with Douglas Fairbanks Jr., chair of American Relief for Korea, Nationalist Chinese consul general P. H. Chang, and New York CCBA president Woodrow Chan.[13] By participating in this Korean War home front effort, New York's Chinese American community claimed membership in the American nation. And yet by framing its contribution as Free China Day and overtly embracing the Chiang regime, it also reinforced its Overseas Chinese subjectivity.

In the months following the People's Republic of China's initiation into the Korean conflict, Chinatown's campaign rapidly coalesced to rally Chinese Americans to the cause and direct public relations efforts. Pei Chu Liu, a KMT official deployed to San Francisco to supervise the stateside publication of the partisan *Chinese Nationalist Daily*, urged Chinatown leaders to organize an official entity "to prove to the American people that we are against communism."[14] They took up his suggestion and established the Chinese Six Companies Anti-Communist League on December 28, 1950, as tangible evidence that "99.7 percent" of Chinatown was on the right side of the Cold War.[15] During the inaugural ceremonies in January 1951, President W. F. Doon outlined the league's three main objectives: to support the United States in Korea and in "upholding democracy"; to back the Nationalist Chinese government's "counter-offensives" against the Chinese Communists; and to "co-operate with Americans in general and help them differentiate between friend and enemy among the Chinese." Vice President Robert S. Lee belabored the last point, encouraging the audience of several hundred that "each and every one of us should consider ourselves as ambassadors of goodwill for our race."[16] One of the league's first major events was a torchlight parade in February 1951 to mark the start of its fifty thousand dollar fund-raising campaign to assist wounded Korean War veterans. An estimated ten thousand people turned out to witness the group's members marching alongside drum corps and drill teams from local schools. Participants carried placards bearing such slogans as "Down with Red Imperialists," "Chinese-Americans Are Loyal Citizens," and "Help Free China." The sponsors distributed thousands of pamphlets to onlookers summarizing the Anti-Communist League's mission, reminding San Franciscans not only of Chinese Americans' patriotism to the United States but also their "industriousness and thrift [as well as] their public and law-abiding spirit." The *San Francisco Chronicle* approvingly concluded, "Their gist is that Chinatown is an American town—at America's service."[17]

FIGURE 4.1 The San Francisco Six Companies' Anti-Communist League torchlight parade, February 13, 1951. Chinatown leaders staged the demonstration to declare Chinese Americans' steadfast patriotism to the United States and dedication to defeating Communism in Asia. Marchers waved signs with such messages as "Down with Red Imperialists," "Chinese-Americans Are Loyal Citizens," and "Help Free China."
  Courtesy of the San Francisco History Center, San Francisco Public Library.

Encouraged by the KMT, Chinese community leaders throughout the country quickly followed suit. Within months the CCBAs of Tucson, Portland (Oregon), Los Angeles, Sacramento, and Chicago instituted similar entities.[18] In Denver, a group of residents founded the Yick Keong Association not only to fight Communism, "forward democracy," and champion the Nationalists but also to facilitate Chinese American integration as a means of eschewing the type of animosity faced by Japanese Americans during World War II.[19] New York Chinatown launched its Anti-Communist Committee for Free China with great fanfare in June 1951. Representatives of sixty area Chinese American civic, business, cultural, and social associations gathered to receive well wishes from Chiang, the mayor of New York City, and Chinese organizations throughout the United States and Cuba. Guest speakers included T. F. Tsiang, Taiwan's delegate to the United Nations, Chinese consul general P. H. Chang, and municipal government representative Charles Hand. Woodrow Chan, president of New York's CCBA, pledged the devotion of its affiliates to democracy: "In a world half slave and half free, we are determined to fight on the side of freedom." He decried the Communist Chinese regime's attenuation of the "bond of friendship" between its people and the United States, and vowed that the new group would work to "restore the unity of China and America."[20]

As the above example illustrates, orchestrators of the anti-Communist crusade utilized mass spectacles as an important proselytizing tool given their potential to reach big audiences. Chinese New Year celebrations became the most prominent of the movement's public relations gestures. Washington, DC.'s Chinatown, for instance, welcomed the Year of the Rabbit (1951) by combining holiday festivities with a commemoration of the fortieth anniversary of the founding of the Republic of China.[21] Manhattan's Chinese community observed the occasion with a mass pledge of allegiance to the United States and chorus of patriotic songs. The performance was recorded and wired to President Truman and General Douglas MacArthur as a "document of our faith" in the United States coupled with "our complete repudiation of Communist China."[22] San Francisco's Chinatown coordinated its first public New Year's gala in February 1953 after local entrepreneur H. K. Wong proposed the event as a means to boost the enclave's tourist economy while displaying a carefully constructed image of Chinese American citizenship for the city to see. Festival planners selected US Army corporal Joe Wong, a Korean War soldier who had been blinded in the line of fire, as the parade's grand marshal. Corporal Wong swept down Grant Avenue flanked by US Air Force enlistees Jessie Lee and Anna Tome, and trailed by veterans of three conflicts (World Wars I and II as well as Korea) and musicians from various branches of the military. Completing the lineup were San Francisco's mayor, cars from the CCBA, the Chinese Chamber of Commerce, and the Anti-Communist League, St. Mary's Chinese Drum and Bugle Corps and other Chinatown school bands, dragon dancers, and Miss Chinatown. The affair was a resounding success, counting over a hundred thousand people in attendance.[23]

Emerging Chinese American media also played a role in swaying the general public. Lee and Leong, publisher and editor, respectively, of *Chinese News: America's Chinese Newsmagazine*, timed the release date of the premier issue (February 14, 1953) to coincide with San Francisco's inaugural New Years extravaganza. The journal unabashedly reinforced the themes of the festival and the movement at large, assuring readers, "One certainty among the Chinese-Americans is that the only red tint to be found [during the holiday] is in the gay money tokens called 'layshee.'" During the fourteen-month run of his paper, Leong (who also served as the cochair of San Francisco's Anti-Communist League's English publicity division) aggressively marketed the *Chinese News* to such staunch promoters of Sino-American amity as the Committee for Free Asia, Inc. (for which Leong had briefly served as Chinese relations director). Chinatown leaders acknowledged the significance of Leong's outreach. "As the only Chinese publication in the United States edited and published entirely in the English language, you have both a great opportunity and grave responsibility in recording the progress of the Chinese-Americans in the fight for freedom, not only to your fellow Chinese, but also to our American friends who seek to understand us," approved Anti-Communist League president Doon. And indeed, Chinatown's anti-Communist crusade found a fitting, if ephemeral, mouthpiece in the *Chinese News* as well as the public relations savvy of Leong.[24]

The claims of the anti-Communist campaign fell on receptive ears, and reinforced already-existing sympathies along with the notion of Chinese loyalty and Americanism established during World War II. Ethnic Chinese were not subjected to the wholesale internment that so many had feared but instead experienced quite the opposite of the anti-Nikkei antagonism that had pervaded the Pacific coast in the wake of the Pearl Harbor bombing.[25] Governor Earl Warren—an advocate of Japanese American detention during World War II—pledged his support. San Francisco mayor Robinson reassured the community that construction on two major Chinatown municipal works projects, the Ping Yuen public housing development and Chinese Recreation Center, would continue as "proof and promise of your loyalty and your continued fidelity to the United States of America." The *San Francisco Chronicle* chided all "Caucasians" who had expressed hostility toward local Chinese, arguing that such blanket "prejudice . . . display[s] a lack of respect for American citizenship itself." In the same vein, the city's Council for Civic Unity resolved "to attack the sources of the fear and insecurity which now disturb Americans of Chinese ancestry." In a parallel move, the City Club of Chicago condemned instances of local anti-Chinese hostilities, and affirmed Chinese Chicagoans' Americanism and contributions to the larger community.[26] Newspapers across the country, including the *Des Moines Register*, rallied to Chinese America's defense: "Instead of being un-American, they are helping us to learn the true meaning of Americanism."[27] In sum, the Cold War and its "hot" analog in Korea opened up an avenue of liberation for Chinese in the United States.

Paradoxically, the uncompromising nature of anti-Communism in the 1950s simultaneously restricted the freedoms of ethnic Chinese as it did for all Americans. Little in the public discourse acknowledged Chinese America's political diversity. The liberal journal the *Nation* was one of the few to do so, subtly critiquing the coercions of the McCarthyist climate.

The *Nation* joined in verifying Chinatown's patriotism, but also noted that many US Chinese actually "sympath[ized]" with the People's Republic of China instead of blindly following the CCBA in its "ardent support" of Chiang. Chinese Americans had "every right" to believe whatever they wanted, the editors contended. But they soft-pedaled this assertion by adding a disclaimer: "This does not mean, of course, that they condone Chinese aggression in Korea; much less does it imply—and this is the real point—subversive intentions." Wartime conservatism meant that Chinese Americans could not openly express their true feelings—an issue that all citizens confronted. "Are they to be castigated as 'disloyal' simply because they may object to certain phases of American foreign policy in the Far East?" the *Nation* lamented.[28]

This brief editorial hinted at intracommunity divisions mostly invisible to mainstream society, yet nevertheless crucial to explaining the zeal with which the conservative establishment carried out its anti-Communism campaign. Though the CCBA claimed otherwise, US Chinatown residents had never moved in lockstep on China-related matters. The situation became increasingly divisive after 1927, when Chiang purged Communists from the united KMT-CCP front. The Chinese American Left experienced an upsurge in the 1930s, rallying around criticisms of Chiang and the KMT for their inability to join forces with the CCP against Japanese aggression in China. Workers and students, influenced by the international rise of Marxism and growth of the Popular Front in the United States, organized to challenge the hegemony of the merchant elite and foster democratic reforms within the community while at the same time supporting China's war effort against Japan. Among the most active groups were New York City's Chinese Hand Laundry Alliance, founded in 1933, the San Francisco–based Chinese Workers' Mutual Aid Association, established in 1937, and the Chinese Min Qing (also known as the Chinese American Democratic Youth League of San Francisco or Chinese Youth League), a coalition of San Francisco youth clubs initiated in 1942.[29]

Although Chinese Americans across the range of the political spectrum united around the cause of Chinese "national salvation" during the Sino-Japanese War (1937–45), support for the KMT within US Chinatowns remained uneven at best. Many Chinese Americans disapproved of the rampant corruption within the party and criticized Chiang's obsession with obliterating his Communist opponents as a wrongful diversion from the goal of defeating the Japanese. A proliferation of Chinese- and English-language community newspapers not affiliated with the KMT reflected the mounting dissatisfaction with the party. The KMT, recognizing its need to shore up its base of supporters in American Chinatowns, named high-ranking individuals in the Chinatown establishment as special commissioners to the party.[30]

The CCBA welcomed this opportunity given the decline of its own power vis-à-vis other Chinese Americans. With the flowering of the Left and coming of age of the younger, US-born cohort, membership numbers decreased, and association coffers shrank. Beginning in World War II, Chinese Americans were no longer heavily dependent on community businesses and traditional organizations for employment and resources. Many found work in the mainstream economy and housing outside Chinatown confines. Clan and district associations did not maintain the weighty presence in individuals' lives, as had been the case during the decades of Exclusion. The merchant elites' arrangement with the KMT thus offered a much-needed replenishment of prestige for the CCBA.[31]

The CCP's final defeat of the Nationalists in 1949 supplied the partnership with the impetus and means to tighten its abilities to suppress Chinatown critics. On the evening of October 9, KMT hires crashed a program sponsored by the Chinese Workers' Mutual Aid Association and Min Qing in San Francisco Chinatown to celebrate the founding of the People's Republic of China. Dozens of men rushed into the auditorium where some eight hundred people had gathered, grabbed the Red Chinese flag from the stage, and pelted the audience with eggs and blue dye. The following day, the KMT posted notices announcing a five thousand dollar reward for the deaths of fifteen Chinese Workers' Mutual Aid Association and Min Qing "bandits." The actions loudly threatened any Mao supporters with dire consequences. The intimidation and harassment intensified through the 1950s as federal agents joined forces with the KMT-CCBA. The ranks of the Chinatown Left depleted considerably as many Chinese Americans grew apprehensive about participating in progressive organizations. The Chinese Workers' Mutual Aid Association and New York's progressive China Youth Club, for example, were forced to terminate their activities in 1954 after losing too many members. Pro–People's Republic of China newspapers such as the *China Weekly* and *Chung Sai Yat Po* folded completely. New York's *China Daily News*, published by the Chinese Hand Laundry Alliance, and critical of both the Nationalists and the United States' China policy, witnessed a steep drop in its circulation when KMT affiliates bullied vendors to stop carrying the paper, and the US Treasury Department indicted its editor for violating the Trading with the Enemy Act. For several years, San Francisco's Min Qing weathered FBI surveillance, infiltration, and threats of deportation—all of which dwindled the membership—finally disbanding when right-wing Chinatown leaders pressured the owner of the building not to renew their meeting space lease.[32]

Ultimately, then, the anti-Communist crusade accomplished what its architects had set out to do: it afforded Chinese Americans a way to signal and reinforce perceptions of their loyalty to the United States and

Nationalist China, and it supplied the Chinatown establishment with a forceful means to devastate the community's leftist factions and buttress its intracommunity standing. This constellation of objectives was realized in significant part through the conscious reproduction and deployment of Overseas Chinese identity—a strategy that assumed a sizable risk at a time when Americans often linked foreignness to subversion. *Life* magazine's January 1951 photographic essay "America's Chinese" captured the uncertainty of this dynamic. The feature glimpsed the everyday world of New York Chinatown, an "orderly, well-functioning community" comprised of veterans, students, laborers, and businesspeople who were "in most ways . . . thoroughly American." Yet at the same time, they were "bound to the past" through a "strange" culture, family ties, and especially politics, as illustrated by shots of New York CCBA members congregrated under a large portrait of Chiang juxtaposed with one of the Chinese Youth Club members practicing music in a room graced by a likeness of Mao. (Recycling a claim made by Chinatown leaders, the story emphasized that "the Nationalists outnumber pro-Communists by nearly 99 to 1.") Now with the People's Republic of China's involvement in Korea, this tension assumed an amplified level of poignancy, suggested *Life*. "Today these Chinese are in an ambiguous position. Their homeland, whose people have for so long been friendly with America, is virtually at war with the U.S." It was this unsettledness, rooted in the notion that Chinese Americans were never simply Americans but rather always simultaneously Overseas Chinese, that would continue to frame Chinese American citizenship through the early years of the Cold War, furnishing both opportunities and limitations to secure full membership in the nation.[33]

Overseas Chinese and the Voice of America

With the "loss" of China to the CCP in 1949, the State Department turned its attention to ethnic Chinese throughout Asia as a specific target audience for anti-Communist propaganda efforts. One important medium was the Voice of America (VOA), the US government's international radio broadcasting operation, run under the auspices of the State Department (1945–53) and the US Information Agency after 1953.[34] On learning that the VOA had openings in its Chinese-language unit, Betty Lee Sung, a second-generation Chinese American, applied for a position. Because her linguistic skills were not advanced enough to meet the demands of the job, administrators instead hired her as a feature writer.[35]

When the VOA offered Sung the chance to focus on topics of her choice, she suggested a program on the Chinese in the United States.

"I was just appalled" at the American public's stereotypes of Chinese—
"opium dens, tong wars, coolie labor, yellow peril, highbinders, hatch-
etmen, laundries, waiters, houseboys, slave wages, unassimilable aliens,
and so on ad nauseam," she recalled. "I decided that I wanted to correct
that image."[36] The unit directors were enthusiastic about her idea because
they saw potential in identifying Chinese Americans as Overseas Chinese.
As Sung recounted, "'What,' thought the editorial staff, 'would interest
the Chinese in China and Southeast Asia more than learning about how
their compatriots lived and were treated in a country that represented to
them the 'Mountain of Gold,' the 'Land of the Beautiful,' and presently
archenemy of the Chinese Communists?'"[37] As a result, Sung began a
trial run of *Chinese Activities*, a weekly six-minute segment that featured
stories about Chinese in the United States. The VOA broadcast *Chinese
Activities* first in Mandarin, and later in the dialects of Cantonese, Swa-
tow, Amoy, Hakka, and Shanghai, to ethnic Chinese audiences throughout the Asia-Pacific region.[38] The show enjoyed a positive reception, Sung
recollected. "I began getting fan mail from all over, where it was broadcast to—mostly from Southeast Asia, because they jammed the Voice of
America in China. So when the fan mail came in, [the editors] said, 'Oh,
this is good.' So that they kept it going." She secured her position and
served as head writer from 1949 to 1954.[39]

Although employed by the VOA, Sung did not consider herself to be
producing anti-Communist material per se. "Well, I wasn't doing propaganda. I was doing what they called 'feature scripts.' . . . If I reported on
the events in the Chinese American community or I talked about somebody like I. M. Pei, it had nothing to do [with anti-Communism], no
political tone. They never told me I couldn't write about this, or that, or
the other," she remembered.[40] *Chinese Activities*, then, served as a meeting ground for a convergence of interests: that of Sung, whose goal was to
portray Chinese Americans in a positive light to counter preexisting negative stereotypes, and that of the State Department, which aimed to represent the United States as a free, democratic society where all peoples,
including those of Chinese ancestry, could assimilate and thrive.

Chinese Activities highlighted the accomplishments of individual Chinese Americans, drawing attention to racial minorities' prospects for
achievement in the United States as well as affirming their membership
in the nation. For instance, Sung's profile of architect Pei stated: "It always makes us Chinese in America experience great pride when we see
that another Chinese has attained success or has accomplished something
outstanding." The show extolled Pei as "another example of how the
Chinese are making a place for themselves in this country."[41] The VOA's
Chinese Unit also covered the story of Toy Len Goon, a laundry opera-
tor from Portland, Maine, honored as 1952's American Mother of the

FIGURE 4.2 Betty Lee Sung, head writer (1949–54) for the VOA's *Chinese Activities*, a weekly show broadcast to Chinese diasporic communities throughout the Asia-Pacific region that featured stories about Chinese in the United States. Using the research materials gathered for the VOA, Sung went on to write *Mountain of Gold* (also known as *The Story of the Chinese in America*) to correct the "grossly distorted" public conceptions of her ethnic community.
Courtesy of Betty Lee Sung.

Year by the American Mothers Committee of the Golden Rule Foundation. Widowed, Goon had single-handedly raised and financed the college educations of her eight children, who had since become successful professionals. "America, declared Mrs. Goon, is a land of opportunity. . . . She has set an outstanding example of the honesty, industry, and motherly care; and Mrs. Goon has given to her adopted country eight outstanding young American citizens," concluded the feature.[42] The VOA sequence complemented a story on Goon in *Free World Chinese* magazine, produced by the US Information Service for Overseas Chinese readers.[43] It also matched material disseminated through the State Department's *Wireless Bulletin*, a digest of news items distributed among foreign posts for recirculation in local media. The consulate general in Singapore reported with satisfaction that articles on Goon ran in Malayan newspapers, culled from *Wireless Bulletin* items, had yielded "most gratifying" responses and pressed for the continued inclusion of "Asians" in the federal government's overseas information programs.[44]

In addition to celebrating the achievements of distinguished individuals, the VOA showcased Chinese in the United States as assimilating Others, emphasizing their "most outstanding" doings. Two *Chinese Activities* segments from 1952 focused on Hawai'i's Chinese, a highly integrated group: "practically everyone you meet has a few drops of Chinese in him." One of the stories recited a list of the islands' prominent "overseas Chinese," including entrepreneurs, teachers, physicians, dentists, and members of the territorial legislature. The other commemorated the one hundredth anniversary of the arrival of Chinese to Hawai'i. Persevering through harsh labor conditions on the sugar plantations, the early laborers and their descendants had become a "group of wealth and influence . . . earn[ing] the respect of all by their hard work, their conscientiousness and their level-headedness."[45] The VOA handled the more delicate matter of racism in the United States by presenting the existence of ethnic Chinese organizations and enclaves as a matter of choice as opposed to consequences of segregation. "The Lost Homeland," a political commentary on New York's Chinatown produced by the Chinese Unit, eschewed mention of this history of discrimination by stressing that Chinese resided in "every section" of the city and in all parts of the United States, being "free to live wherever they wish." Those who dwelled in Chinatown did so "by their own desire, because they prefer to live among their own people and to live a Chinese life."[46]

The suggestion that ethnic identity was a voluntary choice served well the purposes of the VOA, which aimed to underscore the freedoms available under American democracy, including the freedom to practice authentic Chinese culture now denied by Red China. Indeed, the VOA emphasized that Chinese in the United States maintained their identity as Overseas Chinese even as they professed Americanism, at moments co-opting Chinese Americans' anti-Communist outreach for the state's own ends. "Lunar New Year" (1953), for instance, described San Francisco Chinatown's first public commemoration of the holiday with a parade whose participants included the mayor and "overseas Chinese" members of the US armed forces. The story featured festival committee chair Paul Louie, who stated, "We feel that we can point out to the rest of the world that China's glorious old traditions have not died just because of the Communist regime in China. We are asserting a dual faith—faith in the traditions of old China and faith in the freedom of America. And we also give thanks—thanks that we are living in a country where we can observe the old customs."[47]

As the VOA conceded, however, Chinese Americans' ties to China were not merely celebratory but also fraught—an observation that critiqued Communism's ramifications. The broadcast "America's Chinese" (1951), borrowing liberally from *Life*'s photo essay of the same name, noted that the majority of Chinese in the United States still hoped to return "home" to their families in mainland China. Finding themselves in "an ambiguous situation" in the wake of the Chinese Revolution, most Chinese Americans hopefully awaited the overthrow of Mao's regime. (Only "1 percent" of the community, stressed the VOA, was "pro-Communist.")[48] "The Lost Homeland" similarly portrayed Chinese Americans' ambivalent relationship with the People's Republic of China. As Overseas Chinese, they continued to consider China their "homeland," even while being "loyal to America." Yet the dream of rejoining their relatives had "vanished," leaving them with "great sadness and homesickness." Many despaired that they "may never see their own country again." While Chinese Americans had initially been optimistic about the potential of Mao's government to modernize China, they quickly became disillusioned after learning of its totalitarian ways. Knowing this, "American Chinese have appreciated the freedom and opportunity they have found in the United States."[49]

Chinese American Cultural Diplomacy

The VOA broadcasts evinced the usefulness of Chinese Americans in manufacturing Cold War narratives to underscore for foreign audiences, especially Overseas Chinese, that the United States stood for justice and equality, and that racism was aberrational rather than a normative condition of American society.[50] Seeing this, State Department officials decided to send individual Chinese Americans on cultural diplomacy tours of the Asia-Pacific region in the 1950s. The selection of artists Jade Snow Wong and Dong Kingman as well as the San Francisco Chinese Basketball Team to serve as the country's representatives abroad reflected the nexus of racial liberalism, cultural pluralism, and anti-Communism that opened up new possibilities for national inclusion. It also obliged the state to legitimate Chinese American citizenship in the mid-twentieth century.

Since the late 1930s, of course, proponents of cultural pluralism had worked to include Chinese Americans as "brothers under the skin" whose distinctive cultural traditions offered valuable diversity to the United States. Impelled by geopolitical considerations, this invocation continued well into the late 1940s. In 1948, the *Saturday Evening Post* followed the Wong Hongs of San Francisco as part of its *How Our People Live* series that examined various ethnoracial households in the United States to promote "tolerance and harmony."[51] "Your Neighbors: The Wongs" charted the family's Americanization process, beginning with patriarch Wong Hong, who emigrated to the United States in 1903. Over the years, Wong Hong learned English, converted to Christianity, built up a clothing factory, and established a home in Chinatown, where his nine children became "spiritually enmeshed in the destiny of the United States." Author George Sessions Perry noted that this process of assimilation unfolded amid a continuous engagement with Chinese culture, which served not as a liability but rather as an asset, contributing to the "nation's strength." Second Oldest Daughter, Jade Lotus, for example, held a position with the civil service; Oldest Son, Blessing from Heaven, performed electric work for the navy; and Second Oldest Son, Forgiveness from Heaven, had served in the US Army's postwar occupation of Japan.[52]

Perry acknowledged that the Wongs were unusual in terms of "personalities, ambitions, and talents," not only as compared to other Chinatown households, but also to American families in general. One child in particular stood out: Fifth Oldest Daughter Jade Snow, who at the age of twenty-six, had already achieved celebrity status. Jade Snow had worked her way through high school and community college, from which she graduated as the highest-ranking female in her class. She then attended Oakland's Mills College on scholarship, where she earned her bachelor's degree and a Phi Beta Kappa key in 1942. After graduation, Jade Snow found work at a naval shipyard, where her duties included research on employee issues. A paper she prepared on absenteeism won first place in a statewide essay contest sponsored by the *San Francisco Chronicle*. Her prize included the honor of christening a liberty ship. But even this admirable feat was not her crowning achievement. Since then, "backed only by her native abilities and the shadow of a Chinese shoestring," Jade Snow had launched a successful pottery business. Her creations were well received: New York's Museum of Modern Art named two of her pieces to its list of 100 objects of fine design in 1947, and the Metropolitan Museum of Art acquired some of her oeuvre for its permanent collection.[53]

While Jade Snow's doings were undeniably precocious by any standards, what made them most novel and interesting was their depiction as the outcome of the successful melding of two cultural systems. In 1948, *Mademoiselle* recognized her with one of its national Merit Awards presented annually to exceptional young women, remarking, "Jade Snow Wong weighs the values in the formal patterns of her Chinese heritage with the enterprise of her American homeland." And like the *Saturday Evening Post*, observers recognized the potential of appropriating Wong's story to shore up cultural pluralist claims. In fact, Perry had borrowed much of his information from Wong's essays first published in *Common Ground*, the journal of the Common Council for American Unity. Her *Common Ground* essays caught the attention of Elizabeth Lawrence, an editor with Harper and Brothers. She approached Wong about writing her memoirs, which the company published in 1950 as *Fifth Chinese Daughter*.[54] The book explored the obstacles confronted and overcome by Wong in her first twenty-four years, especially the tensions between her traditional Chinatown upbringing—characterized by the devaluation of females—and the modern American emphasis on individualism and women's relative freedom.[55]

Building on—and undoubtedly adding to—the momentum of Wong's fast-rising career, her autobiography rapidly became a best seller. Both the Book of the Month Club and the Christian Herald Family Book Shelf named *Fifth Chinese Daughter* as their selection for November 1950; the Commonwealth Club and Theta Sigma Phi, the American women's journalism honor society, bestowed awards on her the following year. KNBC radio adapted *Fifth Chinese Daughter* for its popular *Cavalcade of America* program, and the *New York Times* lauded the work as "a gravely charming and deeply understanding self-portrait by a brilliant young woman who grew up midway between two cultures," extracting "the best points of both systems." These accolades indicate that cultural pluralism remained a viable outlook in the postwar years, boding well for Chinese Americans.[56]

About a year after the book's initial publication, Department of State officials recommended that it be translated and distributed overseas as a means to promote American-style liberal democracy among ethnic Chinese minorities throughout Asia. "*Fifth Chinese Daughter* will interest overseas Chinese (who will receive at least two-thirds of the copies published by this post) as a first-hand account of the life of a Chinese-American. In general, it presents a favorable picture of American institutions with which Miss Wang [*sic*] comes into collision in the process of growing up," contended Walter P. McConaughy, Hong Kong's US consul general.[57]

McConaughy's views were part of a broader concern among US diplomats stationed in the Asia-Pacific region over local perceptions of the status of Chinese in the United States. In February 1952, Hendrik van Oss, the US consul in Kuala Lumpur, suggested that the State Department's efforts at neutralizing Communist propaganda stressing racism in the United States should not only focus on African Americans but also include "other minority groups into the picture, especially Chinese." The Malayan press, he noted, had given considerable (and presumably negative) attention to the recent uproar over the case of Sing Sheng, the Chinese immigrant whose bold proposal to move into a suburban South San Francisco neighborhood was defeated by white area residents.[58] "As the Chinese are our number one target [in Malaya], this subject is of the utmost importance and must be balanced by information showing the other side of the picture," stated van Oss. He proposed that the State Department involve Chinese American organizations in Cold War diplomatic efforts, though he also cautioned that they be implicated selectively because the State Department needed "to show integration of the many peoples that make up the United States." Too much emphasis on "the necessity of racial organizations," he warned, would undermine the objective of demonstrating "the way all Americans, regardless of race, 'play' together, as well as work together."[59]

This escalating urgency spurred the State Department to recruit Wong to be the first Chinese American to tour Asia on a "good will mission."

In February 1952, McConaughy argued that she would especially interest Overseas Chinese and have more impact than visits by "Caucasian"
writers.[60] Washington officials concurred. They approved her visit as part
of the Leaders' and Specialists' Exchange Program, a State Department
initiative established under the Smith-Mundt Act to "increase mutual understanding between the people of the United States and the people of
other countries" through "the interchange of persons, knowledge, and
skills."[61] The Hong Kong bureau happily reaffirmed the decision: "The
appearance of a Chinese-American whose artistic achievements have
been recognized by the American public would be a much-needed testimonial to the opportunities our society offers to citizens of the so-called
'minority races.' "[62]

Wong accepted the government's offer, expressing her conviction that
"much could be gained toward American-Oriental unity on an intercultural level." Apparently she was fully aware that the State Department
had chosen her largely for her ancestry. In her second memoir, *No Chinese Stranger* (1975), she mused:

> The story of a Chinese female who was able to educate herself and
> establish a career in the United States created an unexpected impact
> on foreign readers. Capitalizing on their interest, the State Depart-
> ment wanted to produce the author in the flesh. It would be good
> for the image of the United States and inspiring to Asians searching
> for identities in a new postwar era.

She agreed to participate, motivated by "patriotism," a desire "to contribute towards East-West understanding," and "a moral obligation to
interpret what she knew of the United States to fellow Asians." Accompanied by her husband, Woodrow Ong, she departed from San Francisco
in January 1953 for a four-month speaking tour of Asia with forty-six
stops throughout Japan, the Philippines, Hong Kong, Malaya (including
Singapore), Thailand, Burma, India, and Pakistan.[63]

Faithfully adhering to the State Department's agenda, Wong's messages
to her audiences throughout Asia celebrated the promises of cultural
pluralism in the United States. "Perhaps if I tell you of my early childhood, which was not so different from that of many other children born
to immigrants in America, Asian or otherwise, and how such a beginning could grow into the miracle of standing before you now, I could
somehow tell you the truth concerning America as I have known it,"
her standard speech declared. As in *Fifth Chinese Daughter*, she told
of the conflicts in her upbringing between the "old world" Chinese values and expectations of her parents, such as patriarchy and conformity,
and the "new world" of her US education, which weighted "individuality, self-expression, and analytical thought." She recounted that her time

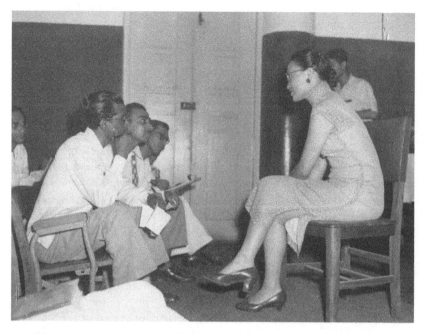

FIGURE 4.3 Jade Snow Wong lectures to an audience in Calcutta, India, during her 1953 Department of State cultural diplomacy tour.
Courtesy of the Jade Snow Wong Collection, Asian American Pacific Islander Collection, Asian Division, Library of Congress.

at Mills College "crystallized in me all the undefined urges toward self-expression," and taught her "how to live and think as an American who could return often and happily to the old familiar Chinese world." In meeting other students,

> I learned that my background as a Chinese was my particular asset, a point of distinction not to be rejected. I learned never to count on the false comfort of racial discrimination to excuse personal failure. There must be some discrimination whenever human beings live together. How easy it would be to say, "I was discriminated against" instead of "I did not work hard enough." But the intellectual honesty I learned through my American education would not permit this easy shifting of blame.[64]

Audiences did not receive her words uncritically. At a gathering in Malaya, one man bluntly confronted her with the question: "From your speech, Miss Wong, do you imply that there is no prejudice in the United States?" After a "sudden silence" among the crowd, Wong acknowledged the racism she encountered in the realms of employment and housing,

but also took pains to stress that "fear of prejudice and the excuse it offers for personal failure are chronically more damaging to a person of a
minority race than to expect the reality of encountering and dealing with
prejudice."[65]

Ironically, various people with whom she came in contact questioned
her identity as an authentic Chinese voice, wondering if she had become
too assimilated to US society. During a press conference in Singapore,
Wong recalled, she was subjected to the suspicions of journalists who
questioned whether or not she was "Chinese 'truly' (and therefore one of
their kind), or Chinese in 'face' only (and really an American)." Likewise,
Julian Harrington of the US consulate in Hong Kong and Paul W. Frillman of the Hong Kong branch of the US Information Service remarked
on the ambivalence and even negativity with which the colony's residents
received her. First, explained Harrington, Hong Kong Chinese, who saw
themselves as "'true' Chinese who through some force of circumstance
are living outside China," considered Wong to be a "'white Chinese'—a
Chinese who has found it possible to divorce herself from the land of her
fathers and take up a new and successful life in the land of her adoption."
This "class distinction" prevented Hong Kongers from "feel[ing] proud
of Miss Wong as a Chinese girl, and developed into the normal feeling of
envy, and even bitterness, for one who has been so successful despite few
opportunities." Frillman mentioned that Wong had been "heckled" by
an audience member "who found it impossible to reconcile her genuine
modesty in the face of such success with his own failure despite every
opportunity." Hong Kong's "prominent Chinese," observed Harrington,
"were even more obvious in their envy for and disapproval of a Chinese-
American girl who had succeeded so well in America. No amount of
modesty or spirit in Miss Wong could resolve this problem, and situations
involving such people were avoided as much as possible."[66] The class,
gender, and age tensions hinted at in these reports belied any assumptions
that the State Department may have had about a monolithic, cohesive
Overseas Chinese identity.

Complaints about Wong's visit registered by State Department officials
further ruptured such presumptions. Eugene F. O'Connor, the public affairs officer of the US embassy in Bangkok, declared her visit ineffec-
tive, with the exception of favorable publicity in local Chinese-language
newspapers. For one, he claimed that short-term visits held little value
for Thailand's US Information Service program because their "impressions" were "at best only fleetingly favorable, and are never of any depth
or lasting importance." He also stated his displeasure that Wong's com-
petency in Cantonese did not match up to the embassy's expectations,
and that she refused to utilize an interpreter or adjust her lecture for
audiences not at "university-level," thereby limiting the range of people

who she could reach.[67] Given this, despite Wong's readiness and willingness to deliver messages appropriate to the federal government's Cold War racial diplomacy designs, State Department officials did not see her tour as an unqualified success in terms of projecting an effective image of Chinese American citizenship. From their perspective, the most useful Chinese American citizen-representative was one who had assimilated and achieved success in the United States, but still retained enough "Chinese" characteristics to be considered "authentic" by Chinese overseas audiences. As State Department personnel came to realize, presumed diasporic ties based on shared ancestry were not enough to fulfill these objectives completely. They also belatedly discovered that individuals who were considered (or considered themselves to be) "authentically" Chinese in the American context might be perceived differently by ethnic Chinese in other diasporic locations, where each population withstood unique, historically contingent, and complicated processes of racialization and assimilation.

State Department officials nonetheless dubbed Wong's tour a triumph, if qualified, for Cold War diplomacy. Personnel in Tokyo and Calcutta described her visit as "worthwhile" and "successful," while the Hong Kong consulate was "reasonably favorably impressed." Singapore's consul noted that "interest in Miss Wong ran so high in Singapore that the usual single press conference after her arrival was insufficient."[68] Van Oss in Kuala Lumpur declared that Wong "handled herself well" and therefore served effectively as "living proof of the ability of a Chinese to become integrated into a non-Chinese society." Details of her itinerary in Malaya provide a sense of how she accomplished her mission. Wong appeared before a diverse range of audiences, including the Malayan-American Society, the staff of the *Young Malayan* (a periodical that serialized *Fifth Chinese Daughter*), the Women's International Club of Malaya, the Rotary Club, the American Methodist–sponsored Anglo-Chinese School in Malacca, the Anglo-Chinese Girls' School in Ipoh, the Penang Discussion Group, and the Penang's Ladies' Chin Woo Association.[69] In northern Malaya, Wong delivered nine lectures to a total of 4,350 persons, while 2,800 individuals visited the US Information Service Library in Penang to see an exhibit of her wares. For those unable to attend Wong's lectures in person, Radio Malaya broadcast interviews, and educators in Ipoh and Penang requested copies of her speeches for distribution. Local press paid favorable attention to her tour, with the *Straits Echo* publishing the entire text of her speech on "My Chinese and American Career," and the *Kwong Wah Yit Poh* reiterating her message that "in America, each community has an independent culture and at the same time can progress and advance with those of other communities without any obstacles."[70]

More informally, Wong and her husband wandered the streets of Kuala Lumpur's Chinese section, where "crowds of people approached [them] excitedly and talked at length." Van Oss stressed, "this type of contact . . . is of inestimable value to American-Malaya relations." Referring to his consulate's initial suggestion that the State Department deploy an "American Chinese" to Malaya, he concluded, "The success of Miss Wong's visit indicates clearly that this request has been more than justified. Miss Wong's life demonstrates the success that Asians can achieve in America. . . . [Her] speech and outlook clearly showed that she is accepted as an American, and this in itself was powerful counteraction to the reports of racial discrimination in America which have received wide publicity here."[71]

Beyond casting US race relations in a positive light, van Oss also noted a second and not unrelated means through which Wong's message could be used to contain Communism in Asia. At this time, the United States aimed to facilitate the local integration of Chinese minorities. Malaya was a prime example. During the period of decolonization in Southeast Asia (the 1940s and 1950s), Malayans feared the political and economic dominance of ethnic Chinese, many of whom comprised a wealthy merchant class. As independence negotiations unfolded, Malayans opposed the granting of full citizenship rights to ethnic Chinese, codifying this stance in the Federation of Malaya Agreement of 1948. Discriminatory treatment of Chinese by their "host" societies, US authorities worried, could result in minority Overseas Chinese populations throughout the region and world casting their lot with Communist China. Indeed, since its inception in 1930, the Malayan Communist Party had gained a considerable following among that country's ethnic Chinese, given its support for such issues as political equality for Malayan Chinese. In the view of US officialdom, then, Wong's "example of a Chinese who has successfully adapted herself to another non-Chinese society" offered Malaya's Chinese an alternative model of non-Communist assimilation.[72]

The State Department clarified this intention when Wong arrived in Kuala Lumpur. In a letter to friends back home, Wong recounted the historic political and social marginalization of ethnic Chinese in Malaya along with the resultant efforts by Nationalist China to "use this citizenship vacuum" in effect to claim the population as subjects of China. "Since it is difficult for them to wrench their loyalty away from China just because it has turned Communist," she wrote, "Communist infiltration and terrorism has been working here, especially directed toward high school level students and teachers." Wong revealed that she was told that "America's interest is to have Malaya emerge a strong nation, divorced from Communist China, somehow with Malays and Chinese cooperation. . . . It was my job to do what I could, in one week, toward American objectives." She reported trying her best to "be all things to all people" over the course of seven "exhausting" days—an effort that earned her the "emphatic approval" of Consul van Oss in his report to Washington.[73]

Wong's complicity as a Cold Warrior should not be overstated, however, nor should her views of American foreign policy be considered one-dimensional. In Burma, she explained, "I skirted myself clear of politics, and simply limited myself to being a girl of Chinese ancestry who had grown up in America, was now traveling as an artist, and the former author of one book which Burmese were reading." She described with humor the invitations extended to her and her husband by both the Ong and Wong Family Associations, resulting in "confusion and official consternation." US government representatives in Rangoon took no issue with the former "pro-KMT" organization. But after Wong discovered that the head of the Wong Association, an educator, used teaching materials supplied by the People's Republic of China, the State Department "had another nightmare." Unbothered, she met with the chair, who asked her to provide copies of her book for his students. "This, I think, sufficiently indicates Asian interest in American life, even though it seems quite comic, when I consider that *Fifth Chinese Daughter* is being distributed in Asia in the hope that the truth about America will counteract Communist propaganda," she reflected.[74]

Mishaps aside, the observed success of Wong's outreach inspired the consulate at Kuala Lumpur to request a second tour by Kingman, a Chinese American watercolorist based in New York. As with Wong, Kingman's trajectory held the potential to resolve the contradictions between liberal democracy and racialized citizenship. In the eyes of State Department officials, Kingman embodied the perfect Cold War cultural diplomat: a veteran who had worked with the Office of Strategic Services during World War II, the father of a son serving with the US Marines in Korea, a "very amiable, humble individual," and a "capable speaker." Assistant Secretary of State Thruston B. Morton clarified Kingman's value for the State Department agenda: "As a former servant, house boy, and employee in a Chinese laundry he exemplifies the opportunity that our land affords men with talent and ability. As a member of one of America's minority races he will be—in all those countries he visits—living refutation of all the distortions and lies the Communists preach about America's 'mal-treatment' of minority groups." Like Wong, the State Department imagined Kingman's Chinese ancestry to be salient to Asia-Pacific audiences. "Because he speaks the language of the oriental, because of his unmistakable oriental features, and because of the success he has attained in America," Morton wrote, "what he has to say about this country's

FIGURE 4.4 Chinese American artist Dong Kingman demonstrates his watercolor technique to a Singaporean audience during his Department of State-sponsored tour of the Far East in 1954.
    Courtesy of Dong Kingman Jr.

aspirations for peace and the dignity of men we believe will gain considerable credence—particularly in those countries of South East Asia and the Far East where everything possible must be done these days to win friends for America and where practitioners of the arts often wield influence and enjoy special prestige."[75]

Kingman's hosts were pleased with the outcome of his visit, concluding that he had ably fulfilled his calling. During four busy days in Taiwan in May 1954, deemed "quite successful" by the US embassy in Taipei, he lectured at a number of receptions hosted by local arts and cultural organizations, and even demonstrated his techniques during the presidential inauguration ceremony for Chiang. Two of his paintings of Taiwanese street scenes were reprinted in *World Today*, a magazine published by US Information Service Hong Kong for Overseas Chinese readers. Yet the artwork, it seems, was of secondary importance to his biography. "He has made many friends here and the story of his humble beginning and his career as a self-made artist has impressed the people much more than his modern-style paintings," noted Taipei embassy staff member K. L. Rankin. "His visit seems to have greatly strengthened the general belief among the local people that the United States is a land of equal opportunity for all." In Hong Kong, where the US Information Service screened films on Kingman, showed his paintings, aired a radio interview, and published features in local periodicals, Consul General Harrington underscored the same points, assessing Kingman as an "extremely successful . . . dramatization of how an American citizen of Chinese descent can make a prominent place for himself in American life while retaining some identification with Chinese culture." In sum, assessed Harrington, Kingman's showing boded well for future visits by Asian Americans, even if "such grantees present some possible pitfalls—local Chinese for example are inclined to view with some disdain their more 'foreignized' Overseas brethren—they are still living refutation of hostile claims that Asians are maltreated in the United States."[76]

As with Wong, the narrative of Kingman's career worked not only to refute charges of racial discrimination in the United States to global witnesses but also to reinforce cultural pluralism and legitimate Chinese American citizenship on the domestic front. *Life* magazine, for example, replicated a sampling of his paintings, including a vista of New York's Chinatown, for the feature "Dong Kingman's U.S.A.," a place where "both worlds come together in cheerful tumult." *Life* portrayed the painter— "born midway between East and West" in Oakland's Chinatown—as an artist whose vision merged "American Scenes" with a "Lively Oriental Flavor." In February 1955, *Life* called its readers' attention to Kingman's tour of the Far East by reproducing thirty-three feet of the forty-foot rice paper scroll he submitted to the State Department as his report for his trip to Japan, Korea, Taiwan, Hong Kong, Singapore, Malaya, Thailand, and India. The same month, *American Artist* lauded Kingman's visit, stating, "We cannot think of a better U.S. Ambassador to the people of the East than Dong Kingman. He likes people and with his outgoing spirit, he invites confidence and trust. He has sown the seed for a great harvest of friendship for the U.S." Significantly, *American Artist* did not refer explicitly to Kingman's Chinese ancestry, describing him simply as a "noted American watercolorist."[77]

Still, the identities of the ethnic Chinese recruited by the federal government as cultural diplomats were far from unequivocally American—a condition that signified Chinese Americans' tenuous social standing. A case in point is the San Francisco Chinese Basketball Team, selected by the State Department to tour Asia in 1956 under its auspices in conjunction with the Amateur Athletic Union. Founded in 1947, the ten-member ensemble boasted an impressive record, winning the National Oriental Tournament in its first two years and placing second in 1949, capturing first place at the California Oriental Championship from 1950 to 1952, and earning the title at the National Oriental Championships from 1952 through 1956.[78] Despite the San Francisco Chinese Basketball Team's exceptional standing among Asiatic sports clubs, however, the State Department sought to deflect attention from its racial homogeneity, reflecting the established concern for downplaying the existence of such entities in the United States. Washington, DC, officials instructed the hosting embassies and consulates that "the team should be billed as the San Francisco Basketball Team. It is composed of American athletes, born and raised in the United States. Team members are all the products of American public education."[79]

Yet clearly to State Department administrators, the team members were not simply "American"; after all, they were recruited to serve as "personal ambassadors" on the basis of their status as racial minorities and ethnic Chinese citizens of the United States. During their seven weeks in Asia, where they played against local teams and conducted youth clinics in Tokyo, Taipei (where they won the Overseas Chinese Presidential Anniversary Cup basketball tournament), Hong Kong, Singapore, Kuala Lumpur, Penang, and Bangkok, team members were seen by spectators as Chinese as well as American. "Among local Chinese fans they were known as 'the American' team," reported Richard M. McCarthy, the Thailand embassy's public affairs officer. "Besides being American, they are also 'overseas Chinese' and their obvious 'American-ness' impressed the local Chinese, who could only draw the obvious conclusion that Chinese in the U.S. were accepted and respected, and enjoyed being Americans." Indeed, the State Department explicitly noted that the goal of the tour was "to enhance U.S. friendly relations with the overseas Chinese Community." In all, State Department officials viewed the expedition approvingly—the team garnered amicable publicity in Chinese newspapers, for instance—noting only a few setbacks, including a "minor riot" against the Bangkok team that they defeated in the Taipei competition and some embarrassment when the players refused to use squat toilets in Haadyai, Thailand.[80]

The significance of the San Francisco Chinese Basketball Team's Asia tour for staking a claim to full citizenship was not lost on the Chinese American community. San Francisco's Chinese Six Companies and Anti-Communist League honored the young men with a luncheon before their departure in October. Readers of the *Chinese World* were able to follow the club's itinerary as columnist H. K. Wong reported the details of their travel. A group of Chinatown leaders assembled to greet the team during their stopover in Honolulu on their way back to California, and the Chinese Six Companies and Anti-Communist League feted them a second time with a welcome home tea, inviting the public to join them in celebrating the athletes' "outstanding record" as well as service as "goodwill representatives of the U.S.A. and Chinatown on the trip."[81]

The state therefore was not the only entity that stood to gain from Chinese Americans' Cold War cultural diplomacy. Wong, Kingman, and the members of San Francisco's Chinese Basketball Team profited by reaping acknowledgment and publicity for their endeavors. Beyond these individual benefits, the community as a whole had its collective citizenship status legitimated in an unprecedented way with the tapping of its members to represent the land.

The enthusiasm with which many residents of US Chinatowns celebrated the team's Far Eastern excursion, in contrast to the mixed reception of Wong during her tour, suggests that the State Department's cultural diplomacy efforts were more persuasive to Chinese Americans than to the intended target audience, Asia's Overseas Chinese. This outcome can be explained in part by noting that Chinese Americans stood to avail from this project in immediate ways, as evident from the embrace by the mainstream press of Kingman's ambassadorship—a clear validation of Chinese American citizenship. The *Chinese News* endorsed Kingman's mission, no doubt with white readers in mind: "Certainly no better cultural representative could be sent to these countries as he exemplified perfectly the opportunity for an Oriental in this country." Chinese Americans understood well the opportunities presented to them by anti-Communism to buttress their claims to unfettered participation in American society.[82]

At the same time, the terms on which Chinese Americans engaged in Cold War cultural diplomacy reproduced their differences as racial minorities and their alien citizenship. In the cases of Wong and Kingman, the focus on their singular achievements—which Wong herself acknowledged was not a "typical story" of Chinese in America—did not address or hold the state accountable for racism in United States. Their exceptionalism actually underscored the limits of racial liberalism in the mid-twentieth century, since so few of their coethnics had achieved their levels of professional eminence.[83]

Reorienting Chinatown Politics

For Cold War–era Chinese Americans, Overseas Chinese identity was a double-edged sword. If it occasioned a means to prove their worth as American citizens, it also kept them bound to foreignness by denoting a split in their loyalties and emotional ties. This presumptive kinship to China, reinvigorated by Chinatown's anti-Communist campaign and Chinese Americans' engagement in cultural diplomacy, fueled the vulnerability of Chinese American citizenship in the mid-1950s.

Federal officials located a powerful reasoning in anti-Communism to halt the continuation of illegal Chinese immigration to the United States. In the aftermath of the Chinese civil war, large numbers of refugees fleeing China applied for visas to emigrate to the United States as the offspring of American citizens. Authorities suspected that the majority of the requests were "paper" petitions—legacies of the strategies of illicit migration that had developed in reaction to the Exclusion laws (1882–1943) barring Chinese laborers from entry into the United States. Such individuals claimed the rights to admission, often fraudulently, based on derivative citizenship status as the sons or daughters of native-born Chinese Americans. In December 1955, Everett F, Drumright, Hong Kong's

American consul general, alleged that the Chinese Communists were manipulating this well-developed "criminal conspiracy" by stealing into the United States on falsified documents and blackmailing paper émigrés who feared exposure. He called for the schema's destruction "for once and for all . . . before Communist China is able to bend that system to the services of her purposes alone."[84] The Immigration and Nationalization Service and FBI agents advanced analogous arguments in order to shore up support for more rigorous investigations of immigration fraud and stricter policing of the Chinese American Left.[85]

These various arms of the federal government, along with the Department of Justice, swiftly coordinated a stateside drive to eliminate illegal Chinese immigration. On February 29, 1956, a US attorney's grand jury subpoenaed thirty-four family and district associations in San Francisco Chinatown, demanding that each immediately produce any and all membership and financial records in the belief that Chinese families belonged to the organizations of their true (rather than paper) surnames. The next day, the Justice Department commenced its hearings. *Chinese Pacific Weekly* editor Woo described the affair as Chinatown's "worst incident since the 1882 Exclusion Act" as the entire community panicked, deserting the enclaves' streets, shops, and restaurants for weeks. In New York City, where the US attorney had impaneled a second grand jury, the CCBA called off all Lunar New Year celebrations.[86]

The mass subpoenas cast all Chinese in the United States under suspicion as both illegal aliens and Communist subversives. Metropolitan newspapers portrayed the "fantastic . . . passport racket" that had enabled illegal admission for "thousands" of Chinese, including suspected CCP agents.[87] Outraged, the Chinese Six Companies, acting as the spokesorganization for Chinese America, denounced these accusations at a press conference on March 16:

> The unreasonableness of requiring the family and district organizations of some 40,000 persons in the Chinese-American community in San Francisco to produce virtually every record, photograph and scrap of paper from the inception of their existence, without specifying what relation they may bear to the inquiry at hand, is incontrovertible. The subpoenas in question can only be used for the obvious purpose of oppressing and intimidating the entire Chinese American community in San Francisco and, whether intentional or otherwise, they are having the effect of stigmatizing the social and family status of a respected community with criminal coloration.[88]

Led by the Six Companies, a coalition of Chinatown organizations, including the Chinese Chamber of Commerce, veterans groups, and the Chinese American Citizens Alliance, protested the state's action, though also promising cooperation with "legitimate" investigation.[89] The ethnic press joined in condemning the probe.[90] On March 20, the US district court conceded that the subpoenas were unconstitutional. Woo commended the decision as "justice for the Chinese people," but cautioned the community not to delude itself into believing that the crisis had passed, noting that the contents of the Drumright report "should make you tremble with fear." And indeed, federal authorities persevered, although they were forced to narrow their inquiry to specific individuals and associations.[91]

The Immigration and Naturalization Service instituted the "Confession Program," whereby paper immigrants could identify themselves to the federal government with the prospect—but no guarantee—of legalizing their presence in the United States. Between 1956 and 1965, a total of 11,336 Chinese came forward and outed an additional 19,124 Chinese in the process.[92] While the majority of the participants were granted legal status, not a few were deported and indicted. Among these, leftists were disproportionately targeted, underscoring yet again the tangling of Cold War imperatives and Chinese American citizenship.[93]

If most of the so-called confessors extracted the heretofore-nonexistent means from this arrangement of freeing themselves from the shackles of legal Exclusion, the Confession Program did little to change persistent cultural notions of Chinese in the United States as foreign and potentially menacing to the national polity.[94] The lurid media coverage of the grand jury investigations had likely produced the opposite effect. For its part, the CCBA had turned to the Nationalist Chinese government's US emissaries for assistance in the throes of the subpoena calamity, but to no avail.[95] The harrowing experience spurred Chinatown leaders to pursue alternative means to shore up the collective position of all US Chinese. In February 1957, New York CCBA president (and KMT member) Shing Tai Liang met with the heads of the San Francisco CCBA and other Chinatown organizations to begin planning for a nationwide summit "to promote, develop, and advance the economic and social status of Chinese persons in the United States."[96]

As the date of the gathering approached, Chinatown opinion makers urged dissociation from China politics in favor of focusing on US immigration and refugee policy and citizenship related concerns. *Chinese World* editor Dai-ming Lee emphasized the "universal desire to find solutions to common problems" among Chinese in the United States, that solutions necessarily "exclude[d] all foreign politics," and that attendees "owe[d] undivided allegiance to the United States."[97] Woo, a longtime proponent of prioritizing US politics over China affairs, echoed Lee: "If some people enjoy a conference on [China] politics, let them go. I strongly advise all citizens of the United States not to be involved. . . . For decades, involvement in China's political struggle has caused endless conflict in the Chinese American community and brought about zero benefit."[98]

Heeding these calls, the participants in the first National Conference of Chinese Communities in America, held in March 1957 in Washington, DC, concentrated on US politics and society as the foremost strategy for securing Chinese American citizenship. The 124 delegates, representing 34 cities including Boston, Detroit, Honolulu, Houston, Seattle, and Tucson, passed a total of 14 resolutions pertaining to immigration and refugee policy reform, such as advocating for an increase in the annual Chinese quota of 105 persons, and securing fairer treatment for those seeking entry into the United States. They also approved a multifaceted vow to improve not only Chinese American lives but also uplift the nation as a whole:

1. To unite the members of all Chinese communities for the promotion of general welfare.
2. To improve immigration legislation and [the] Refugee Relief Act.
3. To contribute towards American cultural heritage.
4. To renew our pledge of loyalty to the United States.[99]

The conference marked a significant departure from the decade's earlier anti-Communist campaigns by advocating a distancing from China politics in favor of focusing on US citizenship-related concerns.[100] An examination of the proceedings reveals this evolution in self-representation, with its portrayals of Chinese as patriotic denizens of the national community who helped build the American West, served in the US military during times of war, and eternally aspired to upstanding citizenship as well as to contribute to the greater good. This scripting of Chinese American history asserted that its actors were integral to the United States and hence deserving of equitable treatment. Only the platform's fifth and final point, "To encourage the fighting spirit of Free China," nodded to international currents, but did so by framing it in terms of the United States' wish to "foster and support the principles of freedom and justice for all peace-loving peoples of the world."[101]

The conferees approved the establishment of the National Council of Chinese Communities, Inc., as the permanent umbrella organization of Chinese in the United States, to be chaired on a rotating basis by the presidents of the country's various CCBAs. In its Certificate of Incorporation (September 1957), the council articulated its main objectives to be the cultivation of Chinese American citizenship, including a "greater appreciation of the American way of life" and fuller participation in "civic

affairs" along with the fostering of "friendly" Chinese American integration.[102] The council's founders strategically omitted any mention of
China.

Cold War politics set the terms of Chinese American citizenship in the
1950s. The era's global alignments meant that both community members
and the state found it useful to superimpose an Overseas Chinese identity on ethnic Chinese in the United States. For Chinese Americans, the
espousal of support for both the United States and Nationalist China's
complementary agendas of Communist containment allowed them to
maneuver adroitly through the Korean War's unnerving climate. For the
federal government, the selection of Chinese Americans as Cold War cultural diplomats was a way to project the state's integrationist imperative
to diasporic Chinese communities throughout the Asia-Pacific region as
well as at home.

The hegemony of anti-Communism, moreover, favored the designs of
the CCBA, Chinatown's traditional establishment. Its ideological reign
narrowed the boundaries of legitimate political affiliation and action for
Chinese in the United States—as was true for all Americans. This con-
traction silenced and criminalized Chinese Americans who championed
the CCP or openly criticized the Chiang regime. The harassment, conviction, imprisonment, and deportation that befell many of these dissenters
spelled out the steep price of dissent. In the end, midcentury politicking
consolidated the power of the conservative merchant elite to represent
the community while facilitating the demise of the Chinatown Left.

But the federal government's drive to end illegal Chinese immigration
in the mid-1950s also revealed a fundamental failing in the CCBA's tactics to promote Chinese American belonging and its own position within
the community. The mass subpoenas emphatically showed that no Chinese Americans, regardless of political persuasion, were immune from
racialization as always-suspect, perpetual foreigners. In this respect, the
crackdown on paper families was not so different from the selection of
Wong—the epitome of the assimilated Other—to represent the nation
abroad not only as an American but also as an Overseas Chinese.

The state's blanket persecution thus forced Chinese Americans to reconsider their embrace of an Overseas Chinese identity—a strategy that
at once undergirded their integration yet also rationalized new modes
of exclusion. In 1957, CCBA members took first steps to distance themselves from China politics and prioritize their concerns as US citizens—an
impermanent enterprise, but a significant move nonetheless. More important, the Cold War immigration crisis hastened the decline of the
establishment's domination over the ethnic community. By highlighting
the inability of the merchant elite to fend off the federal attack, the im-
broglio emboldened Chinatown moderates, liberals, and progressives to

challenge the old guard by cultivating their own political visions through other means. Members of the new Chinese American middle class, inspired by the civil rights movement, also began to develop alternative orientations and institutions. These shifts foretold changes in demographics, US-China-Taiwan relations, and American racial dynamics by the late 1960s that would transform the community's power structure and Chinese America's social standing.[103]

Part II
Definitively Not-Black

In the two decades after World War II, the universe in which Japanese and Chinese Americans dwelled had changed almost beyond their recognition. The regime of Asiatic Exclusion was moribund. Congress had loosened successive laws impeding the admission and naturalization of Chinese (1943), Indian (1946), Filipino (1946), Korean (1952), and Japanese (1952) persons, with token annual quotas granted to each group. Piecemeal legislation after World War II permitted the entry and stay of nonquota immigrants and refugees from Asia, including students and intellectuals stranded after China's Communist revolution in 1949, military brides and fiancées from Japan and other countries, and Korean War orphans adopted by US families. Large-scale migration waves from the region resumed after the passage of the 1965 Immigration Act, replacing its 1924 predecessor that had so effectively barred all aliens ineligible to citizenship from coming into the United States. No longer considered unchangeably strange, Asian Americans also relished a newfound freedom from a host of legal restrictions intended to prevent them from establishing viable livelihoods in the United States, most notably the alien land laws in at least thirteen states. Landmark Supreme Court decisions declared racially restrictive housing covenants (1948) and school segregation (1954) illegal. Bans on racial intermarriages had also begun to be lifted in California (1959) and other western states; in 1967, the *Loving v. Virginia* ruling rendered them all unconstitutional. The United States was unquestionably more open to peoples of Asian ancestry by the 1960s.[1]

Together, this conglomeration of decisions facilitated major demographic shifts in the nation's Japanese and Chinese communities. Between 1952 and 1961, Japanese Americans filed the most applications for naturalization among all Asian ethnic groups. As they became citizens, they were able to petition for their spouses to come on a nonquota basis. Men of all races who served in the postwar occupation of Japan, moreover, sought to bring their Japanese wives back to the United States. From 1952 to 1965, more immigrants landed from Japan than any other Asian nation. The thousands of women who arrived as nonquota spouses tipped the gender balance of the Japanese American community such that women outnumbered men (100 females for every 85 males—an unheard-of ratio in the history of Asian America). Chinese Americans likewise saw a sea change in the gender makeup of their community. Previously considered "bachelor societies" due to their heavily skewed ratios (27 men for every woman in 1890, and 7 to 1 in 1920), the nation's Chinese settlements narrowed much of the gap after World War II. Congress's granting of nonquota status to wives of citizens allowed for stateside "family reunification"; nearly 90 percent of Chinese immigrants between 1946 and 1952 were female. The coming of women enabled the population to grow almost threefold from 125,000 to 360,000 by 1965, and brought down the gender balance to 2 males for every female.[2]

The other big postwar sociological transformation for Asian Americans was their entrée into the society's mainstream. Japanese Americans inarguably attained a higher degree of integration into the mainstream economy as compared to the prewar period. This transition, of course, was not entirely voluntary; the federal government's deliberate dismantling of the ethnic economy had forced many Nikkei to look elsewhere for employment. Furthermore, for many who had toiled in agriculture before the war, the shrinking base and rising prices of open land in the West closed off a return to farming. In 1940, the United States census listed 14.2 percent of the community as farmers and farm managers, 15.1 percent as paid farmworkers, and 9.2 percent as unwaged agricultural laborers (for a total of 38.5 percent in farming). In 1950, those figures had declined to 10.4, 11.6, and 3.5 percent, respectively (for a total of 25.5 percent). They had dropped even further by 1960 to 7.2 percent, 4.8 percent, and an unlisted figure for unpaid farm hands, respectively (for a 12 percent total). Some Nisei, unsure of their prospects, opted to complete their college studies before exploring their career options. At the same time, the demand for semiskilled and skilled labor precipitated by the rapid expansion of the military-industrial complex heralded unforeseen opportunities outside their traditional, segregated niches. Thus for the first time, Nikkei could finally secure positions in fields that corresponded to their university-level education and training.[3]

The concurrent changes in the Japanese American community and primary labor market structured the mass movement of Nikkei into the middle class. A few statistics serve to illustrate this ascent. Of all Japanese Americans in the labor force in 1940, 3.1 percent held professional or semiprofessional occupations, 11 percent were proprietors, managers, or officials, and 10.6 percent were found in clerical and sales work (for a 24.7 percent total). By 1960, 12.9 percent held professional jobs, 7 percent were proprietors, managers, or officials, and 15.2 percent were found in clerical and sales (for a 35.1 percent total). In contrast, the proportion of Nikkei in domestic work, the nondomestic service industry, and nonfarm laboring positions fell from 7.5, 7.5, and 8.2 percent, respectively in 1940 (for a 23.3 percent total), to 3.3, 7.4, and 3.7 percent, respectively (for a 14.4 percent total), in 1960. Education patterns also suggested assimilation. In 1940, 9.5 percent of Japanese Americans had some college education, compared to 12 percent of native-born whites and 3 percent of blacks. Ten years later, 19.1 and 14.7 percent of Nikkei men and women, respectively, had acquired some higher education, compared to 14 percent of all whites, 4.2 percent of black men, 5.2 percent of black women. By 1960, 23.6 percent of Nikkei men and 16.4 percent of Nikkei women had attended college, while only 19.4 percent of white men, 15.5 percent of white women, 6.2 percent of black men, and 7.1 percent of black women had done so.[4]

Chinese Americans exhibited an analogous upswing. By 1960, the proportion of Chinese working in professional and technical occupations had multiplied nearly sevenfold, from 2.5 percent in 1940 to 17 percent in 1960. In comparison, 38.7 percent of employed Chinese worked in domestic, service, farm, blue-collar, and unskilled labor positions in 1960—a steady drop from 49.7 percent in 1950 and 57 percent in 1940. Close to half of all males and over half of all females held white-collar jobs by 1960. The refugee students and intellectuals—dubbed "uptown Chinese" by contemporaries—comprised a small (five thousand) but highly visible proportion of ethnic Chinese in university, corporate, and other highly skilled positions. In terms of education, 28 percent of Chinese men and 24.2 percent of Chinese women had finished some years in college in 1960—a higher rate than among both whites and blacks.[5]

Yet such numbers only tell part of the story. A focus strictly on educational and occupational levels discounts other indicators of mobility. Figures from California in 1960 are particularly illuminating, considering the heavy concentration of both Japanese (60 percent of all Nikkei in United States) and Chinese (49.6 percent of the total US Chinese population) in that state. Generally speaking, Japanese and Chinese Californians were better educated than the state's whites, but their income levels were not commensurate with their years of schooling. Despite having more schooling than whites, in other words, California's Japanese and Chinese earned less money. To cite specifics, among Nikkei, 29 percent of men and 21 percent of women had completed at least one year of college, compared to 24 percent of white men and 20 percent of white women. While California's Japanese American women in 1959 earned a median income of $2,144, exceeding white women's median income of $1,812, Japanese American men had a lower median income ($4,388) as compared to white males ($5,109), despite having higher levels of education, suggesting that Nikkei had not yet achieved economic parity with whites. California's Chinese displayed a bimodal educational distribution. Compared to whites, higher proportions of Chinese men (29.2 percent) and women (23.2 percent) had some college education.

Greater percentages of Chinese men (40.8 percent) and women (38.7 percent), however, had only gone as far as the eighth grade, compared to white men (27.2 percent) and women (24.4 percent). In terms of median income level, Chinese females ($1,997) were higher than their white counterparts ($1,812), but Chinese males ($3,803) earned considerably less than white males ($5,109). On the flip side, Japanese and Chinese in California had higher median incomes than African Americans ($3,553 for men, and $1,596 for women).[6]

Nationally these trends were also the case. To repeat, in 1960, 23.6 percent of Japanese American men and 16.4 percent of Japanese American women were college educated, as were 28 percent of Chinese American men and 24.2 percent of Chinese American women. These exceeded the figures for white men and women (19.4 and 15.5 percent, respectively) and black men and women (6.2 and 7.1 percent, respectively). The Japanese ($3,205) median income was slightly higher than whites' ($3,024), while Chinese ($3,021) and whites median incomes were virtually identical. Again, both Japanese and Chinese earned much higher amounts than African Americans ($1,519). Overall, the census data reveal that growing numbers of Japanese and Chinese Americans were achieving middle-class status (as defined by professional status, education, and income level) at faster rates than African Americans. And as in California, Japanese and Chinese nationwide tended to be more educated than whites, but this difference was not reflected in their earnings. Chinese across the United States, in particular, had a higher ratio of persons without formal schooling (14.7 percent of men, and 15.2 percent of women) compared to whites (7.5 percent of men, and 6 percent of women) *and* blacks (6.2 percent of men, and 7.1 percent of women) nationwide.[7]

Thus, despite their upward mobility, Asians certainly had not achieved economic or social parity with whites. Moreover, educational and occupational statistics do not communicate the many hardships that Japanese and Chinese Americans continued to face after World War II, not only in the labor market, but also in such realms as housing and associational life. In the West, many whites actively repelled or only grudgingly accepted Asian American neighbors.[8] Not a few voluntary organizations, including the National Exchange Club and the American Legion's 40&8 affiliate, refused to allow "Oriental" members—decisions that erupted into highly publicized disputes in the 1950s. In 1956, Northwestern University's Psi Upsilon fraternity ousted pledge Sherman Wu. "They told me that I degrade their house because I am Chinese," he testified. The administration declined to intervene, but public opinion tipped overwhelmingly in Wu's favor. Northwestern's chapter of the American Association of University Professors condemned the incident, as did the school's Interfraternity Council, the NAACP, the *Washington Post*, the Illinois-Wisconsin regional conference of the US National Student Association, and the First Methodist Church of Evanston, Illinois, where the Wu family worshipped. Readers of the *Chicago Daily Tribune* denounced the snubbing as "ignorance," and Rochester University's Psi Upsilon chapter elected to make Wu an honorary brother. In the most creative act of protest, folk singer Pete Seeger sang "The Ballad of Sherman Wu": "As I roved out on the streets of Northwestern / I spied a young freshman dejected and blue, I said / 'Young man—why are you dejected?' / He said, 'I'm Chinese and I can't join Psi U!' "[9]

On the ground, in sum, the post-Exclusion inclusion of Asian Americans proceeded unevenly. Whites were increasingly willing to view Asians as citizens entitled to dignified, equal treatment—an acceptance that translated materially in the lives of ethnic Japanese and Chinese. Nonetheless, whiteness was not an option for assimilating Japanese and Chinese, as it had been for the second and third generations of Southern and Eastern European immigrants. Asians in America remained not-white.

In the mid-1960s, however, not-blackness eclipsed not-whiteness as a signal characteristic of Asian American racialization as African American freedom movements took center stage in the life of the nation. As social observers, politicians, and others—including some Asian American spokespersons—tried to remix the nation's racial order, they paid more attention to the achievements of Japanese and Chinese rather than their continuing struggles. Chapter 5 follows the production and implications of "success story" narratives of Japanese American recovery from internment. Chapter 6 recounts the bifurcated strategy of Chinatown leaders who seized the opportunity to redefine Chinese American identity in the midst of the nation's postwar juvenile delinquency crisis. Finally, chapter 7 examines the Hawai'i statehood debates and their bearing on the new conception of Asian Americans as definitively not-black model minorities.

Chapter 5

Success Story, Japanese American Style

Since JACL's inception, its leaders had intuitively grasped the intimate connection between knowledge and power. This correlation became especially clear during World War II and afterward, when the organization waged its campaign to rescue both Japanese American citizenship and the league's own repute. Through the invention of the iconic Nisei soldier, JACL had shaped a new racial knowledge about its community. The convincing martial patriotism strategy had enabled JACL to tighten its hegemony over Nikkei. Still, JACL leaders did not feel totally secure in either regard. The anti-Japanese hostilities that had flared up in the tense moments of US-Japan postwar relations and the membership's debate about the league's proper stance toward international issues reminded JACL's leaders that the dual objectives necessitated continual reanimation if these aims were to be realized fully.

Writing history—quite literally—would fulfill these imperatives, they decided. As early as 1948, national officers had entertained the idea of producing the "JACL Story" in tandem with the "Issei Story" as a means "to serve as an inspiration to all Americans of the faith we had in the American way and in the ultimate triumph of justice." Lacking funding, the venture stalled until the league ranked public relations as its uppermost priority in 1960. This decision provided a vital impetus for the directors to launch with full force the chronicling of the immigrant generation's "vital contributions" to the United States. As envisioned by the organization, the Issei Story Project (ISP), as it came to be known, would entail conducting oral history interviews along with collecting relevant documents, photographs, and artifacts. In addition to the testimonies and archive, the proposed end products were an academic, definitive history of Japanese America, a social scientific survey of Nikkei life experiences, and a popular account intended for a lay audience. (The directors dropped the overt focus on JACL, perhaps in the interest of choosing a topic less politically contentious and more marketable.)[1]

The ISP's implications would be far reaching, stressed JACL leaders. At the most basic level, the project would execute the league's public relations mission to the "fullest extent and in the best sense of the meaning" by showcasing Nikkei Americanization, good citizenship, and remarkable socioeconomic advancement since World War II. The enterprise thus would also benefit the nation's Cold War agenda. As Boston University sociologist and ISP adviser T. Scott Miyakawa explained, the recent "setback in Japan" had reignited Asians' "bad image" of the United States. A record of Issei accomplishments would go far to mend the damage. At its core, this logic followed a yearning for self-preservation: if the United States could demonstrate that American democracy benefited all its people, including those of Asiatic ancestry, then Japan would be less likely to fall to Communism. By preventing such a turn, Japanese Americans could help to ensure that their precarious citizenship status would not be left defenseless once again.[2]

In seeking to produce new envisagements about Japanese Americans through the ISP, JACL spoke to mid-twentieth-century liberals' confidence in the ability of educational campaigns and social science to transform existing ideas about race and alter the country's racial order. Constituents of the era's race relations complex identified Nikkei citizenship as an American dilemma to be repaired in order to prove the nation's capacity for righting its wrongs, thereby protecting the United States' global position. To this end, academicians, activists, journalists, and politicians generated a series of "recovery narratives" in the 1940s and 1950s, first to facilitate the integration of Japanese Americans into mainstream society after the camps, and then to document and explain the Nikkei's specious rebound from internment's traumas. As policymakers and social witnesses explored new ways of rectifying African American racial inequality in the mid-1960s, the weight of the recovery narratives shifted to contrasting the entry of Japanese Americans en masse into the middle class and the persistence of black poverty. The characterization of Nikkei as a definitively not-black model minority therefore was the result of liberals' concurrent, overlapping attempts to solve both the Negro Problem and the Japanese Problem. It also reflected mass culture's positive depictions of a postwar, reconstructed Japan.

The celebration of Japanese Americans as model minorities seemed to vindicate the assimilationist approach to rehabilitating Nikkei citizenship as espoused by JACL and its allies. Yet at the same moment, the emergence of this image undermined the league's dominant position within the Nikkei community. The organization's prominent role in crafting and circulating the recovery narratives subjected it to heavy fire by many Japanese Americans—including some of its own members—for perpetuating stereotypes and antiblack racism. JACL could no longer claim to speak for the entire community without significant cost. Not coincidentally, JACL's decline mirrored the unraveling of liberal orthodoxy in American political culture as the civil rights movement evolved to emphasize black power and the federal government launched the War on Poverty. If the model minority construct traced its origins to the *liberal* vision for race management, and the recasting of Nikkei into assimilable Others during and after World War II, it gained political purchase by resonating with the burgeoning *conservative* fixation with "law and order" along with the curtailment of structural changes to redress systemic discrimination against African Americans. Hence, the birth of the Japanese American model minority signaled the dawning of reconfigured power relations among Nikkei as well as the emergence of a new racial order in the late twentieth century.

The Social Science of Internment

JACL's turn to knowledge creation as a means to secure Japanese American citizenship reflected the liberal faith in the power of science to fix society's ills. From the turn of the twentieth century onward, this conviction was manifest in the attention devoted by myriad reformers, philanthropists, and academicians to the dislocations of modern life wrought by industrial capitalism. During the Progressive Era, social investigators paid special consideration to populations on the move, including immigrants from Europe, Asia, and Mexico along with African Americans who settled in the urban North as part of the Great Migration. Sociologists at the University of Chicago famously developed a new theory for understanding social interaction that posited "assimilation" as the natural, inevitable outcome of encounters between distinct groups of people.[3]

Social scientific interest in the Negro Problem in particular redoubled as a response to the World War I–era racial violence nationwide. African American intellectuals conducted most of the initial studies as part of the broader struggle for black racial equality. By the 1930s and early 1940s, liberal sociologists had produced an ample body of research to demonstrate African Americans' capability to assimilate to white, middle-class culture and society. This scholarly corpus culminated with the 1944 publication of Swedish economist Gunnar Myrdal's influential *An American Dilemma*—comprehensive findings, commissioned by the Carnegie Corporation, of his extensive, multiyear investigation into American race relations. Synthesizing the conclusions of contemporary social scientists, *An American Dilemma* held white "prejudice" responsible for the enduring inequality of black people in the United States—a breach of the "American Creed," the nation's base beliefs in democracy and equal opportunity. Myrdal, however, maintained optimism that the American Creed would eventually triumph over racism, and proposed social engineering to facilitate the integration and assimilation of blacks into white, middle-class America. With the ideological battle to defeat Nazism and fascism in full swing, and nothing less than the United States' aspirations to global leadership at stake, Mydral's argument persuaded many Americans that their country's racial order needed to be overhauled. *An American Dilemma* defined the major tenets of postwar racial liberalism that would dominate the nation's thinking and policymaking on race until the mid-1960s.[4]

Like African Americans, Japanese Americans presented a quandary to liberals wishing to shore up what Myrdal described as "America's exposed position as the defender of the democratic faith."[5] But if the internment invited the embarrassment that the United States was fighting a "race war," it also offered an opportunity to test the utility of social engineering for achieving the assimilation of racial minorities as championed by Myrdal and like-minded intellectuals and reformers. On the ground, the WRA coordinated the task of integrating the internee population into white, middle-class America. Social scientists observed these efforts for clues on how to influence better group attitudes and behaviors.

In spring 1942, University of California, Berkeley sociology professor Dorothy Swaine Thomas assembled the Japanese American Evacuation and Resettlement Study (JERS) to use the internment as a research laboratory. She recruited a team of white and Nisei investigators—a number of who were internees themselves—to conduct fieldwork inside several of the camps (and later in a number of resettlement areas). Of all the wartime social scientific projects concerned with the incarceration of Nikkei, JERS ultimately became the most influential in shaping ideas about Japanese Americans, and by extension, the nation's racial order.[6] JERS set the framework for postwar examinations of Nikkei citizenship by foregrounding the relationship between culture and assimilation in two published volumes, *The Spoilage* and *The Salvage*.[7] (The former considered the internees deemed "disloyal" by the federal government and consequently segregated into the Tule Lake camp, while the latter focused on the so-called loyal permitted to participate in the resettlement program.)[8] In Thomas's assessment, assimilation begat assimilation; those internees who were relatively assimilated by WRA standards—US born and raised, college educated, Christian or secular (that is, not Buddhist), and hailing from urban rather than agricultural backgrounds—were also the ones most likely to follow the state's directive to shed all signs of Japanese culture in favor of those of the white middle class. It was this strata of Nikkei society—the "salvage"—that comprised the vanguard of integration into mainstream society. For Thomas, internment and resettlement had allowed these Nisei to break free of the ethnic ghetto, and experience "wider opportunity" in terms of job prospects and social interaction with whites. This was a propitious outcome that endorsed the federal government's dispersal strategy, but also liberalism's conception of assimilationism as the key to effectuating racial equality more broadly.[9]

The relationship between culture and assimilation remained a driving question for social scientists at the University of Chicago, the second institutional cluster of scholars concerned with Japanese American resettlement. Since the 1920s, "Orientals" in the United States had fascinated members of the University of Chicago's Department of Sociology. Like Negroes, Orientals posed a predicament because they, too, had not yet been able to achieve full assimilation. The 1940s' Midwest offered a rich opportunity to examine this phenomenon in a very different context from the segregated communities of the Pacific coast. The University of Chicago investigators shared common ground with JERS in that they also found Chicago's resettlers to be assimilating into white society. Collectively, they asserted that the "Oriental Problem" was in fact no longer a problem. They instead asked how Japanese Americans had been able to recover so rapidly and smoothly from the ordeal of internment.[10]

As did Thomas, the Chicago scholars indexed assimilation using cultural and structural measures, mining both quantitative and qualitative evidence of Japanese American mobility. They found, for instance, that by 1947, 60 percent of Chicago's Nisei owned small businesses or held white-collar, skilled-trade, managerial, or professional jobs in the mainstream labor market—a striking contrast to the prewar West, where Japanese Americans had been virtually barred from jobs outside the ethnic economy. Employers and coworkers applauded their "speed, efficiency, honesty, punctuality, willingness to work overtime, general moral standards." On the housing front, the resettlers had started out in undesirable (i.e., black) sections, but had since moved into predominantly white working- and lower-middle-class areas, where neighbors and landlords perceived them as quiet, courteous, and prompt with their payments. To generalize, the Nisei strove to join the ranks of the middle class—an aspiration reflected in such decisions as their choice of "well-groomed," "conservative but chic" dress. Though there remained limits to their ascent—they still lacked intimacy with white, middle-class individuals— they had "achieved more in the space of four years in Chicago than other ethnic groups who had long been in the city, and who appear far less handicapped by racial and cultural differences," as anthropologist William Caudill observed.[11]

In light of these observations, the puzzle for the Chicago scholars was how to explain Nisei mobility given that immigrant parents who had reared them came from a cultural background that seemed to diverge greatly from that of the American middle class. To begin with, the scholars carefully acknowledged the historical circumstances of resettlement as an important factor, especially the absence of established anti-Japanese racism in Chicago and massive wartime labor shortage. But these dynamics alone, they suggested, only accounted for the entrée of Nisei into the mainstream economy. They did not elucidate their progression beyond this starting point.[12]

The Chicago investigators deduced that culture had catalyzed Japanese Americans' upward movement. They hypothesized that the values of Meiji Japan, carried by the Issei generation to their adopted homeland, and the United States' middle class at midcentury overlapped significantly; therefore, Nisei, with their Confucian upbringing, interacted with their social surroundings in ways similar to persons steeped in the mores of the Protestant work ethic. Shared ideals included "politeness, respect for authority and parental wishes, duty to community, diligence, cleanliness and neatness, emphasis on personal achievement of long term goals, importance of terms of address and correct speech." Along with these were "high sensitivity to public opinion" and the tendency toward the "suppression of their real emotional feelings, particularly desires of physical aggressiveness," as "adaptive mechanisms." By exhibiting these characteristics, Nisei conducted themselves in ways acceptable to the white middle class.[13]

In identifying "Japanese culture" as an appreciable factor, Chicago's social scientists redrew the racial boundary between Nikkei and whites. Japanese Americans were becoming like the white middle class, they averred, but they had in no way disappeared into it. This delineation upheld observed common thinking. Chicago-area employers, for example, saw their Nisei workers as culturally and racially distinctive, possessing "Oriental tact," Eastern "psychology," and "typical Japanese politeness," all of which comprised a "Japanese way" that diverged from what they held to be American qualities of independence and rugged individualism. To these owners and managers, this discrepancy was actually a good thing. They commended Nisei for their exemplary conduct, such as a readiness to work longer and harder hours, "minding their own business," and displayed tendencies toward conformity and lack of assertiveness. These traits rendered Nisei especially attractive to businesses seeking tractable labor and at the same time reinforced perceptions of Japanese Americans' racial difference.[14]

Significantly, the Chicago scholars' recognition of Japanese culture as a socioeconomic resource heralded a radical departure from prewar and wartime portrayals. During the Exclusion era, white supremacists marshaled cultural arguments to claim that persons of Japanese ancestry, regardless of their birthplace, were intrinsically incapable of Americanization and therefore should be barred from legal and social citizenship. The same reasoning carried over to the justification of internment, when federal officials bluntly declared that "a Jap is a Jap"—that all Nikkei in the United States were members of a treacherous enemy race whose "racial strains" remained "undiluted" through the generations. Depicting the

Japanese adversary as antithetical to American identity had legitimated the military confrontation in the Pacific, blanket incarceration of Issei and Nisei, and coercive assimilationism of internment and resettlement. By the war's end, however, such representations were no longer tenable. The United States now had geopolitical incentives to reconstruct occupied Japan as Asia's safeguard against the spread of Communism and extend the privileges of national inclusion to its racial minorities, including Japanese Americans. The American public could no longer perceive Japanese culture as defective. Consequently, mass-market periodicals, novels, memoirs, and Hollywood films of the late 1940s and 1950s reconfigured Japan and its people from demonic, alien foes to sympathetic allies capable of joining the fold of liberal democracy. Stateside, social scientists' recasting of Japanese Americans into assimilable others mirrored and reinforced Japan's Cold War transformation. "Japanese culture," then, functioned as a malleable screen onto which various actors could project their political agendas, from validating Exclusion, internment, and resettlement to rehabilitating Japanese American citizenship and reconstructing Japan, depending on the exigencies of the moment.[15]

Narrating Recovery

JERS and Chicago social scientists did not work in isolation but instead were part of a loose confederacy of liberal thinkers and doers committed to disseminating renovated information about Nikkei in the 1940s and 1950s. This alliance—which included religious activists, civic leaders, WRA administrators, and Nisei themselves—stamped its approval on the federal government's plan to rehabilitate Japanese American citizenship through military service and resettlement. JACL, of course, spearheaded the fashioning of the iconic Nisei soldier to emphasize the group's loyalty to the United States. Alongside the league's martial patriotism campaign, liberal advocates of Nikkei generated public conversation about recovery—both of Japanese American lives and democracy itself—meant to facilitate the assimilation of former internees into white middle-class society. Yet the stakes of the mission went far beyond the plight of the internee population. Together, the recovery narratives framed Japanese American social standing as a national concern with international implications inextricably linked to the Negro Problem.[16]

"Now that we have the Japanese evacuated, what are we going to do with them?" asked University of Washington Sinologist George E. Taylor in 1943, voicing a concern of many Americans across the political spectrum. Exclusionists championed perpetual incarceration or mass deportation. But among those who saw themselves as allies of the Japanese

Americans, including WRA administrators, resettlement became the consensus. An engineered scattering would help to mitigate the wartime labor scarcity, but more important, deter the reconstitution of the ethnic enclave, seen as the grand impediment to assimilation.[17]

Believing that public acceptance would be crucial to the success of the operation, WRA administrators distributed pamphlets, brochures, and films with such titles as *A Challenge to Democracy* to educate receiving communities about their new Japanese American neighbors. They worked with local newspapers to run favorable stories and also tapped area residents to promote resettlement. Churches and secular organizations assisted resettlers not only by running hostels, job placement, and housing services; they also introduced civic leaders and prominent individuals to WRA officials and resettlers to cultivate support for the program.[18]

At the national level, resettlement advocates—including Japanese Americans—spoke out, complementing on-the-ground efforts. Librarian Clara E. Breed beseeched *Horn Book* readers to allow Nikkei a "chance to walk our streets, live in our neighborhoods, eat in our restaurants, shop in our stores, and attend our colleges . . . [and] enter the professions" to ensure that "Little Tokyos [are] forever broken up."[19] Likewise, Robert Hosokawa, writing for the *Christian Science Monitor Magazine*, concurred that resettlement would wipe out "the socially undesirable ghetto Lil' Tokyos" and provide Japanese Americans "a chance to prove their assimilability." He described his own transition from camp to a midwestern town as initially trying, but increasingly positive as residents went "out of their way to be kind to us," attesting to his experience that dispersal presented an ideal and feasible solution to the Japanese Problem.[20]

The call for acceptance took on heightened urgency after December 1944, when the War Department rescinded its evacuation orders for the Pacific states and the Supreme Court ruled in *Ex Parte Endo* that the federal government could not continue to detain "concededly loyal" citizens. Anticipating that the internees' release would inflame exclusionist enmity, liberals ratcheted up their pleas for tolerance. When discrimination, violence, and terrorism greeted the first trickle of Japanese Americans returning to their former homes, sympathizers openly chastised nativists' "thoroughly disgraceful attitude." The issue, they contended, was not simply Nikkei's ability to reestablish their households and livelihoods. "It is not a question of whether we want the Japanese-Americans back on the West Coast—it is a question of whether we want democracy," declared one editorial. No less than the very future of democracy—and thus the future of the United States' bid for geopolitical dominance, especially in the Pacific Rim—was at grave risk.[21]

By conceiving internees' return to the Pacific coast in these terms, liberals framed the rehabilitation of Japanese American citizenship as an issue that transcended locality, both in terms of ethnicity and geography, and one that demanded the nation's attention. When Ina Sugihara declared, "No, I don't want to go back to California," she explained that her unwillingness to return was due to her "powerless[ness] to stop the bubbling" of racism in her home state. She implored her fellow citizens to come to the aid not only of Nikkei but also Chinese, Filipinos, and others: "The 'Oriental Problem' is not a Pacific Coast one; though the West initiated it. It is now bigger and far more destructive than the evils existing in any one region alone. It is an American problem." In *Prejudice—Japanese-Americans: Symbol of Racial Intolerance* (1944), the first book-length assessment of the internment, left-leaning social critic Carey McWilliams expressed the hope that a just outcome for the "Japanese issue"—that is, living in the "full stream of American life"—could serve as an entering wedge into dismantling the color line that vexed all the country's minority groups. The demonstrated possibility for resettlers to achieve "full acceptance" outside the boundaries of Little Tokyo had proven the reality and desirability of state intervention in managing race relations. "As a nation, we are beginning to realize that we have a race problem in the United States and not a series of unrelated local issues," McWilliams emphasized. Only federal action, he concluded, could defeat the forces of white supremacy from coast to coast.[22]

McWilliams and fellow liberals conveyed an optimism in the ability of democracy to "correct its own mistakes"—a hopefulness that was at once prescriptive as well as descriptive.[23] "All over the United States . . . battles for democracy are being fought" wherever Nikkei now resided, observed *Parents* magazine. Although discrimination occasionally reared its ugly head, "democracy is winning out against its ancient enemy, race hatred." Hood River, Oregon, provided one of the most striking examples of this turnabout. The town had gained widespread notoriety when its American Legion post deleted the names of Nisei veterans from the municipal honor roll in November 1944. By summer 1946, white residents, some of who had maintained the Nikkei's farms and residences during their absence, were warmly welcoming Japanese Americans returning to the area. This spectacular reversal—a "hate that failed," as the *Saturday Evening Post* put it—was manifest up and down the entire Pacific coast. Exclusionist associations, businesses' refusal to serve returnees, and terrorist acts had been reduced to a "small dying quiver." The West's long-standing Japanese problem was now "largely solved," thanks to the advocacy efforts of the WRA, numerous liberal religious and civic groups (the Catholic Interracial Committee of Los Angeles, Society of Friends, National Council on Race Relations, etc.), and the determination of Japanese Americans themselves to move forward. Nisei resettlers outside the West, depicted as well-adjusted, upwardly mobile, integrated individuals, had reminded many ordinary citizens that "American principles of fair play demand an equal chance for all Americans, regardless of race." These tales of redemption both affirmed and encouraged the nation to live up to Myrdal's conviction that it possessed the capability as well as the will to atone for its misdeeds.[24]

Still, liberals conceded, the rehabilitation of both Japanese America and democracy remained unfinished. Nikkei everywhere had difficulty finding adequate housing—a situation most terrible in the western states, where restrictive covenants and racist real estate agents blocked access to desirable homes. Employment remained a pressing concern, as the evacuation had completely destroyed the ethnic economy. Those who attempted to resume farming, processing, or marketing produce struggled to gain a foothold, contending with the loss of their plants, seeds, and implements. Adding insult to injury were the consumers who waged boycotts and California state officials attempting to confiscate their properties. Nikkei of both generations, driven by "insecurity and a sense of urgency," labored "excessively hard"; those unable to find work (Issei especially faced language barriers and downward mobility) applied for public relief in unheard-of numbers. Observers also noted troubling aspects of Nikkei's social relations, including an "inferiority complex" afflicting many who felt "ill at ease among whites." Crime, delinquency, and alcoholism were ever present. A Nisei couple reporting for *Survey Graphic* decried the presence of zoot-suiters and other "restless" youths in resettlement cities whose "obnoxious" behaviors "invite[d] discrimination not only against themselves, but against the relocatees in general." In *Common Ground*, Robert Cullum, director of the Department of Interior's study of Japanese Americans' postinternment "adjustment," used Nisei's growing attraction to ethnic-specific organizations (sports teams, social clubs, and so forth) as a barometer of their distance from complete assimilation and full citizenship. Only the total abolition of Japanese Exclusion, he argued, would erase their "racial visibility" and assure Nikkei's unencumbered participation in the "mainstream of American life." His cohort of liberal advocates concurred that the nation had a continuing obligation to ensure a "good future" for Japanese America.[25]

By the mid-1950s, the recovery narratives evinced a noticeable shift: the caveats had given way almost entirely to celebration. Of course, much had changed for Nikkei in the decade since the war's end. The legal pillars of Japanese Exclusion—most important, the alien ineligible to citizenship—had been felled. Large-scale structural shifts had pushed and pulled Nikkei out of the ethnic economy and into the primary labor market. More recent stories of recuperation cheered the group's rebound, restoring its historical trajectory to the rightful path of immigrant assimilation. In the photo essay "California's Amazing Japanese," the *Saturday*

Evening Post lauded the "remarkable story" of the former internees, identifying several indicators of Nikkei's successful integration: flourishing careers in traditional and pathbreaking fields, suburban homes and new cars, college degrees, involvement in mainstream community organizations, and greater acceptance by non-Japanese neighbors. The caption under a picture of children proclaimed, "Many Californians who used to say kids like these—of 'Asiatic origin'—were unassimilable, have changed their minds." Similarly, the *Reader's Digest* rejoiced at the "amazing turnabout" that saw Japanese Americans "enjoying a prestige, a prosperity, and a freedom from prejudice that even the most sanguine of them had never hoped to attain within their own lifetime." The *New York Times* likewise noted that Nikkei now occupied a "status close to first-class citizenship," experiencing public opinion so high that they were highly sought after by employers for their "keenness and diligence." *Commonweal* predicted that continued "social acceptability" would foster further movement in this direction.[26]

Like their predecessors, Japanese American "success stories" of the mid- to late 1950s redeemed the nation's missteps and reinforced liberalism's tenets, especially state management of the racial order. This impulse was most apparent in assertions that internment was a "disguised blessing" and, ironically, Nikkei's "greatest opportunity." Military service had allowed them the chance to prove their loyalty to the United States, upset existing notions of their "character," and gain access to socioeconomic mobility through the GI Bill. "As a direct result of the Pacific war, Japanese residents of California have lifted themselves higher in a few postwar years than they had done in the preceding half century. And agitation against them has almost been silenced," the *Saturday Evening Post* triumphantly declared.[27] Resettlement had facilitated the community's "rise out of second-class citizenship," and had precipitated racial, generational, and gendered liberation by breaking up prewar Little Tokyos, halting the "feudalistic control" of Japanese fathers, and "emancipat[ing]" Nikkei women. *Newsweek* proclaimed that Nikkei were "glad" that they had been "pushed into the mainstream of American life," citing one of Chicago's resettlers: "It seemed at the time painful, but now my wife and I feel that the evacuation was a godsend. You know, America gives you a chance, no matter who you are."[28] At the same time, Nikkei's return en masse to the West Coast was cast as a fruitful progression rather than a failure of the dispersal vision, thanks to the evolution in public attitudes. Racial incidents were "rare," Little Tokyo was now a "self-imposed" entity primarily serving the tourist trade, and Japanese Americans had been integrated into "every phase of contemporary California life." By suggesting that the federal government had effectively guided Nikkei to a more integrated existence, these examples offered evidence to quell anxieties surrounding state-mandated desegregation in the wake of the Supreme Court's momentous decision in *Brown v. Board of Education*.[29]

Embedded in these narratives was a second lesson about civil rights: the demand that racial minorities cooperate with rather than oppose the state's handling of race relations. The stories posited Japanese Americans—and JACL in particular—as models of proper political comportment. Given the league's hegemony in shaping Nikkei citizenship through its martial patriotism campaign, it is no surprise that commentators credited the organization as the "architects" of Nisei's "vindication" as well as their "unprecedented prosperity and social acceptance." (JACL assisted in the writing of at least one of these accounts.) Observers extolled Japanese Americas' recuperation as a case in point of the Biblical adage that "the meek shall inherit the earth," adding, "One can imagine all kinds of contrasting eventualities if they had not accepted their wartime tribulations with patience and forbearance." JACL was to be applauded for its foresight in this regard. And although its cooperation with the federal government during the internment and propounding of military service had been controversial decisions, Japanese America's progress had exonerated the league among even its toughest community critics. In adhering to its cultural strategy of *shikataganai* (realistic resignation) and pledge to avoid "arousing antagonisms," JACL had successfully shepherded Nikkei toward full "integration." At one level, such interpretations disparaged the league's longtime adversaries—renunciants, draft resisters, and so forth. At another level—whether intended or not—they implicitly analogized JACL's politics of moderation to the more confrontational tactics of African American civil rights activists. The comparison clearly shone a more favorable light on Nikkei, reinforcing the state's prerogative to set the terms for social change under racial liberalism.[30]

The currency of the recovery narratives, then, can be attributed to their upholding of racial liberalism's imperatives. During and immediately following the war, liberals aimed to illustrate and encourage support for welcoming internees back to civilian life. They also prodded the nation to rectify its treatment of Japanese Americans, and by extension, all minority groups. As the civil rights movement unfolded, the discussion evolved to accommodate nascent misgivings that Americans harbored about the process of state-directed social transformation. While these stories undoubtedly voiced support for racial integration, their elisions of alternative outcomes and critiques of internment indicated to audiences that Japanese Americans had chosen the acceptable, if not ideal, route to assimilation, and thus were rewarded accordingly. The insinuation was that hard work along with unwavering faith in the government and liberal democracy as opposed to political protest were the keys to overcoming racial barriers as well as achieving full citizenship. Recognizing the traction gained by these recovery narratives in the context of the civil rights movement, JACL leaders looked to capitalize on the interest in Japanese American mobility as they inaugurated the ISP.

The Japanese American Research Project

Expecting the ISP to be an ambitious and costly undertaking, JACL leaders deliberated how to secure effectively an institutional home plus funding for the ISP's archives and research activities. After conferring with several distinguished scholars, they decided the best way to garner support for the ISP would be to frame it as a story of "democracy in action" speaking to Cold War geopolitical exigencies. The trick was to persuade university administrators, granting agencies, and other key decision makers that the nation as a whole stood to gain from the project's findings.[31]

With this in mind, the ISP's preliminary proposal posited the Japanese American saga as a triumph of liberal democracy. Despite the "exceptionally strong prejudices, hostility, and cultural differences" during the Exclusion era, Japanese Americans had attained "within a single generation . . . a real measure of 'Success,' greater than many Europeans with far fewer handicaps." As the University of Chicago scholars and liberal advocates of Nikkei had done, JACL linked Japanese American mobility to cultural characteristics, especially Issei's child-rearing practices and their emphasis on educational attainment. The immigrant generation had inculcated their children with the necessary values to foster their rapid Americanization and advance speedily in their chosen careers as discriminatory barriers were removed. Other "outstanding Issei contributions to good citizenship" included unusually low rates of crime, welfare dependency, divorce, and sexual waywardness—claims that had been touted in contemporary mass media, such as the *Better Homes and Gardens* report on the absence of juvenile delinquency among Seattle's Japanese.[32] (Significantly, these assertions belied the gang activity and other youth problems that the Nikkei community confronted in the 1950s.)[33] Nisei's "outstanding" service in World War II and Korea was further testimony to their parents' exemplary standards of family life. As a result of such upstanding conduct, the American public had come to recognize Issei and Nisei as full members of the national community.[34]

JACL leaders, keenly cognizant of the importance of domestic race relations to the United States' pursuit of global dominance, foregrounded the foreign policy implications of this victory. Their pitch suggested that the ISP could smooth diplomatic negotiations with third world nations while facilitating American economic and political interventions in those areas. The proposal stressed that the project could boost the country's reputation in Asia and Africa by underscoring "how American democracy made possible the acceptance of a people with a very different cultural and ethnic background as creative Americans"—an argument with immense "public relations potential" to counter international criticisms of stateside racism and hypocrisy. In addition, Issei "reconcil[ed] Asian and Western heritages" better than just about any other group. Their able synthesis found parallel in reconstructed Japan, "virtually . . . the one non-Western non-totalitarian country which has industrialized." Japan, in other words, was the model nation for the developing world, just as ethnic Japanese were models of assimilation for US minorities. Both could serve as guides as the United States worked to modernize Asian and African societies.[35]

JACL wielded these arguments repeatedly as it worked to find a permanent base for the ISP. In an appeal to University of California, Los Angeles chancellor Franklin D. Murphy, league president Chuman underscored the utility of the study for the United States in terms of international diplomacy. This reasoning helped to persuade university administrators, and in April 1962, Murphy welcomed the ISP to campus.[36]

The newly minted JACL–University of California, Los Angeles partnership occasioned a public retelling of the recovery narrative. Media reports revealed the league's enduring power to shape shared beliefs about Japanese Americans. The *Los Angeles Times* published JACL's press release almost verbatim, including Chuman's statement that "scholarly accounts growing out of the study will deal with the significant story of American democracy in action. It should prove helpful to the United States' relations abroad, especially with Asian and African countries." The *New York Times* incorporated the announcement into a feature about Nikkei with an interpretation that mirrored both the recovery narratives of the 1950s and JACL's history of Japanese America composed for the ISP. Trotting out familiar tropes, the article proclaimed, "Japanese-Americans have triumphed over racial prejudice and achieved notable economic success," and concluded that "the enforced exodus paradoxically led to greater acceptance into American life than ever before," citing the noteworthy careers of outstanding Nisei professionals as examples. Observing "why and how this country's deep anti-Japanese prejudice was so quickly overcome is a question that has excited scholars," the *Times* offered a hypothesis strikingly similar to JACL's: the combination of Issei's "sacrifice[s]" for the sake of their children's education and Nisei's "heroic World War II combat record" had "provided a smashing blow against prejudice."[37]

The highlighting in these narratives of *Nisei* achievements marked a change in the ISP's focus from its originally stated purpose of paying tribute to the immigrant generation. The Issei experience had become relegated to serving as a precursor to Nisei history as Japanese American history. Issei's major contribution was now related as raising patriotic and prosperous American children on "Japanese" cultural values. The rechristening of the initiative from the ISP to the Japanese American Research Project (JARP) reflected the Nisei generation's "discursive takeover"—another instantiation of JACL's intertwining of Nikkei citizenship and its own stature.[38]

Witnessing the receptivity to the ISP/JARP's political justifications, JACL revisited its claims in the quest for additional funding to expand the project's scope. In October 1963, JARP staff members submitted a grant proposal to the Carnegie Corporation requesting one hundred thousand dollars to supplement the original hundred thousand raised by JACL. The Carnegie proposal insisted yet again on Japanese Americans' "success" in assimilation and JARP's potential to "dispel the tenaciously held notion that American democracy limits full citizenship to Caucasians," particularly in response to foreign critics. JACL enlisted prominent academicians to lobby the foundation on its behalf, including Harvard historian Oscar Handlin, who affirmed that the "dramatic recovery" of Japanese Americans was "worthy of understanding." Likewise, University of California president Clark Kerr testified to JARP's "value" for showing the "complete acceptance" of a minority group by whites, offering "significant proof of this country's dedication to democratic principles."[39]

The Carnegie Corporation's decision to award the full amount requested for JARP bears mentioning because the foundation had ceased funding race relations studies since Myrdal's research for *An American Dilemma*, despite numerous requests.[40] This verdict suggests that the philanthropy's officials considered JACL's arguments to be superlatively sound, and that the notion of Nikkei as the success story of the nation's racial minorities had become widely agreed on. Indeed, in its 1964 annual report, Carnegie stated, "Recognizing the contributions that the Japanese have made to American economic and cultural life in spite of the discrimination and injustices that they have suffered, the Corporation believes that an understanding of the immigrants' motivations in coming to the United States and their achievements here may provide clues to ways in which other immigrants may be helped to adapt to life in this country."[41]

The Carnegie funding prompted yet another round of recovery narratives. Reporting the news, the *New York World-Telegram* recited this "most outstanding success story," observing, "Far from being bitter about their treatment, the Issei have raised their children to be loyal and productive citizens. . . . The Issei have taught us all a lesson in democracy." Hawai'i senator Hiram Fong toasted the gift in analogous fashion, rehearsing "one of the outstanding success stories in American history" on the floor of the US Senate and inserting the full text of the *World-Telegram* article along with a similar clipping from the *Pacific Citizen* into the *Congressional Record*.[42]

Through the process of creating JARP, then, JACL fashioned a history of Japanese America with the potential to be used as a pedagogical tool for other immigrants and racial minority groups in the United States, and even third world populations. That the league was able to muster rhetorical endorsements, institutional backing, and financial support by arguing for the significance of the project in terms of race relations as well as geopolitics shows that the narrative of Japanese American recovery reverberated strongly with broader social and political concerns regarding racial liberalism, the Cold War, and the civil rights movement. This synergy meant that by the early 1960s, the Japanese American success story was becoming increasingly accepted as racial common sense.

Japanese America Divided

This was not a frictionless ascent, however. As the Negro Problem hurtled to the front and center of domestic politics, Nikkei and other stakeholders learned the ballooning risks of framing Japanese American history as a racial success story. In September 1957, the *Chicago Daily News* printed a letter from a reader urging African Americans to study the example of Japanese in the United States to learn how "spiritual and moral values alone can lift people upwards." It was through "hard work, honesty and clean living, by loyalty to the United States," and not "pressure group[s]," that "they reached the top as first-class citizens." Dorothy Forde, an African American woman, concurred that Nikkei's "exemplary conduct as citizens . . . earns for them an enviable status." JACL national public relations officer Abe Hagiwara intervened to set the record straight, reminding *Daily News* readers that Nikkei had indeed utilized a pressure group—JACL—to topple racial barriers. For the league, in other words, this type of selective memory imperiled the recognition of its labors. Other respondents submitted different critiques, noting that Japanese had not been enslaved, and that African Americans, as "native-born" citizens, were entitled to all the rights and benefits of first-class citizenship. One woman added, "I dare say there is no other racial group that has greater loyalty to the United States. The Negro has no mother country to divide his loyalty." Such a declaration recalled wartime suspicions of Issei and Nisei, and demonstrated that they might still be dredged up when politically expedient.[43]

Nisei journalist Howard Imazeki magnified the stakes of the narrative in June 1963, when he beckoned African Americans to engage in

"soul searching" about their troubles in an editorial for the Nikkei paper
Hokubei Nichibei—a piece subsequenetly rerun in the *San Francisco Examiner*. He acknowledged that African Americans had experienced levels of "mental suffering and emotional agony" unfathomable to Asian Americans. "We have no intention at all of telling the Negro community leaders, brazenly, to soften their fight for integration and for equal opportunity, for that is our fight too," Imazeki insisted. "But we need to believe that there is a crying need on the part of the Negro community as a whole to make a concentrated effort sincerely to better themselves. And this effort should be made hand in hand with their effort to break down the social and economic barriers." Rather than "blam[ing] society" for their "illegitimate children," "welfare checks," "petty thefts," and "rapes," African Americans ought to "see if their backyards couldn't be tidied up a bit, find if their children couldn't be given a little community push, and examine if there is not one rock too many on their shoulders needlessly." Mentioning attitudinal differences between the two groups—"Oriental" children possessed "long-suffering for education," a trait lacking among black youths—he chided, "Do not say, impatiently, there is no time" to wait for reform. "America will be here for centuries and centuries after we are gone."[44]

The communiqué detonated an instant, national furor. Imazeki reported receiving some 160 letters from people of all races, spanning the vigorously affirmative to the bitterly opposed. One was from a Nisei, reprinted in the *Hokubei Mainichi*, who complimented Imazeki for "hitting the nail on the head, dead center." Louisiana representative Joe D. Waggoner Jr. inserted it into the *Congressional Record* as evidence against the civil rights bill. Newspapers across the country—mass market, black, and ethnic—ran excerpts of the editorial and responses taking different sides on the issue.[45] San Francisco Chinatown's conservative weekly *Young China* commended Imazeki's views as "sane and courageous," offering Chinese "answers" to "questions on the Negro problems." The *Chinese World*, by contrast, expressed "shock" at the *Hokubei*'s "self-righteousness." Confident that Imazeki did not speak for all Nisei, the *Chinese World* added that it hoped to see "Japanese-American, Chinese-American, and all other minority groups in this country not only praise the Negroes for leading the fight for integration but get into that fight themselves."[46] Not surprisingly, a number of African American commentators also decried the edict. Loren Miller, an attorney who had partnered with JACL on numerous civil rights cases, called Imazeki "brainwashed," while a reader of the *Los Angeles Herald-Weekly* likened the column to "slander." In the *Chicago Defender*, another skeptic suggested that his comparison was not a valid one, as African Americans endured more racism than did the Japanese. Chiding Imazeki for trying to pass off his personal views as those of all Japanese Americans, National Urban League trustee George O. Butler pleaded with him to stop "sniping" at those absorbed in a "life and death battle for basic rights."[47]

But it was among Japanese Americans that Imazeki's message seemed to incite the most sensitive criticism. He no doubt had coethnic supporters, such as JACL leader Clifford Uyeda, who praised Imazeki for questioning African Americans' means for seeking social justice. Unlike Issei and Nisei, blacks resorted to "violence and threats"— a methodology that might sink their objectives. "Congress cannot be intimidated into voting for equality," Uyeda frowned. "The most effective persuasion is the proof of good citizenship, loyalty to the country, and especially being good neighbors." Dispatches fired by other Nisei made the reverse case. Jerry Enomoto wrote to the *Pacific Citizen* to refute passionately both Imazeki and Uyeda. "As an American and a national officer of the JACL, I feel that it is my responsibility to do some soul searching of my own. To, as others have already ably put it, be as good a neighbor, fellow worker, etc., to all minorities as I can. . . . I do not feel that it is my responsibility at this time to 'ask' the Negro to look into himself, where there has been, to me, so long standing a need for Japanese Americans to look into themselves." In the *New York Nichbei*, Harlem-based activists Bill and Mary Kochiyama attacked Imazeki's "asinine" opinion: "To say we were shocked, embarrassed, anguished, and enraged could hardly suffice," they countered. They wondered if Imazeki had any real-life exposure to African Americans and the extent of their tribulations. Los Angeles clergyperson George Aki expressed similar sentiments in the *Christian Science Monitor*, commenting that he and other Nikkei felt "deeply hurt and embarrassed" by Imazeki's condescension.[48]

Most unexpectedly perhaps was JACL's riposte. The league distanced itself from Imazeki's exposition via a statement penned by Masaoka for the *Pacific Citizen* just days after the offending piece was published. Masaoka quickly clarified that Imazeki did not speak for JACL as an organization, nor did he represent the views of most of its members. He also pointed out that the league had issued a formal statement in support of the civil rights movement the previous week, although he elided the fact that this particular decision had also been a gravely contentious one among the JACL body. Masaoka carefully proposed that Imazeki had honorable intentions, never anticipating that civil rights opponents would co-opt his words. Regretfully, the editorial was now being used "to create disunity and suspicion among the various minorities," and also "cite Japanese Americans as feeling smugly 'superior' and intolerant of their Negro fellow citizens." The effect was to poison relations between blacks and Nisei. Japanese Americans would do well to remember, however, that they benefited immensely from the hard-fought gains of civil rights pioneers. The ever-elusive "freedom and equality for all Americans," including Nisei, could not be realized without the "leadership and strength" of African Americans.[49] Ironically, Masaoka's hasty redress amplified the intracommunity tensions around the Japanese American recovery narrative that JACL had been promoting with gusto in its quest to launch JARP. Clashes between the Nikkei success story and its discontents—which became proxies for JACL and its detractors—would reach new levels as the black freedom movement intensified.

Coloring Japanese Americans Not-Black

Thanks in no small part to JACL's promotion of JARP and the Imazeki flap, the recovery narratives maintained a steady public presence through the 1960s and beyond. Journalists and social scientists persevered in reporting about Japanese America's astonishing ability to overcome the setbacks of internment. "Even in a country whose patron saint is the Horatio Alger hero, there is no parallel to this success story," proclaimed Univeristy of California, Berkeley sociologist William Petersen in the *New York Times Magazine*. From the *Boston Globe* to *Parade* to Walter Cronkite's CBS documentary *The Nisei: The Pride and the Shame* (1965), watchers marveled at the group's "spectacular comeback."[50] Researchers measured this trend using educational attainment and occupational distribution as benchmarks. Finding Nikkei's numbers generally on par with those for whites, demographer Barbara F. Varon concluded that applying the term minority to Japanese Americans "seem[ed] incongruous," given that they "participate successfully in the economic life of the general population." Some qualified this pronouncement, pointing to continuing bigotry in the realm of housing, discrimination on the job, and income levels below those of whites despite more years of schooling, but nevertheless concurred that "successful acculturation" had taken place. Another principal indication of this trend was that "social pathologies"—crime, delinquency, dependency, and other types of "deviance"—were the lowest for Japanese Americans among all racial or ethnic groups, including whites. Nikkei also had the highest IQ and life expectancy rates of all Americans. "To sum up, the Nisei were squares," as one remarked. Japanese Americans had become so successful that they had not only "outshone other minority groups" but also were now "outwhiting the whites."[51]

Culture remained the preeminent explanation for the resurgence. *Newsweek* pinpointed a host of "traditional Japanese values" including *giri* (sense of group obligation), *gimu* (duty), *enryo* (reserve or restraint), and *gaman* (patience or perseverance), along with "enormous fatalism," "respect for authority," and a willingness to "accommodate to the larger society" to account for Nikkei's collective feat. Equally germane was their reverence for the family and education. In "Success Story, Japanese American Style" (1966), published in the *New York Times Magazine* (and later in expanded form as the monograph titled *Japanese Americans: Oppression and Success* [1971]), Petersen suggested that Issei had imported a Japanese version of the Protestant work ethic. Passed down through the immigrant generations via family and religion, this cultural code emphasized group membership and honor, fear of shame, and respect for authority. Citing the research of George De Vos, one of the University of Chicago's resettlement investigators, Petersen noted that Japanese people in both the United States and Japan demonstrated an "achievement orientation," and that Nikkei's "meaningful links to an alien culture"—the same one that facilitated Meiji Japan's transition into modernity, and more recently, the economic recovery of postwar Japan—had enabled them to surmount the "highest barriers" of American racism. Anthropologist Ronald O. Haak described this phenomenon as an "ancestral reflex pattern of self-sacrifice and cooperation with no reward in sight," while sociologist Stanford Lyman dubbed it the "samurai ethic."[52]

In one sense, the cultural emphasis reflected the American public's postwar appetite for things Japanese in tandem with the reconstruction of Japan. For Nikkei, this had meant the freedom to reclaim their ancestral heritage without fear of negative repercussions. By the late 1950s, community celebrations such as Los Angeles' annual Nisei Week festival openly displayed this embrace, showcasing traditional ceremonies, imported goods, and the manufactures of their Japanese corporate sponsors. Nisei leaders resuscitated the prewar "bridge of understanding" concept, positing themselves as ideal East-West brokers in order to profit from the awakening transpacific trade. Familiarity with Japanese culture was recalibrated as social and financial capital.[53]

Behavioral scientists certainly read it that way. Modifying racial liberalism's coercive assimilationism, these scholars approved of Japanese Americans' congregation—much of it in response to the pressures of internment, resettlement, and return to the Pacific coast. "Ethnic intensification," though, did not mean a wholesale rejection of assimilation; sociologist Harry H. L. Kitano and Petersen underscored that Japanese American success was a consequence of combining acculturation and "independence." Yet overall Nikkei maintained a culture distinctive enough from all others in American society that Petersen described them as a "subnation": a self-conscious, cohesive community of persons with common ancestry enjoying "cultural unity" along with the allegiance of each individual to the group. No member of the subnation acted "without fully considering [the] effect on the 'Japanese image.'" The assemblage, in turn, provided each person "material and moral support"—a "psychological edge" equipping them to overcome all obstacles.[54]

The culture framework did not explicate Japanese American success without consequences. As it had done for decades, it made Nikkei racially distinctive. By attributing their achievements to the practice of an alien culture, the success stories reinscribed Japanese Americans' foreignness. They reproduced the lines that cordoned off the carriers of irreducibly strange thinking and practices from the identity as well as privileges of whiteness. Nikkei in this way continued to be regarded as assimilating Others—even outwhiting the whites—yet still not-white. And in the mid- to late-twentieth-century United States, exclusion from whiteness necessarily meant exclusion from the entitlements of full citizenship.

While this delineation was far from a novel one, the revised culture thesis served to shore up a developing strand of racialization. It positioned Japanese Americans in explicit contradistinction to African Americans—a modification of earlier, more implicit comparisons. Responding to the rise of black power, increasing urban unrest throughout the nation, and the War on Poverty, the updated discourse portrayed Japanese American assimilation as a model for solving the intractable American Dilemma. In sum, it marked Nikkei as definitively not-black by counterposing Japanese American culture with that of African Americans.

Such a juxtaposition was hardly neutral. Since the 1920s, social scientists had conceived of culture as a central factor in understanding poverty. By the following decade, they scrutinized the values and behaviors of indigent black residents of northern ghettos in attempts to right the Negro Problem. Depression-era studies conducted by such scholars as W. Lloyd Warner, St. Clair Drake, Horace Cayton, and especially E. Franklin Frazier identified a discrete black underclass characterized by a cultural "pathology" that deviated from those of the white and black middle and upper classes. Noticeably, Frazier pointed to black "matriarchy" as a consequence of the damages of American racism. In highlighting the aberration of female-headed households, Frazier made the case for the creation of job opportunities for African American men to correct these conditions and allow for the assimilation of the black lower class. His argument greatly influenced Myrdal, who asserted in *An American Dilemma* that poor blacks would remain trapped in a "vicious cycle" of economic deprivation, degraded "manners and morals," and racial discrimination until white Americans interceded through education, legal reforms, and so forth to open the route to assimilation. Postwar scholars (Talcott Parsons, Abram Kardiner, and Lionel Oversey) examining lower-class African American families through the lens of psychology found that black matriarchy's distorted gender roles resulted in corrupted child rearing in the form of personality disorders leading to crime, delinquency, and the perpetuation of destitution. Anthropologist Oscar Lewis coined the term "culture of poverty" to capture this psychological inheritance through the generations and suggest that it could take on a life of its own even in the absence of the structural factors responsible for generating penury in the first place. While researchers and policymakers debated whether or not the black lower-class pathology was inherited or situational, the vast majority did not question its existence, and many found the concept useful in advocating for a more aggressive agenda of social and economic reforms by the 1960s.[55]

All came to a head in August 1965 with the nationwide release of Assistant Secretary of Labor Daniel Patrick Moynihan's paper "The Negro Family: The Case for National Action," just days before Los Angeles' Watts riots. Also known as the Moynihan Report, the document was a liberal call to arms. Moynihan aspired to move federal civil rights policy beyond its signal achievements (the 1964 Civil Rights Act and 1965 Voting Rights Act) toward "equality of results" by focusing federal attention on black poverty. Drawing on the extensive body of midcentury social science literature on race and poverty, he synthesized familiar culture of poverty contentions to claim that the "deterioration of the Negro family"—epitomized first and foremost by black matriarchy—was the root cause of the "deterioration of the fabric of Negro society." The intent of his diagnosis was to mobilize support for structural interventions to establish "stable" black families (i.e., households that conformed to white, middle-class standards of domesticity) as a crucial means to alleviate their wretched circumstances.[56]

Moynihan's convictions were molded in significant part by his reading of Japanese American history. In a private memorandum to President Johnson previewing his conclusions, the assistant secretary candidly expressed optimism in the efficacy of federal family policy for "solv[ing] the Negro problem for once and all." "Many people think the color problem is insoluble. Nonsense," he huffed. Moynihan buttressed this pronouncement with his best example of racial uplift:

A quarter-century ago Japanese Americans were subject to the worst kind of racial discrimination and mistreatment. All of which has practically disappeared before our eyes. The reason is that Japanese (and the Chinese) have become a prosperous middle-class group. They now send twice as large a proportion of their children to college as do whites. Have twice as large a proportion of professional persons. Having solved the class problem, we solved the color problem. One of the reasons it was possible to do the former is that Japanese and Chinese have probably the most close knit family structure of any group in America.[57]

Nikkei had transcended the color line by virtue of their familial habits. With the right kind of political guidance, Moynihan believed, so, too, could black America.

The report's reception was something else altogether. Moynihan's blueprint triggered a tumultuous national debate about racism, poverty, and liberalism's assimilationist vision. Critics discredited his reasoning, fearing that his conclusions would be appropriated by federal officials to "blame the victims" as well as divert attention away from further civil rights action and the War on Poverty. In his own defense, Moynihan turned to the example of Japanese Americans' "family stability and values," elaborating on his brief mention of this theme in the body of the report. Early Japanese immigrants endured dire poverty, he contended, yet "they are today incomparably the highest social and economic group in the nation," citing Nikkei's elevated rates of college attendance. In his view, Japanese Americans fostered "singularly stable, cohesive, and enlightened family life"—the stark opposite of African American households—a culture that laid the groundwork for successful achievement in the face of racial discrimination. The Japanese Americans, in essence, were a model minority whose recovery ought to inspire hope in all Americans for the possibility of eradicating black people's "tangle of pathology."[58]

The Moynihan controversy thus crystallized what had been emerging for two decades: a *national* racial order, merging regional dynamics into a dominant black-white paradigm both complicated and reinforced by Nikkei as a model minority. While the distinction between Japanese and African Americans was not unprecedented—University of Chicago graduate students in the 1940s and 1950s had noted that the city's resettlers were treated as not-black, a status that enabled them access to opportunities from which "Negroes" were barred—higher political stakes characterized comparisons between the two beginning in the mid-1960s.[59] Significantly, some commentators, perturbed by blacks' increasingly uncompromising demands for ending racism and poverty, spelled out divergences between Japanese and African Americans to discredit the latter's insurgency. Just months after the Moynihan Report exploded, Petersen observed that Japanese Americans had evaded the fate of "problem minorities" saddled with the strains of "slum life"—poverty, low educational attainment, high rates of illness and crime, and family instability—stressing that they had amassed their "remarkable record" despite their tortured history and also "by their own almost totally unaided effort." In even more explicit language, Haak asserted, "What helped them most in the long run was the way they chose to earn recognition by performance, rather than by claiming it on principle. They steered clear of demands for radical revisions in the national power structure, in the distribution of wealth, in the ethnic composition of political and policy-making bodies.

They simply worked and endured until their performance overwhelmed without contentiousness, society's negative definitions of their worth." In the mores of Japanese American culture, he underscored, "it is deplorable to . . . tear the country apart over minority rights."[60]

For these observers, the Japanese American example could help to fix the Negro Problem. Nikkei, reflected Petersen, went against the grain of social scientific "generalization[s]" of "ethnic minorities" and therefore merited a close look, seeing as scholars and policymakers "barely" understood how to alter the dismal condition of African Americans. In *Japanese Americans: The Evolution of a Subculture* (1969), Kitano, a Nisei professor of social welfare at the University of California, Los Angeles, proposed that this "story of success Japanese-American style" might be "an illustration of a means of adapting to interethnic contact and conflict with a minimum of bloodshed and chaos." Although he hastened to add that his purpose was not to "sit back smugly and prescribe to others to 'do it the way the Japanese did'" he nonetheless wondered whether "lessons learned" from Nikkei's "remarkable record" would be applicable to other minority groups. And with his observation that Japanese America's basic strategy had been "accommodation" to American society, as opposed to "direct confrontation," the moral for African Americans was hard to miss. *Newsweek* put it most bluntly, quoting George Kobayashi, a Japanese American small business owner and resident of suburban, middle-class Gardena, California: "If they want to get ahead, they have to work—just like the Nisei did."[61]

Yet this was simultaneously an ambivalent prescription. Even as these analysts examined Japanese American history for inspiration, they admitted that the direct application of the Nikkei model to African Americans' situation would be impossible, or what Haak depicted as "an inheritance that is nontransferable." Petersen maintained that blacks lacked the "meaningful ties to an overseas fatherland" that had sustained Japanese Americans through their hardships by providing psychological "refuge." Moreover, social scientists conceded, Japanese America's model minorityness seemed to be specific to the Nisei generation. Delinquency rates among Sansei (third generation) were on the rise, while assimilation threatened to wipe out the group's "collective identity"—the very force to which they attributed Japanese American success.[62]

The contingency of Japanese American achievement in these narratives, then, indicates that the main function of the success stories was to discipline Nikkei themselves. In consistently praising Japanese Americans as the "outstanding exception" among racial minority groups, journalists and academicians reminded them of the social capital that accompanied such an image: their desirability as students, workers, and neighbors translated into access to heretofore off-limits educational opportunities, jobs, and housing. A key component of this desirability was the idea that Nikkei were apolitical. As Kitano wryly noted, "Japanese Americans are good because they conform—they don't 'make waves'—they work hard and are quiet and docile." (Gingerly, he cautioned that this conception could "in the long run, be a drawback as well as a strength.") If Nikkei wished to continue reaping the rewards for "good" behavior, they would need to act accordingly—that is, by not inviting "trouble" and "keep[ing] in their place."[63]

It is perhaps this realization that incentivized JACL to add to the chorus of voices positioning Japanese and African American culture and politics as the antitheses of one another. Significantly, the league served as a consultant to Petersen's seminal essay in the *New York Times Magazine* and reprinted his article in the *Pacific Citizen*.[64] JARP's architects made their role in racializing Japanese Americans as not-black explicit in the design of their national three-generation sociological survey of Nikkei in the United States.[65] One of the most revealing questions posed to interviewees was "Negroes are interested in bettering their position in American society. What advice would you give Negroes, as a race, to achieve their goals?"[66] The assumption underlying this query, of course, was that Japanese Americans' own route to socioeconomic success could and should serve as an exemplar for African Americans. The *Los Angeles Times* underscored this point in its coverage of the JARP survey. The *Times* cited University of California, Los Angeles history professor Robert A. Wilson, JARP's acting director in 1967, who affirmed that information gleaned from "America's most successful ethnic minority" could provide "'useful suggestions' in solving the problems of other minorities."[67]

Nisei: The Quiet Americans?

If JACL leaders were avid promoters of model minority adulation via JARP, other Japanese Americans, including the league's own members, stood among its fiercest critics. Disturbed by the budding stereotype of their community, many Nisei and Sansei vigorously challenged this development. With the impending release of JARP's first major publication, a popular history of Nikkei in the United States, they mobilized to push for what they considered a politically palatable analysis and fitting description of their current social standing. In underscoring the stakes of the representation of Japanese America, the dispute threw into relief JACL's now tenuous hold on its power to speak for the entire Nikkei community.

The production of a Japanese American history for the masses had been a goal of JARP from the beginnings of the ISP. Members of the JARP steering committee agreed that such a volume harbored tremendous public relations potential for both the organization as well as

Japanese America, but diverged over the specifics of the undertaking. As of 1967, the league had contracted with Professor Wilson to pen the manuscript, but a number of officers feared that his style would be "too academic" for the Japanese American and general public.[68] On the other hand, some worried, a popular history might invite skepticism about the book's "basic authenticity" even as it delivered a "great story."[69] Either way, JACL leaders hoped to secure a writer of national prominence—novelist James Michener of *Sayonara* fame was an early candidate—to augment the project's public relations "benefits," boost sales, and perhaps lead to further opportunities such as film adaptations. They weighed this against a desire to choose a "Japanese American to write our side of the story."[70]

Beyond the issue of authorial voice lay the trickier concern of content and interpretation, especially since league directors saw the history of Japanese Americans and that of JACL as essentially inseparable.[71] Conscious of the long-lived antipathy toward JACL, league officials hoped that the book would put critics' charges to rest. JARP administrator Joe Grant Masaoka ruminated, "In my view the role of JACL as evaluated by historians and put into proper perspective will be a unique and distinguished role in the history of Japanese leadership in [the] U.S."[72] Clearly no less than JACL's prestige and organizational future were on the line.

In the end, those who pushed for a Nikkei author won out, as did those propounding the popular bent, when the league commissioned *Denver Post* journalist and longtime JACL faithful Bill Hosokawa to draft the book.[73] As Hosokawa envisioned it, the tome would transcend mere "historical account" to present "the human story of the Japanese in America"—a "chronicle with a happy ending." He affirmed, too, that it would be "JACL's legacy to all Japanese Americans, and of course, in a broader sense to all Americans."[74]

The provisional title used by Hosokawa for the manuscript was *Americans with Japanese Faces*.[75] Editors at publisher William Morrow and Company, however, raised objections to this choice, arguing that the appellation rendered the book difficult to market and possibly offensive to sympathetic whites "who would prefer not to be reminded of the differences" between themselves and Nisei.[76] They proposed instead *A People of Two Worlds*, *The Trial by Fire*, *The Ordeal and the Triumph*, *A Matter of Race*, or *The Strength of Their Heritage*.[77] Hosokawa countered with his own suggestion, *Nisei: The Quiet Americans*, which by his own account, the editors immediately approved. "Both pointed out that such a good title will help the sale considerable [*sic*]. They said it is much more likely that a person will go into a bookstore and ask for 'The Quiet Americans'—there's a familiarity factor involved, too, with reference to 'The Ugly Americans'—than for 'Americans With Japanese Faces,'" he recounted.[78]

Shigeo Wakamatsu, chair of JACL's JARP Committee, decided to put the judgment to the test by conducting a "mini-mini-survey" at his workplace, a Chicago-area chemistry laboratory. He found that his coworkers generally preferred the new title, citing its "intrigue," although those from blue-collar backgrounds preferred Hosokawa's original choice "because it spelled out exactly what the book was about." Most important, *Nisei: The Quiet Americans* did not offend an African American colleague: "Our lab wit, a black chemist who did not object to the 'Quiet' as a possible implied unfavorable comparison to the demonstrating blacks, said: "'Quiet' is good here; it's an 'in' word now. 'Quiet means you don't hit a cop over the head with a brick.'"[79] Wakamatsu's annotation indicated that JACL leaders understood well the social capital of not-blackness.

The optimism of Hosokawa and Wakamatsu's reports belied the adverse reactions of many Japanese Americans. After learning of the selection, Edison Uno, a member of the league's San Francisco chapter, initiated a campaign to pressure William Morrow and Company to change the book's title because it propagated a "negative racial stereotype." Participants in JACL's civil rights workshop in Oakland, California, petitioned the organization's national board to reinstate *Americans with Japanese Faces*, while JACL's National Ethnic Concern Committee (founded in 1968 to improve relations between Nikkei and other minority groups) passed a resolution urging a general boycott of the book if the title was not replaced. Dissenters flooded the editorial offices with letters expressing their disgust. One indicted the title as a "propaganda device to tell Black Americans and Mexican Americans to behave like 'good little Orientals' who know their place." The debate raged in the *Pacific Citizen* for several months. Despite the fracas, Hosokawa, JACL, and William Morrow held steadfastly to their position. "I will not be intimidated by such threats," Hosokawa maintained, likening his opposition to fascist censors in Nazi Germany, wartime Japan, and Soviet Russia. Other defenders argued that the epithet served as a fitting tribute to the second generation's unique, culturally inflected style of tenacity, and that the word quiet did not necessarily denote passivity or submissiveness. The book's publication went ahead as planned.[80]

From the point of view of the league's "old guard"—those who had set the organization's postwar agenda at the national conference in 1946—*Nisei: The Quiet Americans* performed fabulously. Hosokawa's recovery narrative embraced the model minority image. The final section, for instance, observed that the legal, social, and economic obstacles once blocking Japanese American advancement had all but disappeared, as demonstrated by a laundry list of the winners and honorable mentions of JACL's "Nisei of the Biennium" award: Tomi Kanzawa (Metropolitan opera singer), Minoru Yamasaki (architect of the World Trade Center),

FIGURE 5.1 Mr. and Mrs. Bill Hosokawa at Kawafuku restaurant in Los Angeles' Little Tokyo, January 1970. Hosokawa's controversial book *Nisei: The Quiet Americans* rests on the table.
  Photograph by Toyo Miyatake Studio. Gift of the Alan Miyatake Family, Japanese American National Museum. 96.267.1118.

Tommy Kono (1952 and 1956 Olympic gold medalist), Congresswoman Patsy Takemoto Mink (D-HI), and dozens of other distinguished professionals. In the book's closing remarks, Hosokawa briefly meditated on how such feats had been achieved. "It is a question that has been given great pertinency by the often unproductive struggles of other minorities to win social respect and economic security. Looking on the extremes of apathy and militancy among Negroes and Hispanos, some Nisei from the comfort of their upper middle class homes have been led to ask: 'Why can't they pull themselves up by their own bootstraps the way we did?' " Citing Petersen's *New York Times Magazine* essay, Hosokawa proposed that the answer lay in Nisei's cultural heritage. Such an explanation made sense to many in his audience. Assessments commended Hosokawa's "splendid" synthesis of this "great American success story." The *Denver Post* raved, "At a time when other minorities are rushing through the streets with raised fists and crying out against discrimination and injustice, 'Nisei' is remedial reading for Americans of all colors and beliefs."[81]

Just as important, *Nisei: The Quiet Americans* also glorified JACL's "monumental role" in shepherding the community toward full citizenship, thereby fulfilling the league's mandate of self-promotion. The text noted the league's instrumentality in reopening the military to internees and thus the doors to acceptance as Americans of unquestioned national loyalty, while a chapter on "The Dedicated JACL-ers" accentuated their prime position in mediating between the community and the WRA, liberal allies, and racist foes to ensure resettlement's success.[82] Again the message resounded with readers. In a review for the *Chicago Tribune*, Mari Sabusawa Michener, wife of James Michener, observed that her generation had "achieved a voice in American life," and "spoke out for democracy and justice for all minorities" under the stewardship of Masaoka and the league. On the floor of the US Senate, Warren Magnuson accompanied his enthusiastic endorsement of the book with a special mention of JACL's role in "work[ing] quietly but effectively for equality of opportunity [and] citizenship." He appended a recitation of Masaoka's "Japanese American Creed," which he mistakenly and tellingly referred to as the "Japanese American Citizens League Creed." To JACL leaders, these highly public accolades were likely worth the expense of distributing hundreds of complimentary copies to opinion makers and political figures, including the president, vice president, the entire cabinet, all nine Supreme Court justices, and the 350 members of Congress who had Nikkei constituents.[83]

Within Japanese America, however, the book exacted a much higher cost. The issue at hand, as Uno asserted, was "not a mere controversy about a book title" but rather "the entire question as to the relevancy of the JACL to the Japanese American community," given its "authoritarianism" in handling the uproar.[84] In at least two Nikkei periodicals, Mary Tani objected to the "JACL 'powers' . . . purport[ing] to represent Americans of Japanese ancestry thus stereotyping all in the image of JACL" along with its undemocratic elision of Issei, female, and "non-JACLers" perspectives. To her, Hosokawa had acted hypocritically when he had refused to accommodate community demands to change the title on the grounds of principle, while at the same time he had bowed to editorial pressure to jettison *Americans with Japanese Faces*. Tani asked if this "double standard" was motivated by the "$royalties$" that JACL would "rake in" at the cost of "our detriment."[85]

The book's reception among Nikkei progressives betrayed the growing visibility of political fault lines within Japanese America, particularly a rejection of the league's assimilationism. Yuji Ichioka, the young founder of Berkeley's progressive Asian American Political Alliance, was most critical of JACL in his scathing review of *Nisei: The Quiet Americans* written for *Gidra*, a leftist Asian American newspaper. Describing the book as "filiopiestic" and "self-congratulatory," he noted its origins in JARP—a genealogy that "predetermined its content and theme." Ichioka faulted *Nisei: The Quiet Americans* for serving as a narrow paean to the league, rather than maintaining the broader focus as intimated by the book's second subtitle, "The Story of a People."[86]

The fundamental flaw that Ichioka found in the book was the argument that Japanese Americans had "made it" in US society. As a case in point, Ichioka cited at length the book's preface, contributed by former US ambassador to Japan Edwin O. Reischauer:

> No immigrant group encountered higher walls of prejudice and discrimination than did the Japanese. . . . None experienced a more dramatic crisis than they did when . . . one hundred thousand of them . . . were herded from the West Coast into what amounted to concentration camps. None retained greater faith in the basic ideals of America or showed stronger determination to establish their rights to full equality and justice, even when their fellow Americans seemed determined to deny them both. None showed greater loyalty to the United States or greater willingness to make sacrifices on the battlefield or at home for their country. The outcome, of course, has been the great American success story writ large—a Horatio Alger tale on an ethnic scale.[87]

Left untold in Hosokawa's narrative were the "possible psychological damages" inflicted by the internment and the grind of American racism. Ichioka warned that "Sansei should be particularly disturbed by this book," since "the clear implication for them is that they should be grateful." Profoundly disagreeing with JACL's unwavering Americanism, Ichioka observed that *Nisei: The Quiet Americans* appeared,

> ironically, at the very moment when Sansei activists are asking: what have we been integrating into? Into a nation conducting a politically and morally bankrupt war against Vietnamese people in the name of freedom and democracy? A nation bent upon exterminating militant Black leaders? A nation which is moving to the extreme right in the name of law and order? A nation in which the so-called "American Dream" has turned out to be a violent nightmare?

To him, Hosokawa's exaltation of the American dream did not accurately reflect the nation's reality of "racism, super-patriotism, and right-wing politics." Ichioka ultimately dismissed the volume as "an idealized monument to the old guard JACL leaders, justifying their existence and lifetime work." While he conceded that the league had served an "important" role in the past, he opined that *Nisei: The Quiet Americans* had no place in the present, because "old and new problems demand radical approaches, not tired orations." Thus, he concluded, "so having had their testament for posterity written, we bid the old guard to retire as 'quiet Americans.'"[88]

The success of the Japanese American success story was both blessing and curse for JACL. On the one hand, it vindicated the league's ideological underpinnings and assimilationist strategies dating back to the internment, and reaffirmed its status as the spokesorganization for all of Japanese America. On the other hand, JACL's triumphant narrative of recovery roused many Nikkei to criticize noisily the group's power and presumptions. The vocal challenges to *Nisei: The Quiet Americans* not only told of a wider dissatisfaction among Japanese Americans with the model minority pigeonholing but also gestured to alternative visions of community and identity bursting open in the late 1960s and early 1970s. And while JACL would never again experience the same level of organizational dominance that it had enjoyed in the mid-twentieth century, its rendition of Japanese American history would continue to have a lock on narrative representations of Nikkei for decades to come.

Chapter 6

Chinatown Offers Us a Lesson

Trouble punctuated two San Francisco Bay Area Chinese American youth gatherings in February 1949. The sudden appearance of a "gang" at a party hosted by San Mateo's Chinese Youth Organization sparked a melee as the group forced its way into the crowd. President Frank Lee reported being assaulted at knifepoint. The uninvited visitors fled the scene before police arrived. Just days later, a second fight erupted at the Oakland Rollerland Rink.[1]

The outbursts prompted a flood of responses from the ethnic community. The *Chinese Press* chided the instigators for "shatter[ing] in a day" the "goodwill" amassed by San Mateo's Chinese over the past two decades, setting back progress on the integration front. While the editors conceded that such "disturbances" were not unheard of within Chinese American circles, they stressed that the San Mateo affair had attracted more negative attention than ever before, with local newspapers running front-page stories detailing the affray. Action needed to be taken. "Remember that by racial and physical traits, we are easily tabbed as belonging to a minority group. We can be applauded for our achievements. And, conversely, every fault and unfavorable action on our part is magnified. One overt act such as that committed by the San Francisco gang besmirches everyone," they asserted. Comparing the situation to antiblack violence in the South and Los Angeles' zoot suit riots, the *Chinese Press* warned that "Chinatown would be a sorry place" if juvenile delinquency continued to proliferate. "Who is going to think about it, do something about it?" the editors asked. "The parents? The schools? The churches? The civic clubs and organizations? Collectively—the community? *There is a problem. What is the answer?*"[2]

Individual Chinese Americans echoed the concerns. Lee argued that the bunch had brought "disgrace and shame" to Chinatown, and that its actions "should not be tolerated." One onlooker to the Oakland clash advised immediate intervention by community organizations and even law enforcement. Another faulted Chinatown's elite for its neglect of the "less fortunate" and reminded it that class distinctions within the enclave carried little relevance in places where exclusionary forces remained intact: "No matter what they happen to be: a doctor, lawyer, cook, laundryman, beauty queen, etc. a restricted area bars them all regardless."[3]

Millions of Americans agonized over the issue of juvenile delinquency in the post–World War II era. Triggered by the social transformations of wartime, a national panic over a perceived escalation in youth criminality surfaced in the early 1940s, persisted after the cessation of hostilities, and ballooned well into the 1950s. Academic experts, government agencies, and civic associations fed the uproar by launching investigations and spearheading efforts to extinguish its causes and manifestations. The mass media and culture industry heightened anxieties, too, producing scores of articles, books, and films about this social "sickness."[4] Like nearly everyone else in the country, Chinese Americans worried that the currents of deviance were sweeping up their young.

For Chinese in the United States, the issue of juvenile delinquency became an important means through which to stipulate their race and citizenship imperatives after World War II. Chinatown leaders adopted a bifurcated strategy that reflected the ongoing tension between sameness and difference under racial liberalism. In one direction, community managers argued that juvenile delinquency was as much a problem for the Chinese as for other Americans. They stressed their right to state resources to stamp out youth crime as equal and deserving members of the polity.

But high-stakes political considerations, especially Red China's entry into the Korean War and the illegal immigration shakedown of the mid-1950s, ultimately steered Chinatown's custodians down an opposing path. As the nation scrambled to halt the spread of adolescent misconduct, a host of observers celebrated Chinatown as an exemplary enclave comprised of traditional households wherein errant youths simply did not exist.[5] These narratives enjoyed a broad appeal by resonating strongly with Cold War Americans' exaltation of the home as the preeminent site of defense against disorder, material excess, and Communist encroachment.[6] Recognizing the compelling connections between notions of family and ideals of citizenship at midcentury, Chinese American leaders shrewdly appropriated the trope of "nondelinquency" to advance their political, social, and economic interests. In lieu of attempting the Herculean, if not impossible, task of ridding themselves of racial difference, they opted to rewrite their dissimilarity from stigma to virtue. The move succeeded in large part because of its reliance on the valorization of rigidly defined, distinct social roles for males and females. As a constitutive element of racial liberalism, gender conservatism enabled the recasting of Chinese Americans from unassimilable aliens to respectable citizens worthy of emulation.[7]

The conceit of the meritorious Chinatown family constituted a fundamental precondition for the emergence of Chinese Americans as definitively not-black model minorities in the mid-1960s. As they did with

Japanese Americans, social commentators and policymakers depicted Chinese and African American households and communities as absolutely antipodal despite the congruence of their inner-city surroundings. In this way, Chinese Americans arrived at model minority status at the same moment as Nikkei in a parallel response to criticisms of liberalism's approach to race management. The narratives, however, were not interchangeable. Chinese American success stories instead complemented those of Japanese America: whereas Issei and Nisei were lauded for their collective recovery from internment's damages along with their move *away* from the Pacific coasts' Little Tokyos, the nondelinquency discourse underscored the exemplary conduct of Chinese *within* the urban enclave—more Other than assimilating. The dual trajectories of Japanese and Chinese in the United States (integrating versus not-integrating; middle class versus poor/working class), at once divergent but analogous, shored up the model minority's ability to suit an array of shifting political, social, and cultural imperatives. No matter the environment or context, the reconfigured, definitively not-black Asiatic, able to realize the gamut of achievement in American life, now loomed large on the nation's racial landscape.

Chinatown's Juvenile Delinquency Crisis

The San Mateo and Oakland incidents were but two episodes in what many Bay Area Chinese viewed as a youth crime wave. Ethnic media reported steadily on "hooligans" committing vandalism, robberies, petty theft, and assaults and wreaking havoc in the streets of Chinatown. By early 1950, the situation erupted into a full-blown "Punk War," with newspapers noting "gang warfare" at all hours. Area merchants attributed sizable income losses to the turmoil, complaining that rowdyism kept would-be tourists and Chinatown residents away from their businesses.[8] In the pages of the *Chinese Press*, which became a forum for public debate on "misguided youth," a consensus emerged that juvenile delinquency was a calamitous dilemma necessitating immediate consideration. Attributing the rise to families' "disharmonious interpersonal relations" and a dearth of educational and recreational opportunities, sociologist Rose Hum Lee charged families with the responsibility of guiding their young toward "wise use of leisure-time." She further advised San Franciscans to follow the lead of Chicago's Chinatown, where the owner of a vacant storefront had lent the space for use as a youth center—a successful effort that "broke up the 'gangs' and stopped anti-social behavior."[9] Others pressed the community to "improve" the neighborhood's social environment and utilize police more frequently as preventive measures.[10]

After yet another unpleasant encounter, this time between several "ruffians" and members of the Chinese Students Christian Association, one Berkeley resident railed, "We have fought so long for our freedoms and privileges as Chinese-Americans. Are we going to let some silly and sissy punks ruin all our efforts and degrade our people to a lowly, beastly level?" Chinatown's George Yip addressed the "punks" directly, emphasizing the fragility of the recent gains in Chinese America's social standing: "Are you, by your actions, going to dash all that pieces? . . . Society is now looking upon you for the next step. Will it be degradation or integration? Choose wisely for there is no in-between."[11]

Chinatown took action. At the urging of juvenile probation officer Lim P. Lee, residents organized their inaugural Youth Welfare Conference in cooperation with the San Francisco Coordinating Council for Youth Welfare. On June 11, 1949, eighty community leaders, social workers, religious figures, parents, teachers, and students convened at the American Legion Cathay Hall to discuss the roots of the crisis as well as policy recommendations to stem its tide. Speakers and panelists attributed the problem to a range of issues, from the "deterioration" of the home resulting from the waning influence of the church on family life to the alienation of Chinese American minors from both "old Chinese culture" and "true American culture."[12] Discussants also identified the postwar recession as a significant factor, contending that families could no longer provide their children with pocket money, as was the case during the wartime boom. Budgetary constraints coupled with "loose discipline" impelled young people to "secure their needs" through illicit means. And with the recent arrival of war brides and children from China, the neighborhood's social service providers were stretched thin and unable to assist their clientele effectively.[13]

The proposed antidotes were manifold. Participants agreed that Chinatown needed more recreational outlets and "wholesome opportunities." Other suggestions included continuing enrollment in Chinese schools to instill old-world values in children, the improvement of vocational guidance and in-school counseling, aggressive community outreach by religious institutions, and stronger ties between the police department's juvenile bureau and Chinatown squad. Attendees also advocated the creation of more foster homes to care for "abandoned and neglected" Chinese children thought to be at risk of engaging in delinquent behavior, and the establishment of a coordinating body to provide "greater coverage and better efficiency" for youth-targeted social services.[14] On this last point, the conferees followed through by having Chinatown join the Central District Neighborhood Youth Council, an arm of the greater San Francisco Youth Council, which aimed to curb juvenile delinquency throughout the city. With Lim P. Lee on board as the newly elected chair, the Central District Neighborhood Youth Council organized a second Chinatown Youth Welfare Conference in June 1950.[15] In an open invitation to the community to attend the meeting, Lee insisted, "Juvenile delinquency is a social pathology, and it is . . . growing in our community. It will take the combined efforts of all interested individuals . . . to arrive at a workable solution."[16]

Other community initiatives took root as well. The Lee Family Association, the mutual aid organization for area Chinese sharing the Lee surname, opened a youth center stocked with a library, ping-pong tables, and a television to entice its junior members. The group also planned educational programs, athletics, and dancing "to give the young people interests other than roaming around."[17]

These measures were actually a continuation of Chinese Americans' earlier attempts to construct juvenile delinquency as a Chinatown problem demanding civic acknowledgment. The most urgent was the wartime plea for more playground space to accommodate the enclave's dense population. Existing options were scarce. In the 1930s and early 1940s, Chinatown had only three private recreation facilities (the YWCA, YMCA, and Chinese Catholic Center) and a lone public alternative (the Chinese Playground, built in 1927) for its 6,000 children. Moved by these inadequacies, the community rallied to address youths' needs. Some 2,500 residents petitioned San Francisco's Board of Education, Recreation Commission, and Mayor Angelo Rossi in March 1941 to purchase land adjacent to Commodore Stockton Elementary School to better serve its 950 students. Existing playgrounds were simply "inadequate." Given Chinatown's "sub-standard" housing, children spent much of their time outdoors. But with the dearth of public parks and private yards, little ones took to the congested, unsafe streets. Worried parents did not have the means to change the situation; a "large proportion" of mothers worked outside the home and therefore were unable to provide "adequate" after-school "supervision." Without more options for their "dead end kids," the signatories argued, Chinatown's present problems—especially rampant tuberculosis and a recent surge in juvenile delinquency—would only get worse. The same month, Commodore Stockton principal Susie J. Convery along with other community leaders spearheaded the formation of the Chinatown Improvement Association and made the playground their top priority. To their elation, the drive succeeded: in April 1942, the Board of Education purchased the lot, along with a second nearby plot and developed plans for construction.[18]

After World War II, the determination to upgrade Chinatown's recreational options picked up momentum as Chinese Americans fastened their entitlement claims to the postwar juvenile delinquency scare. Undoubtedly emboldened by their military service, home front contributions, and the nation's wartime acknowledgment of their citizenship, Chinatown amplified its request for play space.[19] The passage of a citywide referendum in November 1947 authorizing the sale of bonds to fund recreation facilities provided a timely rallying point. In a guest column for the *San Francisco Chronicle*, Lim P. Lee (himself a veteran and commander of the American Legion Cathay Post) declared that Chinatown, harboring a "new civic consciousness," was "taking stock of its own youth problem" much like everyone else. He noted that myriad community groups (the CCBA, Chinese Chamber of Commerce, Chinatown YMCA and YWCA, Chinese radio station, and neighborhood publishing ventures) had joined forces to collect 4,059 signatures to petition the Board of Supervisors to erect a new recreation facility to "prevent the growth of this social problem." This was a deplorable situation, he added, given that the Chinese Playground, barely a quarter-acre in size, saw nearly 3,000 children weekly. In other words, Lee suggested that the experience of confronting juvenile delinquency reinforced Chinese Americans' sense of belonging to the municipality—no less than being an "integral part of this city's life"—and that this attachment, in turn, proved Chinatown's deservedness of communal funding.[20]

The connection between juvenile delinquency and citizenship reverberated throughout the campaign. In a plea to the San Francisco Board of Education to back the recreation center campaign, Henry S. Louie, chair of the Chinese YMCA's Public Affairs Committee, stressed that the thousands endorsing the project were "vitally interested citizens" as well as "registered and qualified voters" confident that the facility would yield "healthier children" and "less juvenile delinquency."[21] Such arguments sufficiently moved the city's decision makers, who allotted $417,000 for the building and grounds.[22] On November 4, 1951, the Chinese Recreation Center, boasting an array of amenities for all ages, opened its doors at the corner of Washington and Mason streets in Chinatown. Echoing the sentiments of the many who had fought for the space by mobilizing the specter of delinquency, Mayor Robinson affirmed, "The opening of the Chinese Recreation Center has particular significance for parents who are faced with the problem of raising healthy children in one of San Francisco's most congested neighborhoods."[23] Community organizers met similar successes in fighting for the inclusion of playground space in the new Ping Yuen public housing projects as well as the landscaping of Portsmouth Square with sandboxes, slides, swings, and benches.[24]

Chinatown leaders were dismayed to witness that even with the addition of such facilities, misbehaviors remained a visible irritant. In June 1952, twenty boys repeatedly vandalized Commodore Stockton School with BB guns, pipes, knives, and bayonets over a two-week span until caught in the act by plainclothes officers—a scene deplored by the *Chinese*

Pacific Weekly as "one of the worst outbreaks of juvenile delinquency in this community." Contending that parents were ultimately responsible for the actions of their children, CCBA president Robert S. Lee called on educators and public agencies to encourage mothers and fathers to "pay more attention to their children." Chester Fong, youth director of Chinatown's social service agency Cameron House, prodded Chinese schools to redouble their efforts to discipline students. He also asked social workers to "teach older boys to go among the delinquents and be their friends and try to influence them into the better ways of life." Bewailing the "decline of law and order in Chinatown," *Chinese World* editor Dai-ming Lee reiterated the need for sound parental upbringing, community guidance, and appropriate recreational programs to foster the moral training necessary for "self-improvement" plus solid citizenship.[25]

Observers pointed to the children of new immigrant families as a segment of the youth population requiring special monitoring. Both the *Chinese Pacific Weekly* and *Chinese World* reported that the Commodore Stockton incident had involved a fight between "China-borns" and "America-borns." Addressing the Clay Street YWCA Human Relations Forum just days after the episode, Lim P. Lee advised that the postwar boom in San Francisco's Chinese American population might lead to even more serious problems without preemptive measures. Foreign-born youngsters felt alienated from both Chinese Americans and "Caucasians," he noted. Unless agency workers and Chinatown's elite intervened, the "China-born will be exploited by the anti-social organizations or by the subversive groups in the community," he warned. Lee insisted that the skirmish was "not an isolated incident" and that Chinatown must assist the newcomers in the difficult process of "Americanization."[26] The San Francisco Youth Council responded with expanded outreach to this constituency, and the local Columbia Foundation followed suit by funding a study intended to assist the youths' "adjustment."[27] But the desired results might take months, if not years, to effect. Thus, anticipating a continuing surge in new arrivals alongside the maturation of established families, Rose Hum Lee wondered, "Will the next decade see an increase in delinquent, neglected, and dependent Chinese children?"[28]

Keeping Up with the Wongs, Lees, and Engs

Liberal allies of the Chinese, journalists, social scientists, policymakers, and Chinese Americans of influence would likely have answered "no" to Lee's query. These were the people who took part in a national conversation about the nondelinquency of Chinese American youths that emerged in the late 1930s and peaked in the mid- to late 1950s. The discussions encompassed a deluge of representations of Chinatown as an idyllic community comprised of harmonious households that tumbled forth from mainstream periodicals, academic publications, and other outlets. A reading of the nondelinquency exchange reveals that the sundry texts enumerated the same key "facts," themes, and arguments: the seeming contradiction of Chinatown as a ghetto and unblemished record of its youthful denizens; the central role of family and culture in averting waywardness; and the exhortation that Americans "try keeping up the Wongs, Lees, and Engs."[29]

For decades, Chinese in the United States had recognized the impact of criminality on the ways in which they were perceived and treated by authorities and ordinary Americans. As a means of buttressing calls for more stringent immigration enforcement during the Exclusion era, the popular press disseminated sensationalized images of duplicitous Chinese hordes unlawfully entering the country. Chinatowns embodied deviance in the public imagination, the spatial reification of the scientific and common regard of Chinese as naturally inclined to vice, immorality, squalor, disease, and general debasement. The vitality of gambling, prostitution, and opium consumption (industries that catered to non-Chinese as much as they did to Cantonese migrants) reinforced these assumptions, as did the overwhelmingly male gender ratio of Chinese America. The sum of these impressions rationalized the social and political marginalization of Chinese in United States in the late nineteenth and early twentieth centuries.[30]

In attempts to gain both social recognition and political privileges as bona fide citizens, Chinese Americans and their partisans struggled to upend unflattering depictions of Chinatown as a morally suspect "bachelor society." Children and family life were central to these efforts. Around the turn of the twentieth century, immigrant leaders, missionaries, and teachers proclaimed Chinese American schoolchildren as intelligent, respectful, and eager to learn—even preferable to white students—as a way to neutralize anti-Chinese hostility. As the demographics of Chinese America shifted by the 1920s and 1930s with the coming-of-age of the first sizable US-born cohort, community advocates increasingly touted the Americanization of Chinese youths as proof of their assimilability. Reformers and activists, moreover, devoted their energies to cultivating conventional gender roles and heterosexual behaviors among Chinatown residents. San Francisco's Chinese American social workers taught their coethnics white, middle-class standards of parenting, housekeeping, and hygiene as part of a larger project of demonstrating their collective respectability as well as fitness for civic membership. In the process, they effectively reconstructed the local image of the community as one populated by sympathetic, properly Americanizing nuclear families.

Chinatown leaders keenly understood the durable connections between virtuous conduct, normative domesticity, and access to the benefits of citizenship.[31]

By the mid- to late 1930s, new conceptions of Chinese American family life began to circulate extensively. Expatriate scholar Lin Yutang's best-selling *My Country and My People* (1935), an interpretation of Chinese culture for Western audiences, described China's family system as the mechanism that instilled in all "the necessity of mutual adjustment, self-control, courtesy, a sense of duty . . . a sense of obligation and gratitude toward parents, and respect for elders."[32] Social scientists observed that the dearth of juvenile delinquency in China, a product of the "tradition of filial piety," had carried over to diasporic nodes in the United States, where tight-knit families along with "the desire to maintain a good reputation in the American community" accounted for both its depressed rates and the "triviality" of most offenses.[33] Their findings entered popular consciousness through the writings of Carl Glick, the Iowa-born author whose love affair with the Chinese grew out of a brief stint as athletic director for New York Chinatown's Church of All Nations in the early 1930s. Glick's *Reader's Digest* essay "As the Chinese Twig Is Bent" (1938) and its radio adaptation for the US Office of Education's series *Americans All, Immigrants All*, introduced millions of Americans to Eddie Wu, a twelve-year old boy whose classroom antics had prompted a scolding from his teacher. Mortified, Wu skipped school for a week before New York City police found and delivered him to the Children's Court—the first truant Chinese in twenty-three years to appear before the bench. His father pleaded with the judge, "Honorable sir, upon my own ill-mannered self is the blame for my son's misdeeds. I have not properly instructed him in the virtues of scholarship. Therefore sentence *me* to prison. I have lost much face." The astonished judge merely suspended little Eddie's sentence. The elder Wu, however, meted out his own punishment: he refused to speak to his son for two months, confiscated his toys, and grounded him.[34]

Mr. Wu's actions were not at all unusual for his compatriots, Glick promised. In the event of a son's waywardness, the Chinese blamed the father. The patriarch, in turn, lost face (suffered disgrace and humiliation) among family members, friends, and even business associates. But such cases were extremely rare, as "filial piety" was instilled in children from infancy. Furthermore, Chinese children simply had no time to get into mischief. They spent most of their waking hours learning: after a full day at an "American" school, they continued with Chinese instruction, where they were taught history, language, and the moral precepts of Confucius, reinforcing the "respect for the parent and the law" emphasized at home. With all these factors complementing one another, juvenile delinquency was "practically nonexistent" within the Chinese communities of New York City, Boston, New Orleans, Chicago, Los Angeles, and remarkably, San Francisco.[35]

Smitten with his subjects, Glick elaborated on his observations in *Shake Hands with the Dragon* (1941), a handbook to Chinese America for armchair cosmopolitans. The book and its abridged version, also published in *Reader's Digest*, spotlighted the facets of Chinese American culture that made the community inimitably admirable. The bedrock of this uniqueness was the Chinese family, a hierarchical, gendered system of obligation that rewarded compliance with order and security. The absence of juvenile delinquency and crime more generally was but one manifestation. Citing the records of the New York Police Department, Glick pointed out that only 1 Chinese child out of over 500 in the city's Fifth Precinct was arrested in 1936, compared to 275 the same year in the Twenty-Eighth Precinct (Harlem). The rarity of divorce, despite the practice of arranged marriage, was another example. The habit of borrowing money from relatives to raise the necessary start-up capital for new businesses and hiring *hing dai* (cousins) as employees, rendered unions—and therefore labor strikes—unnecessary. (Glick erroneously stated that there had only ever been one single incidence of work stoppage in the history of the Chinese in the United States.) And of perhaps most interest to a nation just beginning to rebound from the ravages of the Great Depression was Chinese America's proven ability to "solve the question of social security" through its Kung Saw, the family associations that provided indigent members with food, lodging, and work. The Chinese were "the one group of so-called foreigners" that did not "burden" the federal government in the 1930s. Glick would later rehearse these claims in his 1943 sequel *Three Times I Bow*.[36]

Glick crafted this string of flattering appraisals with the intent to render the inscrutable scrutable. He neutralized Chinese difference, recasting beliefs and practices once assumed to be strange and vile into innocuous novelties, if not useful treasures. Chinese ways, he avowed, need not remain perpetually foreign but instead might even benefit the nation, as his subjects modeled solutions to society's most perplexing issues. *Shake Hands with the Dragon* thus was an assertion of Chinese Americans' national belonging that fell squarely into racial liberalism's cultural pluralist camp. The book emphasized that Chinese divergences from mainstream society did not undermine assimilation, as demonstrated by the hundreds of Chinese American men lining up to enlist for the army. As Eddie Wu, now grown, proclaimed, "We Chinese are ready to do our part. We are American citizens . . . we want to do our share in making democracy work."[37]

The book's various contentions reappeared in venues that more explicitly championed the overturning of the legal barriers to Chinese immigration, naturalization, and unbridled social participation. Glick, in
fact, was an executive committee member of the Citizens Committee to
Repeal Chinese Exclusion (CCRCE) and assisted in producing its campaign materials. "Our Chinese Wall," one of the CCRCE's pamphlets,
underscored the dearth of juvenile delinquency and crime in Chinatown.
"Our Chinese friends . . . are a law-abiding, peace-loving, courteous people living quietly among us. . . . That they make good citizens, there is no
doubt. They believe in democracy. They want to be a part of this great
country, where all men are free and equal," he wrote. Pearl Buck reiterated his characterizations during the congressional hearings on repeal:
"The Chinese we have here are among our best citizens—they do not go
on relief; their crime record is very low; they are honest and industrious
and friendly."[38]

If the impulse behind *Shake Hands with the Dragon* can be traced to
the rise of racial liberalism and move to repeal Chinese Exclusion, the
longevity of its arguments can be explained by the national mania about
juvenile delinquency at midcentury. After 1941, many Americans feared
that the dislocations of the war mobilization, including mass migration,
the expansion of the defense industry, and increasing numbers of women
in the workplace, had provoked a jump in the frequency of youth mis-
behavior. Anxious to quash the trend, commentators grabbed on to the
notion of nondelinquency and plugged Chinese American family life as
a guide for the nation.[39] *Life* (1946) revisited the story of Eddie Wu to
emphasize the fundamental role of parental responsibility in thwarting
misconduct. Postwar child-rearing manuals and civics textbooks, citing
Glick, likewise upheld Chinese children ("famous for their good behavior") as keys to stamping out the crisis.[40]

Firsthand accounts of Chinese American home dynamics reinforced
these observations with the authority of native informants. Pardee Lowe's
memoir, *Father and Glorious Descendant* (1943), recounted his strict
Confucian upbringing: "[Mother] knew only too well how to wield the
wrong end of a pliant Chinese feather bamboo duster. With this Rod of
Purification she directed our lives, and we became, as our Chinese friends
put it, 'model children who had partaken generously of paternal instruction.' "[41] In Jade Snow Wong's *Fifth Chinese Daughter* (1950), "open re-
bellion" against the protagonist's elders meant an unchaperoned date,
the pursuit of a college education, and the founding of an independent
business—rarities, to be sure, for young Chinese American women of the
day, but certainly a far cry from the typical renderings of youth defiance.[42]
The selection of Maine's Toy Len Goon as the Golden Rule Foundation's

American Mother of the Year in 1952—entailing, among other honors, a trip to the White House to meet First Lady Bess Truman—undeniably buoyed the trope of the exemplary Chinese family as well.[43]

Postwar demographic changes also made it possible to spread the non-delinquency discourse. The repeal of the Chinese Exclusion Acts (1943), an amendment to the 1945 War Brides Act (1946), and the passage of the Displaced Persons Act (1948) and Refugee Relief Act (1953) permitted the entry of over sixteen thousand Chinese women to the United States between 1945 and 1952. The legislation accelerated Chinatown's metamorphosis from a homosocial "bachelor society" to one increasingly populated by conventional nuclear households. These reforms, while not directly causal, likely influenced the general public's perceptions of Chinese Americans even as the community worried about the problems accompanying the sudden influx of "China-born" youths.[44] The synergy of these immigration flows, the mounting dread of incorrigible youths, and high-profile narratives of Chinese American family life, then, primed the idea of nondelinquency to mushroom during the peak of the national panic in the mid- to late 1950s.

Glick's narrative framed these newer iterations. As in *Shake Hands with the Dragon*, the postwar accounts verified that Chinese Americans were a people sans delinquency by furnishing statistical evidence—or more commonly, a lack thereof. At the height of the Chinatown crime wave, the *San Francisco Chronicle* reported that city police were relatively unconcerned, given that only 84 out of 1,450 youth arrests in 1949 were teens of Chinese ancestry. Officers noted the occasional loitering and petty theft, but "aside from an affinity for firecrackers on special occasions," Chinese Americans were "generally law abiding." The *Saturday Evening Post* relayed the tale of a New York judge who swore that not once in seventeen years had he tried a Chinese American minor, and that a survey of his associates throughout the boroughs as well as in San Francisco and Chicago revealed that they, too, had similar (non)experiences. The *New York Post*'s weeklong series on the transformation of Manhattan Chinatown from "problem" community to beau ideal reported that only 9 of the 7,700 delinquents processed by the municipal Children's Court that year were of Chinese ancestry. *Look* marveled that "troublemaking" among New York's Chinese American youths was "so low that the police don't even bother to keep figures on it," while the *Christian Science Monitor* postulated the same for Boston's Chinatown, citing a community leader who vouched, "Never in my 40 years have I ever seen one proven case of juvenile delinquency."[45] Indeed, such proclamations constituted a significant component of evolving representations of Chinatown freed from the evils of its sordid past: opium dens, tong wars, and so forth.[46] The disbanding of San Francisco's 80-year-old Chinatown Squad, the unit of the city's police department charged with handling the Chinese sector, offered further proof that "law and order . . . had triumphed."[47]

The FBI's *Uniform Crime Reports*, annual compilations of data on adult arrests nationwide, seemed to confirm these claims. In 1941, for example, police apprehended 775 Chinese, accounting for a mere 0.00123 percent of all cases. (Of all other races, only Japanese had fewer numbers at 570.) By 1954, the numbers had dropped even lower, with only 363 Chinese arrests, or 0.000215 percent of the total. (Again, Japanese were the lone group with a lower count at 194.) These were direct, if submerged, contrasts to the construction of black criminality through the manipulation of statistical information, foreshadowing the obvious comparisons that would be made in the following decade.[48]

Significantly, nondelinquency examinations focused on the ethnic enclave, suggesting that Chinatown living curbed juvenile delinquency. When the *New York Times Magazine* noted that only 7 out of the 8,714 New Yorkers under age 16 apprehended in 1956 were of Chinese descent—it stressed that they were not "Chinatown Chinese" but rather "boys who lived elsewhere" and likely subjected to the influence of "non-Chinese groups." To the reading public, well versed in the association between urban life, criminality, and color, this finding must have seemed curiously counterintuitive; as one *Washington Post* reader exclaimed, "Sociologists report that the Chinese ghettos of several large West Coast cities are as deplorable as other slums in any large city. The sociologists also tell us that such blighted areas are breeding places for crime. Yet criminologists and sociologists find the incidence of juvenile delinquency among Chinese-Americans in these areas is almost negligible!" Such characterizations effectively de-ghettoized Chinatowns by marking their exceptionalism and divergence from other inner-city minority areas. And by eliding the histories of Chinatowns as products of racial segregation, these omissions dampened contemporary attempts by liberals, civil rights activists, and aspiring minority homeowners to speed the integration of traditionally white residential areas.[49]

Following further in Glick's footsteps, the texts explained the ways in which Chinatown ably prevented the straying of its young. The dual, interrelated theses of family and culture stood at the core of the updated accounts. Family relations, order, and stability were the paramount reasons given for the success of the Chinese in curtailing wrongdoing—arguments that buttressed Cold War domestic ideology. *Coronet* noted that parents and children demonstrated mutual respect for one another, addressing each other at all times with "extreme courtesy" and using honorific titles that underscored each individual's position in the family hierarchy.

Likewise, the *New York Times Magazine* emphasized that Chinese sons and daughters displayed "unquestioned obedience" toward their elders. Children who attempted to defy their parents' authority, according to the *Washington Post*, were simply unsuccessful.[50]

What accounted for the compliance of Chinese American children to parental expectations? The oft-repeated answer to this question, made famous by Glick, was the threat of losing the family's face. Depictions of this self-policing system highlighted the crucial role of family in maintaining social order—a response to the agonizing that the postwar increase in juvenile delinquency was symptomatic of breakdowns in the family unit. Several articles included the explication delivered by Chinese consul P. H. Chang: "Filial piety, the love for parents, is a cardinal virtue my people have brought over from the China that was once free. A Chinese child, no matter where he lives, is brought up to recognize that he cannot shame his parents. . . . Before a Chinese child makes a move, he stops to think what the reactions on his parents will be. Will they be proud or will they be ashamed? Above all other things, the Chinese teen-ager is anxious to please his parents before he pleases himself." As the authors quickly pointed out, the word family for Chinese Americans meant not only the nuclear household but also the extended "clan"—any and all Chinese sharing a surname. Thus a miscreant committing a delinquent act would lose not only their parents' face but the honor of the hundreds, if not thousands, of "cousins" residing in the vicinity as well. Embarrassing the clan, reported *Coronet*, could result in one's ostracization and exclusion from business dealings and other ties. This situation seldom arose, however, given that all of Chinatown was "related in one way or another"—a kin network that deterred the "growth of rival gangs."[51]

A major component of the family thesis was that of stability grounded in a strict gendered order. These representations reproached women who rejected homemaking as their sole or primary occupation by insinuating that mothers who worked outside the home were essentially to blame for delinquent children. The *New York Post* cited the principal of Chinatown's P.S. 130, who observed that Chinese mothers "don't go out to work as much as others." Likewise, the *New York Times Magazine* attributed the stellar record of Chinese American youths to the "sharp division of responsibilities between the male and female"; from their earliest days, boys were socialized toward "breadwinning," while girls were steered toward "homemaking." These statements suggest that the nondelinquency discourse came into its greatest vogue in the mid-1950s by speaking to Cold War Americans' visions of the ideal home, predicated on the gendered division of labor, and serving as a bastion of security from the dangers and uncertainties of an outside world fraught with geopolitical tensions.[52]

In actuality, most Chinatown families of the 1950s lived far outside the parameters of this paradigm. Not only were they neither white, middle class, nor suburban dwellers—the archetypal postwar American family— but many husbands, wives, and even children labored side by side in the commercial niches to which Chinese in the United States had long been confined, particularly restaurants and hand laundries. In New York City, the postwar wave of immigrant Chinese women found employment in the burgeoning Chinatown garment industry. Because families that owned laundries frequently lived on the shop premises, and garment work could at times be completed at home, it is possible that Chinese mothers stayed home more than other American women, but only because Chinatown households often blurred distinctions between the workplace and domestic sphere. Nondelinquency discourse obfuscated the material realities of working-class Chinese Americans.[53]

Blind to (or perhaps purposefully ignoring) such realities, the media instead touted the myriad benefits of Chinese American family life, obscuring both the community's contemporary socioeconomic struggles and historical exclusions. In addition to the nonappearance of juvenile delinquency, reporters noted that Chinatown residents rarely suffered from divorce—a claim belying the domestic discord experienced by the many husbands and wives who vented their frustrations in the pages of Chinese community newspapers.[54] Another popular contention (again, echoing Glick) was that Chinese Americans enjoyed "excellent" physical, mental, and even financial health. A common corollary to the nondelinquency discussion was the allegation that few, if any, Chinese received state welfare payments, since they "look after their own." In an anecdote lifted straight from *Shake Hands with the Dragon*, *Coronet* harkened back to the Depression, recalling that of the ten thousand residents of New York's Chinatown, only seven had been on the relief rolls—and three of them were actually Koreans. What *Coronet* and others failed to mention was that many Chinese were barred from this form of aid, since US citizenship frequently was a necessary precondition for eligibility and Chinese were excluded from naturalized citizenship before 1943. American-born Chinese had actually fought hard to convince government agencies of their deservedness of civic aid, and officials had grudgingly granted them access to subsidized food, emergency shelter, and unemployment compensation only after sustained pressure. Even then, Chinese Americans were shut out from such choice resources as skilled Works Progress Administration positions and high-priority public housing construction.[55]

In conjunction with family, culture played an equally prominent role in these exegeses of Chinese American behavior. Chinese reverence for education meant that Chinatown's youths focused on learning and other constructive pursuits, seemingly impervious to the temptations of teen culture. The principal of Manhattan's P.S. 23 avowed to the *New York Post* that her Chinese students never defaced school property, but if one were to do so, "50 children would report it right away and would form a squad to clean it up." *Look* portrayed seventeen-year-old Wilbert Din, the subject of its photo essay "Americans without a Delinquency Problem" as the prototypical Asian nerd: "Unlike delinquents, who seem to hate to study, Wilbert regards books as his friends. He knows that studying now secures his life for the future." The daily routines of Chinatown's young, including after-school Chinese classes, left little opportunity for misdoing. Any free moments that they did have were spent in activities sponsored by churches, Scouts, and athletic teams, or enjoying meals with their families. Chinese American minors did not waste as much time on dances or movies as their "Occidental contemporaries"—a particularly salient point given prevailing beliefs that the spread of mass consumer culture was much at fault for the spike in juvenile delinquency. The rising generation, like the one before it, possessed a "high moral sense" rather than "cheap, get-rich-quick values" that led to sketchy methods of satiating material desires. Just as important, it rejected drinking and gambling, and harbored "an almost Victorian modesty"—a direct nod to the contemporary nervousness about the links between liberalization of social attitudes and sexual mores and the upswing in youth criminality.[56]

While the flurry of nondelinquency discussion in the postwar era closely resembled Glick's earlier portrait in many ways, an explicitly anti-Communist bent distinguished the 1950s' version from its predecessor. The logic went like this: because Chinese-Confucian tradition directly molded Chinese American ethical sensibilities, the implications of this legacy were important not only for maintaining order among Chinese Americans in the United States but also for America's worldwide battle against Communism. As *Coronet*, quoting Confucius, proclaimed, "When the heart is set right, then the personal life is cultivated; when the personal life is cultivated, then the family life is regulated; when the family life is regulated, then the national life is orderly; and when the national life is orderly, then there is peace in this world." American Chinatowns remained some of the few repositories of "venerable Chinese family tradition" with the victory of the Red Chinese. Mourning this loss, the *Saturday Evening Post* remarked, "More the pity that the 'new China,' in seeking to modernize itself, has felt it necessary to spur this tradition so that, as a Chinese official in their country declared 'for the first time in the history of my country there are tens of thousands of "wild boys" of the road at large.' " In other words, only disciplined and orderly families, as exemplified by Chinese Americans, could ensure secure and stable nations. By destroying this traditional structure, Communism

FIGURE 6.1 *Look* magazine's photo essay "Americans without a Delinquency Problem" (1958) praised the upstanding behavior of Chinese teenagers such as Wilbert Din of New York: "Unlike delinquents, who seem to hate to study, Wilbert regards books as his friends. He knows that studying now secures his life for the future."

Photograph by John Vachon. Courtesy of the *Look* Magazine Photograph Collection, Library of Congress, Prints and Photographs Division. LC-L9-58-7695-FF #18.

in China—and by extrapolation, all other countries behind the iron curtain—fueled chaos and confusion.[57]

It was through the nondelinquency conversations of the 1950s, then, that Chinese Americans came to be seen anew as living within model families and communities—a sentiment succinctly encapsulated by the *New York Times Magazine* headline "Chinatown Offers Us a Lesson." The spread of this racial common sense might be gauged by its appearance in the era's behavioral science scholarship, presence in political discussions, and responses articulated by members of the general public. Not a few social investigators subscribed to this thinking.[58] Nondelinquency narratives stirred public officials as well. Michigan representative Clare E. Hoffman read the *Saturday Evening Post* editorial on the House floor, indicating that the Chinese might inspire a remedy for the crisis. Not to be outdone, his colleague Arthur G. Klein submitted the entire *New York Post* series for reprinting in the *Congressional Record*. Klein praised his New York Chinatown constituents for their "way of life that deserves to be known, applauded, and emulated," including "respect for parents and teachers" as well as a "stable and loving home life," a thirst for education, and "peaceful readjustment"—perhaps meant as an implicit contrast to African American civil rights activists. Individuals around the country, too, reacted to media reports with great enthusiasm. A Wyoming educator, for example, praised *Look* for its feature and suggested that reprints be distributed in "all" high schools, while a *Chicago Daily Tribune* reader proposed that the city thoroughly probe Chinese American family life to spark "workable solutions."[59]

Social science interviews with forty-two young Chinese Californians confirmed the toehold that these representations had gained in the public consciousness. When asked if they felt Chinese Americans to be "more law abiding than any other nationality in your community," half of the group answered in the affirmative. In response to the follow-up question, "How do you know this to be true?" eight youths explained that they had read about it in textbooks, five had seen it in newspapers, two had white friends who had verified this claim, and one had learned of the idea in a speech made by a high school principal. The nondelinquency conversation had reached such a level of visibility that it had traveled full circle back to its young subjects.[60]

Milking Nondelinquency

The explosion of the nondelinquency discourse graphically illustrated the power of representations of children and families to refashion the racialization of Chinese Americans. Like other minority elites, Chinatown leaders had tried for years to harness this power to the community's advantage. At key moments they had also feared its detrimental effects, as during the Bay Area juvenile "crime wave" of the late 1940s and early 1950s. Then, *Chinese World* editor Dai-ming Lee had feared that the unsavory actions of errant boys marred the "good name of the Chinese and Chinatown," and threatened to undo the "considerable effort" by residents to remake the quarter into a major leisure destination. But much more was at issue than simply the tourist dollar: they put all Chinese in the United States at further risk in the wake of the People's Republic of China's intervention in the Korean War. "There is danger of Chinese being misunderstood and being subjected to extraordinary discrimination," Lee advised. "In our relations with other races we must be extremely courteous. And if we would best demonstrate our loyalty to this country we had better exhibit a law-abiding spirit." For Lee, this was crucial to placing Chinese American social standing on sure footing. By purging juvenile delinquency from its midst, Chinese America might serve as an example for the rest of the nation and therefore earn recognition of its deservedness of full equality. "If we give the police the cooperation they seek," he urged, "hoodlumism can be eliminated and Chinatown can be made a truly model area."[61]

Lee's prescription augured the Chinatown elite's embrace of the nondelinquency concept as a means to advance their citizenship goals and other agendas at the national, state, and local levels in the mid-1950s. Rather than continuing to frame juvenile delinquency as a Chinese American problem demanding civic redress, ethnic leaders inverted their previous strategy. Encouraged by the public's proven interest in the phenomenon of nondelinquency, they likely did so out of caution: decoupling Chineseness from crime almost certainly seemed a safer bet than the inverse, as Lee had illuminated in his *Chinese World* editorials.

The illegal immigration crisis of early 1956 clarified the stakes of this decision. With all Chinese Americans, irrespective of class or ideological persuasion, criminalized by the blanket subpoenas and federal grand jury investigations, San Francisco's CCBA moved to shore up the public reputation of the community. The association hired Howard Freeman, a local public relations specialist, to join veteran journalist Charles Leong to coordinate the endeavor. Freeman instructed the CCBA not to air its immigration-related concerns among outsiders; rather, the "considerable problem[s]" were to be managed within the confines of the ethnic community. He and Leong thus devised a blueprint for a comprehensive media publicity blitz, divided into three main categories: "Primary" or "Must-Do," "Desirable" or "Long-Range," and "Projects Presently in Progress." Among their primary proposals was a plan to sway influential figures toward "pro-Chinese attitude[s]" by hosting social events for William Randolph Hearst and other prominent publishers. They also recommended providing *Reader's Digest* (which, they noted, had the largest circulation of any magazine in the world) with material for a "positive" look at Chinese America. Another idea was an internal educational program for young Chinese Americans—those most likely to interact with whites—to inculcate them with "the story we are attempting to tell." Long-range goals included assembling a speakers bureau, the establishment of a Chinese American historical society, cooperation with other minority groups for mutual betterment, and the cultivation of non-Chinese sponsorship of Chinatown's athletic teams.[62]

The duo astutely grasped the utility of the notion of the spotless Chinese household for their mission. Freeman had rushed to incorporate the concept into a press release prepared for the launching of the CCBA's protest against the Department of Justice. "For over a hundred years, beginning with the historic Gold Rush of 1849, the Chinese in America, headquartered in San Francisco, have been responsible, law-abiding citizens who have contributed greatly to the growth of this country, and especially the West Coast. . . . The family is the foundation and strength of the social system of the Chinese people," the statement declared.[63] By June, one of their projects in progress was a feature "WHY CHINESE DO NOT HAVE JUVENILE DELINQUENTS," to be published in *Woman's Home Companion* as a way "to reach a wide reaching audience with a constructive article underscoring the *family system* and its benefits, and painting an extremely favorable picture of the Chinese-American people." The deliberate emphasis on the Chinese family system's ability to provide a fail-safe defense against criminality was particularly striking given the context of the government's crusade against unlawful *family* based immigration streams.[64]

Leong's engagement with the publicity initiative revealed the flexibility with which Chinatown leaders approached the relationship between juvenile delinquency, family, and race. As the operation's codirector, he deliberately concealed the very problem that he had actively constructed through his newspaper, the *Chinese Press*, just a few years prior. Clearly, to Chinatown's decision makers, pushing the image of nondelinquency now made more political sense than harping on the community's deviance after the subpoena fiasco. Signally, Leong assisted Albert Q. Maisel in writing "The Chinese among Us" for *Reader's Digest* (1959), thereby accomplishing one of the goals that he and Freeman had set. The article celebrated the assimilation and achievements of renowned Chinese Americans, and concluded by spotlighting the "age-old Chinese tradition of family unity" most discernible in the "amazingly low delinquency rate." Maisel cited Lim P. Lee—the same probation officer who had rallied San Francisco to address Chinatown's escalating youth crisis after World War II—to deliver the familiar explanation that Chinese parents instilled in their children an "ever-lasting determination" not to shame the family name.[65] Witness, too, the contrast between Lee's *Reader's Digest* statement and a contemporaneous study that he conducted on the social service needs of Chinese in the United States in which he documented a rise in the numbers of delinquency cases recently handled by San Francisco's juvenile court. Lee and coauthor Chinese YMCA executive secretary Henry S. Tom warned, "Per capita as compared w/the general population, these figures *are still low*, but one cannot say that there is NO delinquency among the Chinese children. It is a growing problem year by year." Their proposal that Chinese Christian churches provide the spiritual, moral, and intellectual stewardship necessary to steer young people toward the proper path of assimilation suggests that stakeholders in the juvenile delinquency discussions modified their positions—even espousing contradictory viewpoints—depending on their audience and context. "Insider" discussions within Chinatown circles were likely to have been more frank about the existence of juvenile delinquency as opposed to statements aimed at cultivating agreeable public impressions.[66]

Thus Chinese Americans came to rely on the trope of nondelinquency to advance their social-political ambitions—a tactic that enabled a reconciliation of claims to full citizenship with the replication of racial distinction. The delegates to the first National Conference of Chinese Communities in America in 1957 made this point in a letter to President Eisenhower, stressing their desire to "increase Chinese contribution and participation in American communities and to inspire better citizenship" by continuing to cultivate the traditional emphasis on home life that had enabled Chinese America to "eliminate" juvenile delinquency. *Chinese World* editor Lee endorsed the move, which took up his advice that compatriots tap their cultural assets (especially "family training," "respect for the law," and "low percentage of crime and juvenile delinquency") to raise the community's profile and belabor their value to the United States.[67]

Economist S. W. Kung foregrounded these themes in *Chinese in American Life: Some Aspects of Their History, Status, Problems, and Contributions* (1962), a popular treatise aimed at persuading the nation to reform its restrictive immigration quotas and treat Chinese as social equals. He made the case that Chinese Americans were not only "law-abiding" (behold their "admirable paucity of juvenile delinquency") but also industrious, frugal, patriotic, and eager to assimilate—all characteristics of "excellent citizens . . . of great value to the US."[68] The same arguments served as useful rhetorical materiel for Anna Chennualt, president of Chinese Refugee Relief, an organization that advocated the resettlement of persons fleeing Communist China to the United States. In testimony before the Senate Judiciary Committee's Subcommittee on Escapees and Refugees in 1962, she reassured Congress that those seeking entry would not become liabilities to their receiving communities. "We Chinese-Americans can point with pride to the fact that because of the strong family bonds that characterize the Chinese people, juvenile delinquency is almost unknown in Chinese-American communities, and that Chinese-American citizens are not found on American relief rolls," she propounded.[69]

At the local level, Chinese Americans retread the nondelinquency contention for the sake of economic survival, as seen in the *Chinatown Handy Guide: San Francisco* (1959), a source of "complete information for sightseers." Besides the more predictable examinations of dim sum, the origin of chop suey, how to use chopsticks, and so forth, its producers intended to boost the flagging tourist economy by selling "Chinatown's Pride: No Juvenile Delinquency Problem," "San Francisco Hail Chinese as Law-Abiding," and "Mutual Love of Children and Elders Is the Basis of Chinese Family Life." Unlike other communities in San Francisco, bragged the *Handy Guide*, "Chinatown is not concerned with finding a *cure* for juvenile delinquency. It has a *preventive* in its exemplary family life."[70]

The Battle to Speak for Chinese America

It would be too facile to suggest that nondelinquency supplied an easy, catchall solution to the problems of Chinese American race and citizenship at midcentury. Its valorization of Chinese culture, for one, bothered those who subscribed to racial liberalism's assimilationist vision. Among nondelinquency's discontents was Massachusetts resident Donald D. Dong, who expressed disapproval of the *Christian Science Monitor*'s reporting on Boston Chinatown. "Rather than article[s] describing only the good points of the Chinese traditional 'status quo' and their lack of juvenile delinquency, I would prefer to hear criticisms," he opined. Pointing to the many "corruptions" still thriving in the enclave, Dong encouraged honest explorations of "our inefficiency, our lacks, our challenges" so that Boston's Chinese might embrace "Western ideas" to facilitate "more significant" contributions to American society.[71] In Dong's view, the nondelinquency pigeonhole impeded Chinese American assimilation by dismissing any imperatives for cultural and behavioral modification.

This obstruction haunted Rose Hum Lee, who repeatedly insisted that the "timeworn" nondelinquency trope was a fiction. As its most vocal dissenter, Lee accused Chinese Americans of "hid[ing]" their youth problems, or seeking only temporary stopgaps due to their need to "save face" coupled with the reluctance of extended kin, friends, and neighbors to interfere in domestic matters. She challenged the prevailing narrative's emphasis on nonexistent numbers by pointing out that instances of Chinese in the juvenile justice system were frequently lumped together with those of "Other Races" or all "Orientals," and that with the exception of Northern California, the country simply did not have large concentrations of Chinese American minors prior to the end of World War II. To substantiate her claim, she produced statistics documenting delinquency in the San Francisco region, noting 170 cases handled by the city's Juvenile Court from 1943 to 1949. There also were discrepancies between Chinese and American definitions of waywardness. By her account, the Chinese believed that children's duties to their families took precedence over anything else. Thus, if one engaged in illegal activities for the sake of household advancement, community members would not report the child to authorities. Historically, she added, Chinese had shied away from involving law enforcement, because doing so might expose their paper immigration trails.[72]

Lee reserved her most virulent criticisms for the Chinatown establishment, labeling CCBA leaders as deliberate purveyors of falsehoods. In *The Chinese in the United States of America* (1960), the culmination of her decades of research, Lee indicted them with seeking to "woo public opinion" in order to offset the "unsavoury publicity" tied to the "slot racket," narcotics smuggling, exploitation of Chinese laborers by co-ethnic employers, and other corruptions. "Counterpropaganda" efforts stressed the "happy Chinese family" free of disharmony, divorce, and especially juvenile delinquency. Moreover, the media's tendency to focus on Chinese American communities outside the Bay Area sidestepped the "steadily mounting" crimes committed by Chinese adolescents in the vicinity. In general, she lamented, Americans knew little, if anything, about different Chinese "subgroups" and readily accepted these manufactured "clichés" out of ignorance.[73]

At first glance, Lee's devotion to exposing what she saw as a calculated conspiracy by Chinatown's elites may seem odd or perplexing. The nondelinquency idea, after all, had afforded Chinese America a forcible apparatus to brace their petitions for full citizenship. Yet her screed is more legible when set against the backdrop of her assimilationist beliefs. Seeing "racial distinctiveness" as the ultimate hurdle blocking "complete integration," Lee advocated total acculturation and assimilation as a solution to the Oriental Problem. This meant a wholehearted commitment to the obliteration of any cultural and ultimately physical differences between Chinese and whites. She therefore aggressively condemned the continuing existence of Chinatowns in the United States with the hope that they would eventually disappear from the nation's urban landscape. Nondelinquency discourse suggested that Chinatown and Chinese Americans had no problems, and justified white laissez-faire attitudes, whereas admitting faults might convince society that Chinatowns needed to be abolished. While she conceded that racism was a major factor in propagating the inferior status of Chinese Americans, Lee held Chinatown's inhabitants, especially the merchant elite, most responsible for the failure of Chinese to integrate fully into American society. In her view, members of the Chinatown establishment were unwilling to facilitate this process because they did not want to relinquish their control of Chinese American organizations and their role as community spokespersons.[74]

Lee channeled considerable energy toward uncovering this scheme and educating the public on the true state of Chinese America.[75] After the *California Liberal* (aka the *Californian*) published its February 1960 cover story describing the Chinese as "the most unassimilated ethnic group in the United States today," Lee congratulated editor Burton H. Wolfe for his "very fine research," wishing that Chinese Americans would use the story as a rallying point for "effecting the assimilation and eventual integration which they really want but cannot effect because of the clan-district-benevolent association-tong combination." Lee must have been elated to read Wolfe's findings, which corroborated her own sociology. He first portrayed Chinatown as a "city within a city" where residents maintained their own language, customs, and governance system—all of which greatly reduced their prospects for "amalgamation." Wolfe then attested to the rise of juvenile delinquency in recent times as tongs successfully lured alienated immigrant youths with the promise of material rewards. And third, he concluded that Chinatown's "major problem" was "the necessity for its very dissolution." While whites needed to accept the Chinese as equals to make this happen, the Chinese also had to cut loose their separatist "desire."[76]

Wolfe's coverage of Chinatown provoked a spar between Rose Hum Lee and San Francisco juvenile probation officer Lim P. Lee. The latter vehemently objected to Wolfe's treatment as an oversimplification and sensationalization of a complex situation for the sake of increasing the *Californian*'s circulation.[77] In the following issue, Rose Hum Lee charged that Lim P. Lee, acting as a "public relations man for the Six Companies," had "elected to show his emotional flare-up over what Chinese know to be the truth." She noted that the probation officer had forecast a decade ago the problems of "China-born" youths, and that the Columbia Foundation's final recommendations from its study of this population were never implemented because Chinatown's leaders were more concerned with maintaining their intracommunity hegemony rather than improving the welfare of the people.[78] For months, she persisted in condemning Lim P. Lee. When the *San Francisco Examiner* printed a story in April 1961 on the growing incidences of gang activity in Chinatown, including Lim P. Lee's statement, "If the parents don't do anything about it, it will really be a problem in the next five years," she distributed a critical annotation of the article. Rose Hum Lee accused him of "talk[ing] from both sides of his mouth" and asserted that he had been "feeding the 'no delinquency line' more frequently than any Chinese," using his multitude of political connections—from an "in" with the governor to seats on "every committee at the municipal, county, state, and federal level whenever a Chinese is included"—to do so.[79]

In the end, Rose Hum Lee's fixation with the juvenile delinquency issue bespoke a claim to speaking on behalf of the race. Lee fought an uphill battle: as a native of Butte, Montana, she had grown up far from the centers of Chinese America and hence was an outsider to the major enclaves that she studied. Furthermore, she was both US-born and female—two

FIGURE 6.2 Rose Hum Lee, the most prominent Chinese American sociologist at midcentury. Lee earned her doctorate at the University of Chicago and went on to chair the sociology department at Roosevelt University.

Courtesy of Rose Hum Lee papers (Collection Number 1002), Department of Special Collections, Charles E. Young Research Library, UCLA.

distinct disadvantages in a world of Chinatown elites that had always been dominated by foreign-born men. Lacking access to positions of power within the institutions that had traditionally acted as Chinese American spokesorganizations, Rose Hum Lee established her authority as an expert on Chinese America in the academy—an alternate universe. She forged a career path in this realm that was truly remarkable for a woman of color in the mid-twentieth century. Lee earned a PhD from the University of Chicago, and in 1956 she became the first woman and first Chinese American chairperson of a sociology department in the United States. Her accomplishments were due in part to her self-stylizing as an insider-expert on Chinese culture and Chinese American society—a type of knowledge deemed valuable by her peers as well as lay audiences. (She lectured for the Adult Education Council of Chicago's Speakers Bureau on such topics as "Chinese Customs Old and New," "America as Seen through Chinese Eyes," and "The Chinese in America.") The saturation of the nondelinquency concept undermined her claim to this cultural fluency and put her professional reputation on the line, while simultaneously tightening the Chinatown establishment's hold on mediating between the Chinese American masses and the public at large. (Tepid-to-critical reviews of her monograph in academic journals and the Chinese American press expressing skepticism about her analytic framework as well as her objectivity did not help matters.)[80] For the moment, Lee's fervent pleas could do little to place her in the pole position as the representative voice of Chinese America.[81]

From Nondelinquent to Not-Black

Embattled as she was, Lee was not alone among Chinese Americans in trying to complicate the nondelinquency paradigm. Mark R. Chan, president of Chicago's Chinese American Youth Organization, expressed pride in the "fact" that Chinese American delinquency rates were "extremely low," yet also feared that this record might be fleeting given the era's social and political flux. He encouraged his peers to avoid the "the so-called 'wrong crowd'" and join his group as a way to mold themselves into "stronger citizens for a stronger America and a stronger Free World."[82] In 1962, Stuart Cattell of New York's Community Service Society released a report on Manhattan Chinatown's health, welfare, and social organization, concluding that the stereotype of Chinese Americans as strict adherents to a traditional Confucian culture emphasizing filial piety meant that private and state agencies tended to ignore real problems within the community. The Cattell findings stirred Chinese Americans to action. The *Chinese-American Times* editorialized that the city's Chinese population would soon have "juvenile delinquents in more numbers than we can shake a stick at if we don't start taking preventive measures." New York Chinatown's True Light Lutheran Church heeded this advice, sponsoring an open forum on the topic in June 1964.[83]

Across the country, community affairs took similar turns. The *Chinese World* frequently covered the surge of "lost children" and invited readers to tackle the issue. After a series of fights between Chinatown and North Beach teens, San Francisco Chinese YMCA youth secretary Alan S. Wong urged "every concerned citizen" to follow Cattell's suggestion of establishing "constructive programs" to combat the neighborhood's "cancerous growth." Chinatown responded by sending a delegation to lobby Mayor George Christopher for social service resources. And in the wake of the San Francisco police's capture of the "Bugs" gang members for perpetrating nearly fifty burglaries in the Chinatown vicinity, the *Young China* newspaper mourned, "American Chinese have long been praised for their law-abiding and low crime records. However, such a good record has been broken in recent decades, and it is a fact which can no longer be concealed. . . . There is almost one case of juvenile delinquency every day. Some teen-aged Chinese young girls even shamelessly commit shoplifting crimes. Their doings have put a dirty spot on the clean Chinese record and reputation of the American Chinese." (Vitally, the guiding hand of the *Young China*'s English section was none other than Leong, former *Chinese Press* editor and codirector of the postsubpoena publicity drive.)[84]

The renewal of the alarm over public perceptions had a material basis. Cattell's report facilitated mainstream media attention on Chinese America's problems. CBS television broadcast a three-part documentary in 1963 on Manhattan Chinatown with special attention on youth issues, and the *New York Times* mentioned Cattell's forecasting of gang activity. The *New York Herald Times* noted that "police and school records show definite indications that Chinese ancestry is no longer absolute immunity against felonious tendencies," particularly among the recent wave of immigrants and refugees. In San Francisco, the soaring rate of youth offenses (up 25% from 1964 to 1965) prompted the *Chinese World* to dub juvenile delinquency Chinatown's "Number One Challenge" in 1966.[85]

Perhaps sensing an ominous sea change in their social standing, some Chinese Americans leapt to the defense of the nondelinquency paradigm. A number of New York Chinatown residents indignantly objected to Cattell's conclusions as "entirely wrong" and "exaggerated." As one high school teacher averred, "I don't see any juvenile delinquency. The kids don't play hookey. They are respectful, and they don't like rock 'n' roll." In Massachusetts, Chinese community spokespersons lectured on "Why No Delinquent Children in All Chinatowns in the USA" before churches and civic organizations, while San Francisco's *Young China* celebrated Boston Chinatown as a place where juvenile delinquency remained unknown thanks to a "deeply ingrained" reverence for elders."[86]

These were the voices that won out. As with Japanese Americans, Chinese Americans were drawn into the national controversy resulting from the Moynihan Report on the parlous black family. In the same moment that Moynihan extolled the accomplishments of Issei and Nisei, he applauded the progress made by Chinese immigrants since their arrival in the nineteenth century. "No people came to our shores poorer than the Chinese," he avowed, yet their descendants had gone on to remarkable heights of educational attainment *despite* continued concentration in urban centers. And like Nikkei, a "singular stable, cohesive, and enlightened family life" paved the way for socioeconomic mobility. Chinese Americans were definitively not-black.[87]

The nondelinquency trope thus had evolved to respond to yet another imperative after the mid-1960s: that of the country's enduring Negro Problem. The notion of Chinatown as a place of "voluntary segregation" and a "non-slum," popularized through the nondelinquency discourse, urban studies, and the period's poverty knowledge (Michael Harrington's *The Other America* was a famous example) tantalized those who wished to discredit African American entitlement to state resources.[88] A December 1966 feature in *U.S. News and World Report* titled "Success Story of One Minority Group in U.S." captured this nexus. As with its many antecedents, *U.S. News* underlined the low rates of crime, delinquency, and welfare usage in the Chinatowns of San Francisco, Los Angeles, and New York. The writers cited psychologist Richard T. Sollenberger, whose National Institute of Mental Health–funded research concluded that Chinese American children were raised in households that fostered exemplary comportment and communities that were "haven[s] of law and order" despite their impoverished surroundings.[89] While these were familiar refrains, to be sure, "Success Story" differed from its many antecedents in explicitly contrasting Chinese and African Americans: "At a time when it is being proposed that hundreds of billions be spent to uplift Negroes and other minorities, the nation's 300,000 Chinese-Americans are moving ahead on their own—with no help from anyone else." *U.S. News* underscored that the people of Chinatown depended on their "traditional values of hard work, thrift, and morality" rather than welfare checks to overcome their difficulties. "What you find . . . [with] this remarkable group of Americans is a story of adversity and prejudice that would shock those now complaining about the hardships endured by today's Negroes," the periodical added, launching into a history of anti-Chinese hostility and discrimination. Although Chinatown residents continued to face challenges like overcrowding ("worse than in Harlem"), many chose to stay in the enclave "because they prefer their own people and culture"—the foundations of which were none other than the tight-knit family networks that served as economic safety net and moral policing apparatus preventing juvenile delinquency and other social ills.[90]

Chinatown, in short, was not Watts. And in the throes of the black urban unrest gripping the nation in the second half of the 1960s, this was a stark and forceful contrast hinging on the dual themes of family and criminality. An unintended consequence of attempts made by Chinese Americans and friends in the 1940s and 1950s to buttress their claims to full citizenship, this latest twist in the career of nondelinquency now served to reproduce associations between household deviancy, lawlessness, welfare abuse, and African Americans.[91] As such, these assertions simultaneously reflected and manufactured the emergent national racial order of the late twentieth century that slotted Chinese Americans—like Japanese Americans—into the position of model minority vis-à-vis African Americans. Chineseness worked to define blackness while blackness worked to define Chineseness in ways more visible than ever before.

Chapter 7

The Melting Pot of the Pacific

Americans have long been enamored with Hawai'i as paradise: lush flora and fauna, dreamy topography, and temperate clime. Beyond these natural splendors, Yankee fantasies have also latched on to the exoticism of the islands' people and their putative culture, especially the notion of a welcoming, feminized, and sexually available aloha spirit. This imagination has operated to justify the United States' continued domination of the archipelago since the mid-nineteenth century.[1]

By the early twentieth century, this fascination had come to encompass the idea of Hawai'i as a *racial* paradise.[2] In the 1920s and 1930s, intellectuals began to tout the islands' ethnically diverse composition—including the indigenous population, white settler colonists, and imported labor from Asia and other locales—as a Pacific melting pot free of the mainland's social taboos on intermingling. After World War II, the association of Hawai'i with racial harmony and tolerance received unprecedented national attention as Americans heatedly debated the question of whether or not the territory, annexed to the United States in 1898, should become a state. Statehood enthusiasts tagged the islands' majority Asian population, with its demonstrated capability of assimilation, as a forceful rationale for admission. Americans everywhere heralded Hawai'i as a model for race relations as well as a valuable meeting ground between East and West. With the Cold War in full swing, sketching the territory as proof of American multiracial "democracy at work" and a vital link to Asia proved to be a winning strategy. Hawai'i became the fiftieth state on August 21, 1959.

Hawai'i's bid for statehood occupies a central place in the story of the origins of the model minority, paralleling and reinforcing critical changes in the racialization of continental Asian Americans. Like the postinternment reconstruction of Nikkei as heroic soldiers and "Quiet Americans" along with the far-flung praise for Chinatown's exemplary families and nondelinquent children, the statehood campaign was one of the most high-profile sites for remaking the image of Asian Americans after World War II, capturing the interest of countless individuals in the arenas of formal politics and mass culture.[3] Given that Americans conceived of Hawai'i as a distinctly "Eastern" space in the 1940s and 1950s, the statehood question served as a national referendum on the problem of post-Exclusion Asiatic race and citizenship—a symbolic proxy for Asian Americans' place in the nation. Through admission coupled with the sending of ethnic Japanese and Chinese representatives from the state of Hawai'i to the US Congress, Americans came to regard people of Asian ancestry as model minorities. Statehood, in short, emblematized the nation's investment in the emergent paradigm.

Until World War II, many—if not most—Americans could not fathom Hawai'i's entry into the Union, given its physical distance from the continent, its sizable Asian presence, and the struggle between the United States and Japan for domination in the Pacific. But with Hawai'i's importance as a battleground during the war and new diplomatic imperatives after 1945, Cold War liberals repitched the islands' Oriental Problem as a geopolitical asset. That the vast majority of the US population approved of statehood by the late 1940s and early 1950s suggests that many people accepted the logic of racial liberalism and were willing to reposition the boundaries of the national community to include persons of Asian ancestry.

While contemporaries celebrated Hawai'i's admission as the moment elevating "Oriental citizens" to "full equality," this act of inclusion generated its own constellation of racial exclusions affecting Native Hawaiians, African Americans, and Asian Americans themselves. As with the concurrent processes of transmuting Asian Americans into model minorities on the mainland, statehood was *both* a solution to the conundrum of reconfiguring the nation's racial order in the mid-twentieth century and a seed for new dilemmas of racial management that would plague the nation in the post–civil rights era.

Hawai'i's Oriental Problem

Hawai'i's racial makeup precluded any real possibility of statehood before the 1940s. White planters had little interest in altering the territorial status that enabled them to horde the islands' wealth and power. The oligarchy and its mainland allies regarded Hawai'i's Asiatics as a menace on several fronts: economic, social, political, and military. In myriad ways, whites' construction of Hawai'i's Oriental Problem mirrored anti-Asian animus in the US West. Opposition to statehood therefore can be understood as a facet of the Asiatic Exclusion regime spanning the late nineteenth and early twentieth centuries.

The roots of Hawai'i's Oriental Problem lay in the māhele—literally, "division"—of 1848, the revolutionary privatization and redistribution of land masterminded by New England missionary-merchants (or haole in local terminology). At the expense of indigenous peoples, the haole elite acquired substantial tracts that it aimed to transform into industrial sugar plantations. But doing so required cheap and plentiful labor. The rapid decimation of the native population since the introduction of Western diseases in the late eighteenth century and intractability of those who survived obliged growers to look offshore for workers. Consequently, from the 1850s through the 1930s, plantation owners recruited over four hundred thousand laborers to the islands, mainly from China, Japan, and the Philippines, with smaller numbers from Portugal, Korea, Puerto Rico, Norway, Russia, Germany, Spain, and various Pacific islands.[4]

Whites and Native Hawaiians felt ambivalent about the influx of Far Eastern workers. Asiatic immigration, of course, had made possible the large-scale cultivation of sugar. The independent Hawaiian kingdom had actually encouraged labor recruitment, hoping that an uptick in the Asian population would offset haole domination. Nonetheless, haole and some natives expressed apprehension of an Oriental invasion, leading the Kingdom to pass its own version of US Chinese Exclusion laws in 1886. This hostility extended to the exploding Japanese population, brought in as a replacement labor force. Anti-Asian antagonism by the late 1890s infused the annexation deliberations. Americans who desired the formal colonization of the islands by the United States warned of the "danger of Asiatic ascendancy" and urged their compatriots to preempt a takeover by Japan. Annexation's detractors concurred that the islands were disturbingly Orientalized, but drew the opposite conclusion: that the yellow peril necessitated that the United States abandon its imperialist designs, lest Hawai'i seek statehood in the future. As Missouri representative Champ Clark implored his congressional colleagues, "How can we endure our shame when a Chinese Senator from Hawaii, with his pigtail hanging down his back, with his pagan joss in his hand, shall rise from his curule chair and in pigeon [sic] English proceed to chop logic with George Frisbie Hoar or Henry Cabot Lodge?"[5]

Although the expansionists prevailed in the end, the acquisition of Hawai'i was far from an unmitigated defeat for the opposition. They could find solace in the imposition of the Exclusion regime, including the all-important classification of Asians as aliens ineligible to citizenship (or in the case of Filipino colonial subjects, as nationals rather than citizens). Cultivating a predominantly noncitizen labor force offered a critical advantage to planters: barred from naturalization, Asian workers could not exercise the franchise to advance their class interests.[6]

Still, Asiatic Exclusion had its limits. While Asian migrants were relegated outside the legal bounds of citizenship, their Hawai'i-born offspring confronted no such restrictions, since all persons born in the United States were entitled to birthright citizenship under the Fourteenth

Amendment. The haole elite cast nervous eyes on this new generation, particularly Nisei, who had the potential to dominate the electorate. At the time of territorial incorporation in 1900, the Japanese comprised the largest single ethnic group on the islands. If the Oriental invasion was no longer sustained by immigration, whites now feared Japanese Americans' permanent settlement and their fecundity.[7]

Haoles' concern with the shifting demographics on the islands helps to explain the absence of any sustained push for Union admission in the early decades of the twentieth century. Beginning in 1903, proposals for statehood surfaced at regular intervals in the territorial legislature, but met little success because the oligarchy supposed that such a change would erode its hegemony. Its power derived directly from sugar production, with the heads of the Big Five (Hawai'i's main sugar corporations) and related concerns (banking, transportation, shipping, etc.) wielding an economic monopoly under the territorial system. Big Five executives and their allies likewise controlled the territorial government, holding major sway over the principle public offices appointed by Congress and the president. Territorial governors, in turn, possessed sweeping authority to name their choice of candidates to local offices and determine a slew of major policies impacting the gamut of island life. With little incentive to disturb the status quo, the haole elite viewed the growing Japanese American population as an elemental reason to oppose admission. Once they came of age, Nisei could unravel the islands' interlocking network of white dominance through democratic state elections.[8]

Hawai'i's Oriental Problem, then, became virtually synonymous with the "Japanese Question" by the 1910s and 1920s. In addition to birthrate calculations, the growing labor militancy of Issei and Nisei further reinforced this perception among the ruling class. The local press and ethnic rivals accused Tokyo of plotting to "Japanize" the territory through control of the sugar industry. Military intelligence and the Hawaii Labor Commission deemed the territory's entire ethnic Japanese population as suspect, if not dangerously loyal to Japan. Territorial policymakers launched an Americanization campaign, strictly regulating Japanese-language schools, Nikkei newspapers, and Buddhist churches as a way to demand undivided allegiance to the United States. They also emphasized the cultivation of "American" values among Nisei schoolchildren and pressured those members of the second generation who held dual citizenship to renounce their Japanese nationality.[9]

Ironically, the yellow peril panic turned into a nuisance for the planter class as political winds shifted in the mid-1930s. In 1934, Congress passed the Jones-Costigan Act, subjecting Hawaiian sugar bound for the mainland to quota restrictions that disadvantaged island growers.

Convinced that territorial status subjected them to economic discrimination by federal legislators, the Big Five turned to Union admission as a means of guaranteeing voting representation in Congress and therefore more political clout. The territorial governor formed the Hawaii Equal Rights Commission to coordinate an official statehood campaign, and territorial delegate Samuel Wilder King introduced an admission bill in Congress in June 1935. Although the movement quickly energized, statehood advocates promptly discovered that the Japanese Question's firm toehold in Hawai'i's culture posed an insurmountable obstacle. Despite finding strong support for statehood and ample evidence that the territory met the standards for admission, congressional committees that investigated the matter in 1935 and 1937 hesitated to endorse immediate entry. Both times detractors persuaded the panels that Japanese in Hawai'i were incapable of becoming "unequivocally American," their political allegiances would always remain unreliable, and Nisei sullied democracy with their extreme likelihood of bloc voting. Worsening relations between the United States and Japan fed this reluctance. A January 1941 Gallup poll found that significant numbers of Americans remained hostile to the possibility of sending "Japanese Senators" and "Japanese Representatives" to Congress.[10]

Anti-Japanese acrimony in Hawai'i reached its terrible crescendo after the bombing of Pearl Harbor. On the evening of December 7, 1941, the army imposed martial law on the entire territory. Japanese Americans bore the brunt of this rule, subjected to unparalleled levels of surveillance and restrictions on working and everyday living. For their part, Japanese Americans sought to convince their fellow islanders of their exclusive loyalty to the United States by participating in the war mobilization, sponsoring the Speak American Campaign, and jettisoning all personal displays of Japanese culture. None of this, however, was enough to reverse the military's orders to close Nikkei institutions and incarcerate nearly fifteen hundred Japanese American elders. Hence, at the outset of World War II, the prognosis for statehood seemed highly improbable.[11]

Hawai'i's Unorthodox Race Doctrine

Although Hawai'i's Oriental Problem commandingly structured haole-Asian relations in the late nineteenth to early twentieth centuries, it was never all pervasive. From the 1920s onward, religious leaders, intellectuals, and social commentators furnished a competing discourse by touting the islands as variously a racial frontier, racial laboratory, and racial paradise where the Asiatic presence was innocuous, if not beneficial. Their diagnoses established the liberal position on race in Hawai'i—a standpoint that would prove critical to the admission argument after World War II.

The beginnings of this alternate framework can be traced to white American missionaries who feared that domestic discord on the Pacific coast negatively impacted their overseas conversion attempts. Consequently, they attempted to disprove popular beliefs that "Orientals" were incapable of assimilating to American life—the ideological core of anti-Asian xenophobia. To do so, they enlisted the expertise of social scientists, including Robert E. Park of the University of Chicago, author of the influential "interaction cycle" theory—positing competition, conflict, accommodation, and assimilation as the four stages of encounter between two groups—to understand why Asians had been unable to move beyond the conflict stage.[12]

To answer this question, elite thinkers looked to Hawai'i, "the one place where [racial] injustice does not glare." Its seeming tranquillity despite its diversity, especially its unusually high rates of interracial marriage, suggested the possibility of intercultural accord everywhere. Intellectuals perceived the islands as "the ultimate racial laboratory," where the end stage of the race relations cycle (assimilation) had already been reached. Chicago School sociologists and their scholarly descendants—especially the University of Hawai'i's sociology department—soon developed a preoccupation with Hawai'i's unique culture of intermingling. Led by University of Hawai'i professor Romanzo Adams, social scientists upheld the romance of the islands as racially enlightened, in spite of the haole-planter ruling class. Adams attributed the origins of the "unorthodox" "doctrine" to the native Hawaiian ethos of aloha (reciprocal love and generosity) and willingness of Anglo-American settlers to abide by such a code.[13]

In advancing the racial equality thesis, social scientists posited a radical departure from exclusionists' claim that Orientals were fundamentally incompatible with American culture and democracy. They assumed that Asiatic assimilation was both the normative and inevitable outcome of contact between Asians, Hawaiians, and whites in the crucible of Hawaiian society. Their research proved that Asian islanders had embraced "occidental culture," as indexed by growing numbers of voters and middle-class professionals, an increase in residential dispersion, and rising rates of intermarriage. As one concluded, "They are oriental in appearance, but not in reality."[14]

All the same, they were not oblivious to the territory's anti-Asian racism. They instead actively sought to dispel the fear that Orientals, especially Japanese, constituted a singular menace to Hawai'i. At both the 1935 and 1937 congressional statehood hearings, Adams commended the "Japanese family system" for effectively preventing waywardness and indigence, and stressed that Hawai'i's Asians were "being made over into Americans, for they just can't help themselves." Beyond battling what they saw as racist misperceptions, the social scientists made the plea that persons of Asian ancestry in the United States deserved to be considered full citizens of the nation. With the outbreak of the Pacific War, they raised the stakes of this entreaty even higher. University of Hawai'i sociologist Andrew Lind beseeched fellow islanders to treat Japanese Americans as they would all other citizens, arguing that racial profiling spoiled the fundamental American ideals of fairness and meritocracy.[15]

Intellectuals' advocacy efforts mirrored an analogous focus in the popular press. Akin to the social scientists, journalists and commentators depicted Hawai'i as a racial paradise that fostered a culture of assimilation characterized by the commonplace of interracial marriage and mixed-race peoples. The ethnic and religious conflicts of the 1930s and World War II provided fertile ground for this idea to flourish. In June 1942, *Life* magazine featured a pictorial of individual women representing Hawai'i's various racial "combinations," such as Filipino Chinese, Hawaiian white, and Hindu Dane, meant to depict Hawai'i as a "melting pot bubbling comfortably to produce a fine healthy stew." The photo spread was based on the research of Swedish race biologist William W. Krauss, who located in Hawai'i "an atmosphere of interracial peace and harmony." In recounting his findings, *Life* joined the growing chorus proposing that Hawai'i's amicable relations be upheld as "a striking object lesson in racial accommodation" for other nations beset with strife.[16]

The statehood debate picked up as proponents couched the notion of Hawai'i's distinctive racial environs as a potential asset for American diplomacy in the troubled Pacific. *Asia* contributor Elizabeth Green contended that Hawai'i's people, with their "peculiar qualifications of heritage, birth and upbringing," were especially equipped to "go out as interpreters *of* East and West alike, *to* East and West alike, on a mission of rational human understanding of vast future significance." Writing for *American* magazine in 1937, Webb Waldron echoed this vision, asserting that Hawai'i's entry into the Union might prevent war between the United States and Japan.[17]

Yet the internationalist argument remained a secondary line of reasoning as anti-Japanese agitators forced statehood supporters to rebut their charges of Nikkei disloyalty and unassimilability. Champions of admission attested to the loyalty of Hawai'i's Japanese Americans, pointing to their World War I military service, their eagerness to enlist for their armed forces, and Nisei's rush to expatriate from Japanese dual citizenship as evidence that they would undoubtedly side with the United States in the event of war with Japan. Promoters vigorously accentuated the fitness of Hawai'i's Japanese for citizenship, characterized by thrift, industry, and the absence of criminality. Overall their message stressed equality and sameness. If the case could be made that Hawai'i's people, with its majority of Japanese Americans, were no different than the rest of nation, went the logic, then there would be no justifiable grounds on which to deny the territory a promotion.[18]

When the war broke out, the Japanese Question finally left the realm of speculation. Home front efforts of such groups as the all-Japanese Honolulu Civic Association and Varsity Victory Volunteers of the US Army Corps of Engineers coupled with the European theater service of the all-Nisei 100th Infantry Battalion (which later merged with the 442nd Regimental Infantry) provided indisputable evidence of Japanese Americans' allegiance to the United States for many on the islands and in the nation at large.[19] By the closing months of the war, popular opinion had strikingly evolved. "Our American citizens of Japanese ancestry have acted in uniform and out of uniform, in daily occupation and in the stress and test of battle, just as have our Americans of other ancestries. The basic argument against admission . . . has been answered," declared the *Honolulu Star-Bulletin* in February 1945.[20]

World War II, then, radically altered the social, cultural, and political terrain on which the statehood question would be fought after 1945. Nikkei sacrifice inspired the resolution of Hawai'i's Japanese Question. In the name of antifascism and national unity, liberal leaders and thinkers promoted cultural pluralism as a desirable and appropriate ethos modeled most effectively by Hawaiian society. Hawai'i itself came to be seen by Americans as an integral part of the nation—a point ardently underscored by the Pearl Harbor attack. Too, its geographic location had rendered it the sensible launching point for US troops deployed throughout the Pacific as well as a site of defense industry growth, and the war years witnessed the circulation of tens of thousands of mainlanders through the islands. All these dynamics coalesced to increase an awareness of Hawai'i and its significance among the general public. Moreover, the military's suspension of constitutional rights under marital law convinced many locals that only statehood could guarantee such a scenario would not be repeated in the future. And emboldened by their contributions to the war effort, the territory's Asian Americans—not only Japanese, but also ethnic Chinese, Filipino, and Korean residents—felt more entitled than ever before to political equality and first-class citizenship, and looked to admission as the key to securing their aspirations. This confluence of factors animated statehood advocates, who looked to the postwar years in anticipation of imminent victory.[21]

Resolving the Japanese Question

Predictably, the Japanese Question immediately resurfaced when the statehood debates resumed just after the war's end. The *Washington Post* warned that statehood might open the door to Japanese control of the state government. At preliminary hearings conducted by the US House of Representatives in Honolulu in 1946, a vocal minority of participants opposed immediate statehood, fastening their misgivings to the familiar specter of the yellow peril. Territorial senator Alice Kamokila Campbell, a Native Hawaiian and leading opponent of admission, warned, "The Japanese situation . . . is a serious menace to good American government," given Nikkei's "allegiance to alien parentage" as well as their "numerical, financial, and political majority."[22]

But statehood proponents had cause for optimism. The racial basis of opposition in the 1930s—really, the proposal's main stumbling block— had lost much of its potency as the nation recognized Nisei for their exemplary wartime showing of patriotism during the war. Anti-Japanese testimony no longer held the same weight, as became clear during the 1946 House hearings. A diverse cross-section of Hawaiian society, from Governor Ingram M. Stainback to local housewives, declared faith in Japanese Americans' patriotism and assimilability, citing in dozens of instances the "heroic record" of Nisei in uniform. Lind dismissed the possibility of racial bloc voting by Japanese Americans as "remote" and affirmed that all Asian Americans were entitled to full citizenship. These pronouncements effectively persuaded House investigators to urge "immediate consideration" of admission. "The people of the Territory of Hawaii have demonstrated beyond question not only their loyalty and patriotism but also their desire to assume the responsibilities of statehood," they concluded.[23]

This emphasis on unflinching devotion to the United States became a mainstay of the popular media's examination of the statehood bid. Newspapers agreed that the political sympathies of Hawai'i's Japanese were no longer in doubt, thereby removing any reservations about admission.[24] Scores of periodicals acclaimed these "Jap-Yanks" for their loyalty "beyond question."[25] Nonfiction works by dedicated racial liberals reiterated the same points to mainlanders, including Lind's monograph *Hawaii's Japanese* (1946) and *Hawaii: The 49th State* (1947), a mass-market book by *Reader's Digest* editor Blake Clark, one of Nikkei's most passionate supporters. Clark gushed that Japanese Americans "stand today as the nation's strongest single testament to the fact that Americanism is not a matter of race, color, or religion, but of the heart. Sakamaki, Shimogaki, Awakuni, Nakahara—they have the American heart!"[26]

The burgeoning consensus on Japanese Americans also wound through congressional hearings, reports, and floor debates on Hawai'i statehood between 1947 and 1959. Political leaders posited admission as an earned reward for wartime sacrifice. Successive secretaries of the interior, military officials, representatives and senators, and sundry witnesses continually lavished praise on the "splendid" combat performance of the 100th and 442nd battalions. After 1950, their exuberance covered Nisei's "unmatched record" in the Korean War. While skeptics continued to express anti-Japanese hostility throughout the deliberations, their objections never reached the same levels of influence as they had during the prewar years.[27]

The resolution of statehood's Japanese Question thus functioned as a key locus for the refashioning of Japanese Americans' race and citizenship standing after World War II, at once drawing from and enlivening JACL's soldier-focused, mainland public relations campaign. Correlating to its concurrent push for postinternment recovery and Issei naturalization rights, the league likewise stressed that Hawai'i's Nisei had earned statehood through their participation in the armed forces. As Masaoka asserted before the Senate Committee on Interior and Insular Affairs in 1953, "They have purchased with their blood . . . equal status not only as individual Japanese-Americans but also for their homeland, the Territory of Hawaii." Statehood, then, should be "a recognition of the magnificent gallantry in combat which won for them the admiration of every group with whom they were associated."[28] JACL also underlined the outstanding conduct of Nikkei off the battlefield, such as their lack of criminal activity and their "ability . . . to stay off relief rolls and to take care of [their] own"—a move that echoed its publicity for JARP. The merging of these various strands worked not only to strengthen arguments for admission but also to begin stitching together regional racializations into a national, post-Exclusion racial order.[29]

Cold War Contradictions

While the events of World War II greatly improved Hawai'i's chances for admission, statehood was far from being an open-and-shut case after 1945. The start of the Cold War introduced new considerations that galvanized stakeholders on both sides of the debate. Most decisively, anti-Communism and race defined the postwar negotiations. As powerful but also malleable languages, they simultaneously functioned as the main catalysts for reworking Hawai'i's Oriental Problem into diplomatic advantage and blunt instruments with which detractors perennially frustrated entry. The political contradictions resulting from the ability of the opposing factions to appropriate the two concepts for their respective ends were major factors that protracted the decision-making process. In fact, of the thirty-seven territories considered for statehood after the original thirteen, Hawai'i was "the most thoroughly studied, the most exhaustively investigated, and the most frequently rejected by Congress."[30]

As the Soviet-American rivalry picked up in the late 1940s, admission's foes latched on to a likely means to cloud the campaign. The rise of organized labor in postwar Hawai'i set the stage for the debates' own Red Scare as detractors bent anti-Communism to fit their designs. Union membership in the territory boomed after agricultural workers gained the right to collective bargaining in 1945. As the International Longshoremen and Warehousemen Union (ILWU) rapidly expanded its membership rolls—going from nine hundred members in 1944 to thirty-three thousand two years later—it began to rival the Big Five in political influence. Voting with their feet as well as their ballots, ILWU workers helped to elect an unprecedented number of liberals to local office, inaugurating a shift in the territorial balance of power away from the traditional Republican-haole elite that culminated in the "Democratic Revolution" of 1954. Large-scale strikes in the late 1940s provided statehood opponents with potent ammunition to raise McCarthyist objections to entry. Decriers charged that the territory had fallen under the "firm grip" of Communists and admission would cede control of Hawai'i's government to the Kremlin.[31]

Critics inflated these accusations by joining them to older yellow peril fears. Racializing antilabor and anti-Communist sentiments was easy to do; the vast majority of the rank and file came from Japanese or Filipino ancestral backgrounds. Some suggested that local American-born Chinese elected to the future state legislature would be manipulated by Red China, or that the "Japs" who "control[l]ed" the islands would infect the US Congress and American society with "Asiatic concepts of life." Even worse, statehood might provide the catalyst for Hawai'i's Chinese and Japanese to "merge under the banner of Communism," and together undermine US global leadership—an "unthinkable" outcome.[32]

But race—like anti-Communism—could work in favor of statehood as well as against it. Nearly everyone who weighed in on the issue agreed that the isles were markedly "Oriental." Detractors, of course, posited this as a political and social burden. For promoters, in contrast, the archipelago's Far Eastern roots were a huge selling point in the context of the worldwide decolonization movement and nascent Soviet-American duel. To review briefly, for many in Asia and Africa, World War II was a fight against not only fascism but also imperialism, with occupied peoples struggling to unseat their colonial masters. Chapter 11 of UN Charter, cosigned by the United States in 1945, declared the signatories' duty "to develop self-government" in their territories. In light of this agreement, Hawai'i's colonial relationship with the United States—like stateside racial inequality—posed a problem for America's geopolitical tug-of-war with the Soviet Union. President Truman's Committee on Civil Rights maintained that international relations ranked as one of three reasons impelling the nation to fix its "domestic civil rights shortcomings." Should the nation fail to act, the United States' adversaries would hasten "to prove our democracy an empty fraud, and our nation a consistent oppressor of underprivileged people." Truman responded by including Hawai'i statehood in his comprehensive agenda for racial reform. "The present political status of our Territories and possessions impairs the enjoyment of civil rights by their residents," he declared before Congress in February 1948. Without this change, the United States might well lose the Cold War.[33]

Statehood supporters presciently anticipated these concerns. In 1946, the territorial government reactivated the prewar Hawaii Equal Rights Commission as the Citizens' Statehood Committee (CSC). The committee accented the global implications of statehood in its publicity literature, promising that entry would serve as a "concrete example of self-determination influencing all the peoples of the Pacific." The following year, the Citizens' Statehood Committee morphed once more into the Hawaii Statehood Commission. Based in Honolulu and Washington, DC, the Hawaii Statehood Commission coordinated an extensive, formalized drive for statehood from 1947 to 1959. During this time, the commission persistently lobbied every member of Congress, disseminated as many as forty thousand individual promotional items annually, and communicated regularly with federal officials and agencies, businesses, civic organizations, educational institutions, national magazines, and over seventeen thousand newspapers. Following the lead of its predecessor, the Hawaii Statehood Commission foregrounded the nation's global exigencies in its public relations materials, such as the booklet "The State of Hawaii" (1956): "Old-world colonialism has run its course in Asia, leaving its people with a choice—a free way of life, or Communism. Our national policies will be judged in no small measure by the decisions we make in respect to the people of Hawaii." Other proponents also utilized the stigma of empire to good effect. Joseph R. Farrington, Hawai'i's territorial delegate to Congress, likened territorial rule to "the discredited pattern of European colonialism" and dramatically proclaimed that he would settle for "nothing" short of statehood.[34]

It is difficult to overstate the prominence of Cold War diplomatic imperatives in the statehood deliberations. Seemingly countless remarks of witnesses participating in congressional hearings and floor debates both acknowledged as well as further reinforced the persuasiveness of the rationale. Secretary of the Interior Julius Krug opened the first postwar statehood hearings, held in Washington, DC, in 1947, by emphasizing that prompt admission would "enhance the prestige of this Nation in world affairs and specifically in Pacific affairs." The Department of State's interventions throughout the duration of the debate in particular drove home the point that American policymakers connected the issue of Hawai'i's admission to the United States' geopolitical designs. Officials repeatedly verified that admission would fulfill the United Nations mandate to foster self-determination and refute "Communist propaganda" claiming anti-"Oriental" racism in US governance.[35]

Proponents depicted Hawai'i as a place with enormous ambassadorial potential, given that the ancestries of Hawai'i's inhabitants essentially endowed them to serve as the ideal brokers between the United States and the Pacific world. Supporters wielded an eclectic assortment of metaphors to configure the territory as an indispensable bond to millions in Asia: a "gateway," "springboard," and "logical stepping stone" to the East; a "hub" and "meeting ground"; a "funnel" through which Eastern and Western "influences" traversed in both directions; and the "catalyst" joining Orient and Occident. Most typically, enthusiasts depicted Hawai'i as some form of "bridge"—whether as a "bridge of understanding," a "cultural and political bridge to the Orient," or a "strong bridge with the people of the yellow race." As with justifying statehood in terms of anticolonialism and civil rights reform, the concept of Hawai'i as a racial, cultural, and geographic borderland looked to forward the United States' Cold War agenda of wooing the newly independent third world nations to its camp. "Hawaii's Americans of Oriental ancestry are a strong, urgent reason for Statehood, rather than the reverse," territorial congressional delegate John A. Burns insisted. The United States' relations with Asia would only grow in importance in the postcolonial era, and no group was better equipped or better positioned to forge these ties.[36]

Statehood's backers envisioned the pinnacle of this brokerage to be the election of Asian Hawaiians to the US Congress. Inverting the exclusionist trope of the Oriental senator, the Hawaii Statehood Commission avowed that immediate admission would "immeasurably benefit the Union" by installing legislators with "an intimate knowledge of the Pacific ocean area at their fingertips." Territorial delegate Joseph Farrington and his congressional colleagues incorporated this point into myriad speeches, public appearances, and written testimonies promoting Hawai'i's entrance to the Union. Outside Washington, DC, opinion makers willingly dispensed with the long-standing bugaboo. "Likely enough, Hawaii will send a Senator Watanabe to Washington," mused the Los Angeles Times.

"What's so bad about that? . . . A Hawaiian delegation which included men of Oriental descent would be a strong weapon in our hands against Communist preachings to the Asiatics." Quoting a University of Hawai'i professor, *Newsweek* concurred, "Imagine a Chinese in the U.S. Senate—how would Red China like that?"[37]

To be sure, the willingness to embrace the seating of ethnic Chinese and Japanese in the highest legislative offices signaled an unprecedented welcoming of Asian Americans into the national community. Perhaps nothing could more fittingly symbolize the end of Asiatic Exclusion than these figures embodying the ultimate manifestation of belonging. Yet the motivation for this acceptance—the belief that Hawai'i's denizens were inherently as well as best fit to play the role of racial and cultural go-betweens—simultaneously propagated their otherness. Like the State Department's use of Chinese American cultural diplomats or social scientists' reliance on "Japanese" culture to explain Nikkei mobility, the racial reasoning undergirding Hawai'i's admittance to statehood upheld older, Orientalist ideas of Chinese and Japanese difference from whites. And as long as Asian Americans' racial distinction from whites continued to be assumed and invoked, the citizenship status of Asian Americans would remain susceptible to the vagaries of US foreign policy.

In these narratives, Hawai'i's distinctiveness stemmed from not only its Far Eastern heritage but also its harmonious race relations. Mass-circulation magazines entrenched the racial paradise ideal in the public imagination and provided a rhetorical resource on which the statehood campaign could draw. *Life*'s November 1945 photo essay "Hawaii: A Melting Pot" exemplified this vein of representation. *Life* dubbed Hawai'i "the world's most successful experiment in mixed breeding . . . unmatched in today's world for interracial tolerance and affection." The captions suggested that the islands' diversity rendered "prejudice" unfeasible. Accompanying pictures featured white-Chinese, Japanese-Hawaiian, Filipino, and black-Japanese families; a motley Boy Scout troop; and head shots of pretty young women in a multitude of racial combinations (Portuguese Irish Hawaiian and Korean Spanish English). These illustrated the birth of "the new mixed race of Hawaii—tolerant, healthy, and American," while also neutralizing fears of interracial marriage by depicting this integration as feminine, exotic, and sexually desirable.[38]

Sociological data confirmed these observations. Lind characterized 31 percent of all marriages in Hawai'i as "interracial" by 1953, with the ratio for some ethnic groups reaching even greater numbers. Nearly 77 percent of Hawaiian men and 78 percent of Hawaiian women wed outside the race. Korean males and females followed closely, with 68 and 72 percent, respectively, as did Puerto Rican grooms and brides with 48 and 60 percent, respectively, and Chinese with 41 and 43 percent, respectively. The two groups with the lowest rates—white men at 36 percent and white women at 15 percent; Japanese men at 7 percent and Japanese women at 18 percent—nonetheless outmarried at phenomenally higher rates than any found on the mainland, where many states barred interracial unions through law and custom. (The US census classified a mere 0.4 percent of all American marriages as interracial in 1960.) Lind also observed a steady decrease in the proportion of births of "single ethnic stock." In 1931, 78 percent of all territorial births claimed one ancestral race; the figure had fallen to 67 percent by 1950. The process of "biological fusion," Lind concluded, was "moving irresistibly forward."[39]

With strong discursive and statistical foundations, then, the racial paradise conceit became ubiquitous throughout the life of the statehood deliberations. It maintained a visible presence on editorial pages across the country in newspapers of all circulation sizes and target markets, from major dailies to the African American press.[40] Niche-market and general-interest periodicals fed the groundswell.[41] On Capitol Hill, racial harmony, cooperation, and tolerance became proverbial refrains in testimonies by Hawai'i residents, territorial leaders, cabinet officials, and members of Congress favoring admission.[42]

All offered reassurance that Hawai'i's population would in no way introduce another race problem into a nation already grappling with the vexing issue of black civil rights. The camp in favor of statehood carefully intimated that interracial sex and marriage on the archipelago, though admirable, would be safely contained. The isles were not a microcosm of United States, North or South, but rather a "cultural outpost" whose sociological reality was "irreplaceable."[43] This argument worked because Hawai'i, after all, was no more than a string of small islets literally in the middle of ocean, thousands of miles from the mainland. Its geographic noncontiguousness spatially reinforced the notion of its social uniqueness: the one place where race mixing proved the promise of US democracy, albeit in a foreign, exotic way. Hawai'i—and Hawai'i alone—had succeeded in its otherness, and this success should be rewarded with statehood.

Advocates needed to underline the delimited nature of Hawai'i's race mixing because the most steadfast resistance to statehood came from white supremacists who saw the admission of a non-Anglo-majority and racially fluid territory as a serious threat to the republic's future. A vocal minority of Americans, especially powerful southern lawmakers, persistently stalled the bid on racial grounds. Moreover, they tied the race issue to sectional interests; statehood would sap not only the nation's whiteness but also southern influence in Washington, DC—indispensable to the protection of states' rights and Jim Crow. Statehood foes tried a range of approaches to thwart their adversaries, such as mobilizing the fear of disproportionality. Virginia congressperson Howard W. Smith alleged that if Hawai'i were to become a state, "1 Chinaman" would have "the same power in the United States Senate as 31 American citizens in the State of New York." The representation issue helped to sustain proposals to amend the US Constitution to allow for new states to be entitled to one senate seat instead of two to correct what some legislators deemed Hawai'i's "unfair" pull in Congress. After the Supreme Court's *Brown v. Board of Education* ruling in 1954 mandating school desegregation, disputants increasingly bared their explicitly racist agenda without pretense. Some inserted antistatehood activism into the "massive resistance" crusade against civil rights. Southern congressional leaders affirmed their constituents' views by emphasizing that the "complete foolhardiness" of statehood would saddle the United States with the impossible conundrum of assimilating peoples whose ancestry, culture, customs, and history were radically dissimilar to those of whites.[44]

Responding to such refusals, believers argued that the territory's people were sufficiently assimilated. Their claim that Hawai'i was American enough for admission—that its people had shed their strange ways—rested in part on proving that its Asiatic population had acculturated to white, middle-class standards, behaviors, and orientations.[45] Such a point was an especially critical one to impress, given that the campaign walked a fine line between convincing mainlanders of islanders' commonalities and trumpeting their differences as an asset for international relations. The Hawaii Statehood Commission took care to dwell on the former by suggesting that locals were virtually indistinguishable from their continental counterparts: speaking English, practicing Christianity, joining Parent-Teacher Associations, attending football games, eating hot dogs, and watching television—"They're Americans, through and through."[46] Statehood advocates often coded the resemblance in the language of "modernity," noting the many features of up-to-the-minute living in Hawai'i, including air-conditioned suburban homes, abundant supermarkets, and snarled freeway traffic.[47] They also stressed that the public education system prepared its youths well for their responsibilities as citizens of the future state, and the "patriotic devotion" of Honolulu's denizens was identical to that of people in Topeka, Galveston, or New York City.[48]

Perhaps most crucially, exponents' assessments of Hawai'i's "Americanism" necessarily accentuated anti-Communism. This was a point that needed to be explicitly detailed in light of the territory's contentious but relatively successful postwar labor struggles. Hodding Carter, the same liberal southern journalist who won the 1946 Pulitzer Prize for his editorials including "Go for Broke," ardently swore to readers of the *Saturday Evening Post* in 1954 that "Hawaii is no more Red than is New York or

California or Michigan or any other American area where communists or fellow-travelers have infiltrated into unions whose membership once had or still has legitimate grievances and objectives." Statistically speaking, the proportion of card-carrying Communists to the total population was only half that of the mainland. Carter conceded that left-wing leaders exercised considerable influence, yet countered by mentioning that not all union members were "party-liners." To the contrary, workers joined the ILWU because it had a proven track record of improving labor conditions and wages—one that had secured "the homes, automobiles, and education . . . considered by many Hawaiians as good insurance against Communism." Hawai'i's leaders and citizens, too, had demonstrated their resolve to defeat the red menace. In 1950, the House Un-American Activities Committee had investigated the islands, leading to the arrest of seven suspected Communists, including ILWU regional director Jack Hall. Carter noted that a local, multiracial jury had convicted the accused for advocating the overthrow of the US government. Furthermore, the territorial legislature had initiated a committee on subversive activities, while its proposed state constitution would be the first in the nation to bar Communists from political office. "None of this sounds like communist domination or unawareness of communism," he deduced.[49]

More and more, Americans agreed with Carter's assessment as McCarthyism fell out of fashion in mid-1950s and Hawai'is leftists pursued their progressive agenda through politically acceptable channels (i.e., the territory's Democratic Party). The Smith Act convictions had undeniably weakened the local Communist Party, and the ILWU's numbers had shrunk with the technical advances in sugar production and the economic move away from agriculture toward tourism and other industries. After 1956, the specter of Communist subversion, while still present in the debates, no longer presented an obstacle to statehood.[50]

Besides interracial marriage, cultural compatibility, and Americanization (with its concomitant anti-Communism), statehood's champions used socioeconomic advancement to measure assimilation. As Lind explained, changing structural conditions presented novel opportunities for workers who had historically been confined to sugar and pineapple production. On the one hand, plantation work itself had become increasingly mechanized, requiring (and paying for) handlers possessing technical knowledge. Putting a positive spin on labor militancy, he argued that the growing strength of Hawai'i's unions after World War II enabled members to secure the highest agricultural wages in the world, thereby making these positions even more attractive. On the other hand, the overall economic shift on the islands from a plantation economy to one built on commerce, tourism, and defense opened up new positions in clerical work, the professions, and public administration, including the military. While Lind found that the territory's various ethnicities and races had left the plantations unevenly, generally speaking the proportion of agricultural hands had declined since 1940, corresponding to an uptick in the ranks of white-collar workers. In 1950, haoles remained the most advantaged of all groups (16.9 and 8.9 percent, respectively, of all professionals and laborers). Chinese were not far behind, comprising 10.7 percent of Hawai'i's professionals (compared to just 0.5 percent in 1910) and only 5.3 percent of laborers. Japanese made up 5.5 percent of all professionals and 32.8 percent of all laborers. Filipinos, who tended to be less affluent and educated than Chinese and Japanese, still evidenced this upward trend, going from 0.7 to 1.2 percent, respectively, of all professionals from 1940 and 1950, and 80.1 to 53.6 percent, respectively of all laborers in the same ten-year span. The *New York Times* highlighted this movement, quoting Lind's observation that the "rise from coolie to millionaire," while not an everyday occurrence, had happened enough times among Hawai'i's Asians "to partially justify the local Horatio Alger myth." By contrast, Native Hawaiians were nearly absent in these discussions, save for the rare mention of their desires for independence and fears of increasing marginalization, or a nod to their "culture" as an obstacle preventing their advancement. This obscurity simultaneously reinforced the notion of Hawai'i as an Asiatic locale while minimizing the downward mobility of indigenous peoples under US rule.[51]

The ascendance of racial liberalism grounded the extraordinary traction gained by the racial paradise paradigm and its attendant themes of assimilation and Americanization in the postwar statehood deliberations. If the Negro Problem posed the greatest domestic American Dilemma of the mid-twentieth century, then Hawai'i offered a glimpse of its possible resolution through racial liberalism's major tenets: assimilation, integration, and state intervention. Hawai'i validated the liberal approach to black civil rights, even if the territory's precise formula for a multi-hued, peaceable existence (especially race mixing) could be applied only to itself. (Plainly, except for the occasional mention of African American transplants—usually soldiers or veterans stationed in the Pacific—descriptions of Hawai'i's people did not foreground the "amalgamation" of blacks.) Mid-century liberals habitually addressed the existence of racism in American life by distinguishing between the nation's realities and its ideals, so that racial reform was construed as both an accomplishment and a goal. The incompleteness was only a temporary condition, given the existence of what Myrdal had christened the American Creed—the dedication to securing freedom and equality for all as the driving force in American history. Hawai'i fit securely with this plotline. Depictions of the archipelago as a harmonious melting pot demonstrated what had been achieved under American democracy (equality within Hawaiian society), while upgrading its territorial status presented an opportunity for the nation to bring nonwhite islanders up to parity with citizens on the mainland (equality within US society). Designating statehood as the solution to the problem of Asiatic second-class citizenship, furthermore, upheld liberal thinking by legitimating state intervention in racial reform and by renewing the ideology's emphasis on formal equality in lieu of more far-reaching social, economic, and political change. Hawai'i statehood was not only "safe" in this regard, but also because it rendered Native Hawaiians invisible and allowed Americans to evade an uncomfortable confrontation with the consequences of the United States' colonial occupation.[52]

Cold War justifications buttressed the liberal vision. By constructing Hawai'i as the almost-complete model of multiracial democracy, statehood champions ably conveyed to the nation at large the high stakes of the decision at precisely the time when the United States needed to redress the status of black citizenship in order to convince the world of its qualifications for global leadership. The issue was not about other nations monitoring the actions of the United States per se but rather the ability of the admission campaign to persuade the American people that the votes of their legislators would have reverberations throughout the planet. After all, it would be the senator from Indiana, not the people of India, who would decide the territory's fate.

Anticolonialism, international diplomacy, and racial liberalism clearly struck many mainlanders as issues of consequence, and people of diverse backgrounds and social positions expressed their approval of Hawai'i's proposal to join the Union. The American Institute of Public Opinion found that a sizable majority consistently favored statehood throughout the 1940s and 1950s. Between 1946 and 1958, support for statehood among those sampled ranged from a low of 60 percent to a high of 81 percent in 1950—a spike that institute director George Gallup attributed to the outbreak of the Korean War.[53] (Gallup also found that nearly 55 percent of the respondents in a 1957 poll agreed that the "present trouble between the races in the South has hurt our relations with countries abroad.")[54] Endorsements by scores of organizations nationwide substantiated this conclusion: the NAACP, the Associated Negro Press, the National Education Association, the American Legion, Veterans of Foreign Wars, Disabled American Veterans, AMVETS, the AFL-CIO, the YWCA, the National Association of Real Estate Boards, and Lions Club International. State legislatures including those in Nebraska, Oklahoma, and

New Mexico officially sanctioned statehood, as did over two thousand chambers of commerce, more than 90 percent of continental newspapers, and both the national Republican and Democratic parties.[55] Much of the public, it seemed, had come accept Asiatic *inclusion* as a political reality, if not a necessity.

Cognizant of this phenomenal opportunity to secure their citizenship standing, Asian Americans facilitated the campaign's forward thrust. Some spoke on behalf of their particular ethnic group, while others made the case for statehood's importance to all persons of Asian ancestry in the United States. Calling on its readers to support the cause, San Francisco's *Chinese News* maintained that the "cycle of democracy"—"sparked by the stirring drums of the spirit of '76 and echoed today by the battle-commands of Chinese-American officers and men fighting in Korea"— would not be "fully completed" until Hawai'i achieved statehood and Congress welcomed a Chinese American to its chambers.[56] JACL's Masa-oka told the Senate Committee on Interior and Insular Affairs that after the McCarran-Walter Act, statehood was "the next logical step in that progress for equality of status" for Japanese Americans."[57] Proentry reso-lutions and depositions by a number of Hawai'i-based Asian American organizations, including the 442nd Veterans Club (a crucial part of the political base that instituted Hawai'i's Democratic Revolution), Club 100 (an organization for veterans of the 100th Infantry Battalion), the Fili-pino Federation of America, Inc., the Chinese Chamber of Commerce, the United Chinese Society, and the American Chinese Club, further evinced the direct correlation that many Asian Americans drew between their social status and admission.[58]

After fifty-six years, those in favor of statehood finally overcame resis-tance to the notion in its many guises. Fighting until the end, southern states' rights Democrats did not give up attempting to block admission. As South Carolina senator Strom Thurmond argued during his eleventh-hour attempt to delay statehood's passage on the final day of the senate debate in March 1959, Hawai'i's "Eastern heritage"—one that was "not necessarily inferior, but different"—would forever prevent a true fusion of Hawai'i and the United States. But it was too late. The hegemony of a globally conscious racial liberalism, precedence of Alaska's recent entry into the Union, overwhelming support for statehood on the islands (with the notable exceptions of some conservative haole and numerous Na-tive Hawaiians), and election of mainstream Democratic majorities to the House and Senate in 1958 combined to safeguard approval. When the bill finally passed both chambers of Congress, supporters cheered the verdict, proclaiming it a "miracle" and an "exhilarating climax to the long struggle."[59]

FIGURE 7.1 Six-year-old Dodie Bacon smiles at the *Honolulu Star-Bulletin*'s March 12, 1959 headline celebrating Hawai'i statehood. Shot by her father George Bacon, the iconic photograph—nodding to the popular conception of the islands as a "Pacific Melting Pot" and a "bridge to Asia"—circulated worldwide.

Courtesy of George Bacon Collection, Hawai'i State Archives.

Misters Fong and Inouye Go to Washington, Taipei, and Tokyo

Americans had high hopes for their newest state. At last, here was the unmatched opportunity for the United States to offset "the bad effect of Little Rock in Japan."[60] With no less than the balance of international relations at risk, the nation followed the inaugural contests for Hawai'i's public offices with rapt attention.[61] Asian American aspirants made a strong showing at the polls, capturing forty-two of the eighty-one open positions, including one of the two US Senate seats (by Chinese American Hiram Fong) and Hawai'i's sole berth in the House of Representatives (by Japanese American Inouye). The press saluted the event as "a melting pot election in a melting pot land" while President Eisenhower praised the results as a "very fine example" of "democracy at work." To many, the outcome denoted a watershed in the history of Asian American—and indeed, American—race and citizenship with global implications. As the

New York Times trumpeted, "We can now say to people of the Far East, 'Your brothers and cousins have equal rights with ourselves and are helping to make our laws.' "[62]

Incontrovertibly, the Cold War argument for statehood had primarily been a rhetorical strategy aimed at domestic audiences throughout the debate's duration. Yet a number of Hawai'i's leaders and federal officials had sought to implement this concept into concrete diplomatic outreach in the 1950s. University of Hawai'i president Gregg Sinclair recommended that the VOA broadcast radio and film segments about "the work of American democracy" on the islands. Territorial senator Herbert K. H. Lee, a Chinese American, advised Secretary of State Dean Acheson to utilize Hawai'i's "Americans of Oriental stock" to represent the United States in the Far and Middle East. John Goodyear, the US Consul in Singapore, correspondingly urged the State Department to augment the circulation of Asian Hawaiian "Americana"—depictions of assimilated Asians living harmoniously within island society—throughout his region as a means to foster Southeast Asians' identification with the United States' culture and values.[63] The US Information Agency took up these suggestions, producing an assortment of propaganda pieces with such titles as "Hawaii: A Land of Opportunity" and "Hawaii, U.S.A."[64] The State Department also invited Dr. Richard K. C. Lee, the Chinese American president of Hawai'i's Board of Health, and Lawrence Nakatsuka, the Japanese American press secretary to the territorial governor, to lecture in several Asia-Pacific countries as part of its Leaders' and Specialists' Exchange program. US emissaries favorably assessed the expeditions, applauding both for conveying faith in the "democratic way of life" and displaying "forcible proof" of Asian American upward mobility.[65]

Fong and Inouye willingly inherited this agenda with their respective electoral victories. In October–November 1959, Fong personally financed a multicity fact-finding trip (to Tokyo, Seoul, Taipei, Manila, Singapore, Ipoh, Kuala Lumpur, Saigon, Phnom Penh, Vientiane, Bangkok, Korat, Rangoon, Hong Kong, and Okinawa) with the dual objectives of acquainting himself with the economic, political, social, and military conditions of the various locales along with promoting ties between his host countries and the United States. At each stop, the senator met with high-level dignitaries (Taiwan's first couple, President and Madame Chiang, South Korean president Syngman Rhee, and Philippines vice president Diosdado Macapagal); toured military installations, agricultural projects, and educator training facilities; conducted press conferences, recorded radio broadcasts and telecasts, and spoke before a range of audiences (such as the Korean National Assembly, the Singapore Rotary Club, and a Thailand Fulbright alumni group). During his appearances, Fong invoked the trope of Hawai'i as a racial paradise to underscore opportunities under

US democracy for people of all backgrounds, pointing to his own experiences as evidence. Not least, he repeatedly encouraged Overseas Chinese communities and the Southeast Asian governments to study the example of Chinese in the United States as a guide for assimilating those populations as well as elevating them to full citizenship and equality. Foreign Service officials raved that the visit furthered US interest in the region, spelling out for locals the "meaning of Hawaii statehood and his own success." The embassy in Manila was pleasantly surprised that Fong's address to the Su Yuen Tang Chinese family association stirred several Cantonese Filipinos present to "prais[e] the United States as the bastion of liberty and racial equality."[66]

Like Fong, Inouye stepped into his preordained role as transpacific intermediary with ease. Within days of his election, he announced his wish to travel to Japan as a living example of the possibilities afforded by US democracy and a "bridge of understanding" between the two nations. Inouye spent three weeks in the Far East in December 1959, seeing Tokyo along with Naha (Okinawa), Seoul, Taipei, Hong Kong, and the Philippines. As the centerpiece of his tour, the visit to Japan in particular generated much excitement. Inouye followed a packed itinerary in Tokyo, calling on Prime Minister Kishi, Foreign Minister Fujiyama, Crown Prince Akihito, and Princess Michiko; meeting with members of the Diet; and addressing the Foreign Correspondents Club, using these encounters to promote the economic and political partnership of Japan and the United States and press for the ratification of a mutual security pact. He and his wife, Margaret, also underscored their pride in their US citizenship and appreciation of their Japanese cultural heritage.[67]

State Department officials were delighted with the representative's performance, lauding it as a "major contribution to the strengthening of U.S.-Japan friendship." According to the Tokyo embassy's official report, one gauge of Inouye's impact was the record number of viewers who tuned in to his guest turn on the Japanese television series *Life Is a Drama*. The episode featured his family members, friends, Ambassador Douglass MacArthur II, and the man who saved Inouye's life during combat, all of which resulted in "great emotional impact." Overall, the Inouyes garnered more attention from the Japanese press than any other Americans who visited Japan that year. The representative affirmed this assessment. "The Asians were stunned and thrilled that I was elected," he told *Look* magazine. "My becoming a congressman personified for them our democratic way of life."[68]

Fong's and Inouye's international tours captured the tensions inherent in Asian American citizenship at midcentury. Certainly, the willingness of many Americans to admit Hawai'i to statehood signaled a radical departure from the alarm surrounding the Oriental Problem. But the appearances abroad of the senator and congressman as official emissaries of the United States—the very apex of inclusion—drew on and further consolidated their otherness as not-white and ineradicably foreign. As a case in point, the *New York Times* proclaimed Fong, above all his colleagues, as the best fit for the role of ambassador to the Pacific Rim: "The color of his skin and the shape of his eyes tell his story to an Asian audience before he begins to speak. . . . The appearance in Asia of a United States Senator with Oriental features could hardly be matched in effectiveness." In the same vein, Inouye expected that other members of the House of Representatives would assume him to be knowledgeable about Japan.[69]

Neither Fong nor Inouye explicitly denied this assumption of natural affinity, perhaps because of genuine interest in the region, heartfelt commitments to fighting Communism and improving the future of US-Asia relations, or desires to shore up their own political capital. Certainly Fong did not shy away from claiming racial expertise. Before his trip, he contacted each of the consulates and embassies to inquire about the status and treatment of the Overseas Chinese in those regions. Despite his insistence that he be regarded as a representative of Hawai'i and the United States rather than as "the Senator from Taiwan," Fong actively spoke out on the Overseas Chinese issue at each point on his journey, sometimes to the chagrin of State Department officials, who feared that his interventions would inflame area ethnic tensions. And in his election bids in 1959 and 1964, Fong ran under the campaign slogan "Man of the Pacific." Inouye, too, played up the notion of Asian Americans' essential connection to Asia during his tour by stressing the "special place" of Nisei in advancing US-Japan relations, rekindling the vision that Japanese American leaders had espoused in earlier decades before World War II forced them to abandon the idea.[70]

Hawai'i statehood and the Fong and Inouye tours suggest that even the very height of Asian Americans' inclusion into the nation at midcentury did not necessarily translate into the absence of alienage. In these moments, the state and the public recognized Asians in the United States as uber-Americans while at the same time reinscribing their difference from whites and thus their distance from full citizenship.

Fong, Inouye, and the Invention of the Model Minority

Along with diplomatic duties, Americans envisaged a second task for the fledgling state and its congressmen. In acclaiming Hawai'i as a melting pot and racial paradise, observers saw its utility as an exemplar for domestic relations—tempering the bad effect of Little Rock in Little Rock, as it

FIGURE 7.2 Campaign poster for Senator Hiram Fong.
Courtesy of the collection of the estate of Hiram Leong Fong.

were. The accent on Hawai'i's promise for improving America's racial woes was not entirely new. Liberals, of course, had long noted Hawai'i's "unorthodox race doctrine." As *Life* contended in 1948, "The Islands' contribution to the United States will be an example of warm tolerance and understanding almost unknown in the 48 states now considering Hawaii's bid to join them." Still, Cold War imperatives took precedence over ameliorating the plight of African Americans in arguments favoring statehood before 1959.[71]

Once admission became a certainty, proponents' focus shifted more squarely to Hawai'i's role in advancing a solution to the Negro Problem, given its symbolically closer relationship to the mainland, the prospect of real voting power in Congress, and the press of the civil rights movement. In the final round of hearings conducted by the House in January 1959, Massachusetts representative John W. McCormack emphasized that Hawai'i's unparalleled record in interracial "cooperation" would have a "salutary effect" on similar efforts throughout the mainland. Expectations ran high. The *Chicago Defender* decreed that Hawai'i's citizens must be cognizant of their "mission" to thwart the congressional southern bloc and "bring down the walls of American race prejudice."[72]

While contemporaries generally assumed that as nonwhites, Hawai'i's people would sympathize with black struggles for equality, they nonetheless intimated that islanders would approach race relations in a culturally distinct manner. The ubiquitous James Michener, speaking yet again on behalf of the statehood movement, pointed to the fiftieth state's potential to treat the "grave internal problems" plaguing the South. Hawai'i's congressional emissaries held the possibility of "contribut[ing] to the relaxation of such tensions" through "conciliatory means" and "quiet precept," rather than "shout[ing] and bellow[ing]." Hawai'i's senators and representatives of Chinese and Japanese ancestry, in other words, would set the standard of political conduct to be emulated by both black civil rights activists and the mobs of white massive resistance. Michener's musings previewed the increasing identification of Asian Americans with such cultural traits as moderation and restraint in the coming decade.[73]

As in the realm of international relations, Fong and Inouye shouldered the weight of this anticipation, finding themselves catapulted into the national spotlight. The intersection of their historic responsibilities, the novelty of their racial difference, and their spell-binding personal trajectories riveted the public. This extensive notice positioned them as the most visible Asian American figures of the day—a distinction reified by the duo's immortalization in Washington, DC's Wax Museum of History alongside such notables as Abraham Lincoln and Babe Ruth.[74] In effect, Fong and Inouye became not only the representative faces of Hawai'i but also stand-ins for Asian America in its entirety. Their rise to prominence greatly advanced the crystallization of the model minority concept in the 1960s.

Fong personified the rags-to-riches American meritocracy ideal, prompting the media to label him a "Hawaiian Horatio Alger." Various profiles applauded the determination of this son of immigrant sugarcane laborers to "lift himself out of poverty" from a young age by peddling newspapers, shining shoes, and delivering poi. By his own account, Fong worked his way through his undergraduate studies at the University of Hawai'i, saving just enough to attend Harvard Law School, and then returned home with "10 cents in my pocket" to found his own firm. He diversified his pursuits by running for a seat in the territorial legislature, twice succeeding in 1938 and 1941. With the outbreak of World War II, Fong interrupted his budding political career to serve in the US Army Air Force. After his stint in the military, he returned to government, serving as Hawai'i's speaker and vice speaker of the House. Incredibly, Fong also found time to preside over multiple business ventures in real estate, finance, and bananas, among others.[75] On the eve of his swearing in, *Pageant* magazine eulogized that this "American success story" was "clear proof that racism has no permanent place in America." Fong concurred, "I hope that the American people will see my life as symbolic of the opportunity offered only in a democratic society such as ours." This uplifting narrative decidedly upheld some of midcentury liberalism's most cherished orthodoxies, especially the integration and assimilation of racial minorities.[76]

Fong's relationship to this ideology, however, was not uncomplicated. On the one hand, Fong's odyssey resonated with the liberal impulse to create a multiracial nation. On the other hand, his racial views aligned more closely to conservatives. He expressed a belief in racial equality, but also hesitated to support civil rights law, stating, "We shouldn't rush into a flood of legislation to reform a mode of living that has been going on for years in the South." The African American press in particular conveyed disappointment in the senator's stance. "Don't believe those false reports about the tremendous liberality rampant in Hawaii," responded a *Los Angeles Sentinel* columnist. "Maybe after some Dixiecrat calls him a 'coolie' he'll change his mind fast!" During the 1968 Republican National Convention, the *Sentinel* described Fong as a "Political Jekyll and Hyde" given the disconnection between his racial background and voting record: "Hiram Fong is by no means a 'colored' thinker or senator. Come to think of it what Chinese is?" From this vantage point, Fong was definitively not-black, as was the totality of Chinese America by extrapolation.[77]

Biographies of Inouye embraced a contrasting emphasis: his stature as the consummate Nisei soldier. As a member of the famed 442nd Regimental Combat Team, he rose to the rank of captain and earned numerous decorations (the Purple Heart, a Distinguished Service Cross, and a Bronze Star). While in action, Inouye lost his right arm—a sacrifice unfailingly mentioned by reporters. ("Asked if he would fight to defend America, he holds up his empty sleeve, says, 'The country can have the other one, too.'") The injury extinguished his aspirations to a medical career, and Inouye turned instead to law and government. After attending the University of Hawai'i and George Washington University Law School on the GI Bill, the veteran practiced as an attorney and deputy prosecutor in Honolulu, then secured a seat in the Territorial House as part of the 1954 Democratic Revolution. Inouye won reelection in 1956 before moving to the Territorial Senate in 1958 and then on to Washington, DC, the following year.[78]

The representative's popularity and renown surged quickly. In Hawai'i's first House race, Inouye received 68 percent of the votes cast. He handily reclaimed his position in 1960 with an even more impressive 74 percent landslide. The US Junior Chamber of Commerce ranked him among the ten outstanding young men of 1959, while *Life* magazine named him one of the hundred most influential young members of the "Take-Over Generation" poised to assume leadership in US society, culture, and politics. In 1962, Inouye defeated Benjamin Franklin Dillingham II, scion of one of the islands' most elite haole families, in what *Newsweek* dubbed an "eye-catching race" for Hawai'i's open Senate seat.[79]

As with Fong, Inouye's prodigious climb spoke to what many saw as the growing urgency to defend the tenets of liberal democracy. His life was further evidence that race no longer handicapped individual progress. Inouye's memoir *Journey to Washington*—first published in 1967 and excerpted in *Reader's Digest* in February 1968—spoke directly to this message. In the introduction, Inouye stressed the similarities between the experiences of Americans with roots in the Asia and those whose families originated in Europe. Both groups faced the same challenges of "assimilation": survival, cultural adaptation, upward mobility, and "full acceptance by their fellow-countrymen." Throughout his autobiography,

FIGURE 7.3 Vice President Lyndon B. Johnson administers the Oath of Office to Senator Daniel Inouye in a reenactment of his January 1963 swearing-in ceremony.
Courtesy of the Associated Press.

Inouye repeatedly insisted on this overlap as he retraced his steps from Honolulu's slums to Capitol Hill. The point was that the United States was a nation of immigrants as well as a place that allowed each one "to aspire to the topmost limits of his own talent and energy," regardless of ancestry or background.[80]

Journey to Washington's significance lay in its dual cultural-political intervention at a moment when postwar racial liberalism was coming under heavy fire for its failure to solve the American Dilemma. At its core, the book upheld the vision of race management touted by liberal leaders since World War II: tolerance, civil rights, equality of opportunity, integration, and assimilation. In the first of three forewords, President Johnson praised Inouye's "relentless struggle to achieve freedom of opportunity and equality for Americans of Japanese ancestry, and for all racial and religious minorities." Vice president Hubert H. Humphrey, author of the second prologue, noted that despite their differences in upbringing, he and Inouye "both had the great gift of discovering that there is no limit to the aspirations of an American boy." In the third preface, Senate majority leader Mike Mansfield celebrated the United States' ability to right the past wrongs of Asiatic Exclusion by merging its "Oriental strain" into the "main body of America's humanity," epitomized by Inouye's attainments. The trio of introductions framed Inouye's life history as an allegory of racial progress under US liberal democracy, supplying indisputable attestation of both nonwhite, individual advancement and the corporate achievement of a multiracial nation. More obliquely, *Journey to Washington* also validated the notion of state engineering to address racial inequality—the feature of racial liberalism facing perhaps the most vigorous assault from the Right by the late 1960s. Various moments throughout the text symbolized and vindicated the federal government's actions to facilitate Asiatic integration, especially the formation of the 442nd and Hawai'i statehood.[81]

The book's other main interposition was its portrayal of Inouye as a prototypical model minority figure. While much of the text highlighted the senator's achievements as result of his individual efforts, Inouye acknowledged the importance of the GI Bill and his military pension in providing him access to college, law school, and ultimately the middle class and political elite. By presenting these forms of government assistance as both nonraced and earned by the heroes of the 442nd, however, the memoir forestalled criticisms of Japanese Americans as a coddled minority group profiting from the Great Society's largesse and the War on Poverty's expansion of the welfare state. Inouye's narrative, in other words, placed Japanese Americans in the category of deserving citizens as opposed to that of the undeserving (i.e., black) poor. Moreover, in sculpting the narrative arc as a "Journey *to* Washington," Inouye's story presented Nisei's attainment of full citizenship as participation in mainstream electoral politics. This representation clarified the incipient notion of Asian Americans as not-black by implicitly invoking the foils of African American activism in the civil rights and black power movements.[82]

This is not to say that Inouye deliberately intended to position Asian Americans as model minorities against African Americans. To be clear, he himself was troubled by the increasingly prevalent inclination to counterpose the two groups in the context of the late 1960s' racial politics. Delivering the keynote address at the 1968 Democratic National Convention in Chicago, Inouye recounted, "As an American whose ancestors come from Japan, I have become accustomed to a question most recently asked by a very prominent businessman who was concerned about the threat of riots and of the resultant loss in life and property. 'Tell me,' he said, 'why can't the Negro be more like you?'" "You" in this statement functioned as a rhetorical shorthand, referring both to Inouye as an individual and a representative of all Asians in the United States. Furthermore, without the need for elaboration, "you" conjured up and braced the embryonic stereotype of "Orientals" as politically moderate, patriotic, industrious, and eager to assimilate. Soberly, Inouye challenged this juxtaposition by dismissing the comparison as unsound. "Although my skin is colored it is not black," he declared. Unlike African Americans, Asians in the United States had never endured chattel slavery or been subjected to "systematic racist deprivation" comparable to the extent of Jim Crow. The solution to the American Dilemma therefore could not be achieved by simply having blacks "be like" Asians. In rejecting the suggestion that Asians serve as paragons of conduct for African Americans, Inouye clearly delineated a boundary between the two. Because Asian Americans were definitively not-black, he stressed, they could *not* serve as models for African American assimilation.[83]

Inouye's Democratic National Convention appearance, though, accomplished the opposite effect. Observers interpreted both the message and messenger as confirmation of Asian Americans' model minority status. Journalists noted that the senator disciplined all those who engaged in protest politics, whether in support of civil rights or black power, or against the Vietnam War, in calling on the nation to shun "violence" and "anarchy" in favor of "law and order." When the *Memphis Commercial Appeal* declared, "You don't tell a man such as this that he knows nothing about poverty, discrimination, war, or changing human needs and conditions," it echoed the social commentators and government officials who claimed that Asian Americans had achieved socioeconomic success through hard work and quiet assimilation, notwithstanding a history of intense racial hardship. Grasping the political utility of this comparison, Johnson urged Democratic presidential nominee Humphrey to select Inouye as his running mate: "He answers Vietnam with that empty sleeve. He answers your problems with Nixon with that empty sleeve. He has that brown face. He answers everything in civil rights, and he draws a contrast without ever opening his mouth." Summarily, even as he decried this association, Inouye embodied the new racial wisdom marking Asian Americans as the "good" people of color.[84]

Inouye closed his remarks at the Democratic National Convention by bidding convention delegates "aloha"—a fitting gesture to the spatial corollary of Asian American racialization. After admission, Hawai'i endured in the national imagination as a modern racial paradise, justifying not only the United States' continuing political domination but also its capitalist encroachment. The persistence of this fantasy hinged in part on regenerating the trope of the vanishing native in relation to Asian American "success." Poststatehood accounts of Hawaiian society remarked on the "rapidly" disappearing indigenous population. As Hawai'i's "sophisticated civilization" displaced "old Polynesia," so, too, were "full-blooded" Native Hawaiians destined to fade into the mixed-race population with only vestiges of their traditional culture to remain. Contemporaries juxtaposed the fate of Native Hawaiians to the rise of the "AJA"s (Americans of Japanese Ancestry). They relegated Native Hawaiians to the primitive past, whereas they hailed Japanese Americans as the symbols of the islands' future. While such ruminations were generally celebratory, competing voices could occasionally be discerned. One example was that of Reverend Abraham Akaka, who conveyed the ambivalence toward statehood expressed by many of his fellow Native Hawaiians. On the day after Congress passed the Hawai'i statehood bill, Akaka sermonized, "There are some of us to whom statehood brings great hopes, and there are those to whom statehood brings silent fears. . . . There are fears that Hawaii as a state will be motivated by economic greed, that statehood will turn Hawaii . . . into a great big spiritual junkyard filled with smashed dreams, worn out illusions; that it will make the Hawaiian people lonely, confused, insecure, empty, anxious, restless, disillusioned—a wistful people." Later he mused that "the Hawaiian . . . must chart his own steps, make his own studies, and make up his own mind" to prevent the total erasure of Native Hawaiian "identity."[85]

Such protestations nonetheless remained overshadowed by the dominant discourse of Hawai'i as a racial paradise. Notably, the first report of the US Commission on Civil Rights in 1959 rehearsed the conviction that Hawai'i boasted a culture of tolerance and integration, rooted in "mutual respect, understanding, and widespread appreciation of the dignity and goodness of human beings."[86] By the late 1960s, urban crises breathed new life into this timeworn construct, reshaping the idea of Hawai'i into a definitively not-black melting pot. "In the time of civil rights struggles across the nation on the mainland, Hawaii stands aloof. Only a few exclusive clubs still discriminate against orientals, and few obstacles remain to advancement of a member of any racial group," observed the *Chicago Daily Tribune*. Syndicated newspaper columnist Drew Pearson drew unambiguous contrasts between the islands' Asian Americans and African Americans in northern cities. "What's happened in Hawaii is a healthy reversal of what's happening on the mainland. In Detroit, Newark, and other big cities, it's the young Negro who is the disillusioned troublemaker. In Hawaii, it's the young generation which is building up a loyal citizenry, setting an example of racial understanding."[87] Depictions of Honolulu as an anti-Detroit and anti-Newark replicated and regenerated characterizations of Asian American propriety in contradistinction to

African American lawlessness. More broadly, the mutual constitution of Asian and African American racialization in this geographic comparison corroborated the merging of distinctly regional racial systems (Hawai'i, West, North, and South) into a national order that would continue to depend on juxtapositioning the Asian American model minority and the African American underclass to reproduce white privilege in the post–civil rights era.[88]

The history of Hawai'i's relationship to the United States might be seen as a microcosm of the trajectory of Asian American race and citizenship from the late nineteenth through the mid-twentieth centuries. Once reviled as the islands' Oriental Problem, inhabitants of Asian ancestry resurfaced as model minorities through the course of the statehood debate alongside parallel changes on the mainland. The willingness of so many Americans to admit the territory of Hawai'i as the fiftieth state in the Union was the material counterpart to this discursive shift.

Asian Americans and people of all backgrounds welcomed this change in status with hearty enthusiasm. And yet to reiterate, this seemingly inclusive gesture begat a new set of exclusions and marginalizations. It obscured the very existence of Native Hawaiians and problems that they faced as colonized subjects. It furthered assumptions about the perpetual foreignness of ethnic Asians. And it reinvigorated popular beliefs about the unruliness and criminality of African Americans. These consequences have served to buttress continuing inequalities in the late twentieth and early twenty-first centuries, whether in terms of refusals to recognize indigenous sovereignty claims or denials of human rights.[89]

Hawai'i statehood, finally, illuminates the ongoing narration of US national identity as characterized by exceptionalism in a double sense. The framing of admission as the only possibility for Hawai'i's future in the liberal political discourse of the 1940s and 1950s effectively obfuscated the similarities between the United States' imperial ventures and those of the European empires. In a different vein, but no less troubling, national conversations about statehood set African Americans apart as exceptions to the rule of immigrant assimilation and incorporation. While seemingly discrete, both projects together served to legitimate the spread of the United States' global hegemony by valorizing American democracy as exceptional, benevolent, and superior to alternative arrangements of power.[90]

Epilogue

Model Minority/Asian American

By the twilight of the civil rights era, the success stories of Japanese and Chinese America had themselves become success stories. The cross pressures of exigencies and desires both within and beyond the ethnic communities had effectively midwifed the rebirth of the Asiatic as the model minority. Since then, the model minority has remained a fixture of the nation's racial landscape, ever present yet constantly evolving to speak to a host of new imperatives in the late twentieth century and early twenty-first. Recent iterations depart from the original in notable ways, but retain many of the themes that first coalesced in the postwar period: self-reliance, valorization of family, reverence for education, and political moderation. The persistence of these features suggests that the model minority's durability—like its origins—is about more than just race. Its longevity derives from its ability to adapt to changing historical circumstances. Far from being an outdated vestige of the mid-twentieth century, its periodic resuscitation effectively commands attention because of its flexibility and capaciousness, shape-shifting to respond to the nation's most pressing questions. The reproduction of the model minority as racial truth has posed new obstacles to freedom and equality for Americans from all walks of life. Yet it has also contained the seeds of its own critique, paradoxically serving as a rallying point for the formation of an innovative racial identity—Asian American—grounded in dreams of a different kind of world.[1]

The mid- to late 1960s witnessed the convergence of the postwar trajectories of Japanese and Chinese American racialization. World War II had set the two peoples on distinct, albeit imbricating, paths; both were remade from indelible aliens into assimilating Others in the crucibles of racial liberalism, cultural conservatism, and global wars, although their respective transformations were occasioned by circumstances unique to each. While their merging into definitive not-blackness was neither predictable nor predetermined, it was also not without precedent. White Americans had historically been of divided mind about their samenesses and differences, acknowledging the inimitabilities of the Japanese and Chinese in their midst, while simultaneously conflating them as Orientals, the yellow peril, and aliens ineligible to citizenship. In hindsight, the consolidation of the two into a single cluster of consummate colored citizens was in a sense a mid-1960s' update of an ingrained American Orientalism that held that all Asians really did look—and act—alike.[2]

Subsequently, watchers tagged Japanese and Chinese Americans as model minorities in the same breath with greater frequency, as when the *Senior Scholastic* attributed their concurrent "reversal of fortunes" to a shared reverence for the family and "near-religious belief[s] in formal education as the best ladder for advancement."[3] Cold War imperatives continued to frame these acclamatory portraits. Speaking before Honolulu's East-West Center in 1966, President Johnson noted that the "promise of Asians at home" boded well for "new surge of promise in Asia," especially Vietnam, to modernize under the tutelage of the United States.[4]

Observers increasingly lumped the two together through their descriptions of a categorical not-blackness (and sometimes not-brownness). In myriad meditations about race in the United States, Japanese and Chinese Americans jointly assumed the position as exemplars of colored mobility. At times the comparison was implied, as when a *Chicago Tribune* reader mused, "There is *another* race that has been subjected to even greater prejudice and discrimination—the Asians." Yet through "quiet dignity," "hard work," and an "order of good citizenship higher than the average white," Asian children stayed in school, were not born out of wedlock, and did not grow up to become criminals or "create slums."[5] More often, the contrast was explicit. Charting the many grievances of America's racial minorities, *Ebony* acknowledged that Orientals faced intermittent barriers in house and job hunting, but concluded that they were "more acceptable to white people" than Native Americans, Mexicans, Puerto Ricans, and blacks.[6] *Pittsburgh Courier* columnist George Schuyler compared the greater economic vitality of the Chinese to his own African American community, provokingly noting, "They talk little, picket nobody, hold no mass meetings, denounce none."[7] In *Beyond the Melting Pot*, one of the era's seminal studies of ethnicity in the United States, sociologist Nathan Glazer accentuated the sluggishness of Puerto Ricans' socioeconomic motility by juxtaposing them with Japanese and Chinese. Puertorriqueños' lack of the "more tightly knit and better integrated systems" as seen in Asian immigrant communities had hobbled their group advancement.[8]

The combination of Japanese and Chinese American racialization marked a decisive moment in the formation of a *national* racial order out of the distinct regional hierarchies that had taken shape in the late nineteenth and early twentieth centuries as concomitants of provincial labor regimes. Like the Negro Problem, the global implications of the Oriental Problem demanded national attention. The solution to both drafted ethnic Japanese and Chinese into the disputes about the most vexing conundrum of American society and politics in the mid-twentieth century: the conditions of black citizenship.

Exchanges during the American Academy of Arts and Science's Conference on the Negro American drove home these decisive innovations in the nation's racial taxonomy. In May 1965, dozens of the era's most distinguished intellectuals and policymakers gathered to strategize the next phase of liberal racial reform. None other than Daniel Patrick Moynihan suggested that the participants scrutinize the "rather astonishing" situation of Japanese and Chinese Americans for inspiration on how to lift the racial "stigma" that impeded black progress. In the course of his research, he explained, he had disaggregated "nonwhite" demographic statistics and uncovered some startling facts. On the one hand, the proportion of Japanese and Chinese lacking any years of formal schooling was ten times greater than for whites. On the other hand, the proportion of Japanese and Chinese with postsecondary training and employed in professional, managerial, and proprietary positions was double that of whites, while their unemployment and divorce rates were only half of whites' levels. Twenty-five years ago, Asians had been "colored"; now, Moynihan asked, "Am I wrong that they have ceased to be colored?" The question hinged on a rhetorical sleight of hand. Japanese and Chinese remained not-white in the eyes of the law, Moynihan conceded. But what mattered for the purposes at hand was that this not-whiteness had been eclipsed by not-blackness. While conferees disagreed on exactly how this divergence came to be (Were Asiatic coolies comparable to African slaves? What about the vast disparity in the numbers of bodies?), the general consensus was that Orientals were not like blacks, and that behavior and culture, especially "strong" families, had made the difference.[9]

Moynihan's exhortation anticipated and assisted the rise of the model minority cottage industry—the production of new racial knowledge about Japanese and Chinese (and eventually other ethnic Asians) emphasizing in tandem socioeconomic advancement and not-blackness. One of its earliest, most enthusiastic evangelizers was syndicated columnist Joseph Alsop, whose writings appeared in over three hundred newspapers nationwide. Citing Moynihan, Alsop repeatedly urged social scientists to examine the "staggering" achievements of Asian Americans for clues to solving the nation's racial divide. In his view, higher education and "exceptionally strong family system[s]" had enabled both peoples to reach the "sunniest heights of American society." For Alsop, the expiry of the "Chinaman's chance" was verification that "prejudice can be defeated" for African Americans, rendering the study of the model minority phenomenon a worthwhile investment.[10] Social scientists obliged, and the question of how Asian advancement and not-blackness had been possible entered numerous research agendas on race after the mid-1960s.[11]

The easy cachet of model minority typecasting rested uncomfortably with many Japanese and Chinese Americans, however. Internal quarrels over such comparisons had brewed for years, reflecting a diversity of opinion about the best way to achieve racial equality. As the 1963 controversy over Imazeki's advice that blacks do some "soul searching" had shown, there was certainly no shortage of individuals who disagreed with the black freedom movement's emphasis on direct action. The same year, JACL's membership had also fiercely debated whether or not the organization should accept the invitation to participate in the March on Washington. The split among the directors and rank-and-file members obliged the leadership to issue an official statement on civil rights. With it, the league formally endorsed "intensified participation in responsible and constructive activities to obtain civil equality, social justice and full economic and educational opportunities as a matter of fundamental right for all Americans." Calling on the membership to meet these aspirations through "constructive activity," JACL pledged to support to the Leadership Conference on Civil Rights and promised to join in the march. The progressive aspects of the platform were counterbalanced by a relatively cautious emphasis on "seeking legislative, judicial, and executive fulfillment of constitutional guarantees of human rights." Japanese American organizations further to the Left blasted JACL for being too "meek," while some of the league's more conservative factions objected to any type of JACL presence at the demonstration. (In the end, only thirty-five or so JACL representatives attended the march, although a few hundred other Nikkei were there under other auspices.)[12]

But for all those who disapproved of the thrust of 1960s' civil rights activism, countless others felt a kinship with African Americans. Since World War II, numerous Japanese Americans had cultivated ties with blacks in solidarity against racial oppression. Individual community members devoted their energies to such causes as the Congress of Racial Equality and interracial Freedom Rides. Regional organizations including New York's Japanese American Committee for Democracy had made African American civil rights a top priority. On the national scene, JACL had stood at the forefront of this alliance in the postwar period, working with the NAACP on landmark civil rights cases (including *Shelley v. Kramer* [1948] and *Brown v. Board of Education* [1954]) and serving as the lone Asian American founding member of the Leadership Conference on Civil Rights lobbying coalition.[13]

Chinese Americans cultivated fewer bonds to the African American civil rights establishment, turning most of their political attention to China politics, US-China relations, and immigration reform between the 1940s and mid-1960s. Local-level clashes over issues such as the integration of Chinatown's new public housing projects in San Francisco, boycotts of Chinese businesses for their hostile treatment of black customers or failure to hire black employees, and the punishing social costs of black-Chinese relationships in places like Mississippi's Delta region had also impeded sustained cooperation. Still, some championed African Americans' quest for freedom. San Francisco's *Chinese World* occasionally ran editorials supporting black civil rights activists. Journalist Gilbert Woo, a staunch critic of US race relations, steadily alerted readers of the *Chinese Pacific Weekly* to antiblack racism, including discriminatory behaviors perpetrated by the Chinese. "We must sympathize with and support the exceptional black struggle for equality. This is the only way, and we are duty bound to follow it," he insisted, praising Chinese clergy who had recently sided with black protesters. Others joining in such coalition-building efforts included San Francisco's Chinese American Democratic Club, which spearheaded a fund-raising drive for the NAACP in 1963. As club president Harry W. Low urged, "In the past decade, Chinese-Americans have gained many new civil rights. Many of these gains are the result of vigorous efforts on the part of Negro leadership. . . . The work of all racial minorities for equality continues."[14]

These earlier rumblings erupted into the grassroots political mobilization known as the Asian American movement between the late 1960s and mid-1970s. Inspired by the era's militant struggles against racism and imperialism at home and abroad, thousands of participants nationwide spiritedly questioned existing arrangements of power and authority. They advanced alternative modes of community living through such diverse actions as opposition to the Vietnam War, worker organization, artistic production, and demanding affordable housing for the poor and elderly. Just as important, movement activists reenvisioned their own racialization as a significant facet of this "one struggle, many fronts." Embracing a new, pan-ethnic "Asian American" identity, they consciously rejected the model minority label as an insidious instantiation of the prevailing racist order. Amy Uyematsu expressed this view in her 1969 manifesto, "The Emergence of Yellow Power in America." In this call to arms, Uyematsu argued that Asians in the United States suffered from problems of "self-identity" by assuming the values and attitudes of the white middle class. She criticized Asians for their complicity in perpetuating racial oppression by "allow[ing] white America to hold up the 'successful' Oriental image before other minority groups as the model to emulate. White America justifies the blacks' position by showing that other non-whites—yellow people—have been able to 'adapt' to the system," she charged. The "Myth of Asian American Success," furthermore, harmed not only others but also themselves by glossing over continuing disparities between Asians and whites. Residents of urban "ghetto communities" remained vulnerable to poverty, tuberculosis, and social isolation. The time had come for the rise of "yellow political power" to address injustices "unique" to Asian Americans.[15]

Uyematsu's dictum signaled the Asian American movement's turn away from racial liberalism and its attendant endorsement of US Cold War hegemony as the ideological grounds on which to claim full citizenship. "Today we question whether we want to accept or be accepted by a society whose values are corrupted by greed, who [sic] perpetuates racism, war, and oppression. . . . We question our 'success' when we see young Asian brothers and sisters getting strung out on drugs, getting busted, fighting each other, and even committing suicide," espoused the Asian American Student Alliance of California State University at Long Beach. Likewise, members of the University of California, Santa Cruz's Third World Political Alliance expressed skepticism about the possibility of unmitigated equality under an assimilationist paradigm: "[We] are allowed to succeed economically, academically, and socially—but only to a certain extent. By an unspoken but real consensus, Asian Americans have not been completely acceptable regardless of how long they have been in this country."[16] Calling attention to Asian America's myriad problems, activists noted that even escape from the traditional inner-city enclaves—the very symbol of assimilation—had not guaranteed dignity and freedom. A feature on Nikkei of Gardena, California, in *Gidra*, the movement's leading publication, drew a portrait of "middle class miseries" plaguing suburban youths, including alienation, an obsession with materialism, and psychological pressures to achieve—the combination of which had led to mounting drug use and suicide.[17]

The movement's repudiation of the model minority and its assimilationist origins necessitated a critical reimagining of the relationship between Asian Americans and other communities of color. Believers deliberately inverted the trope of not-blackness and instead embraced affinities with African Americans, Native Americans, Chicanos, and Puerto Ricans, locating commonalities in their respective histories of exploitation as well as their shared desires for liberation and self-determination. Asian Americans throughout the country were greatly influenced by black thinkers such as Malcolm X and Franz Fanon, and backed an array of causes directly impacting "Third World" populations at home and abroad, ranging from antiprison work and Puerto Rican independence to indigenous sovereignty and especially ending the terrible brutalities in Vietnam. To be sure, cross-racial and transnational identifications were not unheralded. But the political framework within which these linkages were forged was original: Asian Americans made these connections as an integral part of their dual critique of US racism and imperialism in its various guises, including military interventions and anti-Communist nationalism. In connecting the plight of Asian Americans to other racial minorities in

FIGURE E.1 Asian American movement musician-activists Joanne (Nobuko) Miyamoto and Chris Iijima perform during a Martin Luther King Day celebration, Central Park, New York City, February 1971.
  Photograph by Bob Hsiang Photography.

the United States and nonwhite peoples everywhere, they exposed the inextricable interdependencies of domestic and foreign structures of power during the era of Cold War liberalism.

Thus Asian American identity was constituted in significant part by the model minority, even if Asian Americans explicitly denounced the model minority's racist logic. While the model minority gave rise to novel modes of racial subordination, it also opened up new possibilities for racial justice by catalyzing the rise of an Asian American political consciousness. By refusing to allow themselves to be used in upholding the distinction between good and bad minorities, those who adopted an Asian American identity articulated a critique of white supremacy and imperial domination—an intent that was the precise opposite of the ideological work of the model minority.

Animated by these imperatives, one of the most enduring legacies of the movement was the creation and first-phase institutionalization of Asian American studies. Students at San Francisco State College struck in November 1968 to demand the rights of all "Third World" peoples to higher education as well as a curriculum that they considered relevant to their communities. Alongside peers of various races, Asian Americans pushed for open admissions, student control of the hiring process, and the implementation of ethnic studies courses. After five contentious and violent months, the students wrested a monumental, if partial, victory when administrators agreed to open the nation's first School of Ethnic Studies. Actions at other campuses soon followed. Demands for an Asian American Studies Center at the University of California, Los Angeles explicated the desire to generate scholarship that more accurately reflected Asian American realities. "Much has been written and said about the 'success' of the 'Orientals.' . . . But the real experiences of the Asians in this country . . . have received no serious attention."[18] By 1973, movement campaigns had resulted in the opening of Asian American studies courses and programs across the nation—no small victory. But although such programs managed to gain an institutional foothold, they were unable to banish completely the model minority from the nation's racial topography.

These competing visions of racial identification collided on the national stage in January 1972 during a television broadcast of the CBS network's newsmagazine *60 Minutes*. Introducing the segment "100% Americans," correspondent Mike Wallace recited the proverbial narrative:

> "The model minority," they are called. They have scrambled into the American middle class from the economic ruin of the concentration camp. Yankee ingenuity, the will to work, a respect for learning and the law—all of them clichés one has to repeat about those super-Americans, the Japanese-Americans. They've become the very model of the way that white Americans like to think of themselves.

Visiting Southern California, home to the largest mainland concentration of Nikkei, Wallace observed a thriving community melding their ethnic heritage and "Japanese ethic" with the influences of Americanization. Japanese American children were a "schoolmaster's delight," earning top grades and winning disproportionately high percentages of scholarships.[19]

Yet *60 Minutes* also aired the tension between the success image and its discontents. One interviewee pointed out that Japanese Americans dealt increasingly with such ills as divorce and crime. When prodded by Wallace about whether he had ever "*really* suffered from white racism," a young man recalled his military experience in Vietnam, where he was subjected not only to racial epithets ("gook") but also singled out by officers and fellow soldiers as an example of the enemy. Wallace skeptically countered that "the Japanese-American has it made" compared to blacks and Chicanos. Another interviewee disagreed, arguing that a "good stereotype" was nonetheless an infringement of Nikkei's "human dignity," because it denied people the right to be treated as individuals. Unconvinced, Wallace suggested that well-to-do Nisei parents "like the

FIGURE E.2 Asian American movement participants rally to bring Asian American Studies to City College of New York, circa early 1970s.
Photograph by Mary Uyetmatsu Kao.

box they're in," taking pleasure in the material rewards of their industriousness and facing "little real sense of racial discrimination."[20]

60 Minutes foretold the lopsided battle between model minority and
anti–model minority discourse that has persisted since the late 1960s.
Structural changes in US law and global capital have driven the viral
reproduction of the Asian American success story, since expanded to encompass recent immigrant and refugee populations. The most significant
has been the passage of the 1965 Immigration Act. This milestone legislation superseded the national origins quotas, implemented in 1924,
that had altogether cut off migration from Asian and the Pacific to the
United States. The Cold War rendered such blatantly racist barriers to
entry shameful and clearly unsustainable, and liberal members of Congress leveraged this concern to install a new entry schema based on the
formal equality of all countries. The Immigration Act also enacted a preference system favoring the admission of white-collar workers, scientists,
and artists of "exceptional ability" to encourage the nation's evolution
from a manufacturing- to a knowledge- and service-based economy. Additional stipulations allowed for the entrance of business investors. Educated Asian professionals and entrepreneurs of means took advantage of
these reforms in unanticipated numbers. Soon an increasing proportion
of immigrants from Asia also came under family preference categories,
whereby the newly minted US citizens and permanent residents petitioned for the admission of their immediate relatives. Admittees, in turn,
applied for the entry of their immediate relatives, thereby establishing a
"chain migration" of Asians equipped with the educational and financial
capital to enter straightaway the ranks of American middle class. All told,
the post-1965 Asian "brain drain"/US "brain gain" has led to a marked
shift in the socioeconomic composition of Asian American communities,
tilting away from their historical roots in agriculture and labor. Today's
perception of Asian Americans as highly educated and affluent can be
traced directly to these selective immigration policies. As during the ages
of Asiatic Exclusion and racial liberalism, the state remains a preeminent
force in the racialization of Asian Americans.[21]

Model minority discourse of the late twentieth and early twenty-first
centuries simultaneously resembles and revises its original, Cold War–era
formulations. Once again, contemporary mass media and academicians
buttress the gravity of the state's hand in shaping the construction of
Asian America. Journalists have maintained their leading role in vivify-
ing the model minority concept in popular thought. Television programs
and periodicals have extolled "America's Super Minority" outpacing all
others in the classroom and labor force. As with their midcentury pro-
genitors, these updated versions of the nation's "greatest success story"
have emphasized the causal role of Asian-Confucian culture, especially

reverence for the family, in Asian American achievement. Social scientists, too, have continued to shore up these claims with their findings.[22]

Not-blackness has remained a core dimension but has shed its liberal imperatives, adapting instead to the needs of the rightward lurch in political culture. In the 1980s, conservatives who pondered the persistence of urban poverty renewed the comparison between African Americans and Asian Americans by counterposing the culture of the model minority to that of the "urban underclass," depicted as void of family values and impervious to change. Rather than understanding the worsening conditions in inner cities as a product of deindustrialization, apartheid, and other conditions of the global economy, conservatives trotted out indicators of Asian American success to justify reducing or eliminating welfare benefits and public services—cuts that impacted impoverished black and brown people most severely.[23]

During moments of national crisis in recent decades, analysts have dragooned black-Asian juxtapositions to serve an assortment of political ends, especially to excuse state inattention to the plight of the African American poor. Reporting on the 1992 Los Angeles riots, for instance, latched on to the notion of long-simmering black-Korean tensions as a root cause of the upheaval. Journalists and pundits predictably attributed the purported conflict to a clash of cultures: the African American ghetto dweller's propensity to sloth, vice, and lawlessness versus the Korean immigrant-entrepreneur's penchant toward the Confucian ethos of industry and kinship.[24] Coverage of New Orleans' Vietnamese Americans post–Hurricane Katrina in 2005 echoed the same dichotomy. The relatively high return rates of ethnic Vietnamese residents to their devastated homes, churches, and communities along with the speediness of their recuperation drew the attention of hundreds of local and national media outlets searching for feel-good stories to offset the terribleness of the disaster. Implicitly and explicitly, heroic tales of Southeast Asian self-sufficiency, rooted in "culture," contrasted sharply with the depictions of Gulf region African Americans: indigent, desperate, and—most of all—wholly dependent on federal rescue.[25]

The prominence of model minority narratives at these flashpoints offers insights into the (re)making of national identity from the 1970s onward. At a time of general unease about the decline of the United States' world stature, economic instability, and widening social inequalities, these anecdotes sustained the nation's mythology as a land of opportunity for all. Parables of the American Dream told with Asian protagonists dovetailed seamlessly with a nationalist revival among conservatives, who must have appreciated not only these affirmations of the nation's greatness but also their ability to give life to the Right's vision of citizenship. Asian American success stories allowed Reaganites and their political heirs to co-opt a version of the racial diversity championed by their liberal, multiculturalist opponents while making the case for color-blind, individualistic approaches to socioeconomic problems in lieu of expanding the welfare state. Recalling Nisei soldiers and Chinese American cultural diplomats, model citizens of an earlier era, tales of determined Korean small business owners and resilient Vietnamese Catholics modeled the conservative brand of nationalism that demanded traditional family values and hard work to reap the rewards of freedom and social mobility.[26]

For all the laudatory strands of newer model minority discourse that resemble its Cold War civil rights antecedent, an acute ambivalence about Asian American success stands out as markedly different. In lionizing Asian America as the embodiment of capitalist democracy's promise, social commentators have suggested that the entire nation, not just racial minorities, would benefit from mimicking model minority behavior. Many Americans have come to see Asians in their midst as *too* successful, however, outwhiting the whites yet again and again. In the 1980s, social observers warned that Asians were poised to infiltrate, if not supplant, the ranks of the nation's elite. In the middle of the decade, the Asian American Task Force on University Admissions discovered that a number of the nation's top universities had deliberately admitted "overrepresented" Asian American applicants at lower rates than other racial groups to preserve white access to these institutions.[27] Most alarmingly, such resentments have sometimes resulted in open hostility and violence. In 1987, the "Dotbusters," a group of whites jealous of the perceived prosperity of New Jersey's South Asian immigrant small business owners, publicly threatened to "go to any extreme to get Indians to move out." Within weeks, several white men beat Kaushal Sharan unconscious in the streets of Jersey City, leaving him brain damaged, and Latino youths killed Navroze Mody in neighboring Hoboken.[28] These tragedies bring into stark relief the ways in which ostensibly positive racialization can lead to dire—even life-threatening—consequences.

National conversations about the model minority demonstrate that Asian Americans' social standing remains inextricably bound to global forces; what has changed over time is that overseas economic competition has eclipsed geopolitical relations as the primary determining factor. Put bluntly, Americans' anxieties about stateside Asians are inseparable from qualms about marketplace rivalries between the United States and the established and emerging Pacific Rim powerhouses: Japan, the "Four Tigers" (Hong Kong, South Korea, Singapore, and Taiwan), Vietnam, India, and China. This uneasiness played out perhaps most poignantly in the 1982 fatal beating of Chinese American Vincent Chin by two white autoworkers in Detroit. ("It's because of you motherfuckers that we're out of work," bystanders overheard them cursing.)[29]

Arguably the episode that best captured the model minority's conflation of the domestic and foreign was the storm of debate detonated by
Yale law professor Amy Chua's contentious memoir *Battle Hymn of the
Tiger Mother* (2011). An abbreviated account, published in the *Wall Street
Journal* as "Why Chinese Mothers Are Superior," sketched Chua's austere
methods of child rearing to demonstrate "how Chinese parents raise such
stereotypically successful kids"—never mind her problematic identification as a "Chinese mother" as someone born and raised in the United
States. For her two daughters, daily marathon piano and violin practice
sessions were nonnegotiable, while sleepovers, playdates, television, and
video games were verboten. Mama Big Cat demanded perfection—grades
less than A were unacceptable—and claimed no hesitation in coercing,
shaming, or insulting her offspring to push them toward this goal. Hers
was a fundamentally different approach than "Western parents," who
were careful not to infringe on their children's individuality or damage
their self-esteem. "Chinese parents" adopted these methods, she suggested, because they "believe that the best way to protect their children
is by preparing them for the future, letting them see what they're capable
of, and arming them with skills, work habits and inner confidence that no
one can ever take away." Chua's testimonial set the blogosphere ablaze
with debate about her extreme parenting, drawing praise, envy, skepticism, and condemnation. Asian Americans in particular expressed uneasiness with her willingness to reproduce uncritically the model minority
stereotype. The book shot up the best-seller list, spawning Internet paro-
dies and earning Chua a spot among *Time* magazine's "100 most influential people" for 2011. Tiger Mom became an overnight cultural sensation
by invoking the newest yellow peril—the rise of the People's Republic of
China as the main contender poised to oust the United States from its
perch as the world's lone superpower and foremost economy. "With a
stroke of her razor-sharp pen, Chua has set a whole nation of parents to
wondering: Are we the losers she's talking about?" asked *Time*. "Think of
the *Battle Hymn of the Tiger Mother* as a well-timed taunt aimed at our
own complacent sense of superiority, our belief that America will always
come out on top."[30]

Tiger Mom–gate graphically illustrated two salient dimensions of the
model minority in the new millennium: its conceptual work and staying power. Chua's self-styling was not original; she drew on decades
of commonplace ideas about Asian Americans emphasizing family ties,
discipline, and diligence. While shocking to some, her confessional only
reinforced what many already thought to be true. The novelty was not
its argument but rather its delivery and context. Regrettably, the model
minority reigns as the overriding figuration of Asian America—the most
prevalent assumption about how someone who "looks Asian" will be.

For Asian Americans, then, the challenge has become how to live beyond the model minority, how to navigate the world day to day without being constrained by such expectations. Many have steadfastly labored to defy its premises and implications. A leading project on this front remains the interdisciplinary field of Asian American studies. Since its inception in the late 1960s, Asian American studies has produced a substantial body of inquiry to refute what its practitioners have deemed the "myth" of the model minority.[31] The consensus among specialists is that the model minority distorts the material realities and obscures the class diversity of a population that includes substantial numbers of poor and working-class people. Select Asian ethnic groups, such as Hmong and other Southeast Asian refugee communities, experience disproportionately high rates of welfare dependency and unemployment alongside disproportionately low levels of income and education. More generally, working-class individuals comprise a significant portion of immigration from Asia, both documented and undocumented. By being grouped together with the more affluent, these segments of the Asian American population are often rendered invisible, and denied access to social welfare and other assistance opportunities.[32]

Students of Asian America also stress that the statistics invoked to support the model minority thesis are misleading. While Asian Americans ostensibly boast the highest median income of any racial group, Asian American families generally include more workers per household than white families. Asian Americans also tend to concentrate in dense metropolitan areas where the costs of living are well above the national average. Moreover, while certain Asian ethnic groups have completed more years of schooling than other races, Asian Americans as a whole earn less than whites of comparable educational levels.[33] Despite perceptions to the contrary, Asian Americans are not outwhiting the whites after all.

While Asian American studies scholars have rightly called attention to the stakes of ignoring the diversity of Asian America, they have had their blind spots, too. The field ironically has crafted its own mythology of the model minority by insisting that the stereotype originated as an imposition on Asian Americans by others, particularly a handful of mainline journalists and social scientists. Some have further suggested that the model minority was made possible by the "political silence" of Asian Americans. Such explanations deny Asian Americans any agency in the process. Certainly they are not entirely false: the receptivity of outsiders to Japanese and Chinese Americans' claims to decorum and belonging made it possible for the concept to stick. Given that Asian American studies is an enterprise devoted to interracial solidarity with other peoples of color, its disavowal of Asian Americans' centrality to the invention of the model minority is comprehensible. The effect, however, has been that of historical erasure by intimating that Asian Americans were either passive victims or wholly apolitical in the postwar period. It glosses over the multiplicity and complexity of experiences and voices that Asian American studies has aimed to unmask.[34]

What if we strive to reassess this history from the vantage point of its actors, setting aside (as much as we can) the filters of hindsight? In projecting the late-twentieth-century politics of multiculturalism back on Asian Americans of the 1940s through the mid-1960s—one that views assimilationism with heavy suspicion—we risk forgetting that model minority status was for the most part an *unintended* consequence that sprung from many concurrent imperatives in American life. As the nation willed itself to disassemble the structures of Asiatic Exclusion, Japanese and Chinese Americans tried a range of approaches to securing freedom, equality, and dignity. Not everyone agreed on the best course of action, but the political culture of the time guaranteed that some options would be more viable than others. The Left, including Communists, socialists, and social progressives, struggled mightily to gain and retain power as well as influence, but were hampered, as were all Americans, by the extremes of McCarthyism and anti-Communism. Japanese and Chinese Americans also knew to cultivate transnational affiliations with care; those who did not line up with conventional definitions of World War II and Cold War–era American nationalism carried risks of deportation, exile, and other punishments. But even with these avenues foreclosed, Japanese and Chinese Americans found ample room to maneuver within the strictures of racial liberalism and political-cultural conservatism. In the postwar decades, Asian American political activity was many things all at once: forward thinking and cautious, hopeful yet pragmatic. And although racial liberalism was an imperfect vehicle for achieving full citizenship for Asian Americans, it made possible what had been impossible during the Exclusion era. The transformation of Japanese and Chinese from aliens ineligible to citizenship to assimilating Others was a remarkable feat for its time.[35]

A history that, perhaps counterintuitively, takes the politics of the middle on its own terms upends the misconception that Asian Americans are inherently apolitical and therefore definitively not-black. It acknowledges the ideological diversity of Asian America alongside the ethnic and class variations that critics of the model minority stereotype have perceptively brought to light. Today, examples of radical-leftist and progressive activism abound. Asian American communities sustain a vibrant network of organizations dedicated to a dizzying array of causes. Nonagenarians Grace Lee Boggs and Yuri Kochiyama, two women who have devoted their lives to achieving social justice, especially for African Americans, continue to inspire generations of Asian American youths fighting to stop oppression in its myriad guises. Asian Americans have also been some of the most vocal critics of the xenophobia and state repression unleashed by the 9/11 attacks, drawing parallels between Japanese American internment and the intense racial profiling of Muslims and others who "appear" Arab, Middle Eastern, or South Asian.[36]

Of course, not all Asian American political activity can be characterized as grass roots and left leaning. The 1990s and 2000s witnessed the rise of many notable individuals on both sides of the aisle in formal politics at the local, state, and national levels. It is no longer exceptional for Asian Americans—Democrats and Republicans alike—to occupy multiple seats in the US Congress, representing places other than California and Hawaiʻi, win mayoral and gubernatorial races in all regions of the country, and accept nominations to the bench, ambassadorships, and even the presidential cabinet. Many Asian Americans have committed to working within the structures of electoral politics, and their efforts have yielded results. In 2009, President Barack Obama revived the White House Initiative on Asian Americans and Political Islanders, to "improve the quality of life and opportunities for Asian Americans and Pacific Islanders by facilitating increased access to and participation in federal programs where they remain underserved."[37]

Alongside intellectual and political labors, Asian Americans defy racial pigeonholing through artistry and expression that is at once provocative, surprising, and moving. People of Asian ancestry can be found among creators of all genres, from the visual arts, music, and literature to food and fashion. In recent times, Asian Americans' presence in Hollywood has proliferated in terms of visibility and variety as more and more are cast as leads in major motion pictures (think *Harold and Kumar*) as well as in starring or reoccurring roles in television series. Asian American writers and musicians have topped the charts. Technology, too, has opened new avenues for exposure in the media arts, with Internet and social media sites providing springboards for young artists. "It's been a big frickin' deal to see such changes," even if the community has yet to "fully take the reins of our representations," mused cultural critic Oliver Wang in 2011. The one performer who has achieved runaway celebrity status, breaking the bamboo ceiling to become a genuine household name, exploded unexpectedly out of major league basketball rather than the arts: Jeremy Lin. His breathtaking run as a replacement point guard for the New York Knicks in early 2012 jolted pundits and fans alike to reflect on their assumptions about Asian American masculinity. For Asian Americans, "Linsanity" offered up unprecedented excitement and validation as a "true, stunning game-changer"—a phenomenon that glimpsed the possibilities of a different kind of being in American life, acknowledging race yet leaving behind the confines of the yellow peril–model minority binary.[38]

There is much hope to be found in these multifaceted undertakings. In all, they remind us that Asian American identity is neither predictable nor fixed. They press us to "imagine otherwise." They spotlight, too, the centrality of Asian American initiative in defining Asian America—and America and beyond—in the past and present, and undoubtedly the future. We can read these acts, ranging from humble to audacious, as repudiations of the racisms that rob individuals of their full humanity. Such refusals are important steps toward the destruction of a racial and geopolitical order anchored by inequality and exploitation, and the rebuilding of relationships that hold dear visions of a humane and just global community.[39]

Notes

Introduction: Imperatives of Asian American Citizenship

1. "Orientals Find Bias Is Down Sharply in U.S.," *New York Times*, December 13, 1970, 1, 70.

2. Ibid.

3. On the concept of belonging, see Barbara Young Welke, *Law and the Borders of Belonging in the Long Nineteenth Century United States* (New York, 2010).

4. Yuji Ichioka, *The Issei: The World of First Generation Japanese Immigrations, 1885–1924* (New York, 1988), 210–43; Bill Ong Hing, *Making and Remaking Asian America through Immigration Policy* (Stanford, CA, 1993), 17–36; Mae M. Ngai, *Impossible Subjects: Illegal Aliens and the Making of Modern America* (Princeton, NJ, 2004), 37–50.

5. Examples of the vast body of historical literature on the Asiatic Exclusion era include Roger Daniels, *The Politics of Prejudice: The Anti-Japanese Movement in California and the Struggle for Japanese Exclusion* (Berkeley, 1962); Alexander Saxton, *The Indispensable Enemy: Labor and the Anti-Chinese Movement in California* (Berkeley, 1971); Sucheng Chan, *This Bittersweet Soil: The Chinese in California Agriculture, 1860–1910* (Berkeley, 1986); Ichioka, *The Issei*; Charles J. McClain, *In Search of Equality: The Chinese Struggle against Discrimination in Nineteenth-Century America* (Berkeley, 1994); Lucy Salyer, *Laws as Harsh as Tigers: Chinese Immigrants and the Shaping of Modern Immigration Law* (Chapel Hill, NC, 1995); Judy Yung, *Unbound Feet: A Social History of Chinese Women in San Francisco* (Berkeley, 1995); Robert G. Lee, *Orientals: Asian Americans in American Popular Culture* (Philadelphia, 1999); John Kuo Wei Tchen, *New York before Chinatown: Orientalism and the Shaping of American Culture 1776–1882* (Baltimore, 1999); Madeline Y. Hsu, *Dreaming of Gold, Dreaming of Home: Transnationalism and Migration between the United States and South China, 1882–1943* (Stanford, CA, 2000); Yong Chen, *Chinese San Francisco, 1850–1943: A Trans-Pacific Community* (Stanford, CA, 2000); Henry Yu, *Thinking Orientals: Migration, Contact, and Exoticism in Modern America* (New York, 2001); Nayan Shah, *Contagious Divides: Epidemics and Race in San Francisco's Chinatown* (Berkeley, 2001); Lon Kurashige, *Japanese American Celebration and Conflict: A History of Ethnic Identity and Festival in Los Angeles, 1934–1990* (Berkeley, 2002); Erika Lee, *At America's Gates: Chinese Immigration during the Exclusion Era, 1882–1943* (Chapel Hill, NC, 2003); Dorothy B. Fujita-Rony, *American Workers, Colonial Power: Philippine Seattle and the Transpacific West, 1919–1941* (Berkeley, 2003); Ngai, *Impossible Subjects*; Him Mark Lai, *Becoming Chinese American: A History of Communities and Institutions* (Walnut Creek, CA, 2004); Eiichiro Azuma, *Between Two Empires: Race, History, and Transnationalism in Japanese America* (New York, 2005); Mary Ting Yi Lui, *The Chinatown Trunk Mystery: Murder, Miscegenation, and Other Dan-*

gerous Encounters in Turn-of-the-Century New York City (Princeton, NJ, 2005); Moon-Ho Jung, *Coolies and Cane: Race, Labor, and Sugar in the Age of Emancipation* (Baltimore, 2006); Linda España-Maram, *Creating Masculinity in Los Angeles's Little Manila: Working-Class Filipinos and Popular Culture, 1920s–1950s* (New York, 2006); Scott Kurashige, *The Shifting Grounds of Race: Black and Japanese Americans in the Making of Multiethnic Los Angeles* (Princeton, NJ, 2008); Charlotte Brooks, *Alien Neighbors, Foreign Friends: Asian Americans, Housing, and the Transformation of Urban California* (Chicago, 2009); Erika Lee and Judy Yung, *Angel Island: Immigrant Gateway to America* (New York, 2010); Richard S. Kim, *The Quest for Statehood: Korean Immigrant Nationalism and U.S. Sovereignty, 1905–1945* (New York, 2011); Shelley Sang-Hee Lee, *Claiming the Oriental Gateway: Prewar Seattle and Japanese America* (Philadelphia, 2011); Rick Baldoz, *The Third Asiatic Invasion: Empire and Migration in Filipino America, 1898–1946* (New York, 2011); Amy Sueyoshi, *Queer Compulsions: Race, Nation, and Sexuality in the Affairs of Yone Noguchi* (Honolulu, 2012); Nayan Shah, *Stranger Intimacy: Contesting Race, Sexuality, and the Law in the North American West* (Berkeley, 2012); Kornel Chang, *Pacific Connections: The Making of the U.S.-Canadian Borderlands* (Berkeley, 2012).

6. Taishi Matsumoto, "The Protest of a Professional Carrot Washer," *Kashu Mainichi*, August 4, 1937, cited in John Modell, *The Economics and Politics of Racial Accommodation: The Japanese of Los Angeles, 1900–1942* (Urbana, IL, 1977), 138.

7. Studies that incorporate social histories of Asian Americans in the mid-twentieth century include Theresa J. Mah, "Buying into the Middle Class: Residential Segregation and Racial Formation in the United States, 1920–1964" (PhD diss., University of Chicago, 1999); Shah, *Contagious Divides*; Xiaojian Zhao, *Remaking Chinese America: Immigration, Family, and Community, 1940–1965* (New Brunswick, NJ, 2002); Ji-Yeon Yuh, *Beyond the Shadow of Camptown: Korean Military Brides in America* (New York, 2002); Kurashige, *Japanese American Celebration and Conflict*; Catherine Ceniza Choy, *Empire of Care: Nursing and Migration in Filipino American History* (Durham, NC, 2003); Ngai, *Impossible Subjects*; Cindy I-Fen Cheng, "Out of Chinatown and into the Suburbs: Chinese Americans and the Politics of Cultural Citizenship in Early Cold War America," *American Quarterly* 58, no. 4 (December 2006): 1067–90; Chiou-ling Yeh, *Making an American Festival: Chinese New Year in San Francisco Chinatown* (Berkeley, 2008); Kurashige, *The Shifting Grounds of Race*; Brooks, *Alien Neighbors, Foreign Friends*; Meredith A. Oda, "Remaking the 'Gateway to the Pacific': Urban, Economic, and Racial Redevelopment in San Francisco, 1945–1970" (PhD diss., University of Chicago, 2010); Greg Robinson, *After Camp: Portraits in Midcentury Japanese American Life and Politics* (Berkeley, 2012); Cindy I-Fen Cheng, *Citizens of Asian America: Democracy and Race during the Cold War* (New York, 2013).

8. Joyce Appleby, *Liberalism and Republicanism in the Historical Imagination* (Cambridge, MA, 1992), 1–33; Gary Gerstle, "The Protean Character of American Liberalism," *American Historical Review* 99, no. 4 (1994): 1043–73; Alan Brinkley, *The End of Reform: New Deal Liberalism in Recession and War* (New York, 1995); Alan Brinkley, *Liberalism and Its Discontents* (Cambridge,

MA, 1998); Eric Foner, *The Story of American Freedom* (New York, 1999); Gary Gerstle, *American Crucible: Race and Nation in the Twentieth Century* (Princeton, 2001), 192–93; Nikhil Pal Singh, "Liberalism," in *Keywords in American Cultural Studies*, ed. Glenn Hendler (New York, 2007), 139–45.

9. On post–World War II racial liberalism, see Walter Jackson, *Gunnar Myrdal and America's Conscience: Social Engineering and Racial Liberalism, 1938–1997* (Chapel Hill, NC, 1990); Gerstle, "Protean Character"; Brinkley, *The End of Reform*; Nikhil Pal Singh, "Culture/Wars: Recoding Empire in an Age of Democracy," *American Quarterly* 50, no. 3 (1998): 471–522; Ruth Feldstein, *Motherhood in Black and White: Race and Sex in American Liberalism, 1930–1965* (Ithaca, NY, 2000); Gerstle, *American Crucible*; Alice O'Connor, *Poverty Knowledge: Social Science, Social Policy, and the Poor in Twentieth Century U.S. History* (Princeton, 2001); Nikhil Pal Singh, *Black Is a Country: Race and the Unfinished Struggle for Democracy* (Cambridge, MA, 2004); Carol A. Horton, *Race and the Making of American Liberalism* (New York, 2005); Thomas J. Sugrue, *Sweet Land of Liberty: The Forgotten Civil Rights Struggle in the North* (New York, 2008); Daniel Martinez Hosang, *Racial Propositions: Ballot Initiatives and the Making of Postwar California* (Berkeley, 2010); Mark Brilliant, *The Color of America Has Changed: How Racial Diversity Shaped Civil Rights Reform in California, 1941–1978* (New York, 2010).

10. Beyond the legal status signifying one's formal membership in a nation-state, I consider the category citizenship to encompass what T. H. Marshall describes as "full members[hip in a] society," Judith N. Shklar terms "social standing" in a community, Linda Bosniak conceives of as "identity" and "solidarity," and Leti Volpp depicts as "inclusion." T. H. Marshall, *Citizenship and Social Class and Other Essays* (Cambridge, UK, 1950), 8; Judith N. Shklar, *American Citizenship: The Quest For Inclusion* (Cambridge, MA, 1991), 2; Linda Bosniak, "Citizenship Denationalized," *Indiana Journal of Global Legal Studies* 7 (2000): 447–509; Linda Bosniak, *The Citizen and the Alien: Dilemmas of Contemporary Membership* (Princeton, NJ, 2006); Leti Volpp, "The Citizen and the Terrorist," *UCLA Law Review* 49 (2001–2): 1575–91. The field of citizenship studies is a vast one, and scholars and activists by no means agree on their understandings of the term. Bosniak ("Citizenship Denationalized") outlines four distinct strands of citizenship discourse: legal status, rights, political activity, and collective identity and sentiment. For introductions to citizenship studies, see Will Kymlicka and Wayne Norman, "Return of the Citizen: A Survey of Recent Work on Citizenship Theory," *Ethics* 104, no. 2 (1994): 352–81; Bart van Steenbergen, ed., *The Condition of Citizenship* (Thousand Oaks, CA, 1994); Gershon Shafir, ed., *The Citizenship Debates: A Reader* (Minneapolis, 1998). For overviews of citizenship in the US context, see Rogers M. Smith, *Civic Ideals: Conflicting Visions of Citizenship in U.S. History* (New Haven, CT, 1997); Linda K. Kerber, "The Meanings of Citizenship," *Journal of American History* 84, no. 3 (1997): 833–54.

11. Examples of historiography connecting mid-twentieth-century foreign policy concerns with race in the domestic arena include Brenda Gayle Plummer, *Rising Wind: Black Americans and U.S. Foreign Affairs, 1935–1960* (Chapel Hill, NC, 1996); Penny M. Von Eschen, *Race against Empire: Black Americans and Anticolonialism, 1937–1957* (Ithaca, NY, 1997); Mary L. Dudziak, *Cold*

War Civil Rights: Race and the Image of American Democracy (Princeton, NJ, 2000); Thomas Borstelmann, *The Cold War and the Color Line: American Race Relations in the Global Arena* (Cambridge, MA, 2001); Christina Klein, *Cold War Orientalism: Asia in the Middlebrow Imagination, 1945–1961* (Berkeley, 2003); Penny M. Von Eschen, *Satchmo Blows Up the World: Jazz Ambassadors Play the Cold War* (Cambridge, MA, 2004); Singh, *Black Is a Country*; Arissa Oh, "A New Kind of Missionary Work: Christians, Christian Americanists, and the Adoption of Korean GI Babies, 1955–1961," *Women's Studies Quarterly* 33, nos. 3–4 (Fall–Winter 2005): 161–88; Kevin K. Gaines, *American Africans in Ghana: Black Expatriates and the Civil Rights Era* (Chapel Hill, NC, 2006); Ellen D. Wu, "America's Chinese: Anti-Communism, Citizenship, and Cultural Diplomacy during the Cold War," *Pacific Historical Review* 77, no. 3 (August 2008): 319–422; Brooks, *Alien Neighbors, Foreign Friends*; Mary Ting-Yi Lui, "Rehabilitating Chinatown at Mid-Century: Chinese Americans, Race, and U.S. Cultural Diplomacy," in *Chinatowns in a Transnational World: Myths and Realities of an Urban Phenomenon*, ed. Ruth Mayer and Vanessa Künneman (New York, 2011), 81–100; Madeline Y. Hsu, "The Disappearance of America's Cold War Chinese Refugees, 1948–1966," *Journal of American Ethnic History* 31, no. 4 (Summer 2012): 12–33; Arissa H. Oh, "From War Waif to Ideal Immigrant: The Cold War Transformation of the Korean Orphan," *Journal of American Ethnic History* 31, no. 4 (Summer 2012): 34–55.

12. Lisa Lowe, *Immigrant Acts: On Asian American Cultural Politics* (Durham, NC, 1996); Lee, *Orientals*; David Palumbo-Liu, *Asian/American: Historical Crossings of a Racial Frontier* (Stanford, CA, 1999); John Dower, *War without Mercy: Race and Power in the Pacific War* (New York, 1986); K. Scott Wong, *Americans First: Chinese Americans and the Second World War* (Cambridge, MA, 2005); Karen J. Leong, *The China Mystique: Pearl S. Buck, Anna May Wong, Mayling Soong, and the Transformation of American Orientalism* (Berkeley, 2005); Naoko Shibusawa, *America's Geisha Ally: Reimagining the Japanese Enemy* (Cambridge, MA, 2006).

13. On European immigrant assimilation and whiteness, see Gary Gerstle, *Working-Class Americanism: The Politics of Labor in a Textile City, 1914–1960* (Cambridge, MA, 1989); Lizabeth Cohen, *Making a New Deal: Industrial Workers in Chicago, 1919–1939* (Cambridge, MA, 1990); David R. Roediger, *The Wages of Whiteness: Race and the Making of the American Working Class* (London, 1991); Russell A. Kazal, "Revisiting Assimilation: The Rise, Fall, and Reappraisal of a Concept in American Ethnic History," *American Historical Review* 100 (1995): 437–71; Matthew Jacobson, *Whiteness of a Different Color: European Immigrants and the Alchemy of Race* (Cambridge, MA, 1998); Eric Arnesen, "Whiteness and the Historians' Imagination," *International Labor and Working-Class History* 60 (Fall 2001): 3–32; Peter Kolchin, "Whiteness Studies: The New History of Race in America," *Journal of American History* 89, no. 1 (2002): 154–73; Thomas A. Guglielmo, *White on Arrival: Race, Color, and Power in Chicago, 1890–1945* (New York, 2003); Russell Kazal, *Becoming Old Stock: The Paradox of German Identity* (Princeton, NJ, 2004). For a contrasting study that decouples whiteness and the embrace of American identity, see Sarah M. A. Gualtieri, *Between Arab and White: Race and Ethnicity in the Early Syrian*

American Diaspora (Berkeley, 2009). On acculturation without social mobility and whiteness, see George J. Sánchez, *Becoming Mexican American: Ethnicity, Culture, and Identity in Chicano Los Angeles, 1900–1945* (New York, 1993).

14. Klein, *Cold War Orientalism*, 5, 9, 11, 16; Amy Kaplan, "'Left Alone with America': The Absence of Empire in the Study of American Culture," in *Cultures of United States Imperialism*, ed. Amy Kaplan and Donald E. Pease (Durham, NC, 1993), 3–21. On racial rearticulation, see Kurashige, *Japanese American Celebration and Conflict*, 1–11.

15. On gender, sexuality, and political culture during the post–World War II/early Cold War period, see Elaine Tyler May, *Homeward Bound: American Families in the Cold War Era* (New York, 1988); Feldstein, *Motherhood in Black and White*; Margot Canaday, *The Straight State: Sexuality and Citizenship in Twentieth-Century America* (Princeton, NJ, 2009).

16. Kathleen Neils Conzen, David A. Gerber, Ewa Morawska, George E. Pozetta, and Rudolph J. Vecoli, "The Invention of Ethnicity: A Perspective from the U.S.A.," *Journal of American Ethnic History* 12, no. 1 (1992): 3–41.

17. On the coding of race as culture, see Paul Gilroy, *The Black Atlantic: Modernity and Double Consciousness* (Cambridge, MA, 1993), 10; Thomas C. Holt, *The Problem of Race in the 21st Century* (Cambridge, MA, 2000), 71–78.

18. Although other ethnic Asians (Filipinos, Indians, and Koreans) actively promoted themselves as good Americans at this time, they did not receive the same extent of attention from academia, the mainstream media, and the general population. Yu, *Thinking Orientals*, viii.

19. See, for example, Jacobson, *Whiteness of a Different Color*; Arnold Hirsch, *Making the Second Ghetto: Race and Housing in Chicago, 1940–1950* (Chicago, 1983); Thomas Sugrue, *The Origins of the Urban Crisis: Race and Inequality in Postwar Detroit* (Princeton, NJ, 1996); Dudziak, *Cold War Civil Rights*; Robert O. Self, *American Babylon: Race and the Struggle for Postwar Oakland* (Princeton, NJ, 2003).

20. For an explication of the black-white paradigm's historical roots in African slavery, see Barbara Jeanne Fields, "Slavery, Race, and Ideology in the United States of America," *New Left Review* 181 (May–June 1990): 95–118. On the consolidation of the black-white paradigm in the twentieth century, see Matthew Pratt Guterl, *The Color of Race in America 1900–1940* (Cambridge, MA, 2001); Jacobson, *Whiteness of a Different Color*, 246–80.

21. My emphasis on Asian American agency offers a corrective to the dominant explanation that a handful of mainstream journalists in the mid-1960s imposed the model minority stereotype on Asian Americans as a response to the civil rights movement. See especially the widely cited article by Keith Osajima, "Asian Americans as the Model Minority: An Analysis of the Popular Press Image in the 1960s and 1980s," in *Reflections on Shattered Windows: Promises and Prospects for Asian Americans*, ed. Gary Y. Okihiro, Shirley Hune, Arthur A. Hansen, and John M. Liu (Pullman, WA, 1988), 165–74.

22. Two key concepts by Michael Omi and Howard Winant undergird my analysis of the model minority's origins. The first is that of "racial formation," which they define as "the sociohistorical process by which racial categories are created, inhabited, transformed, and destroyed." They argue that racial formation

is a process of historically contingent racial "projects in which human bodies and social structures are represented and organized." Racial projects "do the ideological 'work' of linking structure and representation," and are "simultaneously an interpretation, representation, or explanation of racial dynamics, and an effort to reorganize and redistribute resources along particular racial lines." See Michael Omi and Howard Winant, *Racial Formation in the United States from the 1960s to the 1990s* (New York, 1994), 55–56. For an overview of racialization as an analytic concept, see Karim Murji and John Solomos, "Introduction: Racialization in Theory and Practice," in *Racialization: Studies in Theory and Practice*, ed. Karim Murji and John Solomos (Oxford, 2005), 1–27.

23. See, for instance, Jung, *Coolies and Cane*; Neil Foley, *The White Scourge: Mexicans, Blacks, and Poor Whites in Texas Cotton Culture* (Berkeley, 1999); Natalia Molina, *Fit to Be Citizens? Public Health and Race in Los Angeles, 1879–1939* (Berkeley, 2006); Kurashige, *Shifting Grounds of Race*.

24. Claire Jean Kim's "racial triangulation" framework is a useful starting point for thinking about the relational racialization of Asian Americans, African Americans, and whites. See Kim, "The Racial Triangulation of Asian Americans," *Politics and Society* 27, no. 1 (March 1999): 105–38. But this book moves beyond its limitations by treating "triangulation" more flexibly, with attention to intraethnic/intraracial dynamics as well as the significance of other racializations for Asian Americans, and vice versa. I also challenge Kim's position that the racialization of Asian Americans has rested on "civic ostracism," whereby whites have constructed them as "foreign and unassimilable" by showing how whites in the mid-twentieth century moved to assimilate Asians *because* of their foreignness.

25. In this way, my study corresponds with two important critiques of the triangulation model. Shu-mei Shih ("Comparative Racialization: An Introduction," *PMLA* 123, no. 5 [October 2008]: 1351) observes that triangulation poses the ethical dilemma "of what three terms to place under pressure, on the selective valorization of these three terms over others, and on the consequence of diminishing returns for interracial solidarities." Colleen Lye ("The Afro-Asian Analogy," *PMLA* 123, no. 5 [October 2008]: 1734) finds the triangulation approach limited in its reduction of Asian racialization "to a white supremacy that is by temporal and conceptual priority antiblack." I argue that the antiblack racism was but one of a range of factors grounding the changing racialization of Asian Americans, thus illustrating "the genuine multiplicity of racial logics and racisms." Ibid., 1731.

26. Stuart Hall, "Race, Articulation, and Societies Structured in Dominance," in *Sociological Theories: Race and Colonialism* (Paris, 1980).

27. David Theo Goldberg, *Racist Culture: Philosophy and the Politics of Meaning* (Oxford: Blackwell Publishers, 1993), 148–55.

28. Evelyn Nakano Glenn, *Unequal Freedom: How Race and Gender Shaped American Citizenship and Labor* (Cambridge, MA, 2002), 24.

29. Goldberg, *Racist Culture*, 6. Instructive examples of challenges to what Eiichiro Azuma ("Race, Citizenship, and the 'Science of Chick Sexing': The Politics of Racial Identity among Japanese Americans," *Pacific Historical Review* 78, no. 2 [2009]: 245) calls "the accepted paradigm of unilinear progress" from alien to citizen or exclusion to inclusion are ibid.; Mae M. Ngai, "History as Law and

Life: *Tape v. Hurley* and the Origins of the Chinese American Middle Class," in *Chinese Americans and the Politics of Race and Culture*, ed. Sucheng Chan and Madeline Y. Hsu (Philadelphia, 2008), 62–63; Welke, *Borders of Belonging*. For a contrasting take on Asians and postwar liberal inclusion, see Patricia E. Roy, *The Triumph of Citizenship: The Japanese and Chinese in Canada, 1941–1967* (Vancouver, BC, 2008).

30. Holt, *The Problem of Race*, 19–20.

31. Tomás Almaguer, *Racial Fault Lines: The Historical Origins of White Supremacy in California* (Berkeley, 1994); Ngai, *Impossible Subjects*, 8; Jacobson, *Whiteness of a Different Color*, 246–48.

Part I: War and the Assimilating Other

1. Henry Luce, "The American Century," *Life*, February 17, 1941, 61–65; Robert Latham, *The Liberal Moment: Modernity, Security, and the Making of the Postwar International Order* (New York, 1997); Michael Hogan, ed., *The Ambiguous Legacy: U.S. Foreign Relations in the American Century* (New York, 1999); Odd Arne Westad, *The Global Cold War: Third World Interventions and the Making of Our Times* (Cambridge, MA, 2005).

2. "How To Tell Your Friends from the Japs," *Time*, December 22, 1941, 33; "How to Tell Japs from the Chinese," *Life*, December 22, 1941, 81–82.

3. On the history of internment, see Roger Daniels, *Concentration Camps USA: Japanese Americans and World War II* (New York, 1972); Michi Nishiura Weglyn, *Years of Infamy: The Untold Story of America's Concentration Camps* (New York, 1976); US Commission on Wartime Evacuation and Relocation of Civilians, *Personal Justice Denied: Report for the Committee on Interior and Insular Affairs* (1983; repr., Seattle, 1997); Brian Hayashi, *Democratizing the Enemy: The Japanese American Internment* (Princeton, NJ, 2004); Greg Robinson, *A Tragedy of Democracy: Japanese Confinement in North America* (New York, 2009). The total mainland population of Japanese Americans in 1940 was 126,947. US Bureau of the Census, *Sixteenth Census of the United States, 1940* (Washington, DC, 1943).

4. Ngai, *Impossible Subjects*, 175–77; Colleen Lye, *America's Asia: Racial Form and American Literature, 1893–1945* (Princeton, NJ, 2005), 7.

5. US Department of the Interior, *WRA: A Story of Human Conservation* (Washington, DC, 1946), 24–43, 190; Dillon S. Myer, *Uprooted Americans: The Japanese Americans and the War Relocation Authority during World War II* (Tucson, AZ, 1971), 67–80; Weglyn, *Years of Infamy*, 93–102; Caroline Chung Simpson, *An Absent Presence: Japanese Americans in Postwar American Culture, 1945–1960* (Durham, NC, 2001), 154; Mae M. Ngai, "'An Ironic Testimony to the Value of American Democracy': Assimilationism and the World War II Internment of Japanese Americans," in *Contested Democracy: Freedom, Race, and Power in American History*, ed. Manisha Sinha and Penny Von Eschen (New York, 2007), 237–57.

6. Myer, *Uprooted Americans*, 135, 140; US Department of the Interior, *WRA*, 135. Aside from the general resettlement program, other alternatives included

short-term leaves for medical or personal reasons, seasonal leaves to take up farmwork, and student leaves for Nisei to attend colleges and universities.

7. Toshio Yatsushiro, Iwao Ishino, and Yoshiharu Matsumoto, "The Japanese American Looks at Resettlement," *Public Opinion Quarterly* 8, no. 2 (Summer 1944): 188–201.

8. On resettlement, see Dorothy Swaine Thomas, *The Salvage* (Berkeley, 1952); Charlotte Brooks, "In the Twilight Zone between Black and White: Japanese American Resettlement and Community in Chicago, 1942–1945," *Journal of American History*, 86 (March 2000): 1655–87; Allan W. Austin, "Eastward Pioneers: Japanese American Resettlement during World War II and the Contested Meaning of Exile and Incarceration," *Journal of American Ethnic History* 26 (Winter 2007), 58–84; Lane Ryo Hirabayashi, *Japanese American Resettlement through the Lens: Hikaru Iwasaki and the WRA's Photographic Section, 1943–1945* (Boulder, CO, 2009); Robinson, *After Camp*, 43–66.

9. Thomas, *Salvage*, 125; US Department of the Interior, *The Evacuated People: A Quantitative Description* (Washington, DC, 1946), 46; US Department of the Interior, *People in Motion: The Postwar Adjustment of the Evacuated Japanese Americans* (Washington, DC, 1946), 5–15.

10. US Bureau of the Census, *Sixteenth Census of the United States, Special Report, Population, Characteristics of the Nonwhite Population by Race* (Washington, DC, 1943), 47; *US Census of Population 1950, Vol. IV, Special Reports, Part 3, Chapter B, Nonwhite Population by Race* (Washington, DC, 1953), 3B–42; Yung, *Unbound Feet*, 223; Wong, *Americans First*, 71. In 1950, there were 117,629 Chinese in the mainland United States.

Chapter 1: Leave Your Zoot Suits Behind

1. Louise Suski, "Lack of Manners Noted at Chicago Nisei Dance," *Heart Mountain Sentinel*, December 4, 1943, 8; Tamotsu Shibutani, "The First Year of the Resettlement of Nisei in the Chicago Area: A Preliminary Classification of Tentative Plans for Further Research," March 1, 1944, 172–73, reel no. 072, Japanese American Evacuation and Resettlement Study, Bancroft Library, University of California, Berkeley (hereafter JERS).

2. Sus Kaminaka, interview by Charles Kikuchi, August 12, 1944, transcript, 83, box 48, Charles Kikuchi Papers, Young Research Library Special Collections, University of California, Los Angeles (hereafter CKP); Louise Suski, "Chicagoans Find Way to Keep Rowdy Element from Socials," *Heart Mountain Sentinel*, December 9, 1944, 2; Shibutani, "The First Year of Resettlement," 172–73.

3. On the importance of gender, sexuality, and respectability to the rehabilitation of Japanese American citizenship during internment, see John Howard, *Concentration Camps on the Home Front: Japanese Americans in the House of Jim Crow* (Chicago, 2008).

4. On zoot suit culture, see Mauricio Mazon, *The Zoot-Suit Riots: The Psychology of Symbolic Annihilation* (Austin, TX, 1984); Stuart Cosgrove, "The Zoot-Suit and Style Warfare," *History Workshop Journal* 18 (1984): 77–91; Robin D. G. Kelley, *Race Rebels: Culture, Politics, and the Black Working Class* (New

York, 1994); Shane White and Graham White, *Stylin': African American Expressive Culture from Its Beginnings to the Zoot Suit* (Ithaca, NY, 1998); Edward J. Escobar, *Race, Police, and the Making of a Political Identity: Mexican Americans and the Los Angeles Police Department, 1900–1945* (Berkeley, 1999); Eduardo Obregón Pagán, *Murder at the Sleepy Lagoon: Zoot Suits, Race, and Riot in Wartime L.A.* (Chapel Hill, NC, 2003); España-Maram, *Creating Masculinity in Los Angeles's Little Manila*; Elizabeth R. Escobedo, "The Pachuca Panic: Sexual and Cultural Battlegrounds in World War II Los Angeles," *Western Historical Quarterly* 38 no. 2 (2007): 133–56; Luis Alvarez, *The Power of the Zoot: Youth Culture and Resistance during World War II* (Berkeley, 2008); Catherine S. Ramírez, *The Woman in the Zoot Suit: Gender, Nationalism, and the Cultural Politics of Memory* (Durham, NC, 2009); Kathy Peiss, *Zoot Suit: The Enigmatic Career of an Extreme Style* (Philadelphia, 2011).

5. Myer, *Uprooted Americans*, 135, 140; US Department of the Interior, *WRA: A Story of Human Conservation*, 135; US Department of the Interior, *People in Motion*, 145–57. Chicago was the most popular destination through late 1944.

6. Alvarez, *Power of the Zoot*, 2.

7. Shotero Frank Miyamoto, "Interim Report of Resettler Adjustments in Chicago," March 1, 1944, 179–80, reel no. 071, JERS. "Pachuke" was the Japanese American spin on the Chicano term *pachuco*.

8. On the importance of sexuality and military service to wartime notions of masculine citizenship, see Canaday, *The Straight State*, 137–73; James T. Sparrow, *Warfare State: World War II Americans and the Age of Big Government* (New York, 2011), 201–41.

9. With the key exceptions of Isamu Arifuku Waugh's "Hidden Crime and Deviance in the Japanese-American Community, 1920–1946" (PhD diss., University of California, Berkeley, 1978) and Valerie J. Matsumoto's *Farming the Home Place: A Japanese American Community in California* ([Ithaca, NY, 1993] 131–32), yogore were practically invisible in Japanese American and zoot suit historiography until the publication of Paul Spickard's "Research Note: Not Just the Quiet People: The Nisei Underclass" (*Pacific Historical Review* 68, no. 1 [February 1999]: 78–94). Spickard (ibid., 80) explains that the "conventional portrait" of Nisei ("well-behaved, hard-working, patriotic, and intent upon assimilation") had been heavily influenced by the Japanese American Citizens League's efforts to entrench a "positive image of the Nisei generation in the minds of white Americans." This hegemonic project left little room for competing narratives in the postwar decades. Recently, revisionist scholars have increasingly turned their attention to the significance of Nisei "rowdies" and pachuke. See Brooks, "In the Twilight Zone"; Kurashige, *Japanese American Celebration*; Alvarez, *Power of the Zoot*; Allison Varzally, *Making a Non-White America: Californians Coloring outside Ethnic Lines, 1925–1955* (Berkeley, 2008); Peiss, *Zoot Suit*. Most of this secondary work relies heavily (as do I) on the wartime interviews with yogore conducted by Charles Kikuchi for JERS. On the problems and rewards of using these life histories, see Yuji Ichioka, "JERS Revisited: An Introduction," in *Views from Within*, ed. Yuji Ichioka, 3–27 (Los Angeles, 1989); Dana Y. Takagi, "Life History Analysis and JERS: Re-evaluating the Work of Charles Kikuchi," in *Views from Within*, ed. Yuji Ichioka, 197–216; (Los Angeles, 1989); David Yoo,

Growing Up Nisei: Race, Generation, and Culture among Japanese Americans of California, 1924–1949 (Urbana, IL, 2000), 149–71.

10. Singh, "Culture/Wars." On the Mexican Problem recoded as the pachuco problem in the 1940s, see David G. Gutiérrez, *Walls and Mirrors: Mexican Americans, Mexican Immigrants, and the Politics of Ethnicity* (Berkeley, 1995), 124–25.

11. Ellison quoted in Kelley, *Race Rebels*, 161; Spickard, "Not Just the Quiet People"; Brooks, "In the Twilight Zone."

12. Azuma, *Between Two Empires*, 35–60; Waugh, "Hidden Crime," 70–164.

13. Kurashige, *Japanese American Celebration*, 24–25, 38–39; Azuma, *Between Two Empires*, 124–34, 138–39; Modell, *The Economics and Politics of Racial Accommodation*, 83–85.

14. Kurashige, *Japanese American Celebration*, 39, 60–63; Waugh, "Hidden Crime," 133–59; Modell, *Economics and Politics*, 158; Frank Miyamoto, *Social Solidarity among the Japanese in Seattle* (1939; repr., Seattle, 1984), 65–67; Azuma, *Between Two Empires*, 125.

15. Kurashige, *Japanese American Celebration*, 39; Varzally, *Making a Non-White America*, 5–45; Lester Kimura, interview by Charles Kikuchi, September 6, 1944, transcript, 13, box 48, CKP.

16. Hazel Nishi, interview by Charles Kikuchi, 1944, transcript, 56–57, box 46, CKP; Howard, *Concentration Camps on the Homefront*, 108–09. On class tensions in the camps, see Kurashige, *Japanese American Celebration and Conflict*; Hayashi, *Democratizing the Enemy*.

17. Kimura, interview, 13, 20–21; John Modell, ed., *The Kikuchi Diary: Chronicle from an American Concentration Camp* (Urbana, IL, 1993), 126, cited in Varzally, *Making a Non-White America*, 73; Barry Shimizu, interview by Charles Kikuchi, August 1944, transcript, 29, box 48, CKP.

18. Kaminaka, interview, 51–52.

19. Ibid., 37, 50, 52, 53, 54, 61.

20. Ibid., 60–61.

21. "Plug Chain on a Zoot Suit," *Gila News-Courier*, November 14, 1942, 2; Lane Ryo Hirabayashi, *The Politics of Fieldwork: Research in an American Concentration Camp* (Tucson, AZ, 1999), 25, 27–28, 123; "Zoot Suit Gang Here," *Gila News-Courier*, May 22, 1943, 2.

22. Cosgrove, "Zoot-Suit and Style Warfare," 80; Pagán, *Murder at the Sleepy Lagoon*, 101, 109, 257n47; Alvarez, *Power of the Zoot*, 188; Peiss, *Zoot Suit*, 88–90; Mazon, *Zoot-Suit Riots*; Escobar, *Race, Police, and the Making of a Political Identity*; Sparrow, *Warfare State*.

23. Alvarez, *Power of the Zoot*, 200–34; "Our Conduct on the Outside," *Tulean Daily Dispatch*, June 3, 1943, 2; "Behavior and Unconventional Dress of Denver Nisei 'Zoot Suit' Boys Decried," *Denson Tribune*, June 18, 1943, 5; "Zoot Suit and Jive Music," *Manzanar Free Press*, June 19, 1943, 2; "Leave Your Zoot Suits Behind," *Manzanar Free Press*, July 10, 1943, 2.

24. S. Frank Miyamoto, "Notes of Conversation with Shirrell," June 25, 1943, reel no. 088, JERS; Escobedo, "The Pachuca Panic," Alvarez, *Power of the Zoot*, 104–12; Ramírez, *Woman in the Zoot Suit*.

25. Miyamoto, "Interim Report"; Shibutani, "The First Year of the Resettlement"; "Evacuee Writes 'Leave Zoot Suit, Long Haircut' Here," *Tulean Daily Dispatch*, May 26, 1943, 2; Brooks, "In the Twilight Zone," 1683.

26. War Relocation Authority, *Relocation Handbook*, May 31, 1945, release no. 147, 130.16, "WRA Handbook Supplementing Manual 130" folder, box 3, entry 29, RG 210, National Archives and Records Administration, Washington, DC (hereafter NARA); "Juvenile Code: Eleven Offenses Listed," *Gila News-Courier*, September 2, 1944, 1; "Zoot-Suits, Pachukes to Come under New 'Special Penalties,'" *Heart Mountain Sentinel*, December 16, 1944, 1.

27. Ralph E. Smeltzer, "Present Status of the Community Integration Program in Chicago," typescript, July 9, 1943, box 4, Japanese Relocation Collection, Brethren Archives, Elgin IL (hereafter JRC); "Advisory Committee: Avoid Starting New 'Little Tokios' in Relocating," *Tulean Daily Dispatch*, July 15, 1943; War Relocation Authority, "When You Leave the Relocation Center," n.d., www.densho.org.

28. Weglyn, *Years of Infamy*, 196–99; "Instructions and Procedure regarding the Brethren Relocation Hostel," July 15, 1943, "Hostel Mimeographed and Printed Materials" folder, box 4, JRC; Brooks, "In the Twilight Zone," 1661–62.

29. "Helpful Information about the Hostel," n.d., "Hostel Mimeographed and Printed Materials" folder, box 4, JRC (emphasis in original); War Relocation Authority, Gila River Project, Rivers, Arizona, no title, n.d., "Evacuee and Private Research on Relocation" folder, box 4, JRC; Brooks, "In the Twilight Zone," 1683.

30. My conception of the imagined pachuke is inspired by Pagán, *Murder at the Sleepy Lagoon*, 126–44. See also Mazon, *The Zoot-Suit Riots*; Esobedo, "The Pachuca Panic"; Ramírez, *The Woman in the Zoot Suit*.

31. Shibutani, "The First Year of the Resettlement," 112, 122; Charles Kikuchi, "Japanese Americans in Chicago, 1943–1945" (master's thesis, Columbia University, 1947), 123.

32. Shibutani, "The First Year of Resettlement," 231; Kikuchi, "Japanese Americans," 136; Miyamoto, "Interim Report," 150–51; Setsuko Matsunaga Nishi, "Japanese American Achievement in Chicago: A Cultural Response to Degradation" (PhD diss., University of Chicago, 1963), 161, 186–87; Eugene S. Uyeki, "Process and Patterns of Nisei Adjustment to Chicago" (PhD diss., University of Chicago, 1953), 78–80; John DeYoung, "Final Report of Chicago, Illinois Area," folder 15.102B, box 2, entry 64, RG 210, NARA.

33. Shibutani, "The First Year of Resettlement," 110, 123, 144; Andrew J. Diamond, *Mean Streets: Chicago Youths and the Everyday Struggle for Empowerment in the Multiracial City, 1908–1969* (Berkeley, 2009), 119–51. Sociologists St. Clair Drake and Horace R. Cayton Jr. observed that Chicago's black population grew by sixty thousand during World War II from the influx of southern migrants. See St. Clair Drake and Horace R. Cayton Jr., *Black Metropolis: A Study of Negro Life in a Northern City* (Chicago, 1993), 9.

34. Uyeki, "Process and Patterns of Nisei Adjustment," 80; American Friends Service Committee and American Baptist Home Mission Society, "Report on Chicago Resettlement," November 1944, "American Friends Service Commit-

tee" folder, box 3, JRC; Brooks, "In the Twilight Zone"; Diamond, *Mean Streets*, 119–51.

35. Thomas, *The Salvage*, 498, 504; Miyamoto, "Interim Report," 123, 157; Shibutani, "The First Year of Resettlement," 89; Kikuchi, "Japanese Americans in Chicago," 123.

36. Kimura, interview, 40, 50; Tadashi "Blackie" Nakajima, interview by Charles Kikuchi, March 7, 1944, transcript, 3–4, 61–62, 64, 75, 89, box 47, CKP; Charles Kikuchi, diary entry, February 20, 1944, transcript, 11, box 47, CKP.

37. Shimizu, interview, 40–56; Kaminaka, interview, 3.

38. Kelley, *Race Rebels*, 162–81.

39. Kimura, interview, 48; Nakajima, interview, 66; Kaminaka, interview, 96; Shimizu, interview, 52.

40. Kimura, interview, 26–27; Shimizu, interview, 36–37.

41. WRA, "When You Leave the Relocation Center"; Miyamoto, "Interim Report," 122–23; Shibutani, "The First Year of the Resettlement," 71–73, 125–28; Miyamoto, "Notes of Conversation with Shirrell"; Nakajima, interview, 21–22, 27.

42. Mazon, *Zoot-Suit Riots*, 9; Kaminaka, interview, 81; Thomas, *The Salvage*, 340.

43. Nishi, "Japanese American Achievement," 171; American Friends Service Committee and American Baptist Home Mission Service, "Report on Chicago Resettlement"; Smeltzer, "Present Status of the Community Integration Program in Chicago."

44. Smeltzer, "Present Status of the Community Integration Program in Chicago"; "Evacuee Bulletin to Minister-Counsellors," "Chicago Church Federation and United Ministry to Resettlers" folder, box 3, JRC; Brooks, "In the Twilight Zone"; Miyamoto, "Interim Report," 66–68.

45. American Friends Service Committee and American Baptist Home Mission Service, "Report on Chicago Resettlement" (emphasis in original).

46. Horace R. Cayton Jr., "The Nisei," *Pittsburgh Courier*, May 26, 1945, 7. On relationships between African Americans and Japanese Americans in the 1940s, see Brooks, "In the Twilight Zone"; Robinson, *After Camp*; Matthew M. Briones, *Jim and Jap Crow: A Cultural History of 1940s' Interracial America* (Princeton, NJ, 2012).

47. Setsuko Matsunaga Nishi, "Negro-Nisei Identifications: Observations from Wartime and Postwar Chicago," February 14, 1970, unpublished typescript, in author's possession; Cayton, "The Nisei."

48. On racial liberalism and the Negro Problem in wartime Chicago, see Drake and Cayton, *Black Metropolis*, 263–86. Setsuko Matsunaga Nishi, "Report on the Inquiry into the Relocation of Agencies in the Division on Education and Recreation to Nisei in Chicago," May 1945, folder 4, box 145, Chicago Social Welfare Council Collection, Chicago History Museum Center (hereafter SWC).

49. "Committee on Minority Groups Minutes," May 10, 1945, 2, folder 2, box 145, SWC; "Minutes, Conference regarding Services of Japanese-Americans," June 18, 1945, 2, folder 2, box 145, SWC; "Minutes of the Meeting," July 9, 1945, 2, folder 2, box 145, SWC; Lucy P. Carner, "Report on Special Services Needed by Persons of Japanese Descent and Agencies through Which Needs Might Be Met," October 1945, folder 3, box 145, SWC; "Proposal for a Coordinating Service

for Japanese-Americans as Requested by Conference of Japanese Americans and Agency Representatives," October 1945, folder 3, box 145, SWC; "Minutes of the Meeting of the Executive Committee Division 1," October 10, 1945, folder 3, box 145, SWC; "Minutes of the Meeting of the Japanese American Conference Group," October 17, 1945, folder 3, box 145, SWC; "Minutes of Meeting of the Coordinating Committee on Welfare Services to Persons of Japanese Descent," November 7, 1945, folder 3, box 145, SWC.

50. Nishi, "Negro-Nisei Identifications"; Nishi, "Japanese American Achievement," 172–82; "The Chicago Resettlers' Committee," November 26, 1945, folder 15, box 1, RG 8, Japanese American Service Committee, Chicago (hereafter JASC); Corky T. Kawasaki, "Chicago Resettlers' Committee Report of Activities," September 28, 1946, folder 1, series 1, RG 9, JASC.

51. SAC, "Chicago Resettlement: 1947: A Report," Chicago Resettlers Committee collection (hereafter CRC), Chicago History Museum Research Center; Nishi, "Japanese American Achievement," 182–86, 189–90.

52. SAC, "Chicago Resettlement 1947."

53. Ibid. (emphasis in original).

54. Dillon S. Myer to Corky T. Kawasaki, January 20, 1947, folder 1947, box 3, Dillon S. Myer papers, National Archives and Records Administration, Harry S. Truman Presidential Library, Independence, MO; Myer, *Uprooted Americans*, 282; SAC, "Chicago Resettlement 1947"; Nishi, "Japanese American Achievement," 201; Harold M. Mann and Prudence Ross, "History of the North Central Area, War Relocation Authority," 52, n.d., "North Central Area #2C" folder, box 6, entry 4C, RG 210, NARA; DeYoung, "Final Report of Chicago, Illinois Area."

55. Nishi, "Japanese American Achievement," 199, 225; Nishi, "Negro-Nisei Identifications"; SAC, "Chicago Resettlement 1947."

56. Escobar, *Race, Police, and the Making of a Political Identity*; Pagán, *Murder at the Sleepy Lagoon*; Alvarez, *Power of the Zoot*.

57. "Membership Report of the Chicago Resettlers' Committee," Council of Social Agencies of Chicago, September 23, 1946, box 49, Japanese American Research Project, Young Research Library Special Collections, University of California, Los Angeles (hereafter JARP); CRC Annual Report, 1948, 11, folder 2, series 1, RG 9, JASC; DeYoung, "Final Report of Chicago," 5; Nishi, "Negro-Nisei"; SAC, "Chicago Resettlement 1947"; Nishi, "Japanese American Achievement," 211–44.

58. Nishi, "Japanese American Achievement, 195–97; DeYoung, "Final Report of Chicago," n.p., appendix II, 16–19, 23–24.

59. Setsuko Matusnaga, "The Adjustment of Evacuees in St. Louis" (master's thesis, Washington University, 1944); Michael Daniel Albert, "Japanese American Communities in Chicago and the Twin Cities" (PhD diss., University of Minnesota, 1980); Miyako Inoue, "Japanese-Americans in St. Louis: From Internees to Professionals," *City and Society* 3, no. 2 (1989): 142–52; T. M. Linehan, "Japanese American Resettlement in Cleveland during and after World War II," *Journal of Urban History* 20, no. 1 (1993): 54–80; Mitziko Sawada, "After the Camps: Seabrook Farms, New Jersey, and the Resettlement of Japanese Americans, 1944–47," *Amerasia Journal* 13, no. 2 (1986–87): 117–36; Sandra C. Taylor, "Leaving the Concentration Camps: Japanese American Resetttlement in Utah and the In-

termountain West," *Pacific Historical Review* 60, no. 2 (1991): 169–94; Austin, "Eastward Pioneers," 58–84; Robinson, *After Camp*, 43–66.

60. SAC, "Progress Report," December 1947, Chicago Resettlers Collection, Chicago Historical Society; Abe Hagiwara, "For Participation in the Larger Community: The Recreation-Education Program of the Chicago Resettlers Committee," December 1948, folder 3, box 1, RG 8, JASC; "This Is It!" folder 37, box 1, RG 8, JASC; "New Girls Council Meets: Aims Set," *Chicago Shimpo*, February 18, 1948, 8; "Girls' Clubs Organize Council to Coordinate All Activities," *Chicago Shimpo*, March 19, 1948, 8; Jack K. Yasutake, "Annual Report 1948," folder 2, series 1, RG 9, JASC; Jack K. Yasutake and Abe Hagiwara, "1949 4th Annual Report," folder 3, series 1, RG 9, JASC.

61. Uyeki, "Process and Patterns of Nisei Adjustment," 195, 199–205, 298.

62. SAC, "Progress Report," September 1948, folder 41, box 1, series 1, RG 8, JASC; Yasutake, "Annual Report 1948"; City-wide Committee on Recreation, "Minutes," October 22, 1947, folder 37, box 1, RG 8, JASC; CRC Community Relations Committee, "Minutes," December 14, 1950, folder 19, box 35, RG 3, JASC.

63. Jack K. Yasutake, "1950 5th Annual Report," folder 4, series 1, RG 9, JASC; Kenji Nakane and Daniel Kuzuhara, "1953 7th Annual Report," folder 6, series 1, RG 9, JASC; Abe Hagiwara, "Nisei Recreation in Chicago," *Chicago Resettlers Bulletin*, May 1954, Chicago Resettlers Collection.

64. Brilliant, *The Color of America Has Changed*, 7, 271–72.

Chapter 2: How American Are We?

1. Ngai, *Impossible Subjects*, 175–77.

2. Rose Hum Lee, "Chinese in the United States Today: The War Has Changed Their Lives," *Survey Graphic: Magazine of Social Interpretation*, October 1942, 419, 444; Dolly Rhee, "Chinese Home Front," *San Francisco Chronicle*, December 24, 1942, 6.

3. Bradford Smith to Alan Cranston, June 20, 1942, "Chinese Exclusion Acts" folder, box 1075, entry E222, NC-148, RG 208, NARA; Carey McWilliams, *Brothers under the Skin* (Boston: Little, Brown and Company, 1943), 108, 112.

4. Yung, *Unbound Feet*, 239–340; T. Christopher Jespersen, *American Images of China, 1931–1949* (Stanford, CA, 1996), 11–81; Wong, *Americans First*, 35–44, 61–64; Karen J. Leong and Judy Tzu-Chun Wu, "Filling the Rice Bowls of China: Staging Humanitarian Relief during the Sino-Japanese War," in *Chinese Americans and the Politics of Race and Culture*, ed. Sucheng Chan and Madeline Y. Hsu (Philadelphia, 2008), 133–52.

5. Madame Chiang Kai-Shek, "Fighting for the Same Cause," *Vital Speeches of the Day* 9 (1943): 303; Jespersen, *American Images of China*, 82–107; Leong, *China Mystique*, 106–56; Wong, *Americans First*, 89–109.

6. Yung, *Unbound Feet*, 274.

7. Cited in Yung, *Unbound Voices: A Documentary History of Chinese Women in San Francisco* (Berkeley, 1999) 473–75. During World War II, 360 Chi-

nese worked at Marinship. By 1943, about 5,000 Chinese Americans—or one-fourth of San Francisco's Chinese population—worked in the Bay Area's defense industries.

8. Various historians have offered different estimates of the numbers of Chinese Americans in the armed forces during World War II. See L. Ling-Chi Wang, "Politics of Assimilation and Repression: History of the Chinese in the United States, 1940 to 1970," unpublished manuscript, Berkeley Ethnic Studies Library, (hereafter ESL) 1980; Yung, *Unbound Feet*, 253; Wong, *Americans First*, 58.

9. Christina and Sheldon Lim, *In the Shadow of the Tiger: The 407th Air Service Squadron* (San Mateo, 1993); Peter Phan, "Familiar Strangers: The Fourteenth Air Service Group Case Study of Chinese American Identity During World War II," in *Chinese America: History and Perspectives* (1993): 75–107; Wong, *Americans First*, 162–192. On Chinese Americans serving in other units, see Yung, *Unbound Feet*, 252–260.

10. Fred Riggs, *Pressures on Congress: A Study of the Repeal of Chinese Exclusion* (New York, 1950), 48; Charles Nelson Spinks, "Repeal Chinese Exclusion!" *Asia*, February 1942, 92–94.

11. House Committee on Immigration and Naturalization, *Repeal of the Chinese Exclusion Acts, Hearings on H.R. 1882 and H.R. 2309*, 78th Cong., 1st Sess., May 19, 20, 26, 27 and June 2 and 3, 1943, 68–87, 196–203.

12. Riggs, *Pressures on Congress*, 48–57; Frank D. Campbell, "Race Snobbery," *Christian Century*, March 4, 1942, 290; Harry Paxton Howard, "Justice to Our Allies," *Commonweal*, June 5, 1942, 150–53; Walter Kong, "How We Grill the Chinese," *Asia*, September 1942, 520–23.

13. CCRCE, "Our Chinese Wall," 1943, Box 1, Carl Glick Papers, University of Iowa Libraries Special Collections, Iowa City (hereafter CGP).

14. Riggs, *Pressures on Congress*, 65–118, 210–11; Bruno Lasker, "Our Humiliation—Not Theirs," *Common Ground* 4, no. 1 (Fall 1943): 71–76; Carl Glick, "Citizen Kwong," *Common Ground* 4, no. 1 (Fall 1943): 77–79.

15. Riggs, *Pressures on Congress*, 111–14; Arthur Chin to Carl Glick, June 29, 1943, box 1, CGP; Karen J. Leong, "Foreign Policy, National Identity, and Citizenship: The Roosevelt White House and the Expediency of Repeal," *Journal of American Ethnic History* 22, no. 4 (Summer 2003): 3–30.

16. "EXCLUSION REPEAL: Send Your Petition to This List of Congressmen from Largest Chinese Centers," *Chinese Press*, October 8, 1943, 6; "Write to Your Congressmen on Exclusion Repeal," *Chinese Press*, October 15, 1943, 3; Chen, *Chinese San Francisco, 1850–1943*, 257; Renqiu Yu, *To Save China, to Save Ourselves: The Chinese Hand Laundry Alliance of New York* (Philadelphia, 1992), 130–37; Riggs, *Pressures on Congress*, 111–12, 203–4; Lee, "The Chinese in the United States Today."

17. Leong, "Foreign Policy, National Identity, and Citizenship."

18. Act of December 17, 1943 (57 Stat. 600).

19. Gilbert Woo, "One Hundred and Seven Chinese," *Chinese Times*, September 7, 1943, reprinted in Judy Yung, Gordon H. Chang, and Him Mark Lai, *Chinese American Voices: From the Gold Rush to the Present* (Berkeley, 2006), 221–24; Gilbert Woo, "Repeal of the Chinese Exclusion Act, *Chinese Times*, December 1, 1943; Fong Man-Hee and Cheng Tze-Nan, "A Drop of Chinese Blood," *Asia*

and the Americas, February 1945, 120; Yu, *To Save China*, 136–37; Thomas H. Lee, "Six Months since Repeal," *Asia and the Americas*, July 1944, 322–24.

20. Fong and Cheng, "A Drop of Chinese Blood"; Yu, *To Save China*, 136–37; Chen, *Chinese San Francisco*, 259; Hungwai Ching to Carl Glick, January 26, 1944, box 1, CGP.

21. Philip Gleason, *Speaking of Diversity: Language and Ethnicity in Twentieth-Century America* (Baltimore, 1992); Ngai, *Impossible Subjects*, 230–31; Wendy L. Wall, *Inventing the "American Way": The Politics of Consensus from the New Deal to the Civil Rights Movement* (Oxford, 2007), 89; James Henry Powell, "The Concept of Cultural Pluralism in American Social Thought, 1915–1965" (PhD diss., University of Notre Dame, 1971).

22. Gleason, *Speaking of Diversity*; Ngai, *Impossible Subjects*, 232; Wall, *Inventing the "American Way."*

23. Barbara Dianne Savage, *Broadcasting Freedom: Radio, War, and the Politics of Race, 1938–1948* (Chapel Hill, NC, 1999); "Americans All—Immigrants All, No. 16, the Orientals," Federal Security Agency papers, US Office of Education, Performing Arts Library at Lincoln Center, New York Public Library, cited in Savage, *Broadcasting Freedom*, 32.

24. Savage, *Broadcasting Freedom*, 61–62; Wall, *Inventing the "American Way,"* 69; Michael Denning, *The Cultural Front: The Laboring of American Culture in the Twentieth Century* (London, 1997), 115–18, 128.

25. Alexander Alland, *American Counterpoint* (New York, 1943); "They're All Americans," *New York Times Magazine*, September 5, 1943, 16–17.

26. "Chinese Group Will Be Highlight in Dramatic Institute Radio Series," *Chinese Press*, April 3, 1942, 2.

27. Wong's *Common Ground* essays include "Daddy" (*Common Ground* 5 [Winter 1945]: 25–29), "Jon" (*Common Ground* 6 [Fall 1945]: 39–44), and "The Sanctum of Harmonious Spring" (*Common Ground* 8 [Winter 1948]: 84–91).

28. Denning, *Cultural Front*, 447–49; Ngai, *Impossible Subjects*, 232; Wall, *Inventing the "American Way,"* 70; Lasker, "Our Humiliation—Not Theirs"; Carl Glick, "Citizen Kwong," *Common Ground* 4, no. 1 (Fall 1943): 77–79.

29. "Americans All," *Ladies' Home Journal*, December 1943, 103–7, 125.

30. T. E. Murphy, "Portrait of an American Family," *Reader's Digest*, March 1944, 71–74. The Office of War Information may have had a hand in this story, given that officials had solicited Chinese American community leaders for suggestions on families to profile in mainstream magazines. See Bradford Smith to Ching-Kun Yang, December 30, 1942, folder X-Y-Z, box 1070, RG 208, NARA.

31. "Chinatown, San Francisco: James Wong Howe Focuses His Searching Lens on His People in America," *Look*, December 26, 1944, 22–27, cited in Gordon H. Chang, Mark Dean Johnson, Paul J. Karlstrom, and Sharon Spain, *Asian American Art: A History, 1850–1970* (Stanford, CA, 2008), 332–33; Lui, "Rehabilitating Chinatown at Mid-Century"; Bradford Smith to Dorthoy Ducas, December 16, 1942, folder D, box 1069, RG 208, NARA.

32. Carl Glick, "Shake Hands with the Dragon," *Reader's Digest*, September 1941, 121–34; Carl Glick, *Shake Hands with the Dragon* (New York, 1941), 312; Glick, "Citizen Kwong."

33. Ruth Brown Reed, "Career Girl, Chinese Style," *Independent Woman*, September 1942, 259–60, 286–87; Louise Purwin, "Chinese Daughters of Uncle

Sam," *Independent Woman*, November 1944, 336–37, 353, both cited in Wong, *Americans First*, 47–49.

34. See, for example, "AWVS Chinese Center Opening Set," *Los Angeles Times*, November 27, 1942, A5; Marie Carey, "Chinese War Workers," *San Francisco Chronicle*, December 3, 1942, 10; "47 Chinese Join Army 'to End This Damn War,'" *New York Times*, December 19, 1942, 6; Donovan Bess, "We Are All Cousins," *San Francisco Chronicle*, December 12, 1942, 6; "Chinese in War Work," *San Francisco Chronicle*, December 12, 1942, 6; Rhee, "Chinese Home Front"; Yih Chen, "Chinese New Year Has War Trappings," *New York Times*, February 6, 1943, 15; "Chinese Workers Speed War Goods," *New York Times*, February 20, 1943, 15; "Women in War Work," *Chicago Daily Tribune*, June 7, 1943, 15.

35. Bill Simons, "Chinatown Ready for Any Emergency for She Knows Aggressor," *San Francisco Chronicle*, January 14, 1942, cited in Wong, *Americans First*, 88–89.

36. Lee, "Chinese in the United States Today." William Hoy, "Chinatown Keeps Step With America, Says Guest Writer," *San Francisco Chronicle*, July 1, 1940, 7.

37. Riggs, *Pressures on Congress*, 111–12; House Committee on Immigration and Naturalization, *Repeal of the Chinese Exclusion Acts*, 203–4, 207–11. On the significance of the coolie in US culture, see Jung, *Coolies and Cane*.

38. *Buckley Armorer*, February 4, 1944, 1, 4, cited in Yung, *Unbound Feet*, 252–53.

39. "I Am an American Day," May 20, 1945, "I'm an American Day" folder, box 8, entry 84, RG 208, NARA; "Citizenship Week: American Chinese Have a Part in the Country's 'March of Democracy,'" *California Chinese Press*, May 9, 1941, 2; "'I Am an American': Los Angeles Chinese Joins Citizens' Week," *California Chinese Press*, May 23, 1941, 1; "Citizenship Week: American Chinese Have a Part in the Country's 'March of Democracy,'" *Chinese Press*, May 22, 1942, 2; "'Americans All': Chinese Chi-Hi Presents 2nd Annual Rally at YWCA Saturday Night," *Chinese Press*, May 22, 1942, 2; "I Am an American," *Chinese News*, May 15, 1942, 3; "Chinatown Joins City in 'I Am an American Day' Pageant at Civic," *Chinese Press*, May 14, 1943, 1; Wong, *Americans First*, 87–88.

40. For a history of the Chinese-language press in the United States, see Karl Lo and H. M. Lai, eds., *Chinese Newspapers Published in North America, 1854–1975* (Washington, DC, 1977); H. M. Lai, "The Chinese-American Press," in *The Ethnic Press in the United States: An Historical Analysis and Handbook*, ed. Sally M. Miller (New York, 1987), 27–43; Him Mark Lai, "The Chinese Community Press in Hawai'i," *Chinese America: History and Perspectives* (2010): 95–103. For a list of early Chinese American newspapers, see Thomas W. Chinn, *Bridging the Pacific: San Francisco Chinatown and Its People* (San Francisco, 1989, 294–95). Xiaojian Zhao argues that the independent, liberal *Chinese Pacific Weekly* (established in 1946) was an important exception to the China-oriented immigrant press in advocating engagement with US social and political issues. See Xiaojian Zhao, "Disconnecting Transnational Ties: The Chinese Pacific Weekly and the Transformation of Chinese American Community after the Second World War," in *Media and the Chinese Diaspora: Community, Communications, and Commerce*, ed. Wanning Sun (New York, 2006), 26–41.

41. *United States v. Wong Kim Ark*, 169 US 648, 694 (1898); Lee, *At America's Gates*, 103–6; Sue Fawn Chung, "Fighting for Their American Rights: A History of the Chinese American Citizens Alliance," in *Claiming America: Constructing Chinese American Identities during the Exclusion Era*, ed. K. Scott Wong and Sucheng Chan (Philadelphia, 1998), 95–126; Lai, "The Chinese Community Press in Hawai'i."

42. Lai, "The Chinese Community Press in Hawai'i"; "Introducing Ourselves," *Hawaii Chinese Journal*, November 12, 1937, 1; "87% of Chinese Here Are American Citizens," *Hawaii Chinese Journal*, October 31, 1940, 1; "87% Are American Citizens," *Hawaii Chinese Journal*, October 31, 1940, 1.

43. Lo and Lai, *Chinese Newspapers Published in North America*, 14; Julie Shuk-yee Lam, "The Chinese Digest, 1935–1940," *Chinese America: History and Perspectives* (1987): 119–37. Three mimeographed English-language publications in San Francisco preceded the *Chinese Digest*: *Tri Termly Toots* (est. 1921); *Scout Wig Wag* (est. 1927); *Y-World* (est. 1929). Chinn, *Bridging the Pacific*, 47.

44. On Chinn, see Lam, "The Chinese Digest"; Thomas W. Chinn, "A Historian's Reflections on Chinese-American Life in San Francisco, 1919–1991," California Digital Library, http://www.cdlib.org/. On Lee, see Rose K. Gidley, "This Is Chingwah Lee," *Christian Science Monitor Magazine*, June 8, 1946, 4; Lam, "The Chinese Digest"; Chinn, "A Historian's Reflections."

45. "Why the Digest?" *Chinese Digest*, November 15, 1935; Marjorie Lee, "Hu-Jee: The Forgotten Second Generation of Chinese America, 1930–1950" (master's thesis, University of California, Los Angeles, 1984), 52; Wong, *Americans First*, 27–28.

46. W. H., "Youths Who Think," *Chinese Digest*, May 15, 1936, 8.

47. The Ging Hawk Club was a New York City–based organization for young, mostly college-educated native-born Chinese American women. "Ging Hawk Essay Results," *Chinese Digest*, May 15, 1936, 6. For other discussions of the essay contest, see Yung, *Unbound Feet*, 157–59; Gloria Chun, *Of Orphans and Warriors: Inventing Chinese American Culture and Identity* (New Brunswick, NJ, 2000), 21–33; Wong, *Americans First*, 11–16.

48. "Where Does Our Future Lie?" *Chinese Digest*, May 8, 1936, 8; Robert Dunn, "Does My Future Lie in China or America?" *Chinese Digest*, May 15, 1936, 3–13; "Youths Who Think," *Chinese Digest*, May 15, 1936, 8.

49. Stanford University Chinese Students' Club, open letter to Robert Dunn, *Chinese Digest*, May 22, 1936, 11, 15.

50. Robert Dunn, open letter to members of the Stanford University Chinese Students' Club, *Chinese Digest*, June 12, 1936, 5, 14. Dunn noted that he had asked that an introduction to his essay explaining his decision accompany the reprinting in the *Chinese Digest*, but that his request came too late. Dunn and the club engaged in another round of debate. See Stanford University Chinese Students' Club, letter to Robert Dunn, *Chinese Digest*, July 3, 1936, 5, 14; Robert Dunn, letter to the editor, *Chinese Digest*, July 17, 1936, 14; Wong, *Americans First*, 15–16.

51. Kaye Hong, "Does My Future Lie in China or America?" *Chinese Digest*, May 22, 1936, 3, 14. There were two honorable mention winners (whose essays were not reprinted in *Chinese Digest*): Nora Lee and Yee Don Moon. For another

pro-China view, see George Grace, letter to the editor, *Chicago Defender*, June 19, 1936, 14.

52. Chun, *Of Orphans and Warriors*, 26; Rose Hum Lee, "Chinese Dilemma," *Phylon* 10, no. 2 (second quarter, 1949): 137–40.

53. Grace W. Wang, "A Speech on Second-Generation Chinese in U.S.A.," *Chinese Digest*, August 7, 1936, 6, 14; Wong, *Americans First*, 17–19.

54. Jane Kwong Lee, "The Future of Second Generation Chinese Lies in China and America," *Chicago Defender*, June 5, 1936, 5.

55. See, for example, "Seven Steps to Fame," *Chinese Digest*, December 6, 1935, 8; "A Chinese Design," *Chinese Digest*, March 13, 1936, 8; "What Other People Think of Us," *Chinese Digest*, April 10, 1936, 8.

56. "What Is the Chinese Digest?" *Chinese Digest*, January 1938, 2 (emphasis added); Lee, "Hu-Jee," 53–55.

57. The *Chinese Digest* had a second successor, the *Chinese News* (1940–42), founded by *Chinese Digest* editor Chinn. The *Chinese News* began as one page in San Francisco's *Chinese Nationalist Daily* in spring 1940 before coming out as a separate newsmagazine in October 1940. The first issue of the stand-alone *Chinese News* noted that the publication was "prompted by a desire to furnish reliable news to the Chinese in America," and was "endeavoring to gain the support and indorsement [*sic*] of every Chinese club and organization in America." Most of the content of the *Chinese News* was China related (Chinn was also an affiliate of the Chinese News Service, the Chinese government/Kuomintang Party's official information agency in the United States), although every issue contained local news of San Francisco Chinatown along with occasional reports of Chinese American home front and military participation.

58. "An Announcement," *Chinese Press*, June 6, 1941, 3.

59. Ibid.; "'Chinatown Is Ready': All Out Welcome for 15,000 U.S. Army Guests," *Chinese Press*, October 3, 1941, 1; H. K. Wong, "H. K.'s Column," *Chinese Press*, October 3, 1941, 3.

60. See the following in folder C, box 1069, RG 208, NARA: Smith to Leong, July 28, 1942; Leong to Smith, August 8, 1942; Smith to Leong, August 14, 1942; Smith to Leong, August 31, 1942; Leong to Smith, October 14, 1942; Leong to OWI Press Section, October 17, 1942.

61. "First Four Chinese Named Available for Military Service," *California Chinese Press*, November 22, 1940, 1; "New York's No.1 Draftee Chan Chong Yuen Likes Machine Guns," *California Chinese Press*, November 29, 1940, 1.

62. "William Hoy, Historian," *Chinese Press*, June 12, 1942, 2. See, for instance, William Hoy, "The Story of a Chinese Soldier in the U.S. Army," *Chinese Press*, July 31, 1942, 1. After the *Chinese Press* suspended publication in October 1943, Hoy produced *Gung Ho*, a bilingual newsletter by and for Chinese Americans in the armed forces. On *Gung Ho*, see Wong, *Americans First*, 179–82. The entire run of *Gung Ho* is reproduced in Christina M. Lim, Sheldon H. Lim, and Veterans of the 407th Air Service Squadron, *In the Shadow of the Tiger: The 407th Air Service Squadron, 14th Air Service Group, 14th Air Force, World War II* (San Mateo, CA, 1993).

63. "Editorial," *California Chinese Press*, November 22, 1940, 1; Lee, "Hu-Jee," 56; Wong, *Americans First*, 32–33.

64. See, for example, C. T. Feng, "Story of China's Rebirth: Democracy Fight in Far East Told by Consul General Feng," *Chinese Press*, October 10, 1941, 1, 4; William Hoy, "'Double Ten'—And Revolution—Thirty Years Ago a Man Named Sun Yat-Sen—Exiled in America—Saw the Birth of a New China," *Chinese Press*, October 10, 1941, 3.

65. William Hoy, "The Second-Generation Problem: A Columnist's Viewpoint on It; Through a Chinatown Window," *California Chinese Press*, May 9, 1941, 3; Maxine Chinn, "The Second-Generation Problem: 'We Who Are without a Country!'" *California Chinese Press*, May 9, 1941, 3; Daniel H. Lew, "'Freest Road Is Only One': Answer to Second-Generation Problem by a Harvard Man," *California Chinese Press*, May 23, 1941, 3; Nate R. White, "Crisis in Chinatown," *Christian Science Monitor Magazine*, February 1, 1952, 5, 12; Ernest O. Hauser, "Chinaman's Chance," *Saturday Evening Post*, December 7, 1940, 14–15, 82, 84–87.

66. Paul Louie, "Chinese Christian Youth Conferences in America, with a Focus on the East Coast," *Chinese America: History and Perspectives* (2001): 47–58.

67. *East Wind*'s editorial staff consisted of Henry S. Louie (editor), Eugenia Chen and Paul Louie (associate editors), and Yat Ping Bow, Ruby Lee, Dorothy Chang, and Mamie Louie. Based in Cleveland (1945–46) and then San Francisco (1947–48), the quarterly relied on field correspondents in major cities in the United States and Canada for much of its content. In April 1948, *Windbag*, a monthly supplement was added. *East Wind*'s last issue was published in summer 1948. See "East Wind: In Which We Narrate the History of This Magazine," *East Wind*, June 1946, 15–16; Lee, "Hu-Jee," 61–64.

68. Shelley Mark, "Open Forum: How American Are We?" *East Wind*, June 1945, 3, 4, 21.

69. Shelley Mark, "On Going Back to China," *East Wind*, January 1946,11–12.

70. "This Is My Answer! The Readers of *East Wind* Answer Back to Shelley Mark," *East Wind*, March 1946, 11–13.

71. Henry Louie, "Editorial," *East Wind*, March 1946, 10.

72. Paul Louie, "Editorial: Young America Speaks, 'I Believe . . . '" *East Wind*, June 1946, 17.

73. Andrew Loo, "A Letter of Expression," *East Wind*, Summer 1948, 20.

74. Richard Quey, "Social Integration," *East Wind*, December 1946, 16–19, 25–27; Richard Quey, "Social Integration," *East Wind*, June 1947, 24–27.

75. "Bill Seeks Ban on Race Prejudice in Employment," *Chinese Press*, March 11, 1949, 2; "Northwest FEPC," *Chinese Press*, March 18, 1949, 1; "Illinois Seeks FEPC," *Chinese Press*, March 25, 1949, 1; "House Subcommittee Approves FEPC Bill," *Chinese Press*, June 10, 1949, 1; "Civic Unity Federation Hits California Assembly's Refusal to Consider FEPC," *Chinese Press*, June 24, 1949, 3; "Demos Endorse Fair Employment," *Chinese Press*, December 30, 1949, 2; "'Right to Work' Report," *Chinese Press*, January 20, 1950, 1; "Where Are You Going?" *Chinese Press*, April 28, 1950, 7; "Employment Outlook after June," *Chinese Press*, May 26, 1950, 7; "June '50 Grads Strive for Practical Careers," *Chinese Press*, May 26, 1950, 7; "Chinatown to Help Survey Fair Employment," *Chinese Press*, February 23, 1951, 1; "CIO Council Hits FEPC Plan," *Chinese Press*, April 20, 1951, 1; "Fair Employment Hearing Monday," *Chinese Press*,

April 27, 1951, 3; "FEPC: New Legislation May Affect '51 Graduates," *Chinese Press*, May 4, 1951, 1; "City FEPC Is Still in Talking Stage," *Chinese Press*, May 11, 1951, 1; "Chinese Delegates Want FEPC Legislation OK'd," *Chinese Press*, May 18, 1951, 1; "FEPC Legislation Killed in Stormy Board Session," *Chinese Press*, June 1, 1951, 1; Thomas Wu, letter to editor, *Chinese Press*, November 2, 1951, 4, 6; "Economic Status: No Equal Job Opportunities for Chinese, Survey Finds," *Chinese Press*, April 29, 1949, 2; "Economic Blockade: Orientals Face Many Job Discriminations in SF," *Chinese Press*, May 20, 1949, 1; "Won't Hire Chinese: 75% Discrimination, State Survey Says," *Chinese Press*, January 13, 1950, 1; Rose Hum Lee, "Your Job and You," *Chinese Press*, August 11, 1950, 4; Rose Hum Lee, "Vocational Adjustment: Your Chances for a Job," *Chinese Press*, August 18, 1950, 4.

76. Lim P. Lee, "A Decade of Growth for the Chinese-Americans in California," *Chinese Press*, November 24, 1950, 9; Lee, "Vocational Adjustment"; Rose Hum Lee, "Your Job and You."

77. "Chinese Americans on the Job—No. 1, Engineer-Designer: From the Desk of Wallace Fong Come Plans for Powerhouses," *Chinese Press*, June 29, 1951, 4; "Chinese Americans on the Job—No. 2, Design-Engineer: Eugene Wong Aids in Engineering Development of Boeing Planes," *Chinese Press*, July 13, 1951, 4; "Chinese-Americans on the Job—No. 3, Bus Driver: San Franciscan Martin Tom Takes Your Fare, Takes You Places," *Chinese Press*, July 27, 1951, 4; "Chinese-Americans on the Job—No. 4, Superintendent: Gay Wy Heads Staff of China Station Post Office," *Chinese Press*, August 10, 1951, 4; Edward W. Chew, "Naval Suppliers: They Help Keep the Navy Afloat at Oakland Depot," *Chinese Press*, August 24, 1951, 4; "Chinese-Americans on the Job—No. 6, Instructor: Lawrence Wong Keeps Things Humming in College Cafeteria," *Chinese Press*, September 21, 1951, 4; Jack Lait, "Chinese-Americans on the Job—No. 7, Narcotics Agent: Sam Gon Made Life Tough for Dope Peddlers," *Chinese Press*, November 9, 1951, 4; "On the Job," *Chinese Press*, July 13, 1951, 4.

78. "On the Job," editorial, *Chinese Press*, July 13, 1951, 4.

79. On voting and earning as two pillars of citizenship in the United States, see Judith Shklar, *American Citizenship: The Quest for Inclusion* (Cambridge, MA, 1991).

80. "The People Say," *Chinese Press*, October 22, 1948, 4; "The People Say: Vote As You Please," *Chinese Press*, October 29, 1948, 1; "Chinatown Voting Heaviest in Years," *Chinese Press*, November 5, 1948, 1; "The People Say: Post Election Notes," *Chinese Press*, November 12, 1948, 1.

81. "The People Say: Vote as You Please," *Chinese Press*, May 5, 1950, 1; "The People Say: Americans All," editorial, *Chinese Press*, September 29, 1950, 1; "The People Say: Korea Victory," October 27, 1950, 1; "The People Say: Notes on a Vote," *Chinese Press*, November 10, 1950, 1; "Your Citizens' Rights," *Chinese Press*, August 24, 1951, 4; "Political House-cleaning," *Chinese Press*, September 21, 1951, 4; "The People Say," *Chinese Press*, December 7, 1951, 1.

82. Edward W. Chew, "Election Fever Hot: Candidates Look for Chinese Vote," *Chinese Press*, November 3, 1950, 1; Charles Leong, "The People Say: Vote Notes," *Chinese Press*, September 21, 1951, 1; "The People Say: More Vote Notes," *Chinese Press*, September 28, 1951, 1; "The People Say: On the

Spot?" *Chinese Press*, October 12, 1951, 1; untitled, *Chinese Press*, November 2, 1951, 4.

83. "The People Say: Voice of the People," *Chinese Press*, April 28, 1950, 1.

84. "The People Say: Springtime," *Chinese Press*, April 8, 1949, 1; "Progressive Integration," *Chinese Press*, September 28, 1951, 4.

85. Stanton Jue, "Chinese in California Politics," *Chinese Press*, September 22, 1950, 6; Stanton Jue, "Chinese in California Politics, *Chinese Press*, September 29, 1950, 4.

86. On anti-Chinese racism and Chinese inequality in the post–World War II era, see Wang, "Politics of Assimilation and Repression"; Mah, "Buying into the Middle Class"; Shah, *Contagious Divides*; Cheng, "Out of Chinatown"; Brooks, *Alien Neighbors, Foreign Friends*.

87. *Chinese Press*, press release, July 1, [1948], folder 21, box 3, Charles Leong Papers, Asian American Studies Collection, Ethnic Studies Library, University of California, Berkeley (hereafter CLP); "Chinese Press Revived," *Fortnight: The Newsmagazine of California*, July 16, 1948, 14, folder 25, box 3, ESL.

88. Hua Mei Fu Ban, "The Chinese Press Publishes Again," *Chinese Pacific Weekly*, June 26, 1948, 2. The *Chinese Press* ran advertisements for subscriptions in the *Chinese Pacific Weekly*, indicating that there was an overlap in the readership of Chinese- and English-language newspapers. See "The Chinese Press Announces It Has Begun Publishing Again," *Chinese Pacific Weekly*, April 3, 1948, 2.

89. "Mayor Robinson of San Francisco Greets Return of CHINESE PRESS," *Chinese Press*, August 20, 1948, 3; "Officials and Subscribers Tell Their Opinions of This Paper," *Chinese Press*, October 8, 1948, 4; "PRESS Not Only Publishes News But Makes It Too," *Chinese Press*, October 8, 1948, 4.

90. See untitled, *New Yorker*, September 11, 1948, folder 25, box 3, CLP. See also clippings in folder 36, box 3, CLP, including: Jack S. McDowell, "Memo from Mac," *San Francisco Call-Bulletin*, May 17, 1949; Herb Caen, "It's News to Me," *San Francisco Chronicle*, June 25, 1948; "Chinese Paper," *San Francisco Examiner*, July 2, 1948; "Chinese Paper Reopens in SF," *Alameda Times Star*, July 2, 1948; "SF Chinese Press Published Again," *Orange News*, July 3, 1948; "Chinese Press Resumes Again," *Redland Facts*, July 2, 1948; "Charles Leong Again Publishing Chinese Press," *Watsonville Register-Pajaronian*, July 6, 1948; "Chinese Press Revived," *Fortnight: The Newsmagazine of California*; "Scrutable Chinese," *Beverly Hills Script*, September 1948.

91. On the history of CCBAs/Six Companies, see Lai, *Becoming Chinese American*, 39–76; McClain, *In Search of Equality*; Salyer, *Laws as Harsh as Tigers*; Yucheng Qin, *The Diplomacy of Nationalism: The Six Companies and China's Policy toward Exclusion* (Honolulu, 2009).

92. K. Scott Wong, "Cultural Defenders and Brokers: Chinese Responses to the Anti-Chinese Movement," in *Claiming America: Constructing Chinese American Identities during the Exclusion Era*, ed. K. Scott Wong and Sucheng Chan (Philadelphia, 1998), 3–40.

93. "Leong Back from China, Plans Own Office Here," *Black Kitten* (official bulletin of San Francisco Press Club), January 1948, folder 55, box 1, CLP; "Chinese Press Revived," *Fortnight*; "Charles Leong to Be Speaker for Optimists,"

Watsonville Register-Pajaronian, April 25, 1949, folder 26, box 3, CLP; Charles L. Leong, *The Eagle and the Dragon: A Real-Life Chinese-American Story* (San Francisco, 1976).

94. "The People Say," *Chinese Press*, October 7, 1949, 1; "PRESS Wins Plaudits from World of Journalism," *Chinese Press*, November 24, 1950, 3; "Scrutable Chinese," *Beverly Hills Script*; "PRESS Wins Americanism Award in National Editorial Contest," *Chinese Press*, June 15, 1951, 1; Albert K. Chow to Matthew J. Connelly, November 8, 1950, folder PPF 5560, box 601, President's Personal File, National Archives and Records Administration, Harry S. Truman Presidential Library, Independence, MO; Harry S. Truman to Charles Leong, November 21, 1950, ibid.

95. Charles L. Leong to Yinson Lee, March 3, 1953, folder 31, box 3, CLP.

96. "Editorial: Statement of Policy," *Chinese News*, February 14, 1953, 12; "Good News! For Chinese Americans and Their Other American Friends," *Chinese News*, February 14, 1953, 20.

97. Charles L. Leong to Joe Waugh Jr., April 20, 1953, folder 31, box 3, CLP.

98. "Loyal Americans," *Chinese News*, May 9, 1953, 3; "Roll of Honor," *Chinese News*, March 28, 1953, 16–17.

99. Lizabeth Cohen, *A Consumers' Republic: The Politics of Mass Consumption in Postwar America* (New York, 2003), 11.

100. Charles L. Leong to Dan Shaw, August 16, 1954, folder 32, box 3, CLP.

101. On ethnic brokering, see Mae Ngai, *The Lucky Ones: One Family and the Extraordinary Invention of Chinese America* (New York, 2010); Oda, "Remaking the 'Gateway to the Pacific.'"; Lisa Mar, *Brokering Belonging: Chinese in Canada's Exclusion Era, 1885–1945* (New York, 2010); Chang, *Pacific Connections*.

102. Charles L. Leong to Ruth Price, May 18, 1953, folder 29, box 3, CLP.

103. "Statehood Challenge," *Chinese News*, March 14, 1953, 12.

104. Charles L. Leong to Yasuo Abiko, May 29, 1953, folder 31, box 3, CLP; Charles L. Leong to John Foster Dulles, May 11, 1953, folder 31, box 3, CLP.

105. "29 Northern Californian Freedom Awards," *San Francisco Chronicle*, February 23, 1954, 4.

106. In 1962, Leong took the helm of the Chinese American section for San Francisco's *Young China*. As a Kuomintang organ, *Young China* differed from Leong's earlier, independent ventures by including in its editorial policies an open position on China affairs (support for the "ideals and objectives of the democratic atmosphere of the Republic of China"). But in other ways *Young China* resembled the *Chinese Press* and *Chinese News*. Their contents were similar—stories about Chinese America with special attention to ethnic candidates for public office and issues of assimilation. A public relations mission, additionally, remained central to the enterprise. As board chair W. Fong Yue explained, the English-language section was added not only to serve Chinese Americans but also to provide a means for "other Americans" to learn about the community. See Fong Yue, letter to director, Government Information Office, Taipei, Taiwan, n.d., folder 40, box 3, CLP; "Historic Chinese Daily Paper Adds English-Language Section," press release, May 20, 1962, folder 45, box 3, CLP.

107. Other titles included Fresno's *Chi-Kracs*, Los Angeles' *Chinese Chatter*, Boston's *Cathayan*, San Diego's *New Voice*, Detroit's *China Mail Call*, San Antonio's *Chinese Lantern*, Chicago's *Chinese Progess*, Saint Louis's *Cathay Newsletter*, and Seattle's *Epoch*.

Chapter 3: Nisei in Uniform

1. JACL, "Official Convention Minutes, 1946," 2, folder 3, box 297, JARP.
2. Ibid.
3. Ibid. On the relationship between the *Pacific Citizen* and JACL, see Greg Robinson, *Pacific Citizens: Larry and Guyo Tajiri and Japanese American Journalism in the World War II Era*, ed. Greg Robinson (Urbana, IL, 2012), xxx; Yoo, *Growing Up Nisei*, 124–40.
4. JACL, "Official Convention Minutes, 1946," 3. On the renunciants and draft resisters, see US Commission on Wartime Relocation and Internment of Civilians, *Personal Justice Denied*; Ngai, *Impossible Subjects*; Eric L. Muller, *Free to Die for Their Country: The Story of the Japanese American Draft Resisters in World War II* (Chicago, 2001).
5. Ngai, *Impossible Subjects*, 197.
6. US Commission on Wartime Evacuation and Relocation of Civilians, *Personal Justice Denied*, 258–59.
7. On martial patriotism, see Cecilia Elizabeth O'Leary, *To Die For: The Paradox of American Patriotism* (Princeton, NJ, 1999); Lucy E. Salyer, "Baptism by Fire: Race, Military Service, and U.S. Citizenship Policy, 1918–1935," *Journal of American History* 91, no. 3 (December 2004): 847–76.
8. Lee, *Orientals*; David Eng, *Racial Castration: Managing Masculinity in Asian America* (Durham, NC, 2001).
9. Linda Kerber, *Women of the Republic: Intellect and Ideology in Revolutionary America* (Chapel Hill, NC, 1980).
10. Togo Tanaka, "History of the JACL," chapter 1, reel 84, JERS.
11. Ibid., chapters 1–3, 6.
12. Ibid., chapter 2; Yuji Ichioka, "A Study in Dualism: James Yoshinori Sakamoto and the *Japanese American Courier*, 1928–1942," *Amerasia Journal* 13 (1986–87): 49–81; Azuma, *Between Two Empires*, 138–39, 170.
13. Tanaka, "JACL," chapter 3.
14. Ibid.
15. Tanaka, "JACL," chapters 2–3; Jere Takahashi, *Nisei/Sansei: Shifting Japanese American Identities and Politics* (Philadelphia, 1997), 56–57, 66–74, 79; Kurashige, *Japanese American Celebration*, 82.
16. Tanaka "JACL," chapter 4; Kurashige, *The Shifting Grounds of Race*, 111.
17. Tanaka, "JACL," chapter 4; Kurashige, *Shifting Grounds*, 112; Alice Yang Murray, *Historical Memories of the Japanese American Internment and the Struggle for Redress* (Stanford, CA, 2008), 107.
18. Mike Masaoka to Milton S. Eisenhower, April 6, 1942, reel 83, JERS; Paul R. Spickard, "The Nisei Assume Power: The Japanese [American] Citi-

zens League, 1941–1942," *Pacific Historical Review* 52, no. 2 (1983): 147–74; Kurashige, *Celebration and Conflict*, 83–85; Kurashige, *Shifting Grounds*, 126–30; Murray, *Historical Memories*, 110–12.

19. Arthur A. Hansen and David A. Hacker, "The Manzanar Riot: An Ethnic Perspective," *Amerasia* 2, no. 2 (1974): 112–57; US Commission on Wartime Evacuation and Relocation of Civilians, *Personal Justice Denied* 174, 177–78; Weglyn, *Years of Infamy*, 119–21; Takahashi, *Nisei/Sansei*, 108–11; Hayashi, *Democratizing the Enemy*, 94, 100, 108, 111–12.

20. Masaoka to Eisenhower.

21. Weglyn, *Years of Infamy*, 135; US Commission on Wartime Evacuation and Relocation of Civilians, *Personal Justice Denied*, 187; Bill Hosokawa, *JACL in Quest of Justice: The History of the Japanese American Citizens League* (New York, 1982), 190, 192, 197–201; Muller, *Free to Die*, 42–43; Masaoka to Henry L. Stimson, January 15, 1943, http://www.pbs.org/itvs/conscience/compliance/the_draft/03_service_i.html (accessed November 6, 2010).

22. Salyer, "Baptism by Fire." On military service as an obligation of citizenship, see Linda K. Kerber, *No Constitutional Right to be Ladies: Women and the Obligations of Citizenship* (New York, 1998); Sparrow, *Warfare State*.

23. US Commission on Wartime Evacuation and Relocation of Civilians, *Personal Justice Denied*, 186–91; Muller, *Free to Die*, 45–47.

24. Weglyn, *Years of Infamy*, 140–43; Hosokawa, *JACL*, 210–12; Mike Masaoka with Bill Hosokawa, *They Call Me Moses Masaoka: An American Saga* (New York, 1987), 123–59.

25. Masaoka, *They Call Me Moses*, 131.

26. Hansen and Hacker, "The Manzanar Riot"; Muller, *Free to Die*, 44–45; Kurashige, *Celebration and Conflict*, 75, 85–89; Hayashi, *Democratizing the Enemy*, 134–35.

27. Weglyn, *Years of Infamy*, 143–51; Muller, *Free to Die*, 54–57.

28. Weglyn, *Years of Infamy*, 140–43; Muller, *Free to Die*, 60–63.

29. Muller, *Free to Die*, 62–63, 64–99.

30. See, for instance, "Sgt. Kuroki, Nisei War Hero, Returns to U.S.," *Pacific Citizen*, January 1, 1944, 1, 3; "Story of the Week: Sgt. Ben Kuroki Reveals Escape from Spaniards," *Pacific Citizen*, January 29, 1944, 1; "Japanese American War Hero," *Pacific Citizen*, February 5, 1944, 3.

31. JACL, "Official Convention Minutes, 1946," 8, 11; US Commission on Wartime Evacuation and Relocation of Civilians, *Personal Justice Denied*, 246, 256; Saburo Kido, "The President's Report: JACL Intensified Its Public Relations Activity in 1944," *Pacific Citizen*, December 23, 1944, 10; JACL, "PFC Thomas Higa's Lecture Tour Extended," press release, September 6, 1944, reel 83, JERS.

32. Arthur A. Hansen, "Sergeant Ben Kuroki's Perilous 'Home Mission': Contested Loyalty and Patriotism in the Japanese American Detention Centers," in *Remembering Heart Mountain: Essays on Japanese American Internment in Wyoming*, ed. Mike Mackey (Sheridan, WY, 1998), 153–75.

33. Japanese American Committee for Democracy, "Constitution," n.d., New York Public Library; *NewsLetter*, February 1944, 2; Robinson, *After Camp*, 185.

34. Howard, *Concentration Camps on the Homefront*, 140–49.

35. Saburo Kido, "JACL in Wartime," January 1, 1944, reel 83, JERS; JACL, "Official Convention Minutes, 1946," 11, 93; Hosokawa, *JACL*, 265; JACL, "Ben Kuroki's Story," pamphlet, Salt Lake City, 1944; Kido, "The President's Report."

36. Masaoka, *They Call Me Moses*, 145, 178.

37. Ngai, *Impossible Subjects*, 177–82; US Department of the Interior/WRA, "Nisei in Uniform," n.d., "Minorities-Japanese-Pamphlets, 1943–1945" folder, box 51, Philleo Nash Papers, National Archives and Records Administration, Harry S. Truman Presidential Library, Independence, MO (hereafter PNP). See also US Department of the Interior/ WRA "What We're Fighting For: Statements by United States Servicemen about Americans of Japanese Descent," (Washington, DC, 1945).

38. "Blind Nisei," *Life*, February 7, 1944, 53; Lee Shippey, "Leeside," *Los Angeles Times*, February 2, 1944, A4; "Heroes: Ben Kuroki, American," *Time*, February 7, 1944; "Crapshooters, Jitterbugs," *Crisis*, November 1943, 327.

39. "Network Tells Why Jap Gunner Barred from Air," *Los Angeles Times*, January 27, 1944, 2; Warren B. Francis, "Curb on Jap Evacuee Propaganda Sought," *Los Angeles Times*, August 30, 1944, 12; Selden Menefee, "America at War: Future of the Nisei," *Washington Post*, April 20, 1944, 10.

40. "American Fair Play?" *Time*, March 19, 1945; Linda Tamura, "'Wrong Face, Wrong Name': The Return of Japanese American Veterans to Hood River, Oregon, after World War II," in *Remapping Asian American History*, ed. Sucheng Chan (Walnut Creek, CA, 2003), 107–25; US Department of the Interior, *The Relocation Program* (Washington, DC, 1946), 65–66.

41. See, for instance, Sidney Carroll, "Purple Heart Battalion," *Coronet*, May 1945, 4–9.

42. Blake Clark and Oland D. Russell, "Japanese-American Soldiers Make Good," *American Mercury*, June 1945, 698–703, reprinted as "Hail Our Japanese-American GIs!" *Reader's Digest*, July 1945, 65–67. Russell served as a public relations officer with the 442nd during its training period at Camp Shelby in Mississippi.

43. Clark and Russell, "Japanese-American Soldiers Make Good."

44. Tetsuden Kashima, "Japanese American Internees Return, 1945 to 1955: Readjustment and Social Amnesia," *Phylon* 41, no. 2 (Summer 1980): 107–15; Brooks, "In the Twilight Zone"; Brooks, *Alien Neighbors, Foreign Friends*, 159–93; Kurashige, *Shifting Grounds*, 158–204; Brilliant, *The Color of America Has Changed*, 29–57; HoSang, *Racial Propositions*, 45–47.

45. JACL, "Official Convention Minutes, 1946," 16, 43, 46, 53.

46. Hodding Carter, "Go for Broke," *Delta Democrat-Times*, August 27, 1945; "Delta Prizewinner," *Time*, May 20, 1946.

47. JACL, "Official Convention Minutes, 1946," 87; "Go for Broke," *Time*, July 22, 1946. On the GI Bill, see Cohen, *A Consumers' Republic*, 137–43, 156–60, 166–70; Suzanne Mettler, *Soldiers to Citizens: The G.I. Bill and the Making of the Greatest Generation* (New York, 2005); Canaday, *The Straight State*; Kathleen J. Frydl, *The GI Bill* (Cambridge, UK, 2009); Sparrow, *Warfare State*.

48. "Army General Lauds Nisei Soldiers," *Chicago Defender*, June 8, 1946, 7; Harry Hansen, "Fred Gipson Full of Tales from the Heart of Texas," *Chicago Daily Tribune*, October 20, 1946, G2; "Nisei War Hero Will Address Meeting Tuesday," *Washington Post*, November 24, 1946, M3; JACL, "Official Conven-

tion Minutes, 1946," 87; "Ben Kuroki Continues on 59th Mission to Fight for Tolerance," *JACL Reporter*, May 1946; "Kuroki Appeals for Equal Rights of Nisei Vet at Minority Meet," *JACL Reporter*, May 1946; "Kuroki Pens Editorial for Chicago Bulletin," *JACL Reporter*, May 1946; Ralph G. Martin, *Boy from Nebraska: The Story of Ben Kuroki* (New York, 1946); "JACL Sponsors Sale of Ben Kuroki's Book," *JACL Reporter*, July 1946; W. G. Rogers, "A Nisei Boy in O.D.: Story of a 2-Front War," *Washington Post*, October 27, 1946, S7; J. Mitchell Morse, "Nisei from Nebraska," *New York Times*, November 3, 1946, 167.

49. JACL, "Official Convention Minutes, 1946," 87; "Ben Kuroki Continues on 59th Mission"; "Kuroki Appeals for Equal Rights"; "Kuroki Pens Editorial"; "JACL Sponsors Sale"; JACL, "Official Convention Minutes, 1948," 33–36; "French Dedicate Memorial to U.S. Nisei Unit," *Washington Post*, October 31, 1947, 14; "Renaming Army Transport for Nisei Infantry Hero," *New York Times*, March 7, 1948, 51; "RACES: Home Country," *Time*, March 29, 1948.

50. Hayashi to Satow, November 6, 1949, "Nisei Soldier Memorial Day" folder, box 5, series 1, JACL History Collection, Japanese American National Library, San Francisco (hereafter JACL-JANL); "Dead Niseis to Be Honored," *Omaha Sunday World-Herald*, October 30, 1949, 11A, "Nisei Soldier Memorial Day" folder, box 5, series 1, JACL-JANL.

51. Satow to all JACL chapters, October 13, 1950, folder 7, box 301, JARP; Satow to all JACL chapters, October 16, 1951, folder 7, box 301, JARP; "Two Faiths Join Today to Honor Nisei Heroes," *Chicago Daily Tribune*, October 30, 1949, 12; "Battlefield Exploits of Nisei Paid High Praise at Arlington," *Washington Post*, October 31, 1949, B2; "Jap Americans Honor Nisei Soldiers Tomorrow," *Chicago Daily Tribune*, October 29, 1950, 22.

52. Satow to all JACL chapters, October 4, 1949, "Nisei Soldier Memorial Day" folder, box 5, series 1, JACL-JANL; JACL, "Official Convention Minutes, 1950," 10, folder 5, box 296; JARP.

53. Satow to Akagi, October 12, 1950, "Nisei Soldier Memorial Day" folder, box 5, series 1, JACL-JANL.

54. Satow to all JACL chapters, October 13, 1950; Satow to all JACL chapters, October 16, 1951.

55. Setsuda and Abe to Okada, letter and resolution, January 4, 1950, "Nisei Soldier Memorial Day" folder, box 5, series 1, JACL-JANL.

56. For an analysis of *Go for Broke!* see T. Fujitani, *Race for Empire: Koreans as Japanese and Japanese as Americans during World War II* (Berkeley, 2011), 223–29.

57. Muller, *Free to Die*, 42–43.

58. JACL, "Official Convention Minutes, 1950," 6; Masaoka, *They Call Me Moses*, 215–16; JACL, "Official Convention Minutes, 1952," 12, folder 7, box 296, JARP; JACL, "National Headquarters to All JACL Chapters," March 1, 1951, folder 7, box 301, JARP; Satow to all JACL chapters, March 23, 1951, folder 7, box 301, JARP.

59. JACL, "Official Convention Minutes, 1952," 29–30, 41.

60. *Go for Broke!* program for premiere at the Egyptian Theater, Hollywood, CA, May 9, 1951; *Go for Broke!* oversize press book, n.d.; *A Precio De Sangre*, n.d., Spanish-language press book; Core Collection production file for *Go for*

Broke! Margaret Herrick Library Special Collections, Academy of Motion Picture Arts and Sciences, Los Angeles (hereafter MHL).

61. "Two Hundred 442nd Veterans Will Be Guests at Tokyo Premier of 'Go for Broke!'" *Pacific Citizen*, May 5, 1951, 1; Lawrence Nakatsuka, "Metro's Story of Nisei GI Given Glittering Premier at Honolulu's Waikiki Theater," *Pacific Citizen*, May 5, 1951, 1; Satow to Station KSL-TV, July 3, 1951, folder 7, box 301, JARP; Satow to all JACL chapters, March 23, 1951, folder 7, box 301, JARP; Mae Tinee, "Movie of Nisei in World War Truly Gripping," *Chicago Tribune*, June 8, 1951, folder 3, box 298, JARP; Wood Soanes, "'Go for Broke' a Fit Tribute as a Memorial Day Opener," *Oakland Tribune*, May 31, 1951, folder 3, box 298, JARP; Ezra Goodman, "Film Review 'Go for Broke,'" *Los Angeles Daily News*, May 10, 1951; Core Collection production file for *Go for Broke!* MHL.

62. Fred Childress, "442nd Combat Team's Record Gives Excitement to War Film," *Youngstown Vindicator*, June 17, 1951, C-19 folder 3, box 298, JARP; John McClain, "Mad about Manhattan: American Named Yamato," *New York Journal-American*, May 28, 1951, folder 3, box 298, JARP.

63. "Go for Broke Tells Story of Famed Combat Unit," *Cincinnati Post*, May 25, 1951, 18, folder 3, box 298, JARP; Groverman Blake, "Aisle Say," *Cincinnati Times-Star*, May 25, 1951, 14, folder 3, box 298, JARP; Douglass M. Allen, "Relive Heroic Deeds—Cincinnati Veterans of Famed Combat Team Approve Movie," *Cincinnati Times-Star*, May 25, 1951, folder 3, box 298, JARP; Albert D. Cash, "Proclamation," City of Cincinnati, *City Bulletin*, May 29, 1951, folder 3, box 298, JARP.

64. JACL, "Official Convention Minutes, 1952," 9–30, 41.

65. Larry Tajiri, "Nisei USA: MGM and 'Go for Broke!'" *Pacific Citizen*, May 26, 1951, 4.

66. Satow to Sakada et al., May 8, 1951, "Nisei in Uniform" folder, box 5, series 1, JACL-JANL.

67. George Yamada, "Old Stereotyped Pattern," *Crisis*, January 1953, 17–19.

68. Ibid.

69. Shibutani, "The First Year of the Resettlement of Nisei in the Chicago Area"; Nishi, "Japanese American Achievement," 158; JACL, "Official Convention Minutes, 1946," 12.

70. Kurashige, *Shifting Grounds*, 193; Allan W. Austin, "'A Finer Set of Hopes and Dreams': The Japanese American Citizens League and Ethnic Community in Cincinnati, Ohio, 1942–1950," in *Remapping Asian American History*, ed. Sucheng Chan (Lanham, MD, 2003), 87–105.

71. JACL, "Official Convention Minutes, 1946," 24–27, 43–56, 81–86; JACL, "Official Convention Minutes, 1948," 19–20. The ADC was incorporated under the laws of the State of Utah on July 9, 1946.

72. JACL, "Official Convention Minutes, 1946," 98; Takahashi, *Nisei/Sansei*, 112, 126.

73. President's Committee on Civil Rights, *To Secure These Rights* (Washington, DC, 1947), viii–ix; Masaoka to Carr, March 14, 1947, "JACL Anti-Discrimination Committee, Inc." folder, box 11, RG 220, PNP; Carr to Masaoka, April 23, 1947, President's Committee on Civil Rights, "JACL Anti-Discrimination Committee, Inc." folder, box 11, RG 220, PNP.

74. Masaoka, statement before the President's Committee on Civil Rights, May 1, 1947, "JACL Anti-Discrimination Committee, Inc." folder, box 11, RG 220, PNP; Masaoka to the President's Committee on Civil Rights, April 23, 1947, "JACL Anti-Discrimination Committee, Inc." folder, box 11, RG 220, PNP.

75. Ibid.

76. President's Committee on Civil Rights, *To Secure These Rights*, 158–59, 161–62.

77. Ibid., 34.

78. Theda Skocpol, *Protecting Soldiers and Mothers: The Political Origins of Social Policy in the United States* (Cambridge, MA, 1992); O'Leary, *To Die For*; Kerber, *No Constitutional Right*; Mettler, *Soldiers to Citizens*.

79. JACL, "Official Convention Minutes, 1948," 23, 32, A1, A3, A4.

80. Robert M. Cullum, "Japanese American Audit—1948," *Common Ground* (Winter 1949): 87–89; Robinson, *After Camp*, 195–216; Brooks, *Alien Neighbors, Foreign Friends*, 176–84.

81. Cullum, "Japanese American Audit"; JACL, "Official Convention Minutes, 1948," 22, 26–28.

82. Alfred Steinberg, "Washington's Most Successful Lobbyist," *Reader's Digest*, May 1949, 125–29 (originally published in *Sign*, April 1949).

83. JACL, "Official Convention Minutes, 1948," A1, 6; Nishi, "Japanese American Achievement," 198, 277, 326–30.

84. See the following editorials by Omura in the *Rocky Shimpo*: "The JACL and the Nisei," May 27, 1947; "A Gross Misstatement," June 26, 1947; "JACL Leadership Inadequate," Aug. 2, 1947; "An Ironic Situation," August 19, 1947; "The Count Is 12 to 1," Aug. 27, 1947; "Let's Not Be Duped," September 8, 1947. Special thanks to Art Hansen for these citations. See also David Yoo, *Growing Up Nisei*, 140–47; Arthur A. Hansen, "Return to the Wars: Jimmie Omura's 1947 Crusade against the Japanese American Citizens League," in *Remapping Asian American History*, ed. Sucheng Chan (Walnut Creek, CA, 2003), 127–50.

85. Bill Kitayama, "What Do You Think," *Crossroads*, June 4, 1949. Thanks to Charlotte Brooks for this reference.

86. "Local Nisei-for-Wallace Group Organized," *Crossroads*, May 28, 1948, 1; "Progressive Party Platform Urges Full Equality for Nisei," *Pacific Citizen*, July 31, 1948, 2; Chizo Iiyama, "Chicago Nisei for Wallace to Send Delegates to Convention," *Hokubei Mainichi*, July 17, 1948, 1; Yori Wada, "I Shall Cast My Vote for Wallace," *Hokubei Mainchi*, October 29, 1948, 1; Dyke Miyagawa, "It's Wallace for Me," *Pacific Citizen*, August 21, 1948; T. K. "An Editorial," *Independent*, September 22, 1948, 2; "See New Party Adopt Nisei Planks," *Bandwagon*, August 1948, 1, 3. On Nisei progressives, see also Martha Nakagawa, "Rebels with a Just Cause," *Rafu Shimpo*, December 11, 1997, 1, 4; Martha Nakagawa, "Sakae Ishihara: A Marked Man," *Rafu Shimpo*, December, 12, 1997, 1, 3, 4; Greg Robinson, *After Camp*, 191; Diana Meyers Bahr, *The Unquiet Nisei: An Oral History of the Life of Sue Kunitomi Embrey* (New York, 2007). Kurashige (*Shifting Grounds*, 183–85) notes the formation of the two other short-lived Japanese American political groups in early postwar Los Angeles: the Civil Rights Defense Union and Fair Play United. Kurashige (*Celebration and Conflict*, 134–35) also

points out that Nisei veterans groups became an important constituency in post-war Japanese American communities.

87. "Proposed Constitution and By-Laws of the Nisei Progressives," January 18, 1949, folder 2, box 16, Records of the Independent Progressive Party, Young Research Library Special Collections, University of California, Los Angeles (hereafter YRL); "Nisei Progressive," press release, folder 2, box 16, Records of the Independent Progressive Party, YRL.

88. Nisei Progressives, press release, March 31, 1949, folder 2, box 16, Records of the Independent Progressive Party, YRL; "Nisei Progressives Announce Opposition to Mundt-Nixon Bill," *Pacific Citizen*, April 29, 1950, 3; "Nisei Progressives Ask Nehru Continue Mediation for Korea," *Pacific Citizen*, August 12, 1950, 3; "Nisei Progressives Ask Boycott on Florida Products," *Pacific Citizen*, February 2, 1952, 3.

89. "Truman's Choices," *Bandwagon*, October 1949, 25; "Grins and Groans," *Bandwagon*, November 1949, 21–22.

90. Ngai, *Impossible Subjects*, 237; Takahashi, *Nisei/Sansei,* 127–28.

91. Ibid.

92. Blake Clark, "Why Shouldn't They Be Americans?" *Reader's Digest*, August 1951, 91–94 (originally published in *Freeman*, July 16, 1951).

93. Ibid.; "Rep. Judd Inserts *Digest*'s Article on Issei Citizenship into Congressional Record," *Pacific Citizen*, August 4, 1951, 2, 5.

94. JACL, "Official Convention Minutes, 1954," 19, folder 8, box 296, JARP. The McCarran-Walter Act did not overturn the national origins basis of immigrant selection. President Truman vetoed the bill on the grounds that it perpetuated the racist quota system. Many liberals and leftists, including the Nisei Progressives, also opposed the bill for its repressive measures allowing the federal government increased powers to deport aliens in the name of "internal security." See Ngai, *Impossible Subjects*, 237–39; Kurashige, *Shifting Grounds*, 202–4; Bahr, *The Unquiet Nisei*, 104.

95. "JACL Plays Important Role in Obtaining Passage of Issei Citizenship Legislation," *Pacific Citizen*, July 5, 1952, 1.

96. "Passage of Omnibus Measure Marks Highwater Mark in ADC's Legislative Activity," *Pacific Citizen*, May 31, 1952, 1; "The JACL's Leadership," *Pacific Citizen*, June 28, 1952, 4; "JACL's Legislative Objectives," *Pacific Citizen*, July 5, 1952, 4; "The Issei Dream Realized," *Pacific Citizen*, July 5, 1952, 4; "Mike Masaoka," *Pacific Citizen*, July 12, 1952, 4.

97. "Nisei Progressives Urge Truman Veto of Omnibus Bill," *Pacific Citizen*, June 21, 1952, 3; Aristide R. Zolberg, *A Nation by Design: Immigration Policy in the Fashioning of America* (Cambridge, MA, 2006), 315; Robert A. Divine, *American Immigration Policy, 1924–1952* (New Haven, CT, 1957), 171–74.

98. President's Commission on Immigration and Naturalization, *Hearings before the President's Commission on Immigration and Naturalization* (Washington, DC, 1952), 842–44; Robinson, *After Camp*, 93–101.

99. President's Commission on Immigration and Naturalization, *Whom We Shall Welcome* (Washington, DC, 1953), 46; JACL, "Official Convention Minutes, 1952," 30. On race and the reconfiguration of US-Japan relations after World War II, see Dower, *War without Mercy*; Yukiko Koshiro, *Trans-Pacific Rac-*

isms and the U.S. Occupation of Japan (New York, 1999); Shibusawa, *America's Geisha Ally*.

100. JACL, "Official Convention Minutes, 1952," 35–42, 57.

101. Ibid., 60–61, 91.

102. Ishimaru to Inagaki et al., March 10, 1954, "Committee on J-Am Affairs, 1 of 2" folder, box 6, series 1, JACL-JANL; Wakamatsu to Ishimaru et al., March 26, 1954, "Committee on J-Am Affairs, 1 of 2" folder, box 6, series 1, JACL-JANL; Masaoka to Wakamatsu et al., March 30, 1954, "Committee on J-Am Affairs, 1 of 2" folder, box 6, series 1, JACL-JANL; Satow to Wakamatsu, April 5, 1954, "Committee on J-Am Affairs, 1 of 2" folder, box 6, series 1, JACL-JANL.

103. Masaoka to National Board Members et al., August 4, 1954, "Public Relations Committee, 1954–1962" folder, box 6, series 1, JACL-JANL; JACL, "Official Convention Minutes, 1954," 69–70.

104. JACL, "Official Convention Minutes, 1954," 70–71.

105. "Prisons: Once Again, Tokyo Rose," *Newsweek*, January 16, 1956, 26; Lincoln Yamamoto, "The Meaning of Treason," *Newsweek*, February 20, 1956, 2. On Tokyo Rose, see Masayo Duus, *Tokyo Rose, Orphan of the Pacific* (New York, 1979); Russell Warren Howe, *The Hunt for Tokyo Rose* (New York, 1990); Simpson, *An Absent Presence*; Frederick P. Close: *Tokyo Rose/An American Patriot: A Dual Biography* (Plymouth, UK, 2010); Naoko Shibusawa, "Femininity, Race, and Treachery: How 'Tokyo Rose' Became a Traitor to the United States after the Second World War," *Gender and History* 22, no. 1 (April 2010): 169–88.

106. On the midcentury gendering of Asian American women, see Gina Marchetti, *Romance and the "Yellow Peril": Race, Sex, and Discursive Strategies in Hollywood Fiction* (Berkeley, 1994); Lee, *Orientals*; Shibusawa, "Femininity, Race, and Treachery"; Judy Tzu-Chun Wu, *Doctor Mom Chung of the Fair-Hair Bastards* (Berkeley, 2005). Nisei for Wallace also promoted Issei women as republican mothers. See "Progressive Party Platform Urges Full Equality for Nisei," *Pacific Citizen*, July 31, 1948, 2.

107. Nakahara to Satow, February 29, 1956, "1950s and 1960s" folder, box 8, series 1, JACL-JANL.

108. Nakahara to Cogswell, February 25, 1956; Nakahara to Satow, February 29, 1956, "1950s and 1960s" folder, box 8, series 1, JACL-JANL.

109. "Publication of Letter Arouses Nisei Protest to *Newsweek*," *Pacific Citizen*, February 17, 1956, 1, 8; "Great Disservice to Nisei Committed," *Pacific Citizen*, February 17, 1956, 1; Tats Kushida, "How Low Can You Get?" *Pacific Citizen*, February 17, 1956, 4; "'Lincoln Yamamoto' Letter Reviving Smear against Nisei Seen as 'Most Damaging' to JACL Legislative Efforts in Washington," *Pacific Citizen*, February 24, 1956, 1, 3; "JACL Asks FBI Hunt 'Lincoln Yamamoto,'" *Pacific Citizen*, March 9, 1956; "Majority Opinion," *Newsweek*, March 5, 1956, 2, 6, 8; "Nisei Leaders Storm *Newsweek* Editors with Strong Protests for Printing Letter," *Pacific Citizen*, February 24, 1956, 8; JACL, "Official Convention Minutes, 1956," 12, 41, box 296, folder 9, JARP; Chuman to president and chair of the *Newsweek* board of directors, February 24, 1956, "1950s and 1960s" folder, box 8, series 1, JACL-JANL.

110. Whitman, Ransom, and Coulson to Chuman, February 29, 1956, "1950s and 1960s" folder, box 8, series 1, JACL-JANL; "Majority Opinion," *Newsweek*;

Chuman to Inagaki, March 2, 1956, "1950s and 1960s" folder, box 8, series 1, JACL-JANL; "Influential American Legion Post in Stockton Raps *Newsweek* in Unanimously Passed Resolution for Lincoln Yamamoto Letter," *Pacific Citizen*, April 6, 1956, 8; Helen Mineta, "Sen. Kuchel Denounces Writer of Letter to Magazine on Senate Floor," *Pacific Citizen*, February 24, 1956, 1, 2; "California Congressman Roosevelt Rebukes *Newsweek* for 'Linc' Letter," *Pacific Citizen*, March 16, 1956, 1, 8; "Calif. Congressman Gubser Upholds Nisei Loyalty in Letter to Columnist," *Pacific Citizen*, March 30, 1956, 8; Simpson, *An Absent Presence*, 101–2.

111. Masaoka to Inagaki et al., March 1, 1956, "1950s and 1960s" folder, box 8, series 1, JACL-JANL.

112. JACL, "Official Convention Minutes, 1956," 38, 41, folder 8, box 206, JARP; Walter LaFeber, *The Clash: A History of U.S.-Japan Relations* (New York, 1998), 317.

113. JACL, "Official Convention Minutes, 1956," 55; "Urge Nisei to Foster U.S.-Japan Ties: Rabb Delivers Confab Address," *Pacific Citizen*, September 7, 1956, 1; "JACL's Role among Japanese Americans in the New America," *Pacific Citizen*, September 7, 1956, 3–5; "Relationship with Japan Part of 'Changing Perspectives' Theme," *Pacific Citizen*, September 7, 1956, 8; "Concluding Part of Address by White House Aide," *Pacific Citizen*, September 14, 1956, 3, 10; Lawrence E. Davies, "U.S. Urged to Let Nisei Tell Views," *New York Times*, September 1, 1956, 9.

114. JACL, press release, September 27, 1956, "Committee on J-Am Affairs, 1 of 2" folder, box 6, series 1, JACL-JANL; Fred Hirasuna, unpublished typescript, n.d., "Committee on J-Am Affairs, 1 of 2" folder, box 6, series 1, JACL-JANL.

115. Hirasuna, unpublished typescript. For examples, see "Import Limit Protest by Japanese-Americans Presented to Congress," *Wall Street Journal*, September 20, 1956, 3; Charles E. Egan, "Liberal Tariffs Favored for U.S.," *New York Times*, September 20, 1956, 45.

116. Masaoka, *They Call Me Moses*, 253–55, 267–80.

117. Nishikawa to Masaoka et al., September 25, 1956, "Committee on J-Am Affairs, 1 of 2" folder, box 6, series 1, JACL-JANL; Satow, September 26, 1956; Masoka to Honda et al., September 29, 1956, "Committee on J-Am Affairs, 1 of 2" folder, box 6, series 1, JACL-JANL.

118. Masaoka to Honda et al., September 29, 1956, "Committee on J-Am Affairs, 1 of 2" folder, box 6, series 1, JACL-JANL.

119. Kango Kunitsugu, "The Benchwarmer," *Crossroads*, September 14, 1956, "Committee on J-Am Affairs, 2 of 2" folder, box 6, series 1, JACL-JANL; Nishikawa to Masaoka, September 25, 1956, "Committee on J-Am Affairs, 1 of 2" folder, box 6, series 1, JACL-JANL.

120. Masaoka to Nishikawa, September 29, 1956, "Committee on J-Am Affairs, 1 of 2" folder, box 6, series 1, JACL-JANL.

121. "The U.S.A. Is a Nation, Not Assorted 'Cultural' Groups!" *Saturday Evening Post*, December 1, 1956, 10. See also the following in *Pacific Citizen*, December 28, 1956, 1: "Saturday Evening Post Still Sees Main Point of Editorial as Valid"; "Primary Intents of JACL Stressed in Letter to Satevepost"; "Editorial

Indirectly Casts Doubt on JACL's Primary and Fundamental Loyalty to U.S.";
"Saturday Evening Post Issue Still Bare."

122. See the following issues of *Pacific Citizen*, 1957: September 6 and 27; November 8; December 6. See the following issues of *Pacific Citizen*, 1958: January 10 and 24; February 7 and 28; March 28; April 8; June 6, 13, 20, and 27; July 4; August 1, 8, and 15.

123. Nishikawa to Masaoka, October 12, 1957, "Committee on J-Am Affairs, 1 of 2" folder, box 6, series 1, JACL-JANL.

124. "'Help Japan' or 'Hands Off' Issue Raised by Comments on Satevepost," *Pacific Citizen*, December 14, 1956, 8; "JACL Stand on U.S.-Japan Argued," *Pacific Citizen*, October 4, 1957, 1; " 'Benchwarmer' Asks; Nishikawa Answers," *Pacific Citizen*, October 4, 1957, 1, 8; Harry Honda, "Traditional CL 'Hands-Off' Policy Voiced," *Pacific Citizen*, October 4, 1957, 5; Harry Honda, "Nishikawa Urges Nisei Push for U.S.-Japan Friendship," *Pacific Citizen*, February 28, 1958, 1; Roy Yoshida, "Urge Chapters Give Delegates Free Hand on Voting of JACL's U.S.-Japan Policy," *Pacific Citizen*, August 1, 1958, 5; Kango Kunitsugu, " 'Where Do We Go from Here?' Year of Decision Predicted in '58 as Japan-American Relations Brew Big Question for JACL and Nisei in General," *Pacific Citizen*, December 20, 1957, A7; Nishikawa to Satow et al., September 27, 1957, "Committee on J-Am Affairs, 1 of 2" folder, box 6, series 1, JACL-JANL.

125. "Hollywood Chapter Votes 'No' on JACL in U.S.-Japan Affairs," *Pacific Citizen*, May 23, 1958, 4.

126. JACL, "Official Convention Minutes, 1958," 6, 35, folder 10, box 296, JARP.

127. Ibid., 82.

128. Ibid., 89.

129. On the American Committee on Japan (ACJ), see Mike Masaoka to friend, May 22, 1957, "Masaoka" folder, box 8, Committee for Return of Confiscated Property, Hoover Institution; Masaoka, "American Committee on Japan," *Pacific Citizen*, September 19, 1958, 7–8; "American Committee on Japan Urges Ratification of US-Japan Treaty; Time Most Appropriate Senate Committee Informed," *Pacific Citizen*, June 10, 1960, 8; "Text of ACJ Letter Urging Ratification," *Pacific Citizen*, June 10, 1960, 8.

130. Masaoka to national board members et al., August 4, 1954, "Committee on J-Am Affairs, 1 of 2" folder, box 6, series 1, JACL-JANL.

131. Ibid.; Masaoka to Nishikawa et al., September 29, 1956, "Committee on J-Am Affairs, 1 of 2" folder, box 6, series 1, JACL-JANL; Masaoka, *They Call Me Moses*, 267–80. On Japanese Americans as postwar transpacific intermediaries, see Kurashige, *Celebration*, 137–43; Kurashige, *Shifting Grounds*, 200–201; Oda, "Remaking the 'Gateway to the Pacific.' "

132. Harry Honda, "Future of US-Japan Tie Torn Apart; Kishi Calls Off Ike's Visit," *Pacific Citizen*, June 17, 1960, 1; LaFeber, *The Clash*, 314–24; John W. Dower, "Peace and Democracy in Two Systems: External Policy and Internal Conflict," in *Postwar Japan as History*, ed. Andrew Gordon (Berkeley, 1993), 3–33; J. Victor Koschmann, "Intellectuals and Politics," in *Postwar Japan as History*, ed. Andrew Gordon (Berkeley, 1993), 395–423.

133. JACL, "Official Convention Minutes, 1960," 37, folder 11, box 296, JARP.

134. JACL, "Official Convention Minutes, 1960," 38; Mike Masaoka, "Challenge to JACL," *Pacific Citizen*, June 24, 1960, 7–8.

135. JACL, "Official Convention Minutes, 1960," 36, 38; Masaoka, "Challenge to JACL."

136. JACL, "Official Convention Minutes, 1960," 6, 67–68, 99.

137. JACL, "Official Convention Minutes, 1962," 63–64, folder 1, box 297, JARP.

138. Ibid., 63–64; "Japanese-American Military Service," 88th Cong., 1st Sess., *Congressional Record* 109 (May 21, 1963): 9140–45.

139. JACL, "Official Convention Minutes, 1964," 87–89, folder 2, box 297, JARP.

140. "Tributes to Japanese American Military Service in World War II," 88th Cong., 1st Sess., *Congressional Record* 109 (June 11, 1963): 10657–71.

Chapter 4: America's Chinese

1. Rose Hum Lee, *The Chinese in the United States of America* (Hong Kong, 1960), 115–16, 367; "Cathay, USA: Washington DC: A Shadow of Fear Remains with the Chinese in the Nation's Capitol," *Chinese Press*, June 22, 1951, 4; Gilbert Woo, "Your Rights Aren't Greater Than Ours," *Chinese Pacific Weekly*, December 2, 1950; George I. Beronius, "Chino-Americans Dread Relocation," *Los Angeles Times*, December 16, 1950, A2; "Chinese Here Pledge Their Loyalty," *San Francisco Chronicle*, December 2, 1950, 4; "L.A. Chinese Note Unpleasant Incidents," *Chinese World*, December 27 1950, 2; "Chinese in Los Angeles Are Troubled," *Chinese Press*, December 29, 1950, 1; L. Ling-chi Wang, "Politics of Assimilation and Repression: History of the Chinese in the United States, 1940 to 1970," unpublished manuscript, 1980, ESL; Harold R. Issacs, *Scratches on Our Minds: American Images of China and India* (New York, 1958), 212–37; "Footnote on Korean War; Local Incidents Reported," *Chinese Press*, December 22, 1950, 3; "Chinatown Loyalty," *San Francisco Chronicle*, December 5, 1950, 20; untitled, *Nation*, January 13, 1951, 23; "Texas Chinese Shot; Assailant Says 'I Thought He Was a Communist,'" *Chinese World*, April 3, 1951, 2.

2. "Chinese Here Pledge Their Loyalty," *San Francisco Chronicle*; "L.A. Chinese Note Unpleasant Incidents," *Chinese World*; "Chinese in Los Angeles Are Troubled," *Chinese Press*; "The Chinese Forum: Chinese in America Today," *Chinese Press*, December 15, 1950, 4; "Local Chinese Loyal to U.S., Asserts Chief," *Chicago Daily Tribune*, December 1, 1950, A8; "A Message to the American People," 81st Cong., 2nd Sess., *Congressional Record* 96 (December 18, 1950), A7753; "U.S. Chinese React toward Chinese Reds," *Chinese Press*, December 15, 1950, 1; "N. Y. Displays Anti-Red Poster," *Chinese Press*, January 12, 1951, 3.

3. The phrase Overseas Chinese is the English translation of the Chinese term *huaqiao*, an identity used by various modern Chinese governments to refer to members of the global Chinese diaspora. Huaqiao is a politically loaded term, however, in that it denoted loyalty and patriotism to China, thus rending Chinese

migrants politically and suspect residents of their host societies. The concept also reinforced beliefs in the social-cultural unassimilability of Chinese. As Madeline Hsu explains, "The situation became particularly uncomfortable for Chinese in Southeast Asia after World War II as newly established governments tried to gauge the political loyalties of Chinese 'guests' who might adhere to the leadership of communist China." See Hsu, *Dreaming of Gold, Dreaming of Home*, 153, 227n110; Stephen Fitzgerald, *China and the Overseas Chinese: A Study of Peking's Changing Policy, 1949–1970* (Cambridge, UK, 1972); Wang Gungwu, *China and the Chinese Overseas* (Singapore, 1991); Philip A. Kuhn, *Chinese among Others: Emigration in Modern Times* (Ranham, MD, 2008). My thinking on the "flexibility" of Chinese identity is informed by Aihwa Ong, *Flexible Citizenship: The Cultural Logics of Transnationality* (Durham, NC, 1999).

4. Chinatown conservatives were not the only ones to espouse an Overseas Chinese identity. Members of the Chinese American Left, for instance, belonged to the Overseas Chinese Federation for Peace and Democracy. See Him Mark Lai, *Chinese American Transnational Politics*, ed. Madeline Y. Hsu (Urbana, IL, 2010), 131.

5. Meredith Oyen, "Communism, Containment, and the Chinese Overseas," in *The Cold War in Asia: The Battle for Hearts and Minds*, ed. Zheng Yangen, Hong Liu, and Michael Szonyi (Boston, 2010), 59–93.

6. Oyen, "Chinese Overseas"; Klein, *Cold War Orientalism*, 23–24.

7. This was a fundamental divergence between Chinese American and African American participation in Cold War cultural diplomacy, indicative of the differences in their racialization. The Department of State also tapped black artists and athletes to serve as goodwill ambassadors. But a key distinction was that the federal government declared jazz to be "America's music" and claimed the national identity of black jazz musicians to be "exclusively American." As Kevin Gaines argues, federal policymakers actually tried to "delegitimize and discourage transnational solidarities for black Americans" in the 1950s and 1960s, seeing "this potential mobilization in solidarity with Africa and anticolonialism as an affront to U.S. foreign policy designs and management of desegregation on its own terms." African Americans' cultivation of diasporic sensibilities through cultural diplomacy efforts was thus an unintended consequence of their international tours. See Von Eschen, *Satchmo Blows Up the World*, 5, 250, 256; Von Eschen, *Race against Empire*, 179; Gaines, *American Africans in Ghana*, 24–25.

8. Him Mark Lai, "The Kuomintang in Chinese American Communities before World War II," in *Entry Denied: Exclusion and the Chinese Community in America, 1882–1943*, ed. Sucheng Chan (Philadelphia, 1991), 170–212; L. Eve Armentrout Ma, *Revolutionaries, Monarchists, and Chinatowns: Chinese Politics in the Americas and the 1911 Revolution* (Honolulu, 1990); Yu, *To Save China*; Shehong Chen, *Being Chinese, Becoming Chinese American* (Urbana, IL, 2002).

9. Lye, *America's Asia*, 209; Leong, *The China Mystique*, 1, 169–70; Wong, *Americans First*, 71.

10. Helen F. Rouw, "Americans of Chinese Descent," *Chinese World*, December 8, 1950, 2; "Houston Press, Citizens Laud Chinese-Americans," *Chinese Press*, April 13, 1951, 1.

11. "Views of Chinese in U.S. Expressed by L.A. Consul," *Chinese World*, December 29, 1950, 2; "Express Views of L.A. Chinese," *Chinese Press*, January 12, 1951, 1; "Hawaii Chinese Condemn Red Aggression in Korea," *Chinese Press*, March 9, 1951, 3.

12. "U.S. Chinese React toward Chinese Reds," *Chinese Press*, December 15, 1950, 1; "Mammoth Parade Tonight Highlights Chinatown 10-10 Day Celebration," *Chinese World*, October 10, 1951, 2; "Giant 10-10 Parade Climaxes 40th Anniversary of Republic of China," *Chinese World*, October 12, 1951, 2; "Parade, Mass Meeting Will Mark China's Double-Ten Anniversary," *Chinese Press*, October 7, 1949; 1; "'Double 10' Has Anti-Red Theme," *Chinese Press*, October 13, 1950, 1; "VFW Trophies for 10-10 Day Parade," *Chinese World*, October 4, 1951, 2; "10-10 at Sacramento," *Chinese World*, October 9, 1951, 2; "Sacto Chinese Prepare Gala '10 -10' Rites," *Chinese World*, October 9, 1953, 2; "Oakland Group to Hold Rally Oct 10," *Chinese World*, October 9, 1953, 2; "Sign Up for SF '10-10' Parade," *Chinese World*, October 9, 1953; "Chinatown Is Set for '10-10' Celebration," *Chinese World*, October 9, 1953, 2; "SF Chinese Observe '10-10'; Vow Opposition to Red Chinese Regime," *Chinese World*, October 10, 1953, 2; "'10-10' Cocktail Party at Monterey Army School," *Chinese World*, October 10, 1953, 2; "LA Chinese Consul to Hold '10-10' Reception," *Chinese World*, October 10, 1953, 2; Yung, *Unbound Feet*, 240.

13. "Clothing for Korea Gathered," *New York Times*, November 28, 1951, 8; "Chinese Here Give Clothes to Korea," *New York Times*, November 30, 1951, 22.

14. "Anti-Red Organ Formed in SF," *Chinese Press*, January 5, 1951, 3; Victor G. Nee and Brett de Bary Nee, *Longtime Californ': A Documentary Study of an American Chinatown* (Stanford, CA, 1986), 220. Him Mark Lai presents a slightly different account of the start of the Anti-Communist League movement, noting that as early as March 1950, KMT central committee member Huang Wenshan had proposed the formation of an Anti-Communist National Salvation League with branches throughout the United States. See Lai, *Chinese American Transnational Politics*, 28.

15. Lai, *Chinese American Transnational Politics*, 29; "Anti-Red Chinese Meet Here," *San Francisco Chronicle*, January 15, 1951, 9. Lai notes the absence of open opposition to the league's formation.

16. "S.F. Chinese Form League against Reds," *Chinese Press*, January 19, 1951, 1, 2. In addition to presiding over San Francisco's Anti-Communist League, Doon (a.k.a. Yen Doon Wong) was also director of the Six Companies, the Ning Yung Association, and a central committee member of the KMT general branch in the United States. He became chief liaison between the KMT in the United States and Taiwan, and was named the Nationalist regime's adviser on national affairs in 1960. See Lai, *Chinese American Transnational Politics*, 29.

17. "Anti-Red League Schedules Parade," *Chinese Press*, February 9, 1951, 1; "Torchlight Parade Rallies S.F. Chinese against Reds," *Chinese Press*, February 16, 1951, 1, 2; "The Year of the Hare—with No Dragon," *San Francisco Chronicle*, February 13, 1951, 3.

18. "Anti-Red League for Arizona Chinese-Americans," *Chinese Press*, February 23, 1951, 5; "Anti-Red Meet," *Chinese Press*, April 2, 1951, 1; "New York

Chinese Forms Anti-Communist Group," *Chinese Press*, June 15, 1951, 1; Shih-Shan Henry Tsai, *The Chinese Experience in America* (Bloomington, IN, 1986), 134–35. One notable exception to the anti-Communist crusade was New York's Chinese Hand Laundry Alliance, whose members refused to join that CCBA's campaign. See Lai, *Chinese American Transnational Politics*, 146.

19. Lai, "The Chinese Consolidated Benevolent Association/Huiguan System," 64–65; "Denver Group Organizes to Fight Reds," *Chinese Press*, December 29, 1950, 2; "Denver Chinese Organize to Fight Communism," *Chinese World*, December 26, 1950, 2.

20. "New York Chinese Forms Anti-Communist Group," *Chinese Press*, June 15, 1951, 1, 3.

21. "Chinese New Year in U.S. Capital," *Chinese Press*, February 16, 1951, 1, 2.

22. "Chinatown Less Noisy Than Usual in Greeting Year of Golden Rabbit," *New York Times*, February 7, 1951, 31.

23. Nee and Nee, *Longtime Californ'*, 244–49; Chiou-Ling Yeh, "'In the Traditions of China and in the Freedom of America': The Making of San Francisco's Chinese New Year Festivals," *American Quarterly* 56, no. 2 (2004): 395–420; "S.F. and Chinese Chambers Give $1000 for Festival," *Chinese World*, February 12, 1953, 2; Dai-Ming Lee, "Chinese New Year Fete as a City-Wide Project," *Chinese World*, February 27, 1953, 1.

24. "Kung Hay Fat Choy!" *Chinese News*, February 14, 1953, 2. Leong to Brayton Wilbur, July 28, 1953, folder 32, box 3, CLP; W. F. Doon to Leong, April 2, 1953, folder 30, box 3, CLP.

25. Brooks, *Alien Neighbors, Foreign Friends*, 198.

26. "California's Gov. Warren Assures Chinese-Americans," *Chinese Press*, December 8, 1950, 1; "Mayor Talks on Chinese Contribution," *Chinese Press*, February 9, 1951, 1; "Mayor Robinson on S.F. Chinese Loyalty, Reviews Ping Yuen Project, Play Center," *Chinese Press*, February 9, 1951, 3; "Chinatown Loyalty," *San Francisco Chronicle*, December 5, 1950, 20; "The People Say," *Chinese Press*, February 9, 1951, 1; "Chinese Support Civic Unity Body's Program for 1951," *Chinese Press*, January 26, 1951; "City Club Scores Anti-Chinese Acts," *Chinese Press*, March 9, 1951, 3.

27. "Press Inspires Editorial on SF Chinese-Americans," *Chinese Press*, February 9, 1951. See also W. E. "Spense" Spenser, letter to the editor, *Chinese Press*, December 8, 1950, 1; editorials from *Seattle Post-Intelligencer*, *Seattle Times*, *Knight Newspaper*, *Baltimore Sun*, *Oakland Tribune*, and *Los Angeles Daily News*, reprinted in December 1950 and January 1951 issues of the *Chinese Press*.

28. Untitled, *Nation*, January 13, 1951, 23. Occasionally hints of intracommunity political dissension reached the general public. See, for instance, the report on the conflict between *Chinese World* editor Dai-ming Lee and San Francisco's CCBA in "Chinatown Dispute," *San Francisco Chronicle*, March 5, 1951, 1.

29. On the Chinese Left in the United States, see Nee and Nee, *Longtime Californ'*; Him Mark Lai, "A Historical Survey of the Chinese Left in America," in *Counterpoint: Perspectives on Asian America*, ed. Emma Gee (Los Angeles, 1976), 63–80; Yu, *To Save China*; Josephine Fowler, *Japanese and Chinese Im-*

migrant Activists: Organizing in American and International Communist Movements, 1919–1933 (Rutgers, NJ, 2007); Zhao, *Remaking Chinese America*; Lai, *Chinese American Transnational Politics*.

30. Nee and Nee, *Longtime Californ'*, 208; Yu, *To Save China*, 177–79; Zhao, *Remaking Chinese America*, 94–125.

31. Nee and Nee, *Longtime Californ'*, 208; Yu, *To Save China*, 177–79; Zhao, *Remaking Chinese America*, 94–135; Tsai, *Chinese Experience*, 136–37.

32. "S.F. Chinese Charge 15 on 'Death List,'" *San Francisco Chronicle*, October 13, 1949, 4; Nee and Nee, *Longtime Californ'*, 200–27; Lai, "Survey of the Chinese Left," 72; H. M. Lai, "The Chinese Press in the United States and Canada since World War II: A Diversity of Voices," *Chinese America: History and Perspectives*, 1990; Yu, *To Save China*, 165–97; Zhao, *Remaking Chinese America*, 94–125.

33. "America's Chinese," *Life*, January 8, 1951, 70–77.

34. David F. Krugler, *The Voice of America and the Domestic Propaganda Battles, 1945–1953* (Columbia, MO, 2000).

35. Betty Lee Sung, interview with the author, March 23, 2004, New York.

36. Ibid.; Betty Lee Sung, telephone conversation with the author, April 15, 2003.

37. Betty Lee Sung, *The Story of the Chinese in America* (New York, 1967), 1. This book was published in hardback under the title *Mountain of Gold: The Story of the Chinese in America* (New York, 1967).

38. VOA daily broadcast content reports, 1950–1955, Records of the US Information Agency, RG 306, NARA (hereafter VOABR). State Department officials also referred to *Chinese Activities* as "Overseas Chinese Activities in America" and "Worldwide Chinese Activities."

39. Sung, interview with the author.

40. Ibid.

41. Betty Lee Sung, "Architectural Wonders Designed by Chinese Architect," VOA *Chinese Activities* radio transcript, February 14, 1952, broadcast February 20 and 24, 1952, folder 16, box 2, CLP.

42. "American Mother of the Year," *Washington Post*, May 5, 1952, 2; Mary Ellen Shelton, "Chinese Woman Is American Mother of the Year," VOA Chinese Unit news footnote transcript, May 5, 1952, box 41, VOABR.

43. Oyen, "Chinese Overseas," 81.

44. *Overseas Information Programs of the United States*, hearings before a subcommittee of the Committee of Foreign Relations, 82nd Cong., 2nd Sess., November 20–21, 1952, 203–6.

45. Betty Lee Sung, "The Chinese Schools and Newspapers in Hawaii," *Chinese Activities* radio transcript, June 2, 1952, broadcast June 4 and 7, 1952, box 43, VOABR; Sung, "The First Chinese to Hawaii," *Chinese Activities* radio transcript, August 18, 1952, box 51, VOABR. See also "Voice of America: A Program of Chinese Activities, Events, and Progress," *Chinese Press*, October 5, 1951, 4.

46. Arthur H. Burling, "The Lost Homeland," VOA Chinese Unit political commentary transcript, June 1, 1951, box 19, VOABR.

47. Mary Euyang Loh, "The Lunar New Year," VOA Chinese Branch Shanghai commentary transcript, broadcast February 13, and 16, 1953, VOABR.

48. Helena Kuo, "America's Chinese," VOA Chinese Unit feature transcript, February 11, 1951, box 13, VOABR.

49. Burling, "The Lost Homeland."

50. Dudziak, *Cold War Civil Rights*, 250.

51. George Sessions Perry, "Your Neighbors: The Wongs," *Saturday Evening Post*, October 16, 1948, 24–25, 102, 105–7, 109–10, 112.

52. Ibid.

53. Ibid.

54. Jade Snow Wong, "Growing Up in America between the Old World and the New" (transcript of speech presented to the American University Club, Hong Kong, February 18, 1953), addendum to American consulate, Hong Kong, to Department of State, February 26, 1953, 511.903/2-2653, RG 59, NARA. Her remarks were circulated for domestic audiences in "Growing Up in America between the Old World and the New," *Horn Book* 27 (1951).

55. Jade Snow Wong, *Fifth Chinese Daughter* (New York, 1950).

56. "Jade Snow Wong Studio," broadside, n.d., folder 26, box 21, Nancy Wey Papers, ESL; "Jade Snow Wong Visits Calcutta," press release, April 8, 1953, enclosure to American consulate, Calcutta, India, to Department of State, April 9, 1953, 511.903/4-953, RG 59; "KNBC to Feature Jade Snow Wong Book," *Chinese Press*, June 15, 1951, 8. The transcript of the *Cavalcade of America* segment on *Fifth Chinese Daughter*, written by Robert Soderberg and starring Diana Lynn as Jade Snow Wong, is located in the Dupont Collection, Hagley Library, Wilmington, DE. Thanks to Anne Boylan for this reference. Charles Poore, "Books of the Times," *New York Times*, December 13, 1950, 33.

57. American consulate, Hong Kong, to Department of State, November 30, 1951, 511.46G21/11-3051, RG 59.

58. On the case of Sing Sheng, see Theresa Mah, "The Limits of Democracy in the Suburbs: Constructing the Middle Class through Residential Exclusion," in *The Middling Sorts: Explorations in the History of the American Middle Class*, ed. Burton J. Bledstein and Robert D. Johnston (New York, 2001), 256–66; Charlotte Brooks, "Sing Sheng vs. Southwood: Residential Integration in Cold War California," *Pacific Historical Review* 73 (2004): 463–94; Cheng, "Out of Chinatown and into the Suburbs."

59. Hendrik van Oss, American consul, Kuala Lumpur, to Department of State, February 28, 1952, 511.974/2-2852, RG 59.

60. American consulate, Hong Kong, to Department of State, February 11, 1952, 511.46g21/2-1152, RG 59; American consulate, Hong Kong, to Department of State, February 26, 1953, 511.903/2-2653, RG 59. See also "Operations Memorandum from American Consul General, Hong Kong, to American Consul General," Singapore, February 19, 1952, "Book Translation" folder, box 1, Records of the Foreign Service Posts of the Department of State, RG 84, NARA.

61. Dean Acheson to certain American diplomatic and consular officers, July 16, 1952, "Visiting Persons" folder, box 3, RG 84; Public Law 402, January 27, 1948. The Smith-Mundt Act was also known as the US Information and Educational Act of 1948.

62. American consulate, Hong Kong, to Department of State, July 31, 1953, "Visiting Persons" folder, box 3, RG 84.

63. Jade Snow Wong, conversation with the author, March 5, 2003, San Francisco (notes in author's possession); Jade Snow Wong, *No Chinese Stranger* (New York, 1975), 55. The VOA daily broadcast content report for January 14, 1953 lists the following title for the *Chinese Activities* show: "Jade Snow Wong to Make Good-Will Tour to Orient" (box 62, VOABR). Wong did not visit Taiwan on this trip. A memo circulated by the State Department in July 1952 suggested a two-week stay for her in Taipei, but I have not located any sources that explain why Taipei was ultimately dropped from the itinerary.

64. Wong, *No Chinese Stranger*, 54–55; Wong, "Growing Up." Excerpts of Wong's speech are reprinted in Wong, *No Chinese Stranger*, 94–96.

65. Ibid., 81–82.

66. Ibid., 74; Paul W. Frillman to Harold Howland, February 19, 1953, "Visiting Persons" folder, box 3, RG 84; Julian F. Harrington, American consul general, Hong Kong, to Department of State, February 26, 1953, 511.903/2-2653, RG 59.

67. Eugene F. O'Conner, public affairs officer, American embassy, Bangkok, to Department of State, April 8, 1953, 511.903/4-853, RG 59; Robert J. Boylan, American consul general, Singapore, to Department of State, March 2,1953, 511.903/3-253, RG 59; Charles M. Urreula, American consul, Penang, to Department of State, April 2, 1953, 511.903/4-253, RG 59; Olcott H. Deming, first secretary, American embassy, Tokyo, to Department of State (also enclosure 2, office memorandum from American embassy, Tokyo, to American consulate, Nagoya, February 2, 1953, and enclosure 3, office memorandum from American embassy, Tokyo, to American consul general, Kobe, March 5, 1953), March 20, 1953, 511.903/3-2053, RG 59; Wong, *No Chinese Stranger*, 55, 83, 84, 97.

68. Olcott H. Deming, first secretary, American embassy, Tokyo, to Department of State, March 20, 1953, 511.903/3-2053, RG 59; John H. Esterline, American consul/acting public affairs officer, American consul, Calcutta, April 9, 1953, 511.903/4-953, RG 59; Harrington, American consul general, Hong Kong, to Department of State, February 26, 1953, 511.903/2-2653, RG 59; Robert J. Boylan, American consul general, Singapore, to Department of State, March 23,1953, 511.903/3-2353, RG 59.

69. Kwok Kian Woon notes that the *Young Malayan*, published in Kuala Lumpur from 1946 to 1957, aimed to "'help build up a body of loyal Malayan citizens who would always think of Malaya as their home—whether they happened to be Malays, Chinese, Indians, or any other race.'" See Kwok Kian Woon's entry on "Singapore" in Lynn Pan, ed., *The Encyclopedia of the Chinese Overseas* (Cambridge, MA, 1999), 211.

70. "Miss Jade Snow Wong Arrives in Penang," *Kwong Wah Yit Poh*, March 10, 1953, enclosure 5, Urruela, American consul, Penang, to Department of State, April 2, 1953, 511.903/4-253, RG 59; Jade Snow Wong, "My Chinese and American Career," speech delivered to the Penang Rotary Club, *Straits Echo*, March 12, 1953, enclosure 5, Urruela, American consul, Penang, to Department of State, April 2, 1953, 511.903/4-253, RG 59.

71. Hendrik van Oss, American consul, Kuala Lumpur, to Department of State, March 20, 1953, 511.973/3-2053, RG 59.

72. Ibid. On Chinese in Malaya, see Kam Hing Lee and Tan Chee-Beng, ed., *The Chinese in Malaysia* (New York, 2000); Kuhn, *Chinese among Others*.

73. Connie [Constance Wong aka Jade Snow Wong], letter to people, March 15, 1953, folder 126, box 4, Hamilton Basso Papers, Beinecke Rare Book and Manuscript Library, Yale University (hereafter HBP). Special thanks to Mary Lui for this reference. See van Oss, American Consul, Kuala Lumpur, to Department of State, March 20, 1953.

74. Connie [Constance Wong, a.k.a. Jade Snow Wong], letter to People, April 18, 1953, Folder 126, Box 4, HBP.

75. Department of State, instruction no. CA-4330, to American embassies/consulates in Copenhagen, Helsinki, London, New Delhi, Oslo, Paris, Reykjavik, and Stockholm, February 12, 1954, "032 Kingman, Dong" folder, RG 59; Thruston B. Morton to Representative J. Arthur Younger, April 23[?], 1954, 511.003/4-1954, "032 Kingman, Dong" folder, RG 59.

76. American embassy, Taipei, to Department of State, June 1, 1954, "032 Kingman, Dong" folder, RG 59; American consul, Hong Kong, to Department of State, July 21, 1954, "032 Kingman, Dong" folder, RG 59.

77. "Dong Kingman's U.S.A.," *Life*, May 14, 1951, 100–102; "Official Dispatch," *Life*, February 14, 1955, 66–70; "Dong Kingman Ambassador to the People of Asia," *American Artist*, February 1955, 8–9.

78. The team members included Harvey Y. J. Fong, Sherman Fong, Douglas Hom, Chew Jeong, David Ap Lew, Victor Low, George Chew Lum, Donald Fong, Hanson Quock, and Clifford Wong. The team was managed by Marshall Lee and coached by Percy L. Chu.

79. Department of State, instruction no. CA-2580, to American embassies/consulates in Bangkok, Hong Kong, Kuala Lumpur, Singapore, Taipei, and Vientiane, September 20, 1956, "032 San Francisco Chinese Basketball Team" folder, RG 59; Department of State, instruction no. CA-2749, to American embassies/consulates in Bangkok, Hong Kong, Kuala Lumpur, Singapore, and Taipei, September 26, 1956, "032 San Francisco Chinese Basketball Team" folder, RG 59; H. K. Wong, "H. K.'s Corner," *Chinese World*, December 19, 1956, 2.

80. Richard M. McCarthy, public affairs officer, American embassy, Bangkok, to Department of State, March 5, 1957, "032 San Francisco Chinese Basketball Team" folder, RG 59; H. K. Wong, "SF Chinese Quint Captures President Cup in Taipeh [*sic*] Tourney," *Chinese World*, November 17, 1956, 2.

81. H. K. Wong, "HK's Corner: Ambassador of Sport," *Chinese World*, October 10, 1956, 2; H. K. Wong, "HK's Corner: Chinatown Newsreel," *Chinese World*, October 24, 1956, 2 (see also the photograph of the team, Chinese sec., 3); H. K. Wong, "HK's Corner: Adlai and Fortune Cookies," *Chinese World*, October 31, 1956, 2; H. K. Wong, "Formosa Cagers Drop SF Quint 58–49," *Chinese World*, November 10, 1956, 2; H. K. Wong, "SF Chinese Quint Captures President Cup in Taipei Tourney," *Chinese World*, November 17, 1956, 2; H. K. Wong, "An $8 Letter," *Chinese World*, November 21, 1956, 2; H. K. Wong, "SF Chinese Cagers Break Even with Hong Kong All Stars," *Chinese World*, November 22, 1956, 2; H. K. Wong, "SF's 'Five Tigers' Cagers Roar to 48–43 Win over Hong Kong Stars," *Chinese World*, December 1, 1956, 2; "SF Chinese Cagers Arrival Delayed," *Chinese World*, December 14, 1956, 2; H. K. Wong, "HK's Corner," *Chinese World*, December 19, 1956, 2; H. K Wong, "HK's Corner: Tea for Local Five," *Chinese World*, December 26, 1956, 2.

82. "Dong Kingman," *Chinese News*, February 27, 1954, 8.

83. On alien citizenship, see Ngai, *Impossible Subjects*, 7–8.

84. Everett F. Drumright, "Report of the Problem of Fraud at Hong Kong," Foreign Service dispatch no. 931, December 9, 1955, cited Lai, *Becoming Chinese American*, 27; Ngai, *Impossible Subjects*, 209.

85. Zhao, *Remaking Chinese America*, 160–65.

86. Ngai, *Impossible Subjects*, 212–14; Zhao, *Remaking Chinese America*, 152–84; Wang, "Politics of Assimilation and Repression."

87. "Grand Jurors Probing Alien Entry Frauds," *Washington Post*, February 15, 1956, 13; "Cited in Passport Frauds," *New York Times*, March 8, 1956, 8; "Six Chinese Indicted in Passport Inquiry," *New York Times*, March 14, 1956, 18; "How Thousands of Chinese Get into U.S. Told," *Chicago Daily Tribune*, March 24, 1956, 3; Edward Ranzal, "Chinese Leader Is Indicted Here," *New York Times*, May 4, 1956, 1.

88. Chinese Consolidated Benevolent Association [Chinese Six Companies], "Statement of Principle," pamphlet, March 15, 1956, folder 44, box 1, CLP.

89. Ngai notes that the Chinatown Left was not only conspicuously absent from this coalition but also was too marginalized and depleted to mount its own resistance. Additionally, while the CCBA publicly announced its cooperation, it worked to undermine the operation in ways, such as moving records from true family associations to paper associations. See *Impossible Subjects*, 214, 216, 336n41.

90. Gilbert Woo, "Da peishentuan chuanxun huabu shetuan" [The grand jury subpoenas the records of Chinatown organizations], *Chinese Pacific Weekly*, March 23, 1956. See also the series of editorials by Dai-Ming Lee in *Chinese World*, 1956: "Federal Grand Jury Probes Chinatown Associations," March 3; "Burning Down the Barn to Catch Few Rats," March 7, "Sweeping Investigation Creates Resentment," March 14; "Six Companies Protests Calmuny Heaped on Entire Chinese Community," March 16; "Sino-American Friendship," March 17; "Apprehension in Chinatown," March 19; "War-Time Measure in Peace Time," March 21; "Preservation of Constitutional Guaranties [*sic*]," March 22; "Time for Unity in Chinatown," March 23.

91. Woo, "Da peishentuan chuanxun huabu shetuan."

92. Ngai, *Impossible Subjects*, 221.

93. Ibid., 221–23; Lai, *Becoming American*, 32.

94. Ngai, *Impossible Subjects*, 223.

95. Charlotte Brooks, "'A Voter Cannot Be Neutral, Nor Should He Be': The Chinese American Democratic Club of San Francisco and Cold War Party Politics" (paper presented at the American Studies Association annual meeting, San Antonio, TX, November 18–20, 2010).

96. *National Conference of Chinese Communities in America,* report and proceedings, March 5–7, 1957, Washington, DC, 25; in author's possession.

97. Dai-ming Lee, "Conference in the Making," *Chinese World*, February 12, 1957, 1; Dai-ming Lee, "Chinese in U.S. Schedule Nation-Wide Conference," *Chinese World*, February 15, 1957; Dai-ming Lee, "Adherence to Objective Expected of Conference," *Chinese World*, February 27, 1957, 1.

98. Zhao, *Remaking Chinese America*, 182.

99. *National Conference of Chinese Communities in America*, 14–15.

100. Ngai, *Impossible Subjects*, 218; Zhao, *Remaking Chinese America*, 182–83; Dai-ming Lee, "Problems Needing Solution," *Chinese World*, February 11, 1957; Dai-ming Lee, "Problems of the Chinese in America," *Chinese World*, February 28, 1957, 1.

101. *National Conference of Chinese Communities in America*.

102. "Articles of 'National Council of Chinese Communities, Inc.' Filed," *Chinese World*, November 19, 1957, 1–2; "National Chinese Council Elects First Trustees," *Chinese World*, November 20, 1957, 1–2. The National Council of Chinese Communities, Inc., later became known as the National Chinese Welfare Council. Lai notes, "At first there were high hopes and expectations among Chinese Americans for this organization," but by the council's second convening in 1959, KMT supporters had taken over and redirected its mission to serve the Nationalists. See Lai, *Becoming Chinese American*, 29–30; Lai, *Chinese American Transnational Politics*, 31.

103. Brooks, "A Voter Cannot Be Neutral"; Lai, *Chinese American Transnational Politics*, 33–37; Tsai, *Chinese Experience*, 137–38.

Part II: Definitively Not-Black

1. Hsu, "The Disappearance of America's Cold War Chinese Refugees"; Oh, "From War Waif to Ideal Immigrant"; Ngai, *Impossible Subjects*, 228–64; Chan, *Asian Americans: An Interpretive History* (Boston, 1991), 47; Brooks, *Alien Neighbors, Foreign Friends*, 159–236; Robinson, *After Camp*, 195–216; Peggy Pascoe, *What Comes Naturally: Miscegenation Law and the Making of Race in America* (New York, 2009), 246–84.

2. Hing, *Making and Remaking Asian American through Immigration Policy, 1850–1990*, 46–49, 55–56.

3. Takahashi, *Nisei/Sansei*, 113–25; Brooks, *Alien Neighbors, Foreign Friends*, 168–70; Yoo, *Growing Up Nisei*, 28.

4. US Bureau of the Census, *Sixteenth Census of the United States, Special Report, Population, Characteristics of the Nonwhite Population by Race* (Washington, DC, 1943), 47; US Bureau of the Census, *US Census of Population 1950, Vol. IV, Special Reports, Part 3, Chapter B, Nonwhite Population by Race* (Washington, DC, 1953), 3B–37; US Bureau of the Census, *US Census of Population 1960, Special Reports, Nonwhite Population by Race, Final Report PC (2)-1C* (Washington, DC, 1963), 108. The Japanese American population numbered 464,332, in 1960.

5. Lee, *Chinese in the United States of America*, 89; US Bureau of the Census, *Sixteenth Census of the United States*, 47; US Bureau of the Census, *US Census of Population 1950, Vol. IV, Special Reports*, 3B–42; US Bureau of the Census, *US Census of Population 1960, Special Reports*, 111. The total population of Chinese in the United States in 1960 was 237,292.

6. Roger Daniels argues that for two reasons, statistical data from California offer a more accurate portrait of Japanese and Chinese Americans' socioeconomic situation than national data. First, most Asian Americans lived in California

in 1960, and second, the inclusion of data from the southern states (where few Asians lived) depressed the national averages. See Roger Daniels, *Asian America: Chinese and Japanese in the United States since 1850* (Seattle, 1988), 314–15. US Bureau of the Census, *US Census of Population 1960, General Population Characteristics, United States Summary, Final Report PC(1)-1B* (Washington, DC, 1961), 1–164; California Department of Industrial Relations and Division of Fair Employment Practices, *Californians of Japanese Chinese Filipino Ancestry* (San Francisco, 1965), 11, 14.

7. US Bureau of the Census, *US Census of Population 1960, Special Reports*, 9, 16, 19; US Bureau of the Census, *US Census of Population 1960, General Population Characteristics*, 1–209, 1–228.

8. Shah, *Contagious Divides*, 245–50; Mah, "Buying into the Middle Class"; Brooks, *Alien Neighbors, Foreign Friends*, 159–236.

9. Ellen Dionne Wu, "Race and Asian American Citizenship from World War II to the Movement" (PhD diss., University of Chicago, 2006), 98–110.

Chapter 5: Success Story, Japanese American Style

1. T. Scott Miyakawa, "A Proposal for a Definitive History of the Japanese in the United States, 1860–1960: The Preliminary Outline for Discussion and Review," October 1961, YRL; Wakamatsu to Yoshimura et al., September 28, 1960, "Correspondence—Issei Story—1960" folder, box 520, JARP. JACL leaders variously referred to the ISP as the "Issei History Project," the "Story of the Japanese in America Project," and "The History of the Japanese in America."

2. "Progress Report, History of the Japanese in America, 1860–1960," March 18, 1961, box 520, JARP; JACL, "Official Convention Minutes, 1948," 36, 72, 96, folder 5, box 296, JARP; JACL, "Official Convention Minutes, 1950," 10, folder 6, box 296, JARP; JACL, "Official Convention Minutes, 1952," 14–16, folder 7, box 296, JARP; JACL, "Official Convention Minutes, 1954," 15, 69, folder 8, box 296, JARP; JACL, "Official Convention Minutes, 1956," 56, folder 8, box 296, JARP; JACL, "Official Convention Minutes, 1958," 102, folder 10, box 296, JARP; JACL, "National Convention Minutes, 1960," 77, folder 11, box 296, JARP; Wakamatsu to Yoshimura et al., September 28, 1960, "Correspondence—Issei Story—1960" folder, box 520, JARP; Shig Wakamatsu to Frank Chuman, May 2, 1961, "Correspondence—Issei Story—1960" folder, box 520, JARP.

3. O'Connor, *Poverty Knowledge*, 25–73; Yu, *Thinking Orientals*.

4. O'Connor, *Poverty Knowledge*, 74–98; Gunnar Myrdal, *An American Dilemma: The Negro Problem and Modern Democracy* (New York, 1944); Jackson, *Gunnar Myrdal and America's Conscience*.

5. Myrdal, *An American Dilemma*, 1009.

6. Three separate groups of wartime investigators used the internment as a research laboratory. The Bureau of Sociological Research was located at the WRA Poston camp and headed by psychiatrist Alexander H. Leighton. The Community Analysis Section was a department of applied anthropology formed under the auspices of the WRA to operate at each of the other nine camps. Both the Bureau of Sociological Research and Community Analysis Section aimed primarily

to examine internee life so as to improve camp management. The two projects also amassed data on Japanese culture, and developed broader theories of administration to reappropriate for psychological warfare and the governance of Japan, should the United States win the war. The third project was JERS. See Yuji Ichioka, "JERS Revisited: Introduction," in *Views from Within: The Japanese American Evacuation and Resettlement Study*, ed. Yuji Ichioka (Los Angeles, 1989), 3, 5–6; Orin Starn, "Engineering Internment: Anthropologists and the War Relocation Authority," *American Ethnologist* 13, no. 4 (1986): 700–720; Simpson, *Absent Presence*, 43–75.

7. Ichioka, "JERS Revisited," 3. On JERS, see also the other essays in Ichioka, *Views from Within*; Richard S. Nishimoto, *Inside an American Concentration Camp: Japanese American Resistance at Poston, Arizona*, ed. Lane Ryo Hirabayashi (Tucson, AZ, 1995); Hirabayashi, *The Politics of Fieldwork*; Yoo, *Growing Up Nisei*. It is interesting to note that Thomas was a member of Myrdal's *An American Dilemma* research staff in 1939–40.

8. Dorothy Swaine Thomas and Richard S. Nishimoto, *The Spoilage* (Berkeley, 1946); Thomas, *The Salvage*. The third official JERS publication was Jacobus tenBroek et al., *Prejudice, War, and the Constitution* (Berkeley, 1954). There was also a fourth, unofficial JERS book: Morton Grodzins, *Americans Betrayed: Politics and the Japanese Evacuation* (Chicago, 1949).

9. Thomas, *The Salvage*, 125, 127, 131–50; Ngai, "An Ironic Testimony," 237–57.

10. Yu, *Thinking Orientals*, 5–12, 19–46, 187–88. Several University of Chicago scholars participated in the Japanese American Personality and Acculturation Study. The project began in 1947 with a Julius Rosenwald Fund research grant awarded to William Caudill, an anthropology graduate student, and Setsuko Matsunaga Nishi, a doctoral candidate in sociology, active leader within the city's resettler community, and former JERS staffer. Caudill and Nishi were subsequently joined by Charlotte G. Babcock, a psychoanalyst; George De Vos, a graduate student in clinical psychology; Adrian Corcoran, a master's student in anthropology; Alan Jacobson and Percy Lee Rainwater, master's students in sociology; and Estelle Gabriel, a psychiatric social worker. The main pool of data for the project was drawn from a basic sample of 342 families encompassing 1,022 individuals located through a directory of Chicago-area Japanese American households. The researchers also utilized Thematic Apperception Test records, life history interviews, and a survey conducted by Jacobson and Rainwater of 79 Chicago-area employers of Japanese Americans. See Adrian Corcoran, "Early Child Training Practices by Chicago's Second-Generation Japanese Americans" (master's thesis, University of Chicago, 1950).

11. William Caudill, "Japanese American Acculturation and Personality" (PhD diss., University of Chicago, 1950), 4–6; William Caudill, "Japanese American Personality and Acculturation," *Genetic Psychology Monographs* 45 (1952): 7–8; William Caudill and George De Vos, "Achievement, Culture, and Personality: The Case of the Japanese Americans," *American Anthropologist* 58, no. 6 (December 1956): 1103–5; Alan Jacobson and Percy Lee Rainwater, "A Study of Evaluations of Nisei as Workers by Caucasian Employment Agency Managers and Employers of Nisei" (master's thesis, University of Chicago, 1951), later published as

"A Study of Management Representative Evaluations of Nisei Workers," *Social Forces* 32, no. 1 (October 1953): 35–41; Setsuko Matsunaga Nishi, "Japanese American Achievement in Chicago: A Cultural Response to Degradation" (PhD diss., University of Chicago, 1963).

12. Caudill, "Japanese American Acculturation and Personality," 8; Nishi, "Japanese American Achievement."

13. Caudill, "Japanese American Acculturation and Personality," 11–13, 230; Caudill and De Vos, "Achievement, Culture, and Personality," 1107; Nishi, "Japanese American Achievement"; Yu, *Thinking Orientals*, 187–88.

14. Jacobson and Rainwater, "Evaluations," 125–34; Jacobson and Rainwater, "Study of Management"; Yu, *Thinking Orientals*, 189.

15. Daniels, *Politics of Prejudice*; US Commission on Wartime Evacuation and Relocation of Civilians, *Personal Justice Denied*, 66; Ngai, *Impossible Subjects*, 177–81; Weglyn, *Years of Infamy*, 196–99; Dower, *War without Mercy*; Shibusawa, *America's Geisha Ally*.

16. Robert Shaffer, "Cracks in the Consensus: Defending the Rights of Japanese Americans during World War II," *Radical History Review* 72 (1998): 84–120.

17. George E. Taylor, "The Japanese in Our Midst," *Atlantic*, April 1943, 104–10; WRA, *WRA: A Story of Human Conservation*; Larry Tajiri, "Democracy Corrects Its Own Mistakes," *Asia and the Americas*, April 1943, 213–16.

18. WRA, *WRA: A Story of Human Conservation*, 139–40; Harold M. Mann and Prudence Ross, "History of the North Central Area," 45–46, "North Central Area #1A" folder, box 6, entry 4C, RG 210, NARA; WRA, *A Challenge to Democracy*; War Relocation Authority, "A Challenge to Authority," n.d., RG 210, NARA.

19. Clara E. Breed, "Americans with the Wrong Ancestors," *Horn Book*, July 1943, 253–61.

20. Robert Hosokawa, "American with a Japanese Face," *Christian Science Monitor Magazine*, May 22, 1943, 3, 13.

21. "Second Pearl Harbor," *Commonweal*, December 22, 1944, 244; Vanya Oakes, "Test Case for Democracy," *Asia and the Americas*, March 1945, 147–50; Carey McWilliams, *Prejudice—Japanese-Americans: Symbol of Racial Intolerance* (Boston, 1944), 3–12.

22. Ina Sugihara, "I Don't Want to Go Back," *Commonweal*, July 20, 1945, 330–32; McWilliams, *Prejudice*, 278–79, 284, 286, 289–94; Larry Tajiri, "Farewell to Little Tokyo," *Common Ground* 4, no. 2 (Winter 1944): 90–95.

23. McWilliams, *Prejudice*, 298.

24. Raymond Nathan, "New Neighbors among Us," *Parents*, March 1945, 30; Ann Reed Burns, "Nisei Witch-Hunt Burns Itself Out," *Washington Post*, February 10, 1946, S6; W. L. Worden, "Hate That Failed," *Saturday Evening Post*, May 4, 1946, 22–23; A. W. Moore, "Hood River Redeems Itself," *Asia and the Americas*, July 1946, 316–17; Richard L. Neuberger, "Their Brothers' Keepers," *Saturday Review of Literature*, August 10, 1946, 5–6, 27–28; Bradford Smith, "Experiment in Racial Concentration," *Far Eastern Survey*, July 17, 1946, 214–18; "Accept Evacuees' Return to Oregon," *Christian Century*, May 22, 1946, 669; Lawrence E. Davies, "Nisei Return to the Coast," *New York Times*, Octo-

ber 27, 1946, 103; Mary Hornaday, "Nisei Return," *Christian Science Monitor Magazine*, September 13, 1947, 3; Ed Ritter, "The Japanese Came Back," *Forum*, December 1947, 327–31; Frank J. Taylor, "Home Again," *Colliers*, February 15, 1947, 15; Victor Boesen, "Nisei Come Home to California," *New Republic*, April 26, 1948, 16–19; Elmer R. Smith, "Resettlement of Japanese Americans," *Far Eastern Quarterly*, May 18, 1949, 117–18; Bradford Smith, "Nisei Discover America," *American Magazine*, August 1947, 34–35.

25. Worden, "Hate that Failed"; Smith, "Experiment in Racial Concentration"; "Accept Evacuees' Return," *Christian Century*; Davies, "Nisei Return"; "Between Moves: Glimpses of Japanese American Hostel," *Survey Graphic*, March 1947, 199–201; Hornaday, "Nisei Return"; Taylor, "Home Again"; Smith, "Nisei Discover America"; Lawrence E. Davies, "Pacific Coast," *New York Times*, February 8, 1948, E7; Boesen, "Nisei Come Home"; Robert M. Cullum, "People in Motion," *Common Ground* 8, no. 1 (Fall 1947): 61–68; Sophie and Donald Toriumi, "We're Americans Again," *Survey Graphic*, July 1945, 325–27, 334; "Crisis in Church Relations of Japanese-Americans," *Christian Century*, January 23, 1946, 101; "Between Moves," *Survey Graphic*, March 1947, 199–201; Leonard Bloom, "Will Our Nisei Get Justice?" *Christian Century*, March 3, 1948: 268–69; Joan Smith, "Who Is an American?" *School and Society* 70 (September 17, 1949): 180–83.

26. Demarre Bess, "California's Amazing Japanese," *Saturday Evening Post*, April 30, 1955, 38–39, 68, 72, 76, 80, 83; Albert Q. Maisel, "The Japanese among Us," *Reader's Digest*, January 1956, 182–84, 186, 189, 192, 194, 196; Gladwin Hill, "Japanese in U.S. Gaining Equality," *New York Times*, August 12, 1956, 38; Ted Le Berthon, "Vindication for the Nisei," *Commonweal*, January 16, 1959, 406–9.

27. Bess, "California's Amazing Japanese."

28. Ibid.; "Nisei: Disguised Blessing," *Newsweek*, December 29, 1958, 23.

29. Bess, "California's Amazing Japanese"; Le Berthon, "Vindication for the Nisei"; "20 Years After," *Time*, August 11, 1961.

30. Bess, "California's Amazing Japanese"; Le Berthon, "Vindication for the Nisei"; "20 Years After," *Time*; Hill, "Japanese in U.S. Gaining Equality." Gladwin Hill consulted with JACL in writing the *New York Times* article. See "NY Times Features Story Updating Status of Japanese Americans," *Pacific Citizen*, August 17, 1956, 4.

31. Chuman to Murphy, March 23, 1962, folder 1, box 521, JARP; Miyakawa to Shigeo Wakamatsu et al., June 25 1960, folder 2, box 520, JARP.

32. "The Strange Case of the Seattle Slums: Why Aren't These Kids in Trouble?" *Better Homes and Gardens*, July 1958, 46–47.

33. Kurashige, *Japanese American Celebration*, 148–50; "Teenage Gang War Breaks in Eastside; Two Koshakus Injured," *Rafu Shimpo*, June 26, 1956, 1; "Juvenile Gang Warfare Perils Seinan Residents," *Rafu Shimpo*, June 5, 1957, 1; "Gang Bullet Murders Honor Student at Dance," *Rafu Shimpo*, April 19, 1958, 1; Gerald H. Ikeda, "Japanese American Fight Delinquency," *California Youth Authority Quarterly* 12, no. 2 (Summer 1959): 3–6, all cited in *Japanese American History: An A-to-Z Reference from 1868 to the Present*, ed. Brian Niiya (Los Angeles, 1993), 71–72, 264.

34. Miyakawa, "A Proposal for a Definitive History of the Japanese in the United States."

35. Ibid., 2–7, 44.

36. Chuman to Murphy, March 23, 1962, folder 1, box 521, JARP; Murphy to Chuman, April 9, 1962, folder 4, box 521, JARP.

37. "Japanese-American League Plans History with UCLA's Collaboration," *Los Angeles Times*, May 13, 1962; "Nisei Overcome War Prejudice to Find Greater Acceptability," *New York Times*, October 21, 1962, 123.

38. "UCLA Report on the JARP," July 10 to December 1, 1962, folder 3, box 521, JARP. This report appears to be the first mention of renaming the ISP as JARP. Azuma, *Between Two Empires*, 210–11.

39. "Proposal for Aid to the Japanese American Research Project, University of California, Los Angeles," October 1963, folder 7, box 455, Carnegie Corporation of New York Grant Files, Columbia University Rare Book and Manuscript Library (hereafter CCNY); Handlin to Pifer, October 21, 1963, folder 7, box 455, CCNY; Kerr to Pifer, October 29, 1963, folder 7, box 455, CCNY.

40. David W. Southern, *Gunnar Myrdal and Black-White Relations: The Use and Abuse of An American Dilemma, 1944–1969* (Baton Rouge, LA, 1987), 198; Jackson, *Gunnar Myrdal*, 264.

41. "Carnegie Corporation of New York Record of Interview, Subject: UCLA Japanese American Research Project," September 24, 1963, folder 7, box 455, CCNY; UCLA Office of Public Information, "Carnegie Corp. Gives Grant for Japanese-American Study," press release, April 7, 1964, "Carnegie Materials for Discussion" folder, box 10, T. Scott Miyakawa papers, YRL (hereafter TSM); Carnegie Corporation of New York, "Annual Report," 1964, 40, "Carnegie Materials for Discussion" folder, box 10, TSM. JARP also received an additional $41,000 from the Carnegie Corporation in 1966, and three separate grants from the National Institute of Mental Health totaling $432,035 for 1966–69. See "$41,000 Grant Made to UCLA," *Los Angeles Times*, February 10, 1966, WS4; JARP, "NIMH Supports Project for Third Year," news release, December 5, 1968, folder 4, box 125, Joe Grant Masaoka papers, YRL.

42. *History of Japanese Immigration to United States*, 88th Cong., 2nd Sess., *Congressional Record* 110 (April 29, 1964): 9561–62.

43. "Negro, Japanese in U.S. Compared," *Pacific Citizen*, October 4, 1957, 1, 8.

44. Howard Imazeki, "In Our Voice," *Hokubei Mainichi*, June 29, 1963, cited in Robinson, *After Camp*, 227.

45. Robinson, *After Camp*, 228; "Nisei Paper Advises Negroes to 'Do a Little Soul Searching,'" *New York Times*, July 5, 1963, 33; *Pacific Citizen*, July 12, 1963; "Nisei Tells Negroes to Better Themselves," *Los Angeles Times*, July 6, 1963, 4; "Japanese-American Editor Urges S.F. Negroes to 'Search Souls,'" *Chicago Defender*, July 8, 1963, 4; "Japanese-U.S. Editor Urges S. F. Negroes to 'Search Souls,'" *Atlanta Daily World*, December 8, 1963, A6. The *Hokubei Mainichi* printed responses to Imazeki in nearly every issue during July and August 1963.

46. "Editorial," *Young China*, August 16, 1963, 4; "Mr. Imazeki and Humility," *Chinese World*, August 14, 1963, 1.

47. Robinson, *After Camp*, 228; Neils James Jr., "Negroes Hindered," *Chi-*

cago Defender, July 15, 1963, 15, cited in Robinson, *After Camp,* 228, 298n33; "Negro Press Prints Text," *Pacific Citizen,* August 2, 1963, 1; George O. Butler, "Negro Leader Asks for Understanding," *Pacific Citizen,* August 2, 1963, 2.

48. Clifford Uyeda, "This Is Our Voice," *Pacific Citizen,* July 19, 1963, 2. See also Uyeda, "Rhetorics over Racial Discrimination," *Pacific Citizen,* November 10, 1961, 4, cited in Robinson, *After Camp,* 226; Clifford Uyeda, "This Is Our Voice," *Pacific Citizen,* August 2, 1963, 2; Jerry Enomoto, "Nisei Advises Nisei to do 'Soul Searching,'" *Pacific Citizen,* August 9, 1963, 2; Robinson, *After Camp,* 229–30.

49. Robinson, *After Camp,* 229; Mike Masaoka, "NOT 'Our Voice,'" *Pacific Citizen,* August 2, 1963, 2.

50. William Petersen, "Success Story, Japanese-American Style," *New York Times Magazine,* January 9, 1966, 20–21, 33, 36, 38, 40–41, 43, reprinted in *Minority Responses,* ed. Minako Kurokawa (New York, 1970), 169–78, and Nathan Glazer, ed., *Cities in Trouble* (Chicago, 1970), 158–71; "Melting Pot," *New York World Telegram;* Jack Jones, "Now Millionaires: Japanese American Comeback on West Coast Spectacular," *Boston Globe,* November 25, 1965, 16A, "Themes, Topics, and Theories for JARP" folder, box 4, TSM; "Most Successful," *Parade,* November 28, 1971, "Themes, Topics, and Theories for JARP #2" folder, box 3, TSM; "The Nisei: The Pride and the Shame," *The Twentieth Century* transcript, January 3, 1965, Hirasaki General Collection, Japanese American National Museum.

51. Barbara F. Varon, "The Japanese Americans: Comparative Occupational Status, 1960 and 1950," *Demography* 4, no. 2 (1967): 809–19; Harry H. L. Kitano, "Housing of Japanese-Americans in the San Francisco Bay Area," in *Studies in Housing and Minority Groups,* ed. Nathan Glazer and Davis McEntire (Berkeley, 1960), 178–97; Calvin F. Schmid and Charles E. Nobbe, "Socioeconomic Differentials among Nonwhite Races," *American Sociological Review* 30 (1965): 909–22; Harry H. L. Kitano, *Japanese Americans: The Evolution of a Subculture* (Upper Saddle River NJ, 1969), 47–48, 116–33; William Petersen, *Japanese Americans: Oppression and Success* (New York, 1971), 101–51; Charles Michener, "Success Story: Outwhiting the Whites," *Newsweek,* June 21, 1971, 24–25.

52. Michener, "Outwhiting the Whites"; Petersen, "Success Story, Japanese-American Style"; John Modell, "The Japanese American Family: A Perspective for Future Investigations," *Pacific Historical Review* 37 (1968): 67–81; Ronald O. Haak, "Co-opting the Oppressors: The Case of the Japanese-Americans," *Transaction,* October 1970, 23–31; Stanford M. Lyman, "Japanese-American Generation Gap," *Society,* January–February 1973, 55–62.

53. Kurashige, *Japanese American Celebration and Conflict,* 137–43; Oda, "Remaking the 'Gateway to the Pacific.'"

54. Kitano, *Japanese Americans,* 144; Haak, "Co-opting the Oppressors"; Petersen, *Japanese Americans.* For an extended analysis of Petersen, see David Palumbo-Liu, *Asian/American: Historical Crossings of a Racial Frontier* (Stanford, CA, 1999), 170–81.

55. O'Connor, *Poverty Knowledge,* 74–123; Ellen Herman, *The Romance of American Psychology: Political Culture in the Age of Experts* (Berkeley, 1995), 186–93.

56. Daniel Patrick Moynihan, "The Negro Family: The Case for National Action," reprinted in Lee Rainwater and William L. Yancey, *The Moynihan Report and the Politics of Controversy* (Cambridge, MA, 1967), 39-124; O'Connor, *Poverty Knowledge*; Jackson, *Gunnar Myrdal*.

57. Daniel Patrick Moynihan, "Memorandum for the President," March 5, 1965, in *Daniel Patrick Moynihan: A Portrait in Letters of an American Visionary*, ed. Steven R. Weisman (New York, 2010), 95.

58. O'Connor, *Poverty Knowledge*; Jackson, *Gunnar Myrdal*; Daniel Patrick Moynihan, "A Family Policy for the Nation," *America: The National Catholic Weekly Review*, September 18, 1965, reprinted in Lee Rainwater and William L. Yancey, *The Moynihan Report and the Politics of Controversy* (Cambridge, MA: 1967), 385-394; Thomas Meehan, "Moynihan of the Moynihan Report," *New York Times Magazine*, July 31, 1966, 48.

59. Dave M. Okada, "A Study of Male Nisei Workers in Two Chicago Industrial Plants under Wartime Conditions" (master's thesis, University of Chicago, 1947); Yukiko Kimura, "A Comparative Study of Collective Adjustment of the Issei, the First Generation Japanese, in Hawaii and in the Mainland United States since Pearl Harbor" (PhD diss., University of Chicago, 1952); Eugene S. Uyeki, "Process and Patterns of Nisei Adjustment to Chicago" (PhD diss., University of Chicago, 1950).

60. Petersen, "Success Story"; Haak, "Co-opting the Oppressors."

61. Petersen, "Success Story"; Kitano, *Japanese Americans*, vii, xi, 2–3; Michener "Outwhiting the Whites."

62. Haak, "Co-opting the Oppressors"; Petersen, "Success Story"; Kitano, "Changing Achievement Patterns"; Kitano, *Japanese Americans*, 116–33; Lyman, "Japanese-American Generation Gap."

63. Kitano, *Japanese Americans*, 146, 116.

64. The official minutes of JACL's nineteenth biennial national convention in 1966 noted, "JACL also provided some of the material for the special feature in the *New York Times Sunday Magazine*, for January 9, 1966, entitled 'Success Story: Japanese American Style,' by Professor William Peterson [*sic*] of the University of California, Berkeley, which demonstrated that Japanese Americans, though subjected to the color prejudice of the Negro, the economic fear of the Jew, and more hatred of overseas people than any other immigrant group, have succeeded in gaining acceptance and opportunities in the United States." JACL, "Official Convention Minutes, 1966," 50, folder 3, box 297, JARP.

65. Between 1964 and 1966, JARP staff members interviewed a national sample of 1,047 Issei drawn from approximately 18,000 surviving members of the immigrant cohort who arrived in the United States from Japan before 1924. JARP staff members and affiliates (including trained interviewers from the National Opinion Research Center) then contacted their Nisei children via personal interviews, telephone interviews, and a mail questionnaire between 1966 and 1967. Sixty percent of the Nisei sample, or 2,304 individuals, responded. JARP staff members also attempted to reach the adult (eighteen years old and over) Sansei children of the Nisei respondents. JARP staff members collected data from 802 Sansei between 1966 and 1967. For an overview of the survey's theoretical considerations, methodology, and findings, see Gene N. Levine and Colbert

Rhodes, *The Japanese American Community: A Three-Generation Study* (New York, 1981).

66. The "JARP Nisei Interview Schedule" is reprinted in appendix B and the "Sansei Mail Questionnaire" is reprinted in appendix C of Levine and Rhodes, *The Japanese American Community*.

67. Julian Hart, "Called Most Successful: Japanese-American Study May Help Other Minorities," *Los Angeles Times*, February 17, 1967, folder 4, box 124, JARP.

68. Masaoka to Wakamatsu et al., January 10, 1967, folder 5, box 523, JARP.

69. Chuman to Wakamatsu, February 7, 1967, folder 5, box 523, JARP.

70. Hosokawa to Wakamatsu, April 20, 1961, folder 5, box 520, JARP; Yoshinari to Wakamatsu et al., January 20, 1967, folder 5, box 523, JARP; Joe Grant Masaoka to Mike Masaoka, January 9, 1967, folder 5, box 523, JARP.

71. Masaoka to Wakamatsu et al., January 10, 1967, folder 5, box 523, JARP.

72. Joe Grant Masaoka to Mike Masaoka, January 9, 1967, folder 5, box 523, JARP.

73. Ibid.; JACL, "Japanese History Project Executive Committee Meeting Minutes," February 15–16, 1967, folder 5, box 523, JARP.

74. Hosokawa to JACL History Project Executive Committee, January 16, 1967, folder 5, box 523, JARP.

75. *Americans With Japanese Faces* referenced Nisei sociologist's Charles Kikuchi's anonymous biography, "A Young American With a Japanese Face," published in 1940 as part of cultural pluralism proponent Louis Adamic's anthology of immigrant life histories. See Anonymous, "A Young American With a Japanese Face," in Louis Adamic, *From Many Lands* (New York, 1940), 185–234.

76. Hosokawa to Shig [Wakamatsu] and Mike [Masaoka], March 9, 1969, folder 1, box 524, JARP.

77. Cady to Hosokawa, February 19, 1969, folder 1, box 524, JARP.

78. Hosokawa to Shig [Wakamatsu] and Mike [Masaoka], March 9, 1969, folder 1, box 524, JARP.

79. Wakamatsu to members of [JARP] Executive Committee, March 18, 1969, folder 1, box 524, JARP.

80. "Controversy Goes to Publisher," *Pacific Citizen*, August 1, 1969, 4; Harry Honda, "'Quiet American' Controversy: Boycott Threat Called Censorship," *Pacific Citizen*, September 19, 1969, 1–2, 6; JARP chronology, 1980, "JARP 1980 Reports to JACL" folder, box 2, TSM; Bill Hosokawa, *Nisei: The Quiet Americans; The Story of a People* (New York, 1969). On the debate over the title within JACL, see the *Pacific Citizen*'s "letterbox" between June 1969 and February 1970; Alice Yang Murray, *Historical Memories of the Japanese American Internment and the Struggle for Redress* (Stanford, CA, 2008), 214, 216–17.

81. Hosokawa, *Nisei*, 473–97; Murray, *Historical Memories*, 217–19.

82. Hosokawa, *Nisei*, 359–422.

83. Murray, *Historical Memories*, 217–19; Gladwin Hill, "Nisei," *New York Times*, December 21, 1969, BR4; Mari Sabusawa Michener, "Books Today: Japanese in America," *Chicago Tribune*, December 19, 1969, 26; Magnuson remarks, 91st Cong., 2nd Sess., *Congressional Record* 116 (March 19, 1970): 8052–54.

84. "Controversy Goes to Publisher," *Pacific Citizen*; Honda, "'Quiet American' Controversy: Boycott Threat Called Censorship."

85. Mary Tani, "Shhh! A Nisei Is Speaking," *Gidra*, October 1969, 6; Mary Tani, "Nisei: The Traumatized American," *Gidra*, November 1969, 10; Mary Tani, "'Quiet Americans,'" *Gidra*, December 1969, 14–15; Murray, *Historical Memories*, 219.

86. Yuji Ichioka, "Book Review: *Nisei: The Quiet Americans*," *Gidra*, January 1970, 17.

87. Ibid.

88. Ibid.

Chapter 6: Chinatown Offers Us a Lesson

1. "S.F. Chinese 'Gang' Starts Trouble in San Mateo," *Chinese Press*, February 11, 1949, 3; "Youths Put on Probation in San Mateo Fight Case," *Chinese Press*, March 4, 1949, 1; "The People Say ANSWER WANTED," *Chinese Press*, February 25, 1949, 1; "More Rowdyism: Fight Breaks Up Oakland Chinese Skating Party," *Chinese Press*, February 18, 1949, 3.

2. "S.F. Chinese 'Gang' Starts Trouble," *Chinese Press*; "The People Say BOMBSHELL," *Chinese Press*, February 11, 1949, 1 (emphasis in original).

3. "S.F. Chinese 'Gang' Starts Trouble," *Chinese Press*; "More Rowdyism," *Chinese Press*; "The People Say ANSWER WANTED," *Chinese Press*; "Nine Youths Arraigned in San Mateo Fight Case," *Chinese Press*, February 18, 1949, 2; "Youths Put on Probation," *Chinese Press*.

4. "Juvenile Delinquency: War's Insecurity Lifts Youthful Crime 100%," *Life*, April 8, 1946, 83–93. On the postwar delinquency panic, see James Gilbert, *A Cycle of Outrage: America's Reaction to the Juvenile Delinquent in the 1950s* (Oxford, 1986); William Graebner, *Coming of Age in Buffalo: Youth and Authority in the Postwar Era* (Philadelphia, 1990); Eric Schneider, *Vampires, Dragons, and Egyptian Kings: Youth Gangs in New York* (Princeton, NJ, 1999); Steven Mintz, *Huck's Raft: A History of American Childhood* (Cambridge, MA, 2004). On the connections between juvenile delinquency and race in the twentieth century, see Alverez, *The Riddle of the Zoot*; Diamond, *Mean Streets*; Donna Jean Murch, *Living for the City: Migration, Education, and the Rise of the Black Panther Party in Oakland, California* (Chapel Hill, NC, 2010); Miroslava Chávez-García, *States of Delinquency: Race and Science in the Making of California's Juvenile Justice System* (Berkeley, 2012).

5. Chun's *Of Orphans and Warriors* is one of few the historical studies of Chinese America that considers the nondelinquency concept in the 1950s.

6. May, *Homeward Bound*.

7. Feldstein, *Motherhood in Black and White*, 3.

8. "Chinese Six Companies Wages War on Chinatown Crime Wave," *Chinese Press*, July 16, 1948, 1, 4; "Chinatown Robberies: Action by Chinese Chamber of Commerce, *Chinese Press*, August 6, 1948, 1; "Police and Chinese Groups Disagree on Crime Wave in Chinatown," *Chinese Press*, August 20, 1948, 1; Juvenile Delinquency Rate Is Rising in Chinatown," *Chinese Press*, April 15, 1949, 1; "Cal CSCA Talks on Juvenile Delinquency," *Chinese Press*, March 11, 1949,

9; "Juvenile Delinquency Rate Is Rising in Chinatown," *Chinese Press*, April 15, 1949, 1; "Kid Glove Bandits Try a Soft Touch," *Chinese Press*, November 18, 1949, 2; Edward W. Chew, "Chinatown Crimewave: 'Kid Glove Bandits Linked with Six Robberies,'" *Chinese Press*, December 2, 1949, 1, 2; "Punk War Hurting Business," *Chinese Press*, January 27, 1950, 1, 2; "This, Too, Is Chinatown," *Chinese Press*, February 24, 1950, 1; Edward W. Chew, "Chinatown Problem: 'He Had Nothing to Do'—Now in Trouble with Law," *Chinese Press*, March 24, 1950, 2.

9. Rose Hum Lee, "Community Not Interested in Its Youth, Sociologist Charges," *Chinese Press*, February 17, 1950, 3. 4. See also Rose Hum Lee, "Delinquent, Neglected, and Dependent Chinese Boys and Girls of the San Francisco Bay Region," *Journal of Social Psychology* 36 (1952): 15–34. James Gilbert notes that most juvenile experts of the post–World War II period believed that juvenile delinquency was a problem rooted in the family structure. See Gilbert, *Cycle of Outrage*.

10. "Blame Them Not"; "Bob Lee: CSCA Secretary on SF Hoodlums," *Chinese Press*, May 12, 1950, 2; "Walter Mails, Sports Star Deplores Lack of Playfields in Chinatown," *Chinese Press*, February 4, 1949, 12.

11. "Punks 'Jump' Cal Students," *Chinese Press*, May 5, 1950, 2; "The OPEN FORUM: 'Punk' Fights Harm Community," *Chinese Press*, May 5, 1950, 8; George Yip, "OPEN FORUM: Memo to 'Punks,'" *Chinese Press*, May 1, 1950, 6.

12. "Community Group Plans Chinatown Youth Welfare Conclave June 11," *Chinese Press*, May 29, 1949, 4; "Young Chinese Leaders to Meet June 11 for Welfare Conference, *Chinese Press*, June 3, 1949, 2; Letter to the editor from Jack Chow, Dr. Thomas Wu, Dr. Edwin Owyang, Dr. Theodore C. Lee, Dr. Howard Low, and Rev. T. T. Taam, *Chinese Press*, July 8, 1949; "Chinatown Youth Welfare Confab Set for Saturday, *Chinese Press*, June 10, 1949, 1; "Welfare Confab Hailed a Success," *Chinese Press*, June 17, 1949, 3; "Youth Welfare: A Report on Religion and Chinatown Family Life," *Chinese Press*, July 22, 1949, 4; "Long Range Views: Chinatown Youth Welfare Conference Makes Reports and Recommendations," *Chinese Press*, June 24, 1949, 2.

13. "Chinatown Youths Need Foster Homes, Play Space," *Chinese Press*, August 19, 1949, 2; "Youth Welfare Meet Hears Chinatown Police Report," *Chinese Press*, July 29, 1949, 5.

14. "A Report on Recreation in Chinatown," *Chinese Press*; "Long Range Views," *Chinese Press*; "Youth Welfare: A Report," *Chinese Press*; "Youth Welfare Meet Hears Chinatown Police Report," *Chinese Press*; "Chinatown Youths Need Foster Homes, Play Space," *Chinese Press*.

15. Youth Council Meets to Halt Juvenile Delinquency," *Chinese Press*, January 6, 1950, 1; "Chinatown Joins Council; Hopes for Youth Control," *Chinese Press*, January 13, 1950, 1–2; "Neighborhood Council to Hold Public Mass Meeting," *Chinese Press*, January 20, 1950, 2; "Youth Council Will Elect," *Chinese Press*, February 10, 1950, 4; "Council Ready to Halt Delinquency," *Chinese Press*, March 3, 1950, 1; "Youth Council to Elect Chairman at Today's Meet," *Chinese World*, January 31, 1950, 2; "Youth Council Plans Attack on Delinquency," *Chinese World*, February 3, 1950, 2; "Lim P. Lee Chosen as Chairman of New Youth Council," *Chinese World*, March 2, 1950, 2. The Central District

Neighborhood Youth Council is also referred to as the Central Neighborhood Council in the *Chinese Press*.

16. "Blueprints June Welfare Confab," *Chinese Press*, March 10, 1950; "Youth Confab Sked for June 3," *Chinese Press*, April 28, 1950, 2; "Youth Welfare Speakers Named," *Chinese Press*, May 12, 1950, 2; Lim P. Lee, letter to the editor, *Chinese Press*, May 12, 1950, 2; "Delinquency Is Topic of Welfare Confab," *Chinese Press*, May 26, 1950, 1; "2nd Youth Confab Opens Tomorrow," *Chinese Press*, June 2, 1950, 1; "Delegates Elect Dr. Edwin Owyang to Chairmanship," *Chinese Press*, June 9, 1950; "The People Say . . . The Race," *Chinese Press*, June 9, 1950, 1; "Central District Youth Welfare Conference June 3," *Chinese World*, May 27, 1950, 1; "Youth Welfare Conference Today," *Chinese World*, June 3, 1950, 1.

17. Dick Hemp, "Lees Act on Chinatown's Youth Problem," *San Francisco Chronicle*, April 10, 1950, 17; "Lee Family Assn. Organizes Youth Group," *Chinese World*, March 15, 1950, 2.

18. "Chinatown Recreation," n.a., ca. 1938, folder 21, William Hoy Papers, ESL. Thanks to Charlotte Brooks for this reference. "'Dead End Kids': Chinatown Petitions for New Playground to Combat Delinquency; Here Is the Story of Signature Drive," *Chinese Press*, February 28, 1941; Lim P. Lee, "'Dead End Kids': Chinatown Petitions for New Playground to Combat Delinquency; These Are 'Press Facts and Figures,'" *Chinese Press*, February 28, 1941; "More Playspace for Chinatown's Children Urgently Needed!" *Chinese News*, March 1, 1941, 1–2; "Petition for a New Playground in Chinatown," *Chinese News*, March 1, 1941, 2; "Playground Petition," *Chinese Press*, March 7, 1941; "The Playground Problem: Plans Developed for Intensive Campaign; Dr. Theodore C. Lee Named Chairman of Civic Group," *Chinese Press*, March 8, 1941; "New Playground Petition Signed by More Than 2,000," *Chinese News*, March 15, 1941, 6; "Chinatown Improvement Association Meets," *Chinese News*, April 1, 1941, 8; "Playground: Broad Hearing and Constitution Next Move," *Chinese Press*, April 4, 1941; "Chinatown Civic Victory: Playground Request Approved by Local Board of Education," *Chinese Press*, April 11, 1941; "Chinatown Youth," *Chinese Press*, May 9, 1941; "The Playground Issue: Here's Our Letter of Recommendation," *Chinese Press*, June 13, 1941; "Chinatown Improvement Association Meets," *Chinese News*, June 15, 1941, 3; "Playground for Commodore Stockton School," *Chinese News*, August 1, 1941, 2; "New Playground: Like Christmas—It Should Be Here Definitely This Year," *Chinese Press*, August 8, 1941; "Portsmouth Square: Chinatown May Have a New Playground," *Chinese Press*, October 10, 1941; "School Board Has Purchased the New Playground Site," *Chinese Press*, April 17, 1942; "Playground Seems Certain," *Chinese Press*, August 22, 1941; "Action on the New Playground," *Chinese Press*, July 3, 1942; Thomas W. Chinn, *Bridging the Pacific: San Francisco Chinatown and Its People* (San Francisco, 1989), 133–35; Kathleen S. Yep, *Outside the Paint: When Basketball Ruled at the Chinese Playground* (Philadelphia, 2009).

19. "Recreational Project Takes Shape," *Ching Nien News* 1, no. 6, September 19, 1947, 5, "YMCA" folder, Him Mark Lai Research Papers, ESL; William Hoy, "New Chinese Playground: Site Already Purchased," *Chinese Press*, July 16, 1948, 1; "The People Say . . . HAVING A WONDERFUL TIME," *Chinese Press*,

December 10, 1948, 1; "Walter Mails, Sports Star Deplores Lack of Playfields in Chinatown," *Chinese Press*, February 4, 1949, 12; "Chinatown Needs More Playgrounds," *Chinese Press*, March 10, 1950, 1; Dr. Thomas W. S. Wu, "Study Finds Recreation Facilities Inadequate," *Chinese Press*, March 10, 1950, 3, 7.

20. Lim P. Lee, "In the Districts: Chinatown Fights Juvenile Delinquency," *San Francisco Chronicle*, n.d., folder 6, box 4, CLP.

21. "YMCA Club Successful in Recreation Drive," *East Wind*, Spring 1948, 15; Henry S. Louie, letter to George W. Johns, February 13, 1948, folder 23, William Hoy Papers, ESL. Thanks to Charlotte Brooks for this reference.

22. "Chinatown Wins Fight for Recreation Center," *San Francisco Chronicle*, November 23, 1948.

23. "Chinese Community Wins Fight for New Recreation Center," *Chinese Press*, November 26, 1948, 1; "The People Say . . . CITIZENS IN ACTION," *Chinese Press*, November 26, 1948, 1; "Recreation Center for San Francisco's Chinese Population," *Architectural Record*, September 1949, 138–41; "Recreation Center," *Chinese World*, December 2, 1949, 1; "Many Modern Facilities for Recreational Center," *Chinese Press*, January 13, 1950, 2; "OPEN FORUM: Badminton Club Seeks Facilities Here," *Chinese Press*, February 10, 1950, 2; "OPEN FORUM: Question Rec Center Plans; More 'Pretty Gals' Letters," *Chinese Press*, January 27, 1950, 2; "$417,000 Chinese Recreation Center to Be Dedicated Sunday," *Chinese World*, October 30, 1951, 2; "Recreation Center to Open," *Chinese Press*, November 2, 1950, 1, 7; "Recreation Center to Be Dedicated by Mayor Sunday," *Chinese World*, November 3, 1951, 2; Dai-Ming Lee, "The New Chinatown Recreation Center," *Chinese World*, November 5, 1951, 1; "Chinese Recreation Center: Lillian Yuen, Kenny Kim Named Directors," *Chinese Press*, November 9, 1951, 5; "Chinese Recreation Center: 'A Wonderful Place,' Say the Youngsters," *Chinese Press*, November 9, 1951, 5.

24. "Portsmouth Square: Chinatown May Have a New Playground," *Chinese Press*, October 10, 1941, 1; "Breakdown of Chinatown Play Areas in New Report," *Chinese Press*, April 14, 1950, 2; "Opposes Play Area Cuts," *Chinese Press*, May 12, 1950, 1; "Ten Minutes of Happiness," *Chinese Press*, August 24, 1951, 4; "Plans for Playground Move Ahead," *Chinese Press*, November 2, 1951, 1, 6; "Playground Area Resolution Passed," *Chinese World*, November 3, 1951, 2.

25. "Youths Arrested in B-B Gun War at Grammar School," *Pictorial* [*Chinese Pacific Weekly*], September 14, 1952, 1–2; Dai-Ming Lee, "A Serious Problem in Chinatown," *Chinese World*, June 30, 1952, 1; Dai-Ming Lee, "Decline of Law and Order in Chinatown," *Chinese World*, February 20, 1952, 1.

26. "China-Born Youths May Pose Threat to Community Unless Cared for, Probation Officer Warns," *Pictorial* [*Chinese Pacific Weekly*], June 28, 1952, 1.

27. San Francisco Juvenile Court Department, *San Francisco Youth Guidance Center, Annual Report* (San Francisco, 1952), 65; "Project to Aid China-Born Teenagers," *Chinese World*, November 19, 1954, 2; "Chinese Chamber to Aid China-Born Teenagers," *Chinese World*, December 2, 1954, 2; Stanton Jue, "Columbia Foundation Project Helps China-Born Teen-Agers to Adjust," *Chinese World*, February 10, 1955, 2; Stanton Jue, "A Study on China-Born Teenagers," *Chinese World*, October 26, 1955, 2.

28. Lee, "Delinquent, Neglected, and Dependent."

29. "No Chinese-American J.D.'s," *America: National Catholic Weekly Review*, July 23, 1955, 402; William McIntyre, "Chinatown Offers Us a Lesson," *New York Times Magazine*, October 6, 1957, 49, 51, 54, 56, 59. I borrow the term nondelinquency from Conrad Foo Mar, "Non-Delinquency among American-Chinese Youth: A Pilot Study" (master's thesis, University of the Pacific, 1964). Mar and his fellow investigators considered a nondelinquent to be an "individual who has never been apprehended by law enforcement authorities and brought before a court and declared delinquent."

30. Lee, *At America's Gates*, 165–73; Kay Anderson, "The Idea of Chinatown: The Power of Place and Institutional Practice in the Making of a Racial Category," *Annals of the Association of American Geographers* 77, no. 4 (1987): 580–98; Shah, *Contagious Divides*, 29.

31. Wendy Rouse Jorae, *The Children of Chinatown: Growing Up Chinese American in San Francisco, 1850–1920* (Chapel Hill, NC, 2009), 136–37, 205–7; Shah, *Contagious Divides*, 204–24.

32. Lin Yutang, *My Country and My People* (New York, 1936), 176.

33. Ching-yueh Yeh, "Crime in Relation to Social Change in China," *American Journal of Sociology* 40 (November 1934): 303–4; Norman S. Hayner and Charles N. Reynolds, "Chinese Family Life in America," *American Sociological Review* 2, no. 4 (October 1937): 630–37; Norman S. Hayner, "Social Factors in Oriental Crime," *American Journal of Sociology* 43, no. 5 (May 1938): 908–19.

34. Carl Glick, "As the Chinese Twig Is Bent," *Reader's Digest*, April 1938, 63–64 (originally published in the *New York Herald Tribune*'s *This Week*). On the *Americans All* episode, see chapter 2.

35. Glick, "As the Chinese Twig Is Bent." Glick based his claims on data gathered from law enforcement officers of various cities.

36. Glick, *Shake Hands with the Dragon*, 50, 234, 245, 248; Glick, "Shake Hands with the Dragon," 121–34; Carl Glick, *Three Times I Bow* (New York, 1943), 200–202, 237–47.

37. Glick, *Shake Hands*, 312. The anecdote also concluded the *Reader's Digest* abridged version.

38. Riggs, *Pressures on Congress*, 55–62; CCRCE, "Our Chinese Wall"; House Committee on Immigration and Naturalization, *Repeal of the Chinese Exclusion Acts*, 78th Cong., 1st Sess., May 19, 20, 26, 27 and June 2–3, 1943, 69–70.

39. "Few Bad Boys in Chinatown—Credit Family," *Chicago Daily Tribune*, October 25, 1942, S1; Channing Pollock, "What It Takes," *Los Angeles Times*, April 18, 1943, G2; Perry, "Your Neighbors: The Wongs"; Richard E. Harris, *Delinquency in Our Democracy* (Los Angeles, 1954), 132–35.

40. "Juvenile Delinquency: War's Insecurity Lifts Youthful Crime 100%," *Life*, April 8, 1946, 83–93; Elizabeth Bradford, *Let's Talk about Children* (New York, 1947), 86–90; Theodore P. Blaich and Joseph C. Baugartner, *The Challenge of Democracy* (New York, 1947), 575.

41. Pardee Lowe, *Father and Glorious Descendant* (Boston, 1943), 66.

42. Wong, *Fifth Chinese Daughter*, 130.

43. "American Mother of the Year," *Washington Post*, May 5, 1952, 2; "Mother of the Year," *Chicago Daily Tribune*, May 5, 1952, A2; "Mother of '52 Honored," *New York Times*, May 13, 1952, 25; *PTA Magazine* 46, 1951, 22; "Ameri-

can Mother," *Christian Science Monitor*, May 6, 1952; "We're Proud of Mother," *Portland Press-Herald*, May 10, 1952, cited in 82nd Cong., 2nd Sess., *Congressional Record* 98 (May 12, 1952): A2912–13; Elisabeth Logan Davis, *Mothers of America: The Lasting Influence of the Christian Home* (Westwood, NJ, 1954).

44. Morrison Wong, "Chinese Americans," in *Asian Americans: Contemporary Trends and Issues*, ed. Pyong Gap Min (Thousand Oaks, CA, 1995), 65; Xiaolan Bao, "When Women Arrived: The Transformation of New York's Chinatown," in *Not June Cleaver: Women and Gender in Postwar America, 1945–1960*, ed. Joanne Meyerowitz (Philadelphia, 1994), 24.

45. Hemp, "Lees Act on Chinatown's Youth Problem"; "Why No Chinese American Delinquents? Maybe It's Traditional Respect for Parents," *Saturday Evening Post*, April 30, 1955, 2; Henry Beckett, "Why Chinese Kids Don't Go Bad: Spare the Rod, Love the Child," *New York Post*, July 11, 1955, 4, 20; "Americans without a Delinquency Problem," *Look*, April 29, 1958, 75–81; Albert D. Hughes, "Lichee Nuts, Cowboys, Traditions," *Christian Science Monitor*, September 6, 1960; Ray Pittman, "Chinese Pastor Guiding Spirit of Flock," *Washington Post*, December 17, 1951, B1; McIntrye, "Chinatown Offers Us a Lesson"; Michael Schafer, "Chinatown—Where Kids Behave," *Chicago Daily Tribune*, July 7, 1959, C48.

46. Walter G. Beach, *Oriental Crime in California: A Study of Offenses Committed by Orientals in That State, 1900–1927* (Stanford, CA, 1932); C. N. Reynolds, "The Chinese Tongs," *American Journal of Sociology* 40, no. 5 (March 1935): 612–23; Patricia Page, "Chinatown: Not East, Not West," *New York Times Magazine*, December 15, 1946, 24, 59; Sidney Herschel Small, "No Blood on the Streets of Chinatown," *Saturday Evening Post*, September 27, 1947, 36–37, 90, 93; 95, 97–99; Robert Patterson, "The Tongs of San Francisco," *American Mercury*, February 1952, 12.

47. "Out of the Shadows," *Newsweek*, August 15, 1955, 19–20.

48. FBI, *Uniform Crime Reports for the United States and its Possessions, Fourth Quarterly Bulletin, 1941, Vol. 12, No. 4* (Washington, DC, 1942), 209; FBI, *Uniform Crime Reports for the United States, Annual Bulletin, 1954, Vol. 25, No. 2* (Washington, DC, 1955), 116; Khalil Gibran Muhammad, *The Condemnation of Blackness: Race, Crime, and the Making of Modern Urban America* (Cambridge, MA, 2010).

49. McIntyre, "Chinatown Offers Us a Lesson"; Theodore R. Hudson, letter to the editor, *Washington Post*, October 3, 1953, 8; Mary Kelly, "Three R's for N.Y. Chinese," *Christian Science Monitor*, October 28, 1963, 9. For an example from the African American press, see Claire Cox, "Close Family Ties Stop Juvenile Delinquency, Says Chinese," *Chicago Daily Defender*, July 21, 1958, A15.

50. James C. G. Conniff, "Our Amazing Chinese Kids," *Coronet*, December 1955, 31–36; McIntyre, "Chinatown Offers Us a Lesson"; Ray Pittman, "Chinese Pastor Guiding Spirit of Flock," *Washington Post*, December 17, 1951, B1; Beckett, "Why Chinese Kids Don't Go Bad"; Rhoads Murphey, "Boston's Chinatown," *Economic Geography* 28, no. 3 (July 1952): 244–55; Schafer, "Chinatown—Where Kids Behave."

51. "Why No Chinese American Delinquents?" *Saturday Evening Post*; Beckett, "Why Chinese Kids Don't Go Bad"; "No Chinese-American J.D.'s," *America:*

National Catholic Weekly Review; Conniff, "Our Amazing Chinese Kids"; McIntyre, "Chinatown Offers Us a Lesson"; Sheila Wolfe, "New Ways Replace Old for City's Chinese," *Chicago Tribune*, February 7, 1965.

52. Beckett, "Why Chinese Kids Don't Go Bad"; McIntyre, "Chinatown Offers Us a Lesson"; May, *Homeward Bound*.

53. Zhao, *Remaking Chinese America*; Bao, "When Women Arrived," 19–36.

54. Zhao, *Remaking Chinese America*, 126–51.

55. Glick, *Shake Hands with the Dragon*, 242; Conniff, "Our Amazing Chinese Kids"; "Chinese-Americans Enjoy Highest Credit Ratings," *Chinese World*, June 5, 1956, 2; F. Everett Place, "Rebuilding of Chinatown Favored," *New York Times*, August 15, 1950, 28; "Festival Opens New Center for Chinese Family," *Chicago Daily Tribune*, November 19, 1951, A2; Pittman, "Chinese Pastor"; Carter Zeleznik, letter to the editor, *Look*, June 10, 1958, 8; Robert Glass, "Some of the Best Americans in Chicago Live in Chinatown," *Chicago's American*, January 24, 1964; "America's Chinese," *Life*; Yung, *Unbound Feet*, 185; Brooks, *Alien Neighbors, Foreign Friends*, 86–88, 91–94.

56. Beckett, "Why Chinese Kids Don't Go Bad"; Phyllis Ehrlich, "Chinatown Children Learn Discipline at Home," *New York Times*, October 26, 1963; Kelly, "Three R's for New York's Chinese"; "Americans without a Delinquency Problem," *Look*; "Hard Work at Hip Wo School," *Life*, April 25, 1955, 71–72, 74; Coniff, "Our Amazing Chinese Kids"; McIntyre, "Chinatown Offers Us a Lesson"; Marvin Koner, "Chinatown Family," *Washington Post*, June 19, 1960, AW20; Gilbert, *Cycle of Outrage*; George Chauncey Jr., "The Postwar Sex Crime Panic," in *True Stories from the American Past*, ed. William Graebner (New York, 1993).

57. Conniff, "Our Amazing Chinese Kids"; McIntyre, "Chinatown Offers Us a Lesson"; "Why No Chinese American Delinquents?" *Saturday Evening Post*.

58. Richard Dillon, *The Hatchet Men: The Story of the Tong Wars in San Francisco's Chinatown* (New York, 1962), 366; Lucien Bovet, *Psychiatric Aspects of Juvenile Delinquency* (Geneva, 1951), 5; Murphey, "Boston's Chinatown"; Sophia M. Robison, *Juvenile Delinquency: Its Nature and Control* (New York, 1960), 69–172; Trevor C. N. Gibbens and Robert H. Ahrenfeldt, eds., *Cultural Factors in Delinquency* (London, 1966), 21.

59. "Juvenile Delinquency," 84th Cong., 1st Sess., *Congressional Record* 101 (June 16, 1955), 8547 (originally cited in Sung, *Mountain of Gold*); "Why Chinese Kids Don't Go Bad," 84th Cong., 1st Sess., *Congressional Record* 101 (August 2, 1955), A5668–72 (originally cited in Sung, *Mountain of Gold*); Emil L. Purga, letter to the editor, *Look*, June 10, 1958, 8; Gertrude M. Coleman, "Chinatown's Solution," *Chicago Daily Tribune*, July 12, 1959, F4; A. R. Wagner, letter to the editor, *Stockton Record*, April 5, 1963, 56, reprinted in Mar, "Non-Delinquency"; "The Chinese, Too?" *Waterbury American*, reprinted in *The Young China*, January 11, 1963, 4.

60. Mar, "Non-Delinquency."

61. Dai-Ming Lee, "Peace and Quiet in Chinatown," *Chinese World*, July 12, 1951, 1; "Youth Beaten in Chinatown," *Chinese World*, July 11, 1951, 2; Dai-Ming Lee, "Decline of Law and Order in Chinatown," *Chinese World*, February 20, 1952, 1; "Lee Family Assn. Organizes Youth Group," *Chinese World*, March 15, 1950, 2; "Antidote to Juvenile Delinquency," *Chinese World*, March 16, 1950, 1; Dai-Ming Lee, "Keeping Order in Chinatown," *Chinese World*, July 5, 1951, 1;

"Trio Held in Chinatown Beating Case," *Chinese World*, July 13, 1951, 2; "Police to Crackdown on Chinatown Gangs," *Chinese Press*, June 29, 1951, 1; "A Time for Action," *Chinese Press*, June 29, 1951, 4; "Three Teenagers Jailed in Chinatown Beating," *Chinese Press*, July 13, 1951, 1.

62. Howard Freeman to Joseph A. Quan, June 11, 1956, folder 30, box 3, CLP.

63. Howard Freeman for the Chinese Six Companies, press release, March 15, 1956, folder 12, box 2, CLP.

64. Freeman to Quan. The article was never published; *Woman's Home Companion* folded circa late 1956/early 1957.

65. Albert Q. Maisel, "The Chinese among Us," *Reader's Digest*, February 1959, 203–4, 206, 208–10, 212. The article noted, "In preparing this article Mr. Maisel was assisted in his research by Charles Leong, author of the forthcoming *Chinatown Adventure*."

66. Lim P. Lee and Henry S. Tom, "Supplementary Paper to Addendum to Social Service Needs of the Chinese in the United States," unpublished manuscript, ca. 1958–59, folder 12, box 2, Edwar Lee Papers, ESL. Lee documented the following number of cases of Chinese juvenile delinquency that he had adjudicated as a probation officer: twenty (August 1954); twenty (August 1955); twenty-two (August 1956); twenty-three (August 1957); twenty-four (August 1958).

67. Dai-ming Lee, "The Chinese Conference in Washington," *Chinese World*, March 7, 1957, 1.

68. S. W. Kung, *Chinese in American Life: Some Aspects of Their History, Status, Problems, and Contributions* (Seattle, 1962), xi, 47–52, 255–61. For a critique of Kung's discussion of Chinese American nondelinquency, see Stanford M. Lyman, "Up from the 'Hatchet Man': A Review Article," *Pacific Affairs* 36, no. 2 (Summer 1963): 160–71. For other examples of Chinese Americans who promoted the nondelinquency idea, see Calvin Lee, *Chinatown USA* (Garden City, NY, 1965); Sung, *Mountain of Gold*.

69. Senate Committee on the Judiciary, *Refugee Problem in Hong Kong and Macao*, 87th Cong., 2nd Sess., May 29, June 7, 8, 28, July 10, 1962, 91.

70. John T. C. Fang, *Chinatown Handy Guide: San Francisco*, 1959, PAM 4620, North Baker Research Library, California Historical Society, San Francisco.

71. Donald D. Dong, "New England Comment," *Christian Science Monitor*, October 14, 1960, 2; Edward W. Chew, "Front Line Dispatch: Our Teenagers," *Chinese World*, January 26, 1956, 2.

72. Lee, "Community Not Interested in Its Youth, Sociologist Charges"; Lee, "Delinquent, Neglected, and Dependent"; Lee, *The Chinese in the United States of America*, 111, 157–58; Rose Hum Lee to Henry Evans, October 15, 1960, Rose Hum Lee Papers, Young Research Library Special Collections, University of California, Los Angeles (hereafter RHLP).

73. Lee, *The Chinese in the United States of America* 157–58. The three subgroups identified by Lee were "sojourners," "students and intellectuals," and "American-Chinese."

74. Yu, *Thinking Orientals*, 125–29, 181–82; Katharine Ng, "Fear and Loathing of Chinatown: The 1950s and Rose Hum Lee's Desire for Assimilation" (BA honors thesis, University of California, Los Angeles, 2002); Lee, *The Chinese in the United States of America*, 425–28; Rose Hum Lee, "The Decline of China-

towns in the United States," *American Journal of Sociology* 54 (1948–49): 422–32; Rose Hum Lee, "Chicago Chinatown," *Chicago Schools Journal* 31 (January–February 1950): 153–56.

75. Lee to Henry Luce, February 6, 1959; Lee to Russell Sackett (*Life*), January 11, 1959; Lee to J. Johnson (*Ebony*), December 5, 1960; Lee to Walter Judd, February 7, 1959; Lee to Franklin Williams, Department of Justice, June 24, 1960, RHLP.

76. Burton H. Wolfe, "Chinatown USA: The Unassimilated People—50,000 in a Ghetto; Plus the New Tongs," *California Liberal*, February 1960, 1, 3–5 (the *California Liberal* changed its name to the *Californian* with its April 1960 issue.); L. Y. Ngan (pseudonym for Rose Hum Lee) to Burton Wolfe, March 26, 1960, RHLP; Rose Hum Lee to the editor, *Californian*, April 1960, 2; Ng, "Fear and Loathing of Chinatown."

77. Rose Hum Lee to Elaine Lee, March 22, 1960, RHLP; Lim P. Lee, letter to the editor, *Californian*, April 1960, 2.

78. Rose Hum Lee in "Lee vs. Lee," letter to the editor, *Californian*, May 1960, 2; Gilbert Moy to Burton H. Wolfe, April 30, 1960, RHLP.

79. Moy to Wolfe; transcription of John Bryan, "Chinatown Juvenile Crime Gains: Elders Alarmed at Delinquency," *San Francisco Examiner*, April 9, 1961, with accompanying commentary by Rose Hum Lee, n.d., RHLP.

80. See, for instance, reviews in the *American Journal of Sociology* 66, no. 5 (March 1961): 535–56; *Sociological Quarterly* 2, no. 2 (April 1961): 146–48; *Bulletin of the School of Oriental and African Studies* (London) 24, no. 2 (1961): 383; *Population Studies* 17, no. 2 (November 1963): 202–3; Gilbert Woo, "People to Build Bridges," *Chinese Pacific Weekly*, August 11, 1960.

81. For insightful analyses of Rose Hum Lee's oeuvre, see Yu, *Thinking Orientals*, especially 125–33; Ng, "Fear and Loathing." On Lee's entrepreneurial appropriation of her academic knowledge of Chinese America, see the publicity flyers for her speaking appearances under the auspices of the Adult Education Council of Chicago, ca. 1948–49, "Biographies—College Teachers/Lee, Rose Hum" folder, Him Mark Lai Papers, ESL.

82. Mark R. Chan, "An Open Letter to Chinese American Youth," *Chinese American Progress*, May 1962, 22. Chicago's Chinese American Youth Organization, an affiliate of Chicago's Chinese-American Civic Council, was founded in 1959. See Rosalind Lew, "Chicago's Chinese Youth Organize for Civic Activities," *Chinese American Progress*, October 1959, 6.

83. Stuart H. Cattell, "Health, Welfare, and Social Organization in Chinatown, New York City," report prepared for the Chinatown Public Health Nursing Demonstration of the Department of Public Affairs, Community Service Society of New York, August 1962; "Need: Youth Aid," *Chinese-American Times*, July 1962, 2; "Chinatown Report," *Chinese-American Times*, November 1962, 2; Stuart H. Cattell, "Social Problems," *Chinese-American Times*, November 1962, 2; "To Discuss JD," *Chinese-American Times*, June 1964, 3; "Tackling the Problem," *Chinese-American Times*, July 1964, 2.

84. "Chinese Juvenile Delinquency," *Chinese World*, April 2, 1962, 1; "What Is Wrong With Juvenile Delinquents?" *Chinese World*, May 3, 1962; Michael Wilkes, "Lost Children of Chinatown," *Chinese World*, serial column in February–March 1964; Alan S. Wong, "Letters: Youth Problem Explained by Leader in Chi-

natown," *Young China* January 25, 1963, 4; Alan S. Wong, "The Problem," *Young China*, May 10, 1963, 4; Alan S. Wong, "Similar Problems," *Chinese-American Times*, February 1963, 2; "Problems Grow; Services Unused," *Chinese-American Times*, February 1963, 3; "Our Troubled Youth," *Chinese-American Times*, July 1963, 2; "Youth Problems Discussed by SF Chinese & Mayor," *Young China*, July 12, 1963, 1; "J.D. Is Increasing," *Young China*, November 26, 1964, 6; "Juvenile Crime Wave in Chinatown," *Young China*, February 6, 1965, 6.

85. "CBS-TV Shows NY Chinatown Documentary," *Chinese-American Times*, February 1963, 1; Emma Harrison, "Social Problems Beset Chinatown," *New York Times*, October 11, 1962, 41; Eleanor Middleton Telemaque, "Chinatown in the Year of the Serpent," *New York Herald Tribune*, January 31, 1965, 10–11; "Number One Challenge in Chinatown," *Chinese World*, March 14, 1966, 1.

86. Sylvan Fox, "N.Y. Chinese Refute 2-Year Social Report," *Young China*, November 16, 1962, 4; "Mixed Reactions to C-Report," *Chinese-American Times*, December 1962, 1; Carol Lum, "Point of View," *Chinese-American Times*, February 1963, 2; "Juvenile Crime Rate Low for Boston Chinese," *Young China*, September 7, 1962, 1; "Hooray for Us!" *Chinese-American Times*, April 1963, 3; "Boston Chinese Plan Chinatown Renaissance," *Young China*, December 2, 1964, 1.

87. Moynihan, "A Family Policy for the Nation"; Meehan, "Moynihan of the Moynihan Report."

88. D. Y. Yuan, "Voluntary Segregation: A Study of New [York] Chinatown," *Phylon* 24, no. 3 (1963): 255–65; D. Y. Yuan, "Chinatown and Beyond: The Chinese Population in Metropolitan New York," *Phylon* 26, no. 4 (1966): 321–32; Michael Harrington, *The Other America: Poverty in the United States* (New York, 1962), 140–41 (originally cited in Yuan, "Chinatown and Beyond").

89. Richard T. Sollenberger, "Chinese-American Child-Rearing Practices and Juvenile Delinquency," *Journal of Social Psychology* 74 (1968): 13–23. Other media outlets that cited Sollenberger's findings included "Chinese Lack Delinquency," *Science News*, September 17, 1966, 200; "Why Chinatown's Children Are Not Delinquent," *Transaction Magazine*, September 1968, 3 (originally cited in Stanford Lyman, *Chinese Americans* [New York, 1974], 167–68); Mary Merryfield, "Their Youth Don't Run Away: Why?" *Chicago Tribune*, October 20, 1968, F7.

90. "Success Story of One Minority Group in U.S.," *U.S. News and World Report*, December 26, 1966, 73–76.

91. Paul Gilroy, *'There Ain't No Black in the Union Jack': The Cultural Politics of Race and Nation* (Chicago, 1991).

Chapter 7: The Melting Pot of the Pacific

1. Haunani-Kay Trask, *From a Native Daughter: Colonialism and Sovereignty in Hawai'i* (Honolulu, 1999); Adria L. Imada, *Aloha America: Hula Circuits through the U.S. Empire* (Durham, NC, 2012).

2. Jonathan Y. Okamura, "The Illusion of Paradise: Privileging Multiculturalism in Hawai'i," in *Making Majorities: Constituting the Nation in Japan, Korea, China, Malaysia, Fiji, Turkey, and the United States*, ed. Dru C. Gladney (Stanford,

CA, 1998), 264–84; Lori Pierce, "Creating a Racial Paradise: Citizenship and Sociology in Hawai'i," in *Race and Nation: Ethnic Systems in the Modern World*, ed. Paul Spickard (New York, 2005); Shelley Sang-Hee Lee and Rick Baldoz, "'A Fascinating Interracial Experiment Station': Remapping the Orient-Occident Divide in Hawai'i," *American Studies* 49, nos. 3–4 (Fall–Winter 2008): 87–109.

3. Klein, *Cold War Orientalism*, 245.

4. Lilikala Kame'eleihiwa, *Native Land and Foreign Desires* (Honolulu, 1992); Sally Merry, *Colonizing Hawai'i: The Cultural Power of Law* (Princeton, NJ, 1999), 93–95; Noel J. Kent, *Hawaii: Islands under the Influence* (New York, 1983), 26–34; Jonathan Kay Kamakawiwo'ole Osorio, *Dismembering Lahui: A History of the Hawaiian Nation to 1887* (Honolulu, 2002), 44–50; Noenoe K. Silva, *Aloha Betrayed: Native Hawaiian Resistance to American Colonialism* (Durham, NC, 2004), 39–43; Roger Bell, *Last among Equals: Hawaiian Statehood and American Politics* (Honolulu, 1984), 38–44, 47–48; Gavan Daws, *Shoal of Time: A History of the Hawaiian Islands* (Honolulu, 1968), 209–13, 311–17; Glenn, *Unequal Freedom*, 193.

5. Merry, *Colonizing Hawai'i*, 132–34; Bell, *Last among Equals*, 10–11, 32–33; Daws, *Shoal of Time*, 303–34; Wong, *Americans First*, 129; John W. Foster, *The Annexation of Hawaii* (Washington, DC, 1897).

6. Glenn, *Unequal Freedom*, 196, 203–4.

7. Gary Okihiro, *Cane Fires: The Anti-Japanese Movement in Hawaii, 1865–1945* (Philadelphia, 1992), 57; Bell, *Last among Equals*, 11.

8. Bell, *Last among Equals*, 14–15, 38–45; Daws, *Shoal of Time*, 311–17, 333. In 1903, the territorial legislature approved the first of several resolutions recommending initiation of the admission process. Statehood bills were presented before the US House of Representatives in 1919, 1920, and 1931. The Big Five firms included Alexander and Baldwin, American Factors, Castle and Cooke, C. Brewer and Company, and Theo. Davies and Company. With the exception of the elected congressional delegate and territorial legislature, Hawai'i's major public offices were federally appointed.

9. Okihiro, *Cane Fires*, 45–57, 65–81, 95, 102–62; Dean Itsuji Saranillio, "Seeing Conquest: Colliding Histories and the Cultural Politics of Hawai'i Statehood" (PhD diss., University of Michigan), 10; Eileen Tamura, *Americanization, Acculturation, and Ethnic Identity: The Nisei Generation in Hawaii* (Urbana, IL, 1994), 45–88.

10. Bell, *Last among Equals*, 60–75; Daws, *Shoal of Time*, 332–38; Sidney Lanier, "Against Hawaiian Statehood," *Washington Post*, April 7, 1935, B7; Paul Merton, "Japan and Hawaii," *Washington Post*, October 26, 1938; "Forty-Ninth State?" *Washington Post*, October 5, 1940, 8; L. Alice Sturdy, "Statehood for Hawaii," *Los Angeles Times*, November 6, 1940, A4; "Hawaii—Our 49th State?" *Washington Post*, November 9, 1940, 10; D.D.V., "Hawaii Statehood: Japanese Element Viewed as Reason for Caution," *New York Times*, January 12, 1941, E9; George Gallup, "Hawaii State Bid Favored," *Los Angeles Times*, January 1, 1941, 1A.

11. Okihiro, *Cane Fires*, 230–42, 258–67; Bell, *Last among Equals*, 76–91.

12. Yu, *Thinking Orientals*, 19–30, 187.

13. Ibid., 80–82; Klein, *Cold War Orientalism*, 248–49; William Allen White,

"The Last of the Magic Isles," *Survey Graphic* 56 (May 1, 1926): 176–79, 212; Romanzo Adams, *The Peoples of Hawaii* (Honolulu, 1933); Romanzo Adams, *Interracial Marriage in Hawaii: A Study of the Mutually Conditioned Process of Acculturation and Amalgamation* (New York, 1937); Margaret Lam, "Baseball and Racial Harmony in Hawaii," *Sociology and Social Research* 18 (1933): 58–66; William Carlson Smith, *Americans in Process: A Study of Our Citizens of Oriental Ancestry* (1937; repr., New York, 1970); 20–21; Romanzo Adams, "The Unorthodox Race Doctrine of Hawaii," in *Race and Culture Contacts*, ed. E. B. Reuter (New York, 1934), 148, 150–55; Romanzo Adams, "Race Relations in Hawaii (A Summary Statement)," *Social Process in Hawaii* (1936): 56.

14. Andrew W. Lind, "The Changing Japanese in Hawaii," *Social Process in Hawaii* (1938): 37–40; F. Everett Robison, "Participation of Citizens of Chinese and Japanese Ancestry in the Political Life of Hawaii," *Social Process in Hawaii* (1938): 58–60; Clarence Glick, "The Relation between Position and Status in the Assimilation of Chinese in Hawaii," *American Journal of Sociology* (March 1942): 667–79; Smith, *Americans in Process*, 239, 250.

15. House Committee on Territories, *Statehood for Hawaii: Hearings on H.R. 3045*, 74th Congress, 1st Sess., 1935, 40–41; Joint Committee on Hawaii, *Statehood for Hawaii*, hearings on S. Con. Res. 18, 75th Cong., 2nd Sess., 1935, 436, 483. See also Romanzo Adams, "Statehood for Hawaii," *Social Process in Hawaii* (1935): 4-6; Andrew W. Lind, "The Changing Japanese in Hawaii," *Social Process in Hawaii* (1938): 37–40; Andrew W. Lind, "Hawaii at the Polls," *Asia* (October 1936): 643–46; Romanzo Adams, introduction to *Americans in Process: A Study of Our Citizens of Oriental Ancestry*, by William Carlson Smith (1937; repr., New York, 1970), xii–xiii; Andrew W. Lind, *The Japanese in Hawaii under War Conditions* (Honolulu, 1942), 2, 39–40.

16. William Atherton Du Puy, *Hawaii and Its Race Problem* (Washington, DC, 1932); George H. Blakeslee, "Hawaii: Racial Problem and Naval Base," *Foreign Affairs* 17, no. 1 (October 1938): 90–99; Walker Matheson, "Hawaii Pleads for Statehood," *North American Review*, Spring 1939, 130–41; "Speaking of Pictures . . . Hawaiian Islands Have Many Races, Many Combinations," *Life*, June 22, 1942, 8–9; Klein, *Cold War Orientalism*, 248–49; Gretchen Heefner, "'A Symbol of the New Frontier': Hawaiian Statehood, Anti-Colonialism, and Winning the Cold War," *Pacific Historical Review* 74, no. 4 (2005): 545–74.

17. Elizabeth Green, "Race and Politics in Hawaii," *Asia*, June 1935, 370–74; Webb Waldron, "A New Star in the Union?" *American*, April 1937, 36–37.

18. See, for example, Miriam Allen De Ford, "Japanese in Hawaii," *American Mercury*, July 1935, 332–40; James L. Marshall, "Hawaii Wants a Star: Islands to Vote on Statehood in November," *Colliers*, October 19, 1940, 20, 76, 79; Lawrence McCully Judd, "Hawaii States Her Case: Dreams of Achieving Statehood," *Current History and Forum*, July 1940, 40–42; S. L. Gulick, "Loyalty in Hawaii," *Christian Century*, February 5, 1941, 193; Y. Nakashima, "Dual Citizenship and the Question of Statehood for Hawaii: Japanese Expatriation Law," *Scholastic*, May 12, 1941, 11.

19. Bell, *Last among Equals*, 82–83; Daws, *Shoal of Time*, 348–51; Blake Clark, "The Japanese in Hawaii," *New Republic*, September 14, 1942, 308–10; Blake Clark, "Some Japanese in Hawaii," *Asia and the Americas*, December 1942,

723–25; Blake Clark, "U.S. Soldiers with Japanese Faces," *Reader's Digest*, February 1943, 125–27; Cecil Hengy Coggins, "Japanese-Americans in Hawaii," *Harper's Magazine*, June 1943, 75–83; R. J. Walsh, "Japanese-American Heroes," *Asia and the Americas*, September 1944, 387; John Lardner, "Those of the First Generation: Japanese-Americans," *New Yorker*, March 1, 1945, 46, 48–50, 53–55. On Hawai'i's Japanese Americans during World War II, see Franklin Odo, *No Sword to Bury: Japanese Americans in Hawai'i during World War II* (Philadelphia, 2004).

20. *Honolulu Star-Bulletin*, February 26, 1945, 4, quoted in Bell, *Last among Equals*, 83. Joseph R. Farrington, Hawai'i's delegate to Congress (1943–54) and a leading statehood advocate, owned the *Honolulu Star-Bulletin*.

21. Beth L. Bailey and David Farber, *The First Strange Place: Race and Sex in World War II Hawaii* (Baltimore, 1994), 16, 27; Bell, *Last among Equals*, 84, 86, 91.

22. "Statehood for Hawaii?" *Washington Post*, January 1, 1946, 6; House Subcommittee of the Committee on Territories, *Statehood for Hawaii: Hearings before the Subcommittee of the Committee on the Territories*, 79th Cong., 2nd Sess., January 17, 1946, 484–85, 488. Kamokila Campbell was the most visible and outspoken of Native Hawaiian statehood opponents in the postwar years. In addition to her reservations about Japanese Americans, she also feared the reproduction of Big Five hegemony under statehood. In 1947, she established the Anti-Statehood Clearing House to coordinate an antistatehood campaign. John S. Whitehead, "The Anti-Statehood Movement and the Legacy of Alice Kamokila Campbell," *Hawaiian Journal of History* 27 (1993): 43–63; Dean Itsuji Saranillio, "Colliding Histories: Hawai'i Statehood at the Intersection of Asians 'Ineligible to Citizenship' and Hawaiians 'Unfit for Self-Government,'" *Journal of Asian American Studies* (2010): 283–309.

23. Andrew W. Lind, *Hawaii's Japanese: An Experiment in Democracy* (Princeton, NJ, 1946), 235; House Subcommittee of the Committee on the Territories, *Statehood for Hawaii Hearings: Hearings before the Subcommittee of the Committee on the Territories*, 79th Cong., 2nd Sess., January 7, 1946, 34, 63, 66; House Committee on Public Lands, *Statehood for Hawaii*, 80th Cong., 1st Sess., March 7, 10–14, 1947, 27–35.

24. See, for example, "The 49th State," *Chicago Daily Tribune*, March 31, 1946, 16; various clippings in Hawaii Statehood Commission, "Editorial Comment on Statehood for Hawaii," April 15, 1947, "Public Opinion—Surveys of Editorial Comment, 1947–1950" folder, box 2, Hawaii Statehood Commission Collection, Hawai'i State Archives (hereafter HSCC).

25. Hoyt McAfee, "Hawaii Bids for Statehood," *Travel*, December 1946; "Hawaii Today . . . The 49th State Shapes Up," *Navy News*, June 1951; Joseph Rider Farrington, "Hawaii's Goal, Statehood," *Christian Science Monitor Magazine*, June 7, 1947, 8; "Territories: Knock on the Door," *Time*, December 22, 1947; "Hawaii Moves Ahead," *Scholastic*, December 14, 1949; "Hawaii: Stalled Statehood," *Newsweek*, November 27, 1950; Hodding Carter, "The Case for Hawaii," *Saturday Evening Post*, June 12, 1954, 32–33, 164, 166.

26. Lind, *Hawaii's Japanese*, 235; Blake Clark, *Hawaii: The 49th State* (Garden City, NY, 1947), 147.

27. Miller remarks, 83rd Cong., 1st Sess, *Congressional Record* 99, no. 2 (March 10, 1953): 1827; Senate hearings before the Committee on Interior and Insular Affairs, *Statehood for Hawaii*, 85th Cong., 1st Sess., April 1, 1957, 9; House hearings before the Committee on Interior and Insular Affairs, *Statehood for Hawaii*, 86th Cong., 1st Sess., January 26, 1959, 23; Bell, *Last among Equals*, 257–58.

28. Senate hearings before the Committee on Interior and Insular Affairs, *Statehood for Hawaii*, 83rd Cong., 1st and 2nd Sess., part 2, July 2, 1953, 256.

29. House hearings before the Committee on Interior and Insular Affairs, *Statehood for Hawaii*, 86th Cong., 1st Sess., January 27, 1959, 72–82.

30. Heefner, "New Frontier," 548; Bell (*Last among Equals*) argues that partisan politics were also a major factor in drawing out the debates. Only New Mexico remained a territory (1850–1912) longer than Hawai'i.

31. Bell, *Last among Equals*, 139–41, 164–67, 201–2; Daws, *Shoal of Time*, 357–81; Moon-Kie Jung, *Reworking Race: The Making of Hawaii's Interracial Labor Movement* (New York, 2006); Gerald Horne, *Fighting in Paradise: Labor Unions, Racism, and Communists in the Making of Modern Hawai'i* (Honolulu, 2011); T. Michael Holmes, *The Specter of Communism in Hawaii* (Honolulu, 1994); Hugh Butler, *Statehood for Hawaii: Communist Penetration of the Hawaiian Islands, Report to Committee on Interior and Insular Affairs*, 80th Cong., 2nd Sess., 1949. On the "Democratic Revolution," see George Cooper and Gavan Daws, *Land and Power in Hawaii: The Democratic Years* (Honolulu 1990).

32. Ann K. Ziker, "Segregationists Confront American Empire: The Conservative White South and the Question of Hawaiian Statehood, 1947–1959," *Pacific Historical Review* 76, no. 3 (439–65); Zacharias letter, 83rd Cong., 2nd Sess., *Congressional Record* 100, no. 3 (March 18, 1954), 3485; George Sokolsky, "The Days: The Problem of Hawaii," *Washington Post*, November 23, 1956, A13; Richard Lloyd Jones, "Stop Statehood for Hawaii," *Tulsa Tribune*, March 30 1957, reprinted in Senate hearings before the Committee on Interior and Insular Affairs, *Statehood for Hawaii on S. 50 and S. 36*, 85th Cong., 1st Sess., April 1–2, 1957, 99–100; Drew L. Smith, *The Menace of Hawaiian Statehood* (New Orleans, 1957), 24–25, cited in Ziker, "Segregationists."

33. Heefner, "New Frontier," 560–61, 552; Dudziak, *Cold War Civil Rights*, 80; Harry S. Truman, "Special Message to the Congress on Civil Rights, February 2, 1948," *Public Papers of the Presidents of the United States* (Washington, DC, 1948).

34. Citizens' Statehood Committee, "Statehood for Hawaii," n.d., "Hawaii Citizens' Statehood Committee" folder, box 28, HSCC; Hawai'i Statehood Commission, "The State of Hawaii," 1956, HSCP–Hamilton Library, University of Hawai'i at Manoa (hereafter UHM); "Should Hawaii Be Admitted to Statehood Now?" *Town Meeting*, October 4, 1949; Farrington remarks, 83rd Cong., 1st Sess., *Congressional Record* 99, no. 12 (July 22, 1953): A4557; Bell, *Last among Equals*, 121–24; Saranillio, "Seeing Conquest," 143–47.

35. House hearings before the Committee on Public Lands, *Statehood for Hawaii*, 80th Cong., 1st Sess., March 7, 1947, 38–42; Senate hearings before the Committee on Interior and Insular Affairs, *Hawaii Statehood*, 81st Cong., 2nd Sess., May 1, 1950, 50–51, 92; Heefner, "New Frontier," 560–61, 563–64.

36. Citizens' Statehood Committee, "Statehood for Hawaii"; House hearings before the Committee on Interior and Insular Affairs, *Hawaii-Alaska Statehood*, 84th Cong., 1st Sess., January 25, 1955, 88; House hearings, *Statehood for Hawaii*, 1947, 38–42, 59; "Hawaii—A Bridge to Asia," *Business Week*, May 13, 1950, 128, cited in Klein, *Cold War Orientalism*, 251; Sieminski and Farrington remarks, 83rd Cong., 1st Sess., *Congressional Record* 99, no. 2 (March 9, 1953), 1700, 1789; Miller remarks, 81st Cong., 2nd Sess., *Congressional Record* 96, no. 2 (March 6, 1950), 2871; Curtis remarks, 85th Cong., 2nd Sess., *Congressional Record* 104, no. 10 (July 14, 1958), 13736; House hearings on H.R. 50 and H.R. 888 before the Committee on Interior and Insular Affairs, *Statehood for Hawaii*, 86th Cong., 1st Sess., January 26–28, 1959, 31–32; John A. Burns, "Asia and the Future," letter to the editor, *Commonweal*, August 9, 1957, 474–75; Senate hearings, *Statehood for Hawaii*, 1957, 10; Heefner, "New Frontier," 561, 565–66.

37. "Should Hawaii Be Admitted to the Union? (Prince H. Preston Jr. and Joseph R. Farrington)," *Talks*, October 1947; Farrington remarks, 80th Cong., 1st Sess., *Congressional Record* 93, no. 2 (June 30, 1947), 7198; House hearings before the Subcommittee on Territories and Insular Possessions of the Committee on Interior and Insular Affairs, *Statehood for Hawaii*, 83rd Cong., 1st Sess., February 23, 1953, 70. See also Judd remarks, 80th Cong., 1st Sess., *Congressional Record* 93, no. 2 (June 30, 1947), 1799; House hearings, *Statehood for Hawaii*, 1947, 76–79, 86; "Why Delay Statehood?" *Los Angeles Times*, March 14, 1950, A4; "Enchanting 'State,' " *Newsweek*, February 23, 1959, 29–32.

38. "Hawaii: A Melting Pot," *Life*, November 26, 1945, 103–8 (also cited in Klein, *Cold War Orientalism*, 249; Heefner, "New Frontier," 571); James A. Michener, "Hawaii," *Holiday*, May 1953, 34–45, 88, 90–92, 95; G. M. White, "Youth in Hawaii," *Ladies' Home Journal*, October 1955, 70–71, 202–4; William W. Davenport, "Hawaii—Showcase for Americanism," *House Beautiful*, September 1958, 118–19, 138.

39. Andrew W. Lind, *Hawaii's People* (Honolulu, 1955), 102–7; US Bureau of the Census, *1960, 1970, and 1970 Subject Reports on Marital Status and 1991 and 1992 Current Population Reports*, P20, nos. 461 and 468 (Washington, DC, 1998). By comparison, only 12 out of 170,636 marriage licenses granted in Los Angeles County between 1924 and 1933 were interracial, and at the time of the *Loving v. Virginia* Supreme Court decision in 1967, only 0.7 percent of all US marriages were classified as interracial. Pascoe, *What Comes Naturally*, 152, 295.

40. See, for example, "Hope for Hawaii," *Washington Post*, July 6, 1947, B4; "Hawaii as an Asset," *Washington Post*, March 9, 1953, 8; Hubert H. White, "Hawaii's Statehood Fight Seen as Vital to American Negroes," *Los Angeles Sentinel*, July 31, 1947, 2; Louis Lautier, "In the Nation's Capital," *Atlanta Daily World*, May 17, 1953, 6. Members of Congress often inserted reprints of these opinions into the *Congressional Record*. See, for instance, Henry G. Ellis, "Hawaii: Ten Good Reasons Why It Should Be a State," *Rochester Times-Union*, July 8, 1953, in 83rd Cong., 1st. Sess., *Congressional Record* 99, no. 12 (July 17, 1953): A4437; C. W. Snedden, "Give Hawaii Her Chance," *Fairbanks Daily News-Miner*, n.d., in 85th Cong., 2nd Sess., *Congressional Record* 104, no. 11 (July 16, 1958): 13959; "Congress Owes It to the Nation to Make Hawaii Our

50th State," *Denver Post*, February 24, 1959, in 86th Cong., 1st Sess., *Congressional Record* 105, no. 3 (March 11, 1959): 3858.

41. "Hawaii Moves Ahead," *Scholastic*, December 14, 1949; "Hawaii: Stalled Statehood," *Newsweek*, November 27, 1950; Carter, "The Case for Hawaii"; James A. Michener, "Hawaii—The Case for Our 50th State," *Reader's Digest*, December 1958.

42. House hearings before the Subcommittee on Territorial and Insular Possessions of the Committee on Public Lands, *Statehood for Hawaii*, 81st Cong., 1st Sess., March 3, 1949, 32; Johnson remarks, 83rd Cong., 1st Sess., *Congressional Record* 99, no. 2 (March 9, 1953): 1778.

43. Heefner, "New Frontier," 570–71.

44. Ziker, "Segregationists"; Bell, *Last among Equals*, 133–34, 206–7, 222; Smith remarks, 83rd Cong., 1st Sess., *Congressional Record* 99, no. 22 (March 5, 1953): 1652–53; Wolverton remarks, 83rd Cong., 1st Sess., *Congressional Record* 99, no. 9 (March 10, 1953): A1210–11; Smith, "Menace," 11, 28; Smith remarks, 84th Cong., 1st Sess., *Congressional Record* 101, no. 5 (May 10, 1955): 5934; Smith remarks, 86th Cong., 1st Sess., *Congressional Record* 105, no. 3 (March 12, 1959): 4015; Senate hearings, *Statehood for Hawaii*, 1957, 88.

45. Heefner, "New Frontier," 569–72.

46. Hawaii Statehood Commission, "Hawaii U.S.A.: Showcase for Americanism," 1954, HSCC-UHM; Hawaii Statehood Commission, "Hawaii Statehood and Contiguity," 1959, HSCC-UHM; Hawaii Statehood Commission, "Statehood for Hawaii," 1959, HSCC-UHM; Joseph Rider Farrington, "Hawaii's Goal, Statehood," *Christian Science Monitor Magazine*, June 7, 1947, 8; "The 49th State," *Life*, February 9, 1948, 97–109; Farrington remarks, 83rd Cong., 2nd Sess., *Congressional Record* 11, no. 3 (March 31, 1954): 4301.

47. "Hawaii: Stalled Statehood," *Newsweek*, November 27, 1950; "Hawaii Today . . . The 49th State Shapes Up," *Navy News*, June 1951; "They Copy Us and Some of Us Copy Them," *Life*, February 22, 1954, 26–27; Davenport, "Hawaii"; Michener, "Hawaii"; "Enchanting 'State,'" *Newsweek*; "Hawaii—Beauty, Wealth, Amiable People," *Life*, March 23, 1959, 58–72; Heefner, "New Frontier," 571–72.

48. Hawaii Statehood Commission, "Hawaii U.S.A. and Statehood"; Willard E. Givens, "Statehood for Hawaii," *NEA Journal*, March 1948, 165; Javits remarks, 85th Cong., 2nd Sess., *Congressional Record* 104, no. 10 (July 10, 1958): 11318; Ch'eng-K'un Cheng, "Assimilation in Hawaii and the Bid for Statehood," *Social Forces* 30, no. 1 (October 1951): 16–29.

49. Carter, "The Case for Hawaii."

50. Bell, *Last among Equals*, 227, 262–63; Holmes, *Specter of Communism*, 215–19; Horne, *Fighting in Paradise*, 15, 277–322.

51. Lind, *Hawaii's People*, 70–79; Andrew W. Lind, "Changing Race Relations in Hawaii, *Social Process in Hawaii*, 1954; Walter Kolarz, "The Melting Pot in the Pacific," *Social Process in Hawaii*, 1955; "Orientals Better Status in Hawaii," *New York Times*, April 7, 1957, 6; "Harmony in Hawaii," *Newsweek*, April 30, 1951; Carter, "The Case for Hawaii"; "Hawaii: The 49th State?" *Fortnight: The Magazine of the Pacific Coast*, February 1956.

52. Singh, *Black Is a Country*, 39; "At Last, a 49th State of the Union?" *Newsweek*, February 15, 1954, 49–50; Dudziak, *Cold War Civil Rights*, 13; Ngai, *Impossible Subjects*, 242–45.

53. George Gallup, "Public Backs Admission of Hawaii," *Los Angeles Times*, August 1, 1950, 10.

54. Gallup poll no. 589, September 19–24, 1957, http://institution.gallup.com (accessed November 11, 2010).

55. Bell, *Last among Equals*, 122, 236; House hearings, *Statehood for Hawaii*, 1947, 288–90; Senate hearings, *Statehood for Hawaii*, 1950, 525, 528–29; House hearings, *Statehood for Hawaii*, 1955, 408; Senate hearings before the Committee on Interior and Insular Affairs, *Alaska-Hawaii Statehood, Elective Governor, and Commonwealth Status*, 84th Cong., 1st Sess., February 21, 22, 28, 1955, 151–53; Senate hearings, *Statehood for Hawaii*, 1957, 107, 111; House hearings, *Statehood for Hawaii*, 1959, 100–101.

56. "Statehood Challenge," *Chinese News*, March 14, 1953, 12.

57. Senate hearings, *Statehood for Hawaii*, 1953, 257.

58. See various resolutions in "Public Opinion—Resolutions 1947–1949" folder, box 2, HSCC; Senate hearings before the Subcommittee on Territories and Insular Affairs of the Committee on Public Lands, *Statehood for Hawaii*, 80th Cong., 2nd Sess., January 9, 1948, 241–43.

59. In 1958, 27 percent of Native Hawaiians opposed statehood. See Whitehead, "Anti-Statehood Movement," 46; Ziker, "Segregationists"; Klein, *Cold War Orientalism*, 247; Bell, *Last among Equals*, 234–69; "The Miracle of Hawaii," *New York Times*, March 13, 1959, 28; "Hawaii's In!" *Washington Post*, March 13, 1959, A18.

60. Douglas H. Mendel Jr., "59-Year Pledge Kept: Hawaii Statehood Benefits America," *Los Angeles Times*, March 18, 1959, B4; James T. Rogers, "ABC of Hawaii—The State and Its People," *New York Times*, March 15, 1959, E7; "Hawaii Speaks for America," *New York Times*, March 15, 1959, E8; "Our Fiftieth State," *Los Angeles Sentinel*, March 19, 1959, A6; "Hawaii: The New Breed," *Time*, March 23, 1959; "Hawaiian Statehood," *Commonweal*, March 27, 1959, 661–62; George B. Leonard Jr., "Hawaii: State-to-Be Where Many Bloodlines Blend in Beauty," *Look*, May 12, 1959, 29–31.

61. Kyle Palmer, "Political Kettle Bubbles in HI," *Los Angeles Times*, May 10, 1959, B4; "Hawaii Expects Oriental Winner," *New York Times*, June 7, 1959, 83; "Hawaii: Almost In," *New York Times*, June 29, 1959, 28; "Melting Pot," *Washington Post*, June 30, 1959, A16; "Campaign, Hawaiian-Style," *New York Times Magazine*, July 26, 1959, SM22; Robert Alden, "Congress Gets 2 of Asian Descent," *New York Times*, July 30, 1959, 15; "The Unique Hawaiian Look in Politics," *Life*, August 17, 1959, 41–42, 44, 46.

62. "Hawaii's Melting Pot Election," *Los Angeles Times*, July 30, 1959, B4; "Ike Calls Hawaii Action in Election 'Fine Example,'" *Chicago Defender*, August 8, 1959, 1; "Elections in Hawaii: 'Democracy at Work,'" *U.S. News and World Report*, August 10, 1959, 19; "The Election in Hawaii—Meaning of Republican Gains," *U.S. News and World Report*, August 10, 1959, 58; "The State of Hawaii Votes," *New York Times*, July 31, 1959, 22.

63. See in decimal file 1950–54, RG 59, NARA: Sinclair to Acheson, August 8, 1950, folder 511.11A/8-850; Lee to Acheson, October 22, 1951, folder 511.90/10-2251; Goodyear to Department of State, October 2, 1951, folder 511.9021/10-251.

64. "Hawaii: A Land of Opportunity," VOA Chinese Unit transcript, broadcast May 3 and 5, 1951, box 17, VOA daily broadcast content reports, RG 306, NARA; "Hawaii, U.S.A.," "Hawaii U.S.A." folder, entry A1 1098, box 13, RG 306, NARA.

65. See in decimal file 1955–59, RG 59, NARA: Webster, American embassy, Taipei to Department of State, July 5, 1955, folder 511.903/7-555; Noonan, American consulate general, Kuala Lumpur, to Department of State, August 1, 1955, folder 511.903/8-155; Noonan, American consulate general, Kuala Lumpur, to Department of State, September 8, 1955, folder 511.903/9-855; Riley to King, January 25, 1956, folder 511A.803/1-2556.

66. Robert Trumbull, "Senator Fong Shows Asia the Twain Meet," *New York Times*, October 11, 1959, 1, 20. For details of Fong's tour, see the following in folder 033.1100-FL/3-3155, box 146, RG 59, decimal file 1955–59, NARA: MacArthur, American embassy, Tokyo, to Department of State, October 16, 1959; Gilstrap, American embassy, Seoul, to Department of State, October 16, 1959; Abbott, American embassy, Manila, to Department of State, October 23, 1959; Nelson, American embassy, Taipei, to Department of State, October 27, 1959; Koren, American embassy, Manila, to Department of State, November 6, 1959; Smith, American embassy, Vientiane, to secretary of state, November 10, 1959; Ranard, American embassy, Seoul, to Department of State, November 18, 1959; Wright, American embassy, Rangoon, to Department of State, November 19, 1959; Hackler, American consulate general, Singapore, to Department of State, November 20, 1959, Koren, American embassy, Manila, to Department of State, November 23, 1959; Holmes, American consulate general, Hong Kong, to Department of State, December 1, 1959; Guthrie, American embassy, Bangkok, to Department of State, December 8, 1959; Ranard, American embassy, Seoul, to Department of State, December 29, 1959.

67. Milton Viorst, "Rep.-Elect Inouye Arrives, Declares Hawaii Will Be Nation's Bridge to Asia," *Washington Post*, August 10, 1959, A2. For details of Inouye's tour, see the following in folder 033.1100-HU/11-358, box 152, RG 59, decimal file 1955–59, NARA: Department of State memorandum, September 11, 1959; MacArthur, American embassy, Tokyo, to Department of State, telegram, December 7, 1959; Kidd, American embassy, Tokyo, to Department of State, December 28, 1959.

68. MacArthur to Department of State; Kidd to Department of State; C. Brossard, "Daniel Inouye: First Japanese American in Congress," *Look*, March 1, 1960, 28–30.

69. Heefner, "New Frontier," 573; Trumbull, "Senator Fong"; "Duty in Congress Cited by Hawaiian," *New York Times*, August 10, 1959, 18; Kidd to Department of State.

70. See Department of State reports on Fong's trip as cited above; "'Man of the Pacific' Opens Senate Campaign," *Hawaii Chinese Weekly*, May 14, 1959, 1; Robert Trumbull, "Inouye Stresses 'Bridge' to Japan," *New York Times*, December 7, 1959, 9.

71. "The State of Hawaii Votes," *New York Times*, July 31, 1959, 22; Robert Alden, "Congress Gets 2 of Asian Descent," *New York Times*, July 30, 1959, 15; "The 49th State," *Life*, February 9, 1948, 97–109.

72. House hearings, *Statehood for Hawaii*, 1959, 24–25; "Hawaii's Statehood," *Chicago Defender*, March 18, 1959, A11; "Fiftieth Star in the Flag," *Los Angeles Times*, March 13, 1959, B4; "No Sharp Lines in Hawaii: Negro Just Another Citizen," *Atlanta Daily World*, May 26, 1959.

73. James A. Michener, "'Aloha' for the Fiftieth State," *New York Times Magazine*, April 19, 1959, SM14, cited in Klein, *Cold War Orientalism*, 249–50.

74. Rasa Gustaitis, "Hawaiian Senators Find Being Immortalized for Wax Museum Is Chance to Better Image," *Washington Post*, October 12, 1963, C1.

75. "New Faces in Congress," *Time*, August 10, 1959; "Elections in Hawaii: 'Democracy at Work,'" *U.S. News and World Report*, August 10, 1959, 19; "Hawaii Legislator Pledges Rights Aid," *Chicago Defender*, August 15, 1959, 21; John Ramsey, "All Capitol Eyes Will Be on Long, Fong, and Inouye," *Washington Post*, August 21, 1959, B2; Dillon Graham, "Fong Arrives, Welcomed by Nixon," *Washington Post*, August 24, 1959, A8.

76. "New Faces in Congress," *Time*; Marie Smith, "Hawaii's Senior Senator: His Ties to Home Are Doubly Strong," *Washington Post*, August 1959, 30, F1; "Hawaii Legislator Pledges Rights Aid," *Chicago Defender*, August 15, 1959, 21; David S. Teeple, "Hawaiian Success Story," *Pageant*, August 1959; A.E.P. Wall, "From Shine Boy to Senator: The Busy Life of Hiram Fong," *Honolulu Star-Bulletin*, February 23, 1964, A11.

77. "Senator Fong on Civil Rights," *New York Daily News*, September 1, 1959; A. S. "Doc" Young, "The Big Beat," *Los Angeles Sentinel*, September 3, 1959, C1, C3; "Jackie Robinson," *Chicago Defender*, September 10, 1959, 13; "Hawaiian Senator Starts Wrong," *Chicago Defender*, September 12, 1959, 11; "One 'Political Jekyll and Hyde,'" *Los Angeles Sentinel*, August 8, 1968, A3.

78. Lawrence E. Davies, "A Nisei of Hawaii Aims for Senate," *New York Times*, March 17, 1959, 20; "War Hero Leads in Hawaii Vote," *Washington Post*, July 29, 1959, A1; "Oriental War Hero Is Champion Vote Getter," *Chicago Defender*, July 30, 1959, 3; "Daniel K. Inouye," *New York Times*, July 30, 1959, 14; Milton Viorst, "Rep.-Elect Inouye Arrives, Declare Hawaii Will Be Nation's Bridge to Asia," *Washington Post*, August 10, 1959, A2; "Japanese-American Lost Arm in World War II," *Chicago Defender*, August 15, 1959, 21; "Loss of Arm Makes Politician of Inouye," *Chicago Daily Tribune*, August 16, 1959, 43; Ramsey, "All Capitol Eyes"; Brossard, "Daniel Inouye"; Willard Edwards, "Nisei Hero Brings Battlefield Courage to Senate," *Chicago Daily Tribune*, February 17, 1963, 11.

79. "10 Young Men Cited by Junior Chamber," *New York Times*, January 5, 1950, 27; "A Red Hot Hundred," *Life*, September 14, 1962, 5; "Eye-Catching Race," *Newsweek*, April 9, 1962, 39–40; "Big Ben and Young Danny," *Time*, October 5, 1962.

80. L. Elliott, ed., "Go for Broke! Condensation of *Journey to Washington*," by Daniel Inouye, *Reader's Digest*, February 1968, 212–48; Daniel K. Inouye with Lawrence Elliott, *Journey to Washington* (Englewood Cliffs, NJ, 1967), xix, 293.

81. Inouye, *Journey to Washington*, v–vi, viii, xi–xv.

82. Ibid., ix, 216. See also "The A.J.A.'s: Fast-Rising Sons," *Time*, October 20, 1975.

83. "Transcript of the Keynote Address by Senator Inouye Decrying Violent Protests," *New York Times*, August 27, 1968, 28.

84. "The Empty Sleeve," *Harper's Magazine*, March 2009; "An American Speaks," *Memphis Commercial Appeal*, reprinted in *Chicago Tribune*, August 31, 1968, 8; Philip Warden, "Keynoter Inouye—from Japanese Ghetto to Senate," *Chicago Tribune*, August 25, 1968, O11; "Hawaii's Sen. Inouye: Racial Gap Spanned by Keynote Speaker," *Los Angeles Times*, August 26, 1968, 16; "White House-Backed Keynoter: Daniel Ken Inouye," *Chicago Tribune*, August 27, 1968, 28.

85. Gene Sherman, "Hawaii's New Horizons: Isles Melting Pot of the Pacific," *Los Angeles Times*, May 21, 1963, 2; Akaka quoted in Whitehead, "The Anti-Statehood Movement"; William J. Lederer, "The 50th State, at 5, 'Goes Mainland,'" *New York Times Magazine*, April 16, 1964, SM24.

86. US Commission on Civil Rights, *Report of the U.S. Commission on Civil Rights* (Washington, DC, 1959), 370, 447.

87. Samuel Jameson, "Hawaii, 6 Years a State, Booming," *Chicago Daily Tribune*, December 19, 1965, A1; Drew Pearson, "A State of Racial Harmony," *Los Angeles Times*, September 5, 1967, A5. See also "Racial Equality Works," *Chicago Defender*, August 10, 1963, 8; "Hawaii: The Golden Land," *Life*, October 8, 1965, 84–99, 101–2; Samuel Jameson, "Hawaii's Races 'All Mixed Up' and Happy," *Chicago Daily Tribune*, December 26, 1965, A1; J. P. Jankowiak, "Hawaii's Racial Mixture and How It Works," *Chicago Defender*, November 26, 1966, 6; Drew Pearson, "Hawaii: A Model in Race Relations," *Washington Post*, September 5, 1967, D11.

88. Nancy Abelmann and John Lie, *Blue Dreams: Korean Americans and the Los Angeles Riots* (Cambridge, MA, 1995).

89. For critical views of the relationships between Hawai'i's ethnic Asian population and Native Hawaiians, see Haunani-Kay Trask, "Settlers of Color and 'Immigrant' Hegemony: 'Locals' in Hawai'i," *Amerasia Journal* 26, no. 2 (2000): 1–24; Candace Fujikane and Jonathan Y. Okamura, ed., *Asian Settler Colonialism: From Governance to the Habits of Everyday Life in Hawai'i* (Honolulu: University of Hawai'i Press, 2008).

90. Klein, *Cold War Orientalism*, 1–17; Saranillio, "Colliding Histories."

Epilogue: Model Minority/Asian American

1. Henry Yu, "The 'Oriental Problem' in America, 1920–1960," in *Claiming America: Constructing Chinese American Identities during the Exclusion Era*, ed. K. Scott Wong and Sucheng Chan (Philadelphia, 1998), 191–214; Kandice Chuh, *Imagine Otherwise: On Asian Americanist Critique* (Durham, NC, 2003), 1–27.

2. On American Orientalism and the racialization of Asian Americans, see Lee, *Orientals*; Tchen, *New York before Chinatown*; Yu, *Thinking Orientals*; Klein, *Cold War Orientalism*.

3. "Americans from Asia: The East Came to the West," *Senior Scholastic*, April 25, 1969, 12–17.

4. "Johnson's Speeches in Washington and Honolulu at Start of His 17-Day Tour," *New York Times*, October 18, 1966, 16.

5. Austin Herschel, "Asian Prejudice," *Chicago Tribune*, September 9, 1963, 20 (emphasis added).

6. "All the Natives Are Restless," *Ebony*, February 1962, 80.

7. George S. Schuyler, "Views and Reviews," *Pittsburgh Courier*, June 8, 1963, 21.

8. Nathan Glazer and Daniel Patrick Moynihan, *Beyond the Melting Pot: The Negroes, Puerto Ricans, Jews, Italians, and Irish of New York City* (Cambridge, MA, 1963), 90.

9. "Transcript of the American Academy Conference on the Negro American—May 14–15, 1965," *Daedalus* 95, no. 1 (Winter 1966): 287–441; Daniel Geary, "Racial Liberalism, the Moynihan Report, and the Daedalus Project on the 'Negro American,'" *Daedalus* (Winter 2011): 53–66.

10. Joseph Alsop, "Matter of Fact: July 4!" *Washington Post*, July 3, 1967, A17; "Chinese, Japanese, Jews Show Way to Advance in US," *Washington Post*, February 12, 1969, A21; "Alsop on Black Studies," *Washington Post*, March 10, 1969, A20; "Failure of Negro Education Seen in Berkeley Statistics," *Washington Post*, April 11, 1969, A25; "Photo Indicts Sociologists," *Washington Post*, January 11, 1971, A17; "Alsop Answers Critics," *Washington Post*, January 30, 1971, A17; "The Wasps' Decline," *Washington Post*, March 1, 1972, A19.

11. See, for example, Chia-Ling Kuo, "The Chinese on Long Island: A Pilot Study," *Phylon* 31, no. 3 (Fall 1970): 280–89; James W. Loewen, *The Mississippi Chinese: Between Black and White* (Prospect Heights, IL, 1971); Ivan H. Light, *Ethnic Enterprise in America: Business and Welfare among Chinese, Japanese, and Blacks* (Berkeley, 1972).

12. Robinson, *After Camp*, 224–35.

13. Briones, *Jim and Jap Crow*; Varzally, *Making a Non-White America*; Robinson, *After Camp*; Brilliant, *The Color of America Has Changed*.

14. Scott H. Tang, "Becoming the New Objects of Racial Scorn: Racial Politics and Racial Hierarchy in Postwar San Francisco, 1945–1960," in *The Political Culture of the New West*, ed. Jeff Roche and David Farber (Lawrence, KS, 2008), 219–45; Dai-ming Lee, "Race Riots in Dixie over Integration," *Chinese World*, September 7, 1956, 1; "Selma and the Law," *Chinese World*, March 18, 1965, 1; Gilbert Woo, "Heiren de Douzheng" (The black struggle), *Chinese Pacific Weekly*, June 6, 1963; Harry W. Low, "Time to Remember Our Friends," *Chinese World*, June 25, 1963, 1.

15. Amy Uyematsu, "The Emergence of Yellow Power in America," *Gidra*, October 1969, 8–11. On the Asian American movement, see "Salute to the 60s and 70s; Legacy of the San Francisco State Strike," commemorative issue, *Amerasia Journal* 15, no. 1 (1989); Yen Le Espiritu, *Asian American Panethnicity: Bridging Institutions and Identities* (Philadelphia, 1992); William Wei, *The Asian American Movement* (Philadelphia, 1993); Glenn Omatsu, "The 'Four Prisons' and the Movements of Liberation: Asian American Activism from the 1960s to 1990s," in *The State of Asian America: Activism and Resistance in the 1990s*, ed. Karin Agu-

ilar San Juan (Boston, 1994), 19–69; "Yellow Power," *Giant Robot*, Spring 1998, 61–81; Fred Ho, *Legacy to Liberation: Politics and Culture of Revolutionary Asian Pacific America* (San Francisco, 2000); *Asian Americans: The Movement and the Moment*, ed. Steve Louie and Glenn Omatsu (Los Angeles, 2001); Daryl J. Maeda, *Chains of Babylon: The Rise of Asian America* (Minnesota, 2009).

16. Asian American Student Alliance, California State University, Long Beach, "Brothers and Sisters," *Yellow Journalism*, September 1970, 2–3, part II, reel 2, Steve Louie Asian American Movement Collection, YRL (hereafter SLC); Asian Americans of the Third World Political Alliance, University of California, Santa Cruz, "Asians in America," *Stevenson Libre: A Forum for Unrestricted Expression*, n.d., part II, reel 2, SLC.

17. Pei-Ngor Chin, "Chinatown Ferment," *Gidra*, February 1971, 16; L. Ling-chi Wang, "Chinatown and the Chinese," *Asian American Political Alliance*, November–December 1968, 1–2; Steve Tatsukawa, "Gardena Part One: A Saga of Youth, Drugs, and Middle Class Misery," *Gidra*, July 1973, 6–8; Steve Tatsukawa, "Gardena Part Two: 'Everybody Needs a Helping Hand,'" *Gidra*, September 1973, 1, 5–8; "Editorial," *Taishu: Japanese American Journal*, April 1973, 2.

18. "Proposal for an Asian-American Studies Center," n.d., part II, reel 2, SLC.

19. "100% Americans," *60 Minutes* transcript, vol. 4, no. 12, January 9, 1972, Mike Wallace Collection, Bentley Historical Library, University of Michigan.

20. Ibid.

21. Sucheng Chan, *Asian Americans: An Interpretive History* (New York: 1991), 145–47; Hing, *Making and Remaking Asian America*, 40–41, 82; Vijay Prashad, *The Karma of Brown Folk* (Minneapolis, 2000), 69–82; Ngai, *Impossible Subjects*, 61–263, 267.

22. Ronald Takaki, *Strangers from a Different Shore: A History of Asian Americans* (Boston, 1989), 474–80; Frank H. Wu, *Yellow: Race in America beyond Black and White* (New York, 2002), 39–78.

23. Abelmann and Lie, *Blue Dreams*, 170–75.

24. Ibid., 165.

25. Eric Tang, "Boat People," *Colorlines*, March 21, 2006; Karen J. Leong et al., "Resilient History and the Rebuilding of a Community: The Vietnamese American Community in New Orleans East," *Journal of American History* (December 2007): 770–79; Helen Heran Jun, *Race for Citizenship: Black Orientalism and Asian Uplift from Pre-Emancipation to Neoliberal America* (New York, 2011), 149–56; Eric Tang, "A Gulf Unites Us: The Vietnamese Americans of Black New Orleans East," *American Quarterly* 63, no. 1 (2011): 117–149.

26. Abelmann and Lie, *Blue Dreams*, 148–80.

27. Dana Y. Takagi, *Retreat from Race: Asian-American Admissions and Racial Politics* (Rutgers, NJ, 1993); Don T. Nakanishi, "A Quota on Excellence? The Asian American Admissions Debate," in *The Asian American Educational Experience: A Source Book for Teachers and Students*, ed. Don T. Nakanishi and Tina Yamano Nishida (New York, 1995), 273–84.

28. Deborah N. Misir, "The Murder of Navroze Mody: Race, Violence, and the Search for Order," *Amerasia Journal* 22, no. 2 (1996): 55–76.

29. Christine Choy and Renee Tajima-Peña, dirs., *Who Killed Vincent Chin?* (1987).

30. Amy Chua, "Why Chinese Mothers Are Superior," *Wall Street Journal*, January 8, 2011; "Tiger Moms: Is Tough Parenting Really the Answer?" *Time*, January 20, 2011.

31. The anti–model minority literature is too vast and far reaching to allow for a comprehensive bibliography here. Representative works include Prashad, *The Karma of Brown Folk*; Wu, *Yellow*.

32. Asian Americanists' critiques speak to Evelyn Brooks Higginbotham's argument that the "metalanguage of race" obscures social and power relations operating within racialized groups. See Evelyn Brooks Higginbotham, "African-American Women's History and the Metalanguage of Race," *Signs* 17, no. 2 (1992): 251–74.

33. National Commission on Asian American and Pacific Islander Research in Education and College Board, "Asian Americans and Pacific Islanders: Facts, Not Fiction—Setting the Record Straight," 2008, http://professionals.collegeboard. com/profdownload/08-0608-AAPI.pdf (accessed March 4, 2013); Tamar Lewin, "Report Takes Aim at 'Model-Minority Stereotype' of Asian Students," *New York Times*, June 10, 2008.

34. Osajima, "Asian Americans as the Model Minority"; Lee, *Orientals*, 151.

35. As Susan Koshy argues, "The range of political strategies adopted in different contexts highlights the liminality of [Asian American as an] intermediary racial category and the complex patterns of resistance and complicity that have shaped its historical emergence" in the triangulated relationship between white-black-Asian. See Susan Koshy, "Morphing Race into Ethnicity: Asian Americans and Critical Transformations of Whiteness," *boundary 2* 28, no. 1 (2001): 159. For a useful comparison see also David G. Gutiérrez, *Walls and Mirrors: Mexican Americans, Mexican Immigrants, and the Politics of Ethnicity* (Berkeley, 1995).

36. Prashad, *Karma of Brown Folk*, 185–203; Helen Zia, *Asian American Dreams: The Emergence of an American People* (New York, 2001); Grace Lee Boggs, *Living for Change: An Autobiography* (Minneapolis, 1998); Grace Lee Boggs with Scott Kurashige, *The Next American Revolution: Sustainable Activism for the Twenty-First Century* (Berkeley, 2011); Diane C. Fujino, *Heartbeat of Struggle: The Revolutionary Life of Yuri Kochiyama* (Minneapolis, 2005); Tram Nguyen, *We Are All Suspects Now: Untold Stories from Immigrant Communities after 9/11* (Boston, 2005); Russell C. Leong and Don T. Nakanishi, eds., *Asian Americans on War and Peace* (Los Angeles, 2002); Volpp, "The Citizen and the Terrorist."

37. http://www.whitehouse.gov/administration/eop/aapi/about (accessed September 19, 2011).

38. Austin Considine, "For Asian-American Stars, Many Web Fans," *New York Times*, July 29, 2011; Oliver Wang, "Notes of a Native Tiger Son, Part I," *Atlantic*, January 19, 2011; Oliver Wang, "Lin Takes the Weight," *Atlantic*, March 1, 2012.

39. Chuh, *Imagine Otherwise*.

Archival, Primary, and Unpublished Sources

Government Publications

California Department of Industrial Relations, Division of Fair Employment Practices. *Californians of Japanese Chinese Filipino Ancestry*. San Francisco: Division of Fair Employment Practices, 1965.

Congressional Record

Du Puy, William Atherton, US Department of the Interior. *Hawaii and Its Race Problem*. Washington, DC: US Government Printing Office, 1932.

Federal Bureau of Investigation. *Uniform Crime Reports for the United States, Annual Bulletin 1954*. Vol. 25, No. 2. Washington, DC: US Government Printing Office, 1955.

Federal Bureau of Investigation. *Uniform Crime Reports for the United States and Its Possessions, Fourth Quarterly Bulletin 1941*. Vol. 12, No.4. Washington, DC: US Government Printing Office, 1942.

President's Committee on Civil Rights. *To Secure These Rights*. Washington, DC: US Government Printing Office, 1947.

US Bureau of the Census. Various reports.

US Commission on Civil Rights. *Report of the U.S. Commission on Civil Rights*. Washington, DC: US Government Printing Office, 1959.

US Commission on Wartime Evacuation and Relocation of Civilians. *Personal Justice Denied: Report of the Commission on Wartime Relocation and Internment of Civilians*. Washington, DC: US Government Printing Office, 1983. Reprint, Seattle: Civil Liberties Public Education Fund and University of Washington Press, 1997.

US Congress. Joint Hearings before the Subcommittees of the Committees on the Judiciary. *Bills to Revise the Laws Relating to Immigration, Naturalization, and Nationality*. 82nd Cong., 1st Sess., March 6–9, 12–16, 20–21, and April 9, 1951. Washington, DC: US Government Printing Office, 1951.

US Congress. Senate. Committee on the Judiciary. *Refugee Problem in Hong Kong and Macao: Hearings Before the Subcommittee to Investigate Problems Connected with Refugees and Escapees*. 87th Cong., 2nd Sess., May 29, June 7, 8, 28, July 10, 1962. Washington, DC: US Government Printing Office, 1962.

US Department of the Interior. *The Evacuated People: A Quantitative Description*. Washington, DC: US Government Printing Office, 1946.

US Department of the Interior. *People in Motion: The Postwar Adjustment of the Evacuated Japanese Americans*. Washington, DC: US Government Printing Office, 1946.

US Department of the Interior. *The Relocation Program*. Washington, DC: US Government Printing Office, 1946.

———. *WRA: A Story of Human Conservation*. Washington, DC: US Government Printing Office, 1946.

US Department of the Interior/War Relocation Authority. "Nisei in Uniform." Washington, DC, n.d.

US Department of the Interior/War Relocation Authority. "What We're Fighting For: Statements by United States Servicemen about Americans of Japanese Descent." Washington, DC: US Government Printing Office, 1945.

US President's Commission on Immigration and Naturalization. *Hearings before the President's Commission on Immigration and Naturalization*. Washington, DC: US Government Printing Office, 1952.

——. *Whom We Shall Welcome*. Washington, DC: US Government Printing Office, 1953.

Various congressional hearings and reports pertaining to Hawai'i statehood.

Interviews

Sung, Betty Lee. Conversation with author. March 23, 2004, New York.

Wong, Jade Snow. Conversation with author. March 5, 2003, San Francisco.

Manuscript and Archival Collections

Academy of Motion Picture Arts and Sciences, Margaret Herrick Library Special Collections, Los Angeles (MHL), *Go for Broke!* file

Bancroft Library, University of California, Berkeley, Japanese American Evacuation and Resettlement Study (JERS)

Beinecke Rare Book and Manuscript Library, Yale University, Hamilton Basso Papers (HBP)

Bentley Historical Library, University of Michigan, Mike Wallace Collection

Brethren Archives, Elgin, IL, Japanese Relocation Collection (JRC)

Chicago History Museum Research Center, Chicago

Chicago Resettlers Committee Collection
Social Welfare Council Collection

Columbia University Rare Book and Manuscript Library, New York, Carnegie Corporation of New York Grant Files (CCNY)

Densho Online Archive (densho.org)

Ethnic Studies Library (ESL), University of California, Berkeley, Asian American Studies Collection

William Hoy Papers
Him Mark Lai Research Papers
Edwar Lee Papers
Charles Leong Papers (CLP)
Nancy Wey papers

Hagley Library, Wilmington, DE, Dupont Collection

Hamilton Library, University of Hawai'i at Manoa (UHM), Hawaiian Collection

Hawai'i State Archives, Honolulu, Hawaii Statehood Commission Collection (HSCC)

Japanese American National Library, San Francisco, Japanese American Citizens League History Collection (JACL-JANL)

Japanese American National Museum, Los Angeles, Hirasaki National Resource Center General Collection

Japanese American Service Committee, Chicago (JASC), Legacy Center Archives

National Archives and Records Administration (NARA)

> Foreign Service Posts of the US Department of State, record group 84, College Park, MD
>
> Harry S. Truman Presidential Library, Independence, MO
>> Philleo Nash Papers (PNP)
>> President's Committee on Civil Rights, record group 220 (RG 220)
>> White House Central Files President's Personal File (PPF)
>
> Office of War Information, record group 208 College Park, MD
> US Department of State, record group 59, College Park, MD
> US Information Agency, record group 306, College Park, MD
> War Relocation Authority, record group 210, Washington DC

North Baker Research Library, California Historical Society, San Francisco, General Collection

Performing Arts Library at Lincoln Center, New York Public Library, Americans All–Immigrants All Collection

University of Iowa Libraries Special Collections, Iowa City, Carl Glick Papers

Young Research Library Special Collections, University of California, Los Angeles (YRL)

> Charles Kikuchi Papers (CKP)
> Independent Progressive Party Papers
> Japanese American Research Project (JARP)
> Joe Grant Masaoka Papers
> Rose Hum Lee Papers (RHLP)
> Steve Louie Asian American Movement Collection (SLC)
> T. Scott Miyakawa Papers (TSM)

Periodicals

Alameda Times-Star
America: National Catholic Weekly Review
American Artist
American Journal of Sociology
American Magazine
American Mercury
Asia
Asia and the Americas
Asian American Political Alliance
Atlanta Daily World
Atlantic

Bandwagon
Better Homes and Gardens
Beverly Hills Script
Boston Globe
Business Week
California Chinese Press/Chinese Press (San Francisco)
Californian/California Liberal
Chicago Daily Defender/Chicago Defender
Chicago Daily Tribune/Chicago Tribune
Chicago Herald-American
Chicago Schools Journal
Chicago Shimpo
Chicago Sun-Times
Chicago's American
Chinese American Progress (Chicago)
Chinese-American Times (New York)
Chinese Digest (San Francisco)
Chinese News (San Francisco, 1940–42)
Chinese News: America's Chinese Newsmagazine (San Francisco, 1953–54)
Chinese Pacific Weekly (San Francisco)
Chinese Times (San Francisco)
Chinese World (San Francisco)
Christian Century
Christian Science Monitor
Christian Science Monitor Magazine
Cincinnati Post
Cincinnati Times-Star
Colliers
Common Ground
Commonweal
Coronet
Crisis
Crossroads
Current History and Forum
Denson Tribune
Detroit Free Press
East Wind (San Francisco)
Ebony
Far Eastern Survey
Far Eastern Quarterly
Foreign Affairs
Fortnight: The Magazine of the Pacific Coast
Gidra
Gila News-Courier (Gila, AZ)
Harper's Magazine
Hawaii Chinese Journal (Honolulu)
Hawaii Chinese Weekly (Honolulu)

Heart Mountain Sentinel (Heart Mountain, WY)
Hokubei Mainichi (San Francisco)
Holiday
Honolulu Advertiser
Honolulu Star-Bulletin
Horn Book
House Beautiful
Independent
Independent Woman
JACL Reporter (Salt Lake City)
Japanese American Committee for Democracy Newsletter
Ladies' Home Journal
Life
Look
Los Angeles Daily News
Los Angeles Sentinel
Los Angeles Times
Mademoiselle
Manzanar Free Press (Manzanar, CA)
Navy News
NEA Journal
New Republic
Newsweek
New York Journal American
New York Post
New York Times
New York Times Magazine
New York World Telegram
New Yorker
Oakland Tribune
Omaha Sunday World-Herald
Orange News
Pacific Citizen (Salt Lake City)
Parade
Pittsburgh Courier
Reader's Digest
Redland Facts
Rocky Shimpo (Denver)
San Francisco Call-Bulletin
San Francisco Chronicle
San Francisco Examiner
Saturday Evening Post
Saturday Review of Literature
Scene: The Pictorial Magazine (Chicago)
Scholastic
School and Society
Science News

Senior Scholastic
Social Forces
Social Process in Hawaii
Society
Sociology and Social Research
Survey Graphic
Taishu: Japanese American Journal
This World (San Francisco)
Time
Town Meeting
Transaction Magazine
Travel
Tule Lake Daily Dispatch (Tule Lake, CA)
U.S. News and World Report
Wall Street Journal
Washington Post and Times Herald/Washington Post
Watsonville Register-Pajaronian
Young China (San Francisco)
Youngstown Vindicator (Youngstown, OH)

Unpublished Dissertations, Manuscripts, and Theses

Albert, Michael Daniel. "Japanese American Communities in Chicago and the Twin Cities." PhD diss., University of Minnesota, 1980.

Brooks, Charlotte. "'A Voter Cannot Be Neutral, Nor Should He Be': The Chinese American Democratic Club of San Francisco and Cold War Party Politics." Unpublished paper presented at the American Studies Association annual meeting, 2010.

Caudill, William. "Japanese American Acculturation and Personality." PhD diss., University of Chicago, 1950.

Corcoran, Adrian. "Early Child Training Practices by Chicago's Second Generation JA's." Master's thesis, University of Chicago, 1950.

Jacobson, Alan, and Percy Lee Rainwater. "A Study of Evaluations of Nisei as Workers by Caucasian Employment Agency Managers and Employers of Nisei." Master's thesis, University of Chicago, 1951.

Kimura, Yukiko. "A Comparative Study of Collective Adjustment of the Issei, the First Generation Japanese, in Hawaii and in the Mainland United States since Pearl Harbor." PhD diss., University of Chicago, 1952.

Lee, Marjorie. "Hu-Jee: The Forgotten Second Generation of Chinese America, 1930–1950." Master's thesis, University of California, Los Angeles, 1984.

Mar, Conrad Foo. "Non-Delinquency among American-Chinese Youth: A Pilot Study." Master's thesis, University of the Pacific, 1964.

Ng, Katharine. "Fear and Loathing of Chinatown: The 1950s and Rose Hum Lee's Desire for Assimilation." Bachelor's thesis, University of California, Los Angeles, 2002.

Nishi, Setsuko Matsunaga. "Japanese American Achievement in Chicago: A Cultural Response to Degradation." PhD diss., University of Chicago, 1963.

Oda, Meredith Akemi. "Remaking the 'Gateway to the Pacific': Urban, Economic, and Racial Redevelopment in San Francisco, 1945–1970." PhD diss., University of Chicago, 2010.

Okada, Dave M. "A Study of Male Nisei Workers in Two Chicago Industrial Plants under Wartime Conditions." Master's thesis, University of Chicago, 1947.

Powell, James Henry. "The Concept of Cultural Pluralism in American Social Thought, 1915–1965." PhD diss., University of Notre Dame, 1971.

Saranillio, Dean Itsuji. "Seeing Conquest: Colliding Histories and the Cultural Politics of Hawai'i Statehood." PhD diss., University of Michigan, 2009.

Uyeki, Eugene S. "Process and Patterns of Nisei Adjustment to Chicago." PhD diss., University of Chicago, 1953.

Wang, L. Ling-chi. "Politics of Assimilation and Repression: History of the Chinese in the United States, 1940 to 1970." Unpublished manuscript, Ethnic Studies Library, University of California, Berkeley, 1980.

Waugh, Isami Arifuku. "Hidden Crime and Deviance in the Japanese-American Community, 1920–1946." PhD diss., University of California, Berkeley, 1978.

Wu, Ellen Dionne. "Race and Asian American Citizenship from World War Two to the Movement." PhD diss., University of Chicago, 2006.

Index

accommodation, 6–7; as "cultural" attribute, 168–69; and end of legal exclusion, 74; Hawai'i as example of racial, 215–16; Japanese Americans and, 72–74, 77–78, 95, 173; *shikataganai* (realistic resignation), 161; as stage of social interaction cycle, 51, 215

Acheson, Dean, 231

Adams, Romanzo, 215–16

African Americans: as advocates of Japanese during WWII, 42, 84; and Asian Americans as allies in civil rights struggle, 235–36, 245–46; assimilation and, 152–53, 170; citizenship of, 165, 243–44; civil rights activism and, 165–67, 173, 177, 198, 209, 246; and Cold War diplomacy, 293n7; criticism of Chinese Americans, 235–36; and "cultural pathology," 170–71; "culture clash" with Asian Americans, 252; Double V campaign during WWII, 82; Hawai'i statehood and resolution of "Negro Problem," 227; Imazeki and need for "soul searching" by, 6–7, 165–68, 245; JACL and cooperation with, 96; Japanese and assimilation with, 30; "matriarchal" family structure among, 170–71; model minority trope as rationale for continued racism against, 6–7, 151, 165–68, 170–76, 209, 238–41; negative stereotypes of, 166, 167, 209, 240–41, 252; the "Negro Problem," 6–7, 18, 42, 62, 151–52, 156, 165–68, 170–73, 208, 227; poverty and, 151–52, 170–72, 208–9, 252; racialization in contrast to (*See* "not-black" racialization); as severed from African identity, 293n7; and welfare entitlement programs, 208–9

Akaka, Abraham, 240

Alland, Alexander, 52–53

Alsop, Joseph, 244

American Civil Liberties Union (ACLU), 49, 104

American Committee on Japan (ACJ), 107

American Creed, 152–53, 227–28

American Dream, 179, 252–53

American identity: cultural pluralism and, 51, 52–53; exclusion from, 62–63; race and, 2, 4–5, 9, 220–25

Americanism, 20, 109; education and "inculcation" of, 79; equated with white culture, 24, 26; FDR on, 89; JACL and, 75–77, 79, 100, 150–51, 179

Americanization: and anti-Communism, 226; assimilation and, 51; of Chinese Americans, 51, 126–27, 187–89; in Hawai'i, 213, 225, 226–27; of Japanese Americans, 19, 79, 150–51, 155–56, 162, 213, 249

American Loyalty League, 75

Americans All, Immigrants All (radio series), 52

"Americans without a Delinquency Problem" (photo essay), 196–97

"America's Chinese" (*Life* photo essay), 122

"America's Chinese" (VOA radio segment), 125

An American Dilemma, 152–53, 164, 170

Anti-Discrimination Committee (ADC) of JACL, 92, 94–97, 100

Asian American Movement. *See* civil rights activism *under* Asian Americans

Asian Americans: civil rights activism and, 235–36, 245–46; and Cold War diplomacy, 293n7; and collapse of distinction between Chinese and Japanese, 242–43; "culture clash" with African Americans, 252; identification as, 7, 242–43

Asian American studies, 248–50, 255–56; rejection of the model minority stereotype, 255–56

Asiatic Exclusion. *See* Exclusion

assimilating Others. *See* assimilating Others *under* assimilation

assimilation: African Americans and lack of, 152–53, 170; with African Americans *vs.* whites, 30; Americanization and, 51; Asians as "unassimilable," 1–2, 55–56, 123, 160, 182, 203–4, 215, 216; assimilating Others, 4, 43–44, 85–86, 142, 151–52; Chinese Americans and, 43–44, 51, 55–56, 142; Chinese as unassimilated or unassimilable, 55–56,

Politics and Society in Twentieth-Century America

Series Editors

William Chafe, Gary Gerstle, Linda Gordon, and Julian Zelizer